Our God-Breathed Book--

The Bible

Our God-Breathed Book—
The Bible

By
John R. Rice

Sword of the Lord Publishers
Murfreesboro, Tennessee

ISBN 0-87398-628-8

Library of Congress
Catalog Card Number:
70-107027

Printed and Bound in the United States of America

TABLE OF CONTENTS

AUTHOR'S FOREWORD

The authenticity and authority of a God-inspired Bible is the very foundation of Christianity. Even if it should be admitted that Christ is deity, we have no certain way of knowing the truth about Christ, about the way of salvation, no assurance of Heaven and eternity, no sweet promises, no way to know Christian duty, to grow Christian character, or preach the Christian Gospel, without an inspired Bible. We had as well settle it to start with that it is the Bible *and* Christ or no Bible, no Christ, no salvation, no Christianity.

Here is what the Bible itself teaches about the matter of inspiration, as far as this writer can understand it, taking the Scripture itself at simple face value. We have not tried to adjust the doctrine to fit the theories of men. We have been dogmatic where the Bible speaks with certainty.

Here we acknowledge that we differ with some devout, scholarly men, not on the fact of inspiration but as to whether it sometimes does not guarantee genealogies, scientific matter, or history, or moral perfection of the Scriptures. We differ on whether the Scriptures are progressive in the liberal sense of the first part being imperfect and superseded by later inspiration. We are not thus unbrotherly, we trust, where we insist on what the Bible plainly claims for itself—perfection in every jot and tittle in the original.

Some men, too anxious to please unbelieving scholars, have thus not been impressed as we think they should be, with the undebatable claims of Scripture itself: that the very words were breathed out from God. Some, like Orr, who first made too many concessions to unbelief, and thought evolution was scientifically proved, as its advocates once falsely claimed, later seemed to have been convinced by the work of Hodge, Warfield, Machen, and others. Orr, some nineteen years after writing his book, *Revelation and Inspiration,* had evidently come to regard Warfield's position so highly that he had Warfield prepare the extended article on inspiration, very strong, in the *International Standard Bible Encyclopaedia,* of which Orr was the editor-in-chief.

Many less erudite men, we fear, have written on inspiration who would have done well to first master Gaussen, Warfield, Young, and Engelder, and most of all, to be mastered themselves by what the Scriptures plainly claim for their inspiration.

The great point of difference about inspiration in the last half century and more has been the problem of how to explain the paradox of the Bible's being made up of the very words of God while being also in the words of men. We hope the two chapters here on "Eternal Word of God Settled in Heaven Before It Was Written Down by Men God Prepared" and "God Put His Style Into the Prophets," will help in that matter not very widely taught. And the example of Divine-human involvement in Jesus Christ and in regeneration should shed light on this question, too.

To get the viewpoint of a number of the best Bible-believing scholars, we wrote to some of them the following letter:

> Dear Dr. —————————:
>
> I am writing to you and about twelve other godly scholars concerning a matter of great interest to me and, I think, to you. Because of my faith in your devotion to Christ and the Bible, and my respect for your scholarship, I want your counsel.
>
> I have been working for months on a book on the inspiration of the Bible. There are other good books on inspiration, but because of certain areas about the human sources and color in the Scriptures, some good men keep insisting on a "restudy" of inspiration. There is the seeming paradox that men wrote the Bible, and in it express their hopes and desires, their history, their testimonies, and yet the Bible insistently declares that God gave the very words of the Scripture. In a study of this matter there are thoughts that come to mind, on which I would be deeply grateful if you can counsel with me.
>
> I. DID THE SCRIPTURES EXIST COMPLETELY IN THE MIND AND PLAN OF GOD BEFORE THEY WERE GIVEN FOR MEN TO WRITE DOWN?
>
> 1. Some Scriptures seem to teach so. Psalm 119:89 says, "For ever, O Lord, thy word is settled in heaven." Was all the Word of God, including the part yet unwritten, settled in Heaven when this Psalm was written?

On the same line, Psalm 119:152 says, "Concerning thy testimonies, I have known of old that thou hast founded them for ever." I note the past tense. That seems to teach that they were founded before they were written down.

In Acts 15:18 we read, "Known unto God are all his works from the beginning of the world." That is recorded as a statement of James, but I regard it as an inspired and authoritative statement. If so, does not that mean that all the Bible, in detail, was known unto God from the beginning of the world?

2. Consider the ceremonial law. The Tabernacle in the wilderness, and its furniture and appointments, were evidently copied after a heavenly tabernacle which Moses saw in Heaven. Hebrews 8:2 speaks of Christ as "a minister of the sanctuary, and of the true tabernacle, which the Lord pitched, and not man." And verse 5 says that earthly priests "...serve unto the example and shadow of heavenly things, as Moses was admonished of God when he was about to make the tabernacle: for, See, saith he, that thou make all things according to the pattern shewed to thee in the mount." Would that not mean then that all the ceremonial matters involved, and their spiritual meaning, were already planned out in every detail before the Scriptures were written down?

3. The whole matter of the crucifixion of Christ, the types picturing it, the allusions to it, and the doctrines involved, were evidently planned before God killed innocent animals and made garments for naked Adam and Eve and before righteous Abel offered a sacrifice that pictured Christ. It seems that is involved in the mention of Christ as "the Lamb slain from the foundation of the world" in Revelation 13:8.

I am deeply concerned to see the truth about this, and if what I am suggesting is true, then the Word of God and whatever human color, testimony, feelings and experiences are incorporated in the Word of God were planned of God ahead of time and thus incorporated in the Bible. If I am not understanding these Scriptures correctly in the light of some other Scripture or Bible truth, I honestly want to know it and will welcome any counsel or criticism that may come to mind.

II. HOW MUCH WERE THE BIBLE WRITERS CONDITIONED AND PREPARED AHEAD OF TIME SO THAT THEY WOULD UTTER EXACTLY THE WORDS OF GOD, IN THEIR OWN VOCABULARIES, AND EXPRESS ALSO THEIR OWN CONDITIONS, FEELINGS AND TESTIMONIES?

1. Some Scriptures seem to say that God so prepared His men ahead of time that their personalities, their surrounding condi-

tions and their terminologies, would be distinctive, yet fit exactly the words of Scripture which He would give them.

For example, Isaiah 49:1 and 2, "The Lord hath called me from the womb; from the bowels of my mother hath he made mention of my name. And he hath made my mouth like a sharp sword; in the shadow of his hand hath he hid me, and made me a polished shaft; in his quiver hath he hid me." And verse 5 says, "Now, saith the Lord that formed me from the womb to be his servant, to bring Jacob again to him...." I would think that the beautiful language, the color, the exalted artistry of the writing of Isaiah is involved in this "polished shaft" that God made him and that God made His "mouth like a sharp sword." Thus if God prepared Isaiah with his characteristics, his surroundings, his vocabulary, and if God prepared the Word of God ahead of time, then it would represent Isaiah and God, yet we could say that the Bible is "every word that proceedeth out of the mouth of God" (Matt. 4:4), and that the Scripture is "not in the words which man's wisdom teacheth, but which the Holy Ghost teacheth" (I Cor. 2:13).

A similar thing is said about Jeremiah, in Jeremiah 1:4-9: "Then the word of the Lord came unto me, saying, Before I formed thee in the belly I knew thee; and before thou camest forth out of the womb I sanctified thee, and I ordained thee a prophet unto the nations. Then said I, Ah, Lord God! behold, I cannot speak: for I am a child. But the Lord said unto me, Say not, I am a child: for thou shalt go to all that I shall send thee, and whatsoever I command thee thou shalt speak. Be not afraid of their faces: for I am with thee to deliver thee, saith the Lord. Then the Lord put forth his hand, and touched my mouth. And the Lord said unto me, Behold, I have put my words in thy mouth." Jeremiah was known and sanctified and ordained a prophet before he was formed in the womb, this Scripture says. And then Jeremiah should speak "whatsoever I command thee," the Lord said, and "I have put my words in thy mouth." It seems to me that the eternal Word, already settled in Heaven, and God's prophet, known and sanctified and ordained before he was born, fit together to give to us the Scriptures that are wholly God's words and yet through the words of men (in the original manuscripts).

In the light of the above Scriptures, Galatians 1:15 and 16, regarding the Apostle Paul, may have the same meaning. "But when it pleased God, who separated me from my mother's womb, and called me by his grace, To reveal his Son in me, that I might preach him among the heathen; immediately I conferred not with flesh and blood." Was every detail of Paul's life so governed and controlled and known ahead of time by the Lord that when he wrote Scriptures, the Scriptures would be put in the words and colored by the vocabulary and personality and characteristics which God had already prepared and planned?

2. Romans 8:29 tells us that God did foreknow all those who would be saved. And I Peter 1:2 says that certain Christians are "elect according to the foreknowledge of God the Father." I think that the choice of salvation is offered to all men but that God knows who will be saved. If this be true, as these Scriptures seem to say, that God knows ahead of time about every individual, would it not mean that the writers of the Scripture and the circumstances surrounding them and their characteristics and personality were all known ahead of time so that God would make the eternal Word when it comes in human words, be with the words and color and the human element which He Himself had carefully prepared?

Forgive me for writing at such length, but I need your help. I am not writing for controversy but asking for counsel.

I will be deeply grateful if I may hear from you, and if you will give me your frank opinion about these matters before I should incorporate them in the book.

In Jesus' name, yours,

John R. Rice

Dr. R. Laird Harris, dean of the faculty, Covenant Theological Seminary, St. Louis, wrote as follows:

Dear Dr. Rice:

Thank you for your letter of 19 May and the searching questions that you propose. I am interested that you are writing this study on inspiration, for although the subject has been written on often before, yet we constantly need new treatments to consider and to oppose the new ideas that are everywhere around. May the Lord bless your effort and give it wide usefulness.

I think you have considered very carefully the questions that you raise, and there is really not much more that I need to say. On your first question, "Did the Scriptures exist completely in the mind and plan of God before they were given for men to write down?" I would say that you have argued very cogently that they did. The Scriptures that you quote seem to say so, and the Old Testament types and prophecies would involve the same thing. You are quite right to guard this teaching by remembering that not only was the Word of God fixed in the mind of God, but that this included the human instruments and testimony and feelings and experiences that were to be incorporated in the Bible. These too were planned, and we must insist that they were planned in such a way that what these writers would say was true, God Himself being the author.

On your second question, "How much were the Bible writers conditioned, etc. ...?" again I believe you have given the arguments rightly. God did prepare His prophets and apostles ahead of time. Isaiah wrote in elevated style. The Book of Chronicles is more prosaic. But then God is interested in all kinds of people and uses all kinds of people to give His Word. The only point is that when He gives it, He gives it in truth.

You have mentioned Isaiah and Jeremiah. I would add also Ezekiel, who was given a scroll to eat which God Himself had written. The words of this scroll were to be given out to the people, but obviously they were Ezekiel's words as well as God's words. The result therefore is that the Bible is truly the Word of God and every word in it is God-breathed, and yet it is also the word of men who spoke what God wished them to speak, and spoke in accordance with His will as they themselves naturally would speak with their own characteristics. Only, these characteristics are overridden by the Spirit of God who preserved them from error in fact, doctrine and judgment. You have outlined the problems and answers very well; I simply say "Amen!"

*   *   *

> Sincerely in Christ,
> /s/ Laird Harris
> R. Laird Harris
> Dean of Faculty

Dr. Charles Lee Feinberg, dean of Talbot Theological Seminary, La Mirada, California, wrote the following kind words:

Dear Dr. Rice:

Let me thank you very warmly for having written me at such great length.

It is not often that one sees in written form exactly what one has come to believe through the years with reference to the Word of God. I could write a book on all your paragraphs, but it will have to suffice to say that you have a very high regard for Scripture, and every point that you have made is amply substantiated by the Word of God.

May the Lord give you many years to set forth the truths that are very precious to us. If our view of Scripture be faulty, then everything else must be wrong.

> Yours in His faithfulness,
> /s/ Charles Lee Feinberg
> Charles Lee Feinberg,
> Dean

Dr. S. Maxwell Coder, dean of education, Moody Bible Institute, Chicago, wrote as follows:

Dear Dr. Rice:

Thank you for your very gracious letter of May 14. I am delighted to learn that you are writing a book on the inspiration of the Bible. It is a pleasure and a privilege to comment on the points you have raised.

I have always believed as you do that the Scriptures were known in their entirety in the mind of God before the foundation of the world. I have used Psalm 119:89,152 in support of this. The Holy Spirit has evidently spoken to both of us through these same verses. The content of the Scriptures and the death of the Lamb of God in my understanding are two of the elements in the total plan of God which antedate the foundation of the world.

The Scriptures which you have cited to demonstrate that God prepared the holy men who were used to give us the Bible long beforehand say precisely the same thing to me that they do to you. I am glad to have this listing and these comments which you have prepared.

You and I both know that we are regarded as holding extreme views because we take such verses literally, but I can take no other position, and no one is going to shake my convictions about this.

May the Lord greatly use your book when it is published.

Sincerely yours,
/s/ S. Maxwell Coder
S. Maxwell Coder
Dean of Education

These men, of course, are not responsible for the views expressed in this book except as they have stated their opinions in the letters above. We are grateful for their counsel and that of other men who wrote.

We have two strong words to say in conclusion. One is, in the words of the inspired apostle in Galatians 1:8,9, "Though we, or an angel from heaven, preach any other gospel unto you than that which we have preached unto you, let him be accursed. As we said before, so say I now again, If any man preach any other gospel unto you than that which we have preached unto you, let him be accursed." And any interpretation of Scripture by those who deny the deity, virgin birth, and atoning death of

Jesus Christ to save sinful men, is to be counted accursed. We do not need infidels to teach us about Christ and the Bible.

The next earnest word I would say is that those who are not much concerned about saving sinners, whose great concern is not to obey Christ in winning souls to Him, are not obedient Christians and thus not likely to have the high doctrine of Scripture of soul-winning scholars. A Spurgeon, a Talmage, a Torrey, a Riley, or a Rimmer, who were close to Christ, more filled with His Spirit, obediently winning souls, were far more likely to have the mind of Christ about the Bible than any scholarly scoffers.

The millions of devoted, common Christians who through the centuries have regarded the Bible as the inspired, infallible Word of God, are right. And honest, reverent scholarship will not change nor put questions about that truth but rather reinforce it.

Now we offer humbly, for God's blessing, this book, the result of enormous labor. Since we entered into an active defense of the verbal inspiration of the Bible in a statewide controversy in Texas forty years ago, we have studied everything on this subject by responsible scholars that we could find. And we have, God knows, studied the Scriptures with passion and holy zeal to find all that God claimed for His Word. How many hundreds of pages of notes we have written in longhand! How many months of labor on the manuscript! We humbly commit it to God for His blessing.

JOHN R. RICE
Murfreesboro, Tennessee
1969

CHAPTER I

INSPIRATION: HOLY GROUND: PULL OFF YOUR SHOES!

I. WE ALREADY KNOW THE BIBLE IS THE WORD OF GOD

1. We Have Weighed the Evidence
2. We Are Not Open to Slander and Unbelief Concerning the Word
3. We Have Seen the Miraculous Power of God's Word

II. BUT WE HAVE STUDIED THE "INFALLIBLE PROOFS" TOO

1. God Brought Me to Face the Inevitable Conflict Between Belief and Unbelief
2. We Found That Prophecy, **Archaeology** and Reason Back Up the Bible

III. ONE CAN KNOW CERTAINLY THAT THE BIBLE IS THE WORD OF GOD

1. God Offers to Reveal Himself to Honest Seekers
2. The Tremendous Testimony of Dr. B. H. Carroll
3. Thousands Have Proved That the Honest Heart Can Know Whether the Bible Is True

INSPIRATION: HOLY GROUND: PULL OFF YOUR SHOES!

In the back side of the desert of Midian, Moses saw a burning bush and drew near. But God spoke to Moses out of the bush and said, "Draw not nigh hither: put off thy shoes from off thy feet, for the place whereon thou standest is holy ground" (Exod. 3:5).

That bush burning in the desert signified the miraculous presence of God to speak to man. The Bible is as truly miraculous as that burning bush. The bush had natural branches but they burned with supernatural fire. The Bible has human language, but it nonetheless speaks with the voice of Deity. The Bible had human writers, but they wrote God's words. "Which things also we speak," the Apostle Paul writes, "not in the words which man's wisdom teacheth, but which the Holy Ghost teacheth" (I Cor. 2:13).

So God speaks to us out of His burning Word in this desert world. And we beg the reader to approach this study of the Bible doctrine of inspiration with holy reverence and humility. We are not wise scholars with arrogant assurance passing judgment on a fallible human document. We are poor, frail sinners seeking to examine the very Word of God.

I. WE ALREADY KNOW THE BIBLE IS THE WORD OF GOD

Does someone say that we are not unbiased, that we do not approach the subject of the inspiration of the Bible with an open mind? Certainly we are not without preference and not without convictions. Certainly we are not, with an open mind, as willing to reject the Bible as to accept it. No, we have well-established convictions. We come with reverence, already accepting the Bible as the very Word of God, which it claims to be. We come bowing to its authority as the authority of God and of Christ. We come to believe all its statements, to humbly try to follow its commandments, to claim gladly as many of its promises as our frail faith can claim.

1. We Have Weighed the Evidence

But are we thus coming with no weighing of evidence? Do we thus dethrone reason? Are we thus unscientific in method when we already accept the Bible as the Word of God?

Not at all! Already we have considered ten thousand evidences. Already we have tried its promises and found them true. We have already considered its prophecies and found hundreds of them already fulfilled. We have faced again and again its judgments on sin and found them true. Sin always turns out as the Bible warns, and the sinner suffers as the Word foretold. We have tried this Word in our own heart and found it to be the Word of God with the power and wisdom of God, not simply the word of man with the failures and limited resources of human knowledge and human reason.

Oh, we found more, more, more than that! We have met the Saviour here offered in the Word. He gave peace to the troubled heart, peace that was not human but divine! He made the child of wrath a new creature, a child of God. We know Him intimately. His Holy Spirit lives within us, and innumerable contacts prove Him present. Jesus Christ, becoming my Saviour through the message of His Word, brought me to know God as my Father. Thus I became heir and joint heir with Christ. The truths of God in His Word are revealed by His Spirit, marvelous things that "eye hath not seen, nor ear heard, neither have entered into the heart of man" (I Cor. 2:9). So we do not come without logical, compelling, spiritual and scientific evidence that the Bible is the very Word of God.

2. We Are Not Open to Slander and Unbelief Concerning the Word

Suppose you come to tell us, "Let us now open the subject of whether your mother was a godly, good woman. Let us suppose that she may have been a hypocrite, with no true love for God and no righteousness in her life but an unclean and immoral woman. Suppose we consider the charge that she had no love for you or her family." Do you think I would come to discuss amicably such slanderous opinion of my mother and that I would come without convictions and without well-formed opinions? Could one come or would one want to come with an open mind to consider with evil men their slanderous suppositions?

Let me use the first person. I would scorn the suggestion. I remember the sweet songs she sang as she went about the house. I remember how I wept, just a five-year-old boy, when she sang, "Turned Away From the Beautiful Gate." Oh, what if I should miss Heaven, I thought. I remember when I told her a childish lie, she was so moved that she told me God hated a lie. I remember how she loved us all, how she labored and toiled to care for a big family without modern conveniences, in a country home. I remember standing near her deathbed when she made all promise to meet her in Heaven, when she asked my cousin to sing, "How firm a foundation, ye saints of the Lord, Is laid for your faith in His excellent Word!" I remember now how she lifted glad hands and said, "I can see Jesus and my baby now!" Then she fell asleep in Jesus, not to be sick or poor or to sorrow any more.

I already know more about my godly mother's character than any foolish or wicked detractor, so I am not openminded on that subject and only a fool would expect me to be.

3. We Have Seen the Miraculous Power of God's Word

So we do not come with an unbiased mind about the Bible. When we consider the inspiration of the Bible, we come after fifty-nine years knowing Jesus Christ as our own personal Saviour and God as our Father. We come after preaching the Word and studying it for forty-seven years of public ministry. We have written comments on every chapter in the Bible and on every principal verse. We have acted on faith in God's promises in matters where all logic would expect utter ruin.

But the God of the Bible has abundantly cared for us, has educated our family, provided our needs, put millions of dollars through our hands to get out the Gospel in many millions of copies of my books and pamphlets and on hundreds of radio stations and in marvelous citywide revivals, and for thirty-four years in a Christian magazine.

We have seen tens of thousands of sinners transformed by the Gospel of this Bible. Thousands of the most abandoned sinners have claimed the Christ proclaimed here. Oh, how many drunkards we have seen made sober, how many harlots made pure, how many infidels made into humble believers through the Word of God, as we preached it! We have seen the Gospel work the same among skid row bums, among murderers in prison, among false cultists of every kind. We have seen it work wonders in Japan, in Korea, India and Palestine, when Moslems and Druses, Parsees, Buddhists, Hindus, Catholics, and Jews turned to Christ and were transformed. So it is not with a blank mind, not with unformed opinions that we approach the study of the inspiration of the Bible.

Oh, then, "Put off thy shoes from off thy feet, for the place whereon thou standest is holy ground."

Dr. Arthur T. Pierson gives many strong, intelligent evidences, "infallible proofs," of the inspiration of the Scriptures and urges Christians to be students of these evidences. But he says:

> It is true that many an ignorant disciple has been both firm in faith and rich in service. But even he has studied one kind of evidences, and it is his knowledge of them that makes him strong. The evidences he has mastered are those which are understood by **experience** rather than **argument**. God has made it possible for even the most unlearned to know that the Bible is His Word, by finding it the power of God to their salvation and sanctification. There are simple-minded believers who know nothing of the proofs from prophecy and miracle, who do know that God is faithful to His promises, and see the miracle of the new heart and changed life actually wrought in themselves. Christ is a living Saviour by that most infallible proof—what He has done and is doing for them. He opened their blind eyes to see their sin and need, and His beauty and love; He cleansed the leprosy of their guilt, cured the palsy of their helplessness and the fever of their raging passion, and cast out the demon from their hearts.
> Jerry McAuley, at whose burial thousands sadly gathered, had, in his own conversion, as great an evidence of Christianity as though Christ's word had raised him from the dead! What less than the power of God could in a moment recover such a

man from a life conspicuous for every crime, and not only set him free from the chains of his vices but make him an apostle of grace to rescue other perishing souls![1]

Yes, we rejoice in those overwhelming evidences of *experience.*

II. BUT WE HAVE STUDIED THE "INFALLIBLE PROOFS" TOO

Surely in my young manhood God began to prepare me to "earnestly contend for the faith," as we are commanded to do (Jude 3), even as Paul was inspired to urge the Philippian Christians to be "striving together for the faith of the gospel" (Phil. 1:27).

1. God Brought Me to Face the Inevitable Conflict Between Belief and Unbelief

In Baylor University, I was a young and ardent Christian, but I had been taught and more or less perfunctorily accepted the teaching of evolution. I was assured that the Bible was true, but my vague understanding of the Scriptures about creation and the theory of evolution had not come to sharp contrast and conflict until that time. A professor of sociology taught in classes that man was a product of evolution from brute beasts and that the Bible could not be true. I objected seriously to that, and a great conflict arose in my mind.

Later, when I was a college teacher doing graduate work in the University of Chicago, I heard William Jennings Bryan speak on "The Bible and Its Enemies," and then university authorities, to answer Bryan, put up the head of the Botany Department, a Presbyterian layman who had been moderator of the nationwide assembly, who spoke on "The Evidences for Evolution." I already believed the Bible, but I was shocked to find nothing more than speculation and guesswork and unproved theories to back the evolutionary teaching of unbelievers.

After I heard the professor in Mandel Hall, the university chapel, that day in 1921, I went to speak to him privately, and

---

1. *Many Infallible Proofs,* p. 17.

I boldly put the question, "If the Bible account of creation is not true, then what about Jesus Christ? Is He really God's own Son, deity in human form, as the Bible claims He is?"

To my shocked surprise, the professor who did not believe the Bible turned away scornfully, refusing to give a clear-cut answer and saying it was not worthwhile to answer. When the professor did not stand up for Christ as the virgin-born Son of God, I knew he was wrong and that his teaching was wrong, but I could not then prove it.

When I went out on the steps of Mandel Hall following the lecture, two freshmen lads, each seventeen years old, argued with some heat. One was the son of a university professor; the other, the son of a believing father teaching in Robert College, Constantinople, Turkey. With concern and on the verge of tears, the freshman of the missionary father, said, "I wish my father were here. I have always understood that he believed the Bible is all true, the very Word of God."

And the other young man answered with the university viewpoint, "Well, you have to take scientific facts when you find them. You can't believe all these old-fogy notions." And I saw the ardent young man sadly turn away, his faith shaken in the Bible.

That day I determined I would learn all the evidences that any man needs to know to prove absolutely that the Bible is the very Word of God and that Christ is the Son of God. And you may be sure I have labored at that through these years. Oh, how I have proved the Bible and its promises! I have sought out the scientific and historical evidence.

And I did find out.

2. We Found That Prophecy, Archaeology and Reason Back Up the Bible

I know how Bible prophecies have been fulfilled, proving beyond any doubt that they were written by Deity's knowledge and plan for the future. I know how the scientific facts, recorded in the Bible long before men of science ever discovered them, prove they were written by God. I know how the silly and wicked claims of infidels that Moses could not have written the Pentateuch have been disproved by the Hammurabi code and other archaeological evidences. I know how archaeological discoveries have borne out the Bible. There was a great Hittite nation as the Bible says, though so long disputed by infidels. I know about the Tel el-Amarna tablets.

I know the evidences from Dr. Robert Dick Wilson and Professor Allis and others who have so thoroughly discredited the Graff-Wellhausen theory.

Oh, yes, I have the books of the unbelievers, too. As an editor and defender of the faith, I have books which I do not advise preachers to have, including the infamous and enormous and expensive *Interpreter's Bible* commentary, full of the most ungodly unbelief ever published. I have the books of Nels Ferre, of Oxnam, of Buttrick, of Fosdick, of Georgia Harkness, and many others. I have the lectures of Robert Ingersoll; *The Age of Reason* by Tom Paine. I have read Darwin's *Origin of Species.* In some six thousand volumes on my shelves I have examined all the claims of unbelief and found them false.

I say again that anybody can know whether the Bible is the Word of God and the only people who do not know are those who have not been willing to put it to an honest test with a penitent heart, seeking to know and please God.

So we do not come to a study of the inspiration of the Bible with an open mind. Long ago indisputable facts, "infallible proofs," as the Scriptures call them (Acts 1:3), have proved that Jesus Christ is God the Son, the Saviour, and the Bible is God's Word breathed out of God, the trustworthy Word of God.

III. ONE CAN KNOW CERTAINLY THAT THE BIBLE IS THE WORD OF GOD

We have said plainly that we know beyond any doubt that the Bible has proved itself to be the Word of God. And now we say that every person who wants to know can know the same.

1. God Offers to Reveal Himself to Honest Seekers

There is a clear Bible doctrine that God loves the world, loves men, wants to reveal Himself, wants men to know Him, love

Him and have fellowship with Him. That is inherent, is basic to the whole matter of divine revelation, of God dealing with men. God sought Adam in the Garden of Eden. Adam ran. God loved Israel and sought her again and again in her idolatry, rebellion and sin. God personified as wisdom cries out:

"How long, ye simple ones, will ye love simplicity? and the scorners delight in their scorning, and fools hate knowledge? Turn you at my reproof: behold, I will pour out my spirit unto you, I will make known my words unto you. Because I have called, and ye refused; I have stretched out my hand, and no man regarded; But ye have set at nought all my counsel, and would none of my reproof." — Prov. 1:22-25.

Here God offers that if men will turn from sin, "I will pour out my spirit unto you, I will make known my words unto you." Divine wisdom is here offered to the sinner. Verse 25 above says, "But ye have set at nought all my counsel...." Men can find God; men can know about God's Word.

In James 4:6-8 we are promised that "God resisteth the proud, but giveth grace unto the humble." We are promised, "Draw nigh to God and he will draw nigh to you." But the condition is clear for He says, "Cleanse your hands, ye sinners; and purify your hearts, ye double minded." One who honestly turns his heart away from sin and seeks God can find God. One who draws nigh to God will find God draws near to him. God comes to the darkened mind which seeks light and to the humble heart that wants truth and righteousness.

We remember that Jesus said in John 6:37, "...and him that cometh to me I will in no wise cast out." God has the door open for every contrite and humble heart.

So, concerning the Word of God, we have the promise of John 7:17, "If any man will do his will, he shall know of the doctrine, whether it be of God, or whether I speak of myself." One who wills and chooses to do the will of God will know whether the doctrine in the Bible is of God or not.

2. The Tremendous Testimony of Dr. B. H. Carroll

In a most remarkable and moving article, "My Infidelity and What Became of It," by B. H. Carroll, the great Southern

Baptist theologian, founder of Southwestern Baptist Theological Seminary, tells how, when he faced this verse of Scripture, it led him to give God an honest trial. Dr. Carroll tells how he heard the challenge by a humble country preacher who insisted that he take God up on this promise to be willing to know the truth. Dr. Carroll says:

> I had sworn never to put my foot in another church. My father had died believing me lost. My mother — when does a mother give up a child? — came to me one day and begged, for her sake, that I would attend one more meeting. It was a Methodist camp meeting, held in the fall of 1865. I had not an atom of interest in it. I liked the singing, but the preaching did not touch me.
>
> But one day I shall never forget. It was Sunday at eleven o'clock. The great, wooden shed was crowded. I stood on the outskirts, leaning on my crutches, wearily and somewhat scornfully enduring. The preacher made a failure even for him. There was nothing in his sermon. But when he came down, as I supposed to exhort as usual, he startled me not only by not exhorting, but by asking some questions that seemed meant for me. He said: "You that stand aloof from Christianity and scorn us simple folks, what have you got? Answer honestly before God, have you found anything worth having where you are?"
>
> My heart answered in a moment: "Nothing under the whole heaven; absolutely nothing." As if he had heard my unspoken answer, he continued: "Is there anything else out there worth trying, that has any promise in it?" Again my heart answered: "Nothing; absolutely nothing. I have been to the jumping-off place on all these roads. They all lead to a bottomless abyss."
>
> "Well, then," he continued, "admitting there's nothing there, if there be a God, mustn't there be a something somewhere? If so, how do you know it is not here? Are you willing to test it? Have you the fairness and courage to try it? I don't ask you to read any book, nor study any evidences, nor make any difficult and tedious pilgrimages; that way is too long and time is too short. Are you willing to try it now; to make a practical, experimental test, you to be the judge of the result?"
>
> These cool, calm and pertinent questions hit me with tremendous force, but I didn't understand the test. He continued: "I base my test on these two Scriptures: 'If any man willeth to do his will, he shall know of the doctrine, whether it be of God;' 'Then shall we know, if we follow on to know the Lord.'"
>
> For the first time I understood the import of these Scriptures. I had never before heard of such a translation for the first, and

had never examined the original text. In our version it says: "If any man will do his will, he shall know of the doctrine, whether it be of God." But the preacher quoted it: "Whosoever willeth to do the will of God," showing that the knowledge as to whether the doctrine was of God depended not upon external action and not upon exact conformity with God's will, but upon the internal disposition—"whosoever willeth (or wishes) to do God's will." The old translation seemed to make knowledge impossible; the new, practicable.

In the second Scripture was also new light: "Then shall we know, if we follow on to know the Lord," which means that true knowledge follows persistence in the prosecution of it; that is, it comes not to temporary and spasmodic investigation.

So, when he invited all who were willing to make an immediate experimental test to come forward and give him their hands, I immediately went forward. I was not prepared for the stir which this action created. My infidelity and my hostile attitude toward Christianity were so well known in the community that such action on my part developed quite a sensation. Some even began to shout. Whereupon, to prevent any misconception, I arose and stated that I was not converted, that perhaps they misunderstood what was meant by my coming forward; that my heart was as cold as ice; my action meant no more than that I was willing to make an experimental test of the truth and power of the Christian religion, and that I was willing to persist in subjection to the test until a true solution could be found. This quieted matters.

The meeting closed without any change upon my part. The last sermon had been preached, the benediction pronounced and the congregation was dispersing. A few ladies only remained, seated near the pulpit and engaged in singing. Feeling that the experiment was ended and the solution not found, I remained to hear them sing. As their last song they sang:

> O land of rest, for thee I sigh,
> When will the moment come
> When I shall lay my armor by
> And dwell in peace at home.

The singing made a wonderful impression upon me. Its tones were as soft as the rustling of angels' wings. Suddenly there flashed upon my mind, like a light from Heaven, this Scripture: "Come unto me, all ye that labour and are heavy laden, and I will give you rest." I did not see Jesus with my eye, but I seemed to see Him standing before me, looking reproachfully and tenderly and pleadingly, seeming to rebuke me for having gone to all other sources for rest but the right one, and now inviting me to come to Him. In a moment I went, once and forever, casting myself unreservedly and for all time at Christ's feet, and in a moment the rest came, indescribable and unspeakable, and it has remained from that day until now. [2]

Unbelief then stems from a stubbornness of the will. But one who chooses to do the will of God and humbles his heart to seek God can find out whether or not the Bible is the very Word of God and thus that Christ is the Son of God.

This truth is told in Hosea 6:1-3, as Dr. Carroll found:

"Come, and let us return unto the Lord: for he hath torn, and he will heal us; he hath smitten, and he will bind us up. After two days will he revive us: in the third day he will raise us up, and we shall live in his sight. Then shall we know, if we follow on to know the Lord: his going forth is prepared as the morning; and he shall come unto us as the rain, as the latter and former rain unto the earth."

O, Israel! Backslidden, defeated, punished Israel, return to the Lord and you can know His healing and forgiving and reviving! "Then shall we know, if we follow on to know the Lord."

3. Thousands Have Proved That the Honest Heart Can Know Whether the Bible Is True

Anyone who really wants to know whether the Bible is true or not, whether Christ is deity, virgin born, an atoning Saviour, can find out.

Dr. A. T. Pierson says:

There have been many candid doubters, but never one who had carefully studied the Evidences of Christianity. Mr. Hume confessed himself the prince of sceptics, as Voltaire was the prince of scoffers, and dark indeed were those depths of doubt into which his speculations plunged him. He said of those speculations: "They have so wrought upon me and heated my brain that I am ready to reject all belief and reasoning, and can look upon no opinion even as more probable or likely than another." And yet, though pretending to great diligence in the search after truth, and using all his fine powers and culture to destroy faith in the Gospel, he confessed, as Dr. Johnson tells us, that he had

---

2. *Sword Book of Treasures*, pp. 128-131.

never read even the New Testament with attention.

Whenever an honest doubter comes to me, I feel perfectly safe in calmly saying, to his face, "You have never studied the evidences, and it is likely never attentively examined the Bible." And that arrow never misses its mark.

Some five years since, I was brought into contact with a man who took pride in his sceptical opinions and made a boast of not being misled by the credulity of Christians. I ventured to take the old arrow out of my quiver. I said, "You have never thoroughly studied the Bible, sir." He turned my arrow aside, saying very positively, "You are mistaken there; for I have been familiar with the Bible from my boyhood." And yet within ten minutes he had shown that he did not know the difference between **Job** and **Lot**, but thought it was Job that lived in Sodom and dwelt with his two daughters in the cave!

If there is one candid doubter living who has faithfully studied the Bible and the Evidences of Christianity, he has not yet been found. Before this course of argument is concluded, your attention will be called to two prominent Englishmen who agreed to assault Christianity; but in order to conduct the assault the more successfully and skillfully, they agreed also first to examine it thoroughly; but when they began honestly to search the scriptures, they could no longer doubt that the Bible was the Word of God, and so Gilbert West and Lord Lyttleton became converts and defenders of that same faith they were about to attack. [3]

Just as Gilbert West and Lord Lyttleton set out to study the Bible to answer the claims of the resurrection of Christ and of the conversion of the Apostle Paul, and through the Word of God were convinced and wrote books to preach the truth they once scorned, so may any honest man be convinced who approaches the Bible with an open heart.

Dr. R. A. Torrey again and again faced infidels and skeptics with a challenge that he could show them how to know for sure that the Bible is true and that Christ was the Son of God, the Saviour. Those who accepted his challenge were happily saved; those who backed down, of course, were those who did not want to know the truth because they did not want to turn from their sins.

D. L. Moody, Sam Jones, the late Dr. Bob Jones, Sr., Billy Sunday, along with this writer, have come face to face with unbelief and have challenged the skeptic to face the Word of God and turn with a penitent heart from sin and to see if the

---

3. *Many Infallible Proofs*, pp. 12,13.

Bible were true. And always, the honest heart who seeks light comes to Christ.

Do not count the scholarly unbeliever as being forced by actual evidence to disbelieve the Bible and reject the claims of Christ. No, his trouble is heart trouble, not head trouble, a wicked bias of the heart that chooses darkness instead of light, and by feigned words pretends honesty and scholarship and morality.

CHAPTER II

BEWARE OF "SCHOLARS" WHO DO NOT BELIEVE THE
BIBLE IS GOD'S WORD

I. THERE IS A MORAL GUILT IN UNBELIEF ABOUT
CHRIST AND THE BIBLE

1. A Bias Against the Bible Blinds the Unbeliever

2. Such Unbelieving Scoffers at the Scripture Are Foretold

3. Dr. Fosdick an Example of the "Feigned Words" of
Enemies of the Bible

4. Only the Spirit of God Can Make the Wicked Heart
Open to the Bible

II. ENEMIES OF THE BIBLE ARE WICKED, DECEIT-
FUL MEN

1. Jesus Warned of False Prophets, Wolves Who Come in
Sheep's Clothing

2. False Teachers Are "Deceitful Workers, Transforming
Themselves Into the Apostles of Christ"

3. Paul Warned Timothy of Such Wicked Unbelief

4. Modernists, Liberals "Bring in Damnable Heresies"
Privily, Through Covetousness

5. Bible Deniers Are "Ungodly Men," Denying the Lord
Jesus

6. Infidels in the Church and Out Are Alike Wicked

III. UNCONVERTED MEN CANNOT UNDERSTAND
SPIRITUAL TRUTH

1. The Natural Man Cannot Receive the Things of the
Spirit of God

BEWARE OF "SCHOLARS" WHO DO NOT BELIEVE THE BIBLE IS GOD'S WORD

It is part of the apostasy of this day that unconverted men, not Christians by experience, unbelieving men, not Christians in the historic Christian faith "once delivered," are accepted in many Christian circles. That is wrong morally and it is foolish from the viewpoint of scholarship. Those who do not revere the Bible as the Word of God are not good men and are not reliable scholars.

I. THERE IS A MORAL GUILT IN UNBELIEF ABOUT CHRIST AND THE BIBLE

It is true that God invites the sinner to come and that God meets all who draw nigh. God is found of all who seek Him sincerely with their whole heart. Since one who chooses to do God's will and follows on to know God may know Him, there is a moral guilt to those who do not believe the Bible. A sinful heart blinds a sinful mind. A perverse will that chooses darkness will not find the true light of God.

Jesus stated this great moral law in John 3:18-21:

"He that believeth on him is not condemned: but he that believeth not is condemned already, because he hath not believed in the name of the only begotten Son of God. And this is the condemnation, that light is come into the world, and men loved darkness rather than light, because their deeds were evil. For every one that doeth evil hateth the light, neither cometh to the light, lest his deeds should be reproved. But he that doeth

truth cometh to the light, that his deeds may be made manifest, that they are wrought in God."

One who does not believe in Christ, who does not lovingly trust Him for salvation, "is condemned already, because he hath not believed in the name of the only begotten Son of God." God pronounces a moral condemnation on unbelief in Christ and thus unbelief in the Bible.

We see that the heart that does not trust Jesus Christ is condemned because it chooses not to believe. The deeds of such an one are evil so he does not seek the light. There is no way to divorce the heart attitude choosing sin, from the mind that does not approach Christ in loving trust. And so a love for sin and a choosing of sin blinds one to the truth about the Bible.

There is much talk about "honest doubters." An honest doubter cannot stay a doubter. He can know, if he chooses Christ and righteousness. To choose Christ and to choose righteousness is the same choice. And to choose Christ and righteousness is to come to the light so one's mind can see clearly the spiritual truth.

1. A Bias Against the Bible Blinds the Unbeliever

The heart attitude tends to dictate the mental choice. There are many illustrations of how one's preference influences one's judgment.

For example, the American Cancer Society and the American Medical Society have proved beyond any reasonable doubt that cigarettes tend to bring lung cancer and that several times as many heavy smokers have lung cancer as non-smokers. They say that scientific research definitely connects smoking with increased heart disease and other causes of death.

But at great cost the tobacco companies have set up a foundation to study the same problem. And they keep reporting that a causal relation between cigarette smoking and lung cancer is not yet proved! Why? Because tobacco companies and those who live on the sale of the poison weed do not want to see that they are helping kill their victims. I do not mean that these tobacco men are wholly and maliciously lying. Rather, they deceive themselves and then they hope to deceive others. Men do not willingly believe that they ought to give up their livelihood, give up their profits, give up what they want. They choose to believe what they would rather believe. Men who continue in sin and prefer sin do not willingly consider how bad is their sin.

So scientists, paid by the liquor industry, do not find that about half of the fatal traffic accidents are caused by drink or that a great percentage of major crimes involve drink as a factor. But unbiased police and government agencies do so find.

The fact that the heart, opposed to light, does not get the light is the reason Jesus gave for teaching in parables.

In Matthew 13:9-15, we are told:

"Who hath ears to hear, let him hear. And the disciples came, and said unto him, Why speakest thou unto them in parables? He answered and said unto them, Because it is given unto you to know the mysteries of the kingdom of heaven, but to them it is not given. For whosoever hath, to him shall be given, and he shall have more abundance: but whosoever hath not, from him shall be taken away even that he hath. Therefore speak I to them in parables: because they seeing see not; and hearing they hear not, neither do they understand. And in them is fulfilled the prophecy of Esaias, which saith, By hearing ye shall hear, and shall not understand; and seeing ye shall see, and shall not perceive: For this people's heart is waxed gross, and their ears are dull of hearing, and their eyes they have closed; lest at any time they should see with their eyes and hear with their ears, and should understand with their heart, and should be converted, and I should heal them."

Jesus said it was true in Isaiah's day and it was true in our Lord's ministry also that "this people's heart is waxed gross, and their ears are dull of hearing, and their eyes they have closed; lest at any time they should see with their eyes and hear with their ears, and should understand with their heart, and should be converted, and I should heal them." You see, those who rejected Christ and His truth then, did so because of their choosing to dull their ears and close their eyes. They did not want to be converted so they were not converted. Many, many times the Lord Jesus said, in effect, "He that hath ears to hear, let him hear." It is clearly understood that only those who tune their ears to hear God, hear Him; only those whose will chooses to know God, know Him; only those who are open to believe the Bible come to believe the Bible.

2. Such Unbelieving Scoffers at the Scripture Are Foretold

We are told in II Peter 3:3-7 that scoffers shall arise who "willingly are ignorant" of direct creation and of the world cataclysm of the flood in Noah's day. That Scripture says:

"Knowing this first, that there shall come in the last days scoffers, walking after their own lusts, And saying, Where is the promise of his coming? for since the fathers fell asleep, all things continue as they were from the beginning of the creation. For this they willingly are ignorant of, that by the word of God the heavens were of old, and the earth standing out of the water and in the water: Whereby the world that then was, being overflowed with water, perished: But the heavens and the earth, which are now, by the same word are kept in store, reserved unto fire against the day of judgment and perdition of ungodly men."

So people snatch at the unprovable fantasy of organic evolution instead of believing in direct creation of this world as the Bible reports it. So people choose to suppose millions, even billions, of years of life on the earth as the reasons for fossils instead of believing what the Bible tells of a worldwide flood which caused them and caused the strata in our layers of the earth's surface. Why do they so believe that which is not provable? Because they are "willingly ignorant" of God's revealed truth in the Bible.

There is an old proverb, not in the Bible but which sums up the wisdom of the ages as found by millions: "Convince a man against his will, he's of the same opinion still."

So men lively affirm that they do not believe the Bible, that it could not possibly be the infallible Word of God. Yet these same men never read and will not read the works of Robert Dick Wilson, of Machen, of Allis, which demolish the Graff-Wellhausen theory and other theories of unbelief about the Bible. They stay on the side of unbelief because they choose to stay there.

An example of this bias against the Bible and the essentials of the Christian faith often appears in proponents of evolution who, despite continuing lack of proof, insist on natural origin and development of men from brutes, instead of direct creation as taught in the Bible. Here are such examples of animosity to the Bible, given by Byron Nelson:

> That dislike of the idea of creation is in fact the underlying reason for belief in evolution by many leading evolutionists is apparent from the following statements of evolutionists. Prof. Louis T. More of the University of Cincinnati says, "When we examine the causes of our belief [in evolution] we find that, excepting our **desire to eliminate special creation and, generally, what we call the miraculous,** most of them can be considered only as secondary proofs to confirm a theory already advanced." He also says, "Our faith in the idea of evolution depends on our **reluctance to accept the antagonistic doctrine of special creation.**"
>
> Prof. Bateson who, on account of his high standing in the scientific world, often angered his fellow evolutionists by his frank confessions of the weaknesses of the theory, said, "The evolution theory finds its support **not in direct observation, but in the difficulty of forming an alternate hypothesis.**" On one notable occasion Bateson, at the close of an address entitled "Evolutionary Faith and Modern Doubts," in which he had made some surprising acknowledgements of the weakness of the theory, showed his contempt for the Biblical idea of creation in these words, "When such confessions are made, the enemies of science [believers in the Bible are not enemies of science, but of science 'falsely so-called'] see their chance. If we cannot declare here and now how species arose, they will obligingly offer us the solutions with which obscurantism is satisfied (i. e., creation). Let us then proclaim in precise and unmistakable language that our faith in evolution remains unshaken.... The obscurantist [a term of derision applied to the creationist] **has nothing to suggest which is worth a moment's attention.**" [1]

The statement of Dr. More was in a lecture at Princeton University, January, 1925, page 117.

Dr. William Bateson, named above, was professor in Cambridge University, England, was once president of the British Association for the Advancement of Science, was accepted worldwide as a leading authority on evolution. The statements quoted above are from *Materials for the Study of Variation,* page 4, and from an address before the American Association for the Advancement of Science in Toronto in 1922, published in *Science,* January 20, 1922.

It is obvious that these liberal deniers of the Bible hate the idea of creation and so hate the Bible which calls man to give account to God, and so they do not seek truth with an open

---

1. *After His Kind*, pp. 150,151.

mind. They are unrepentant sinners and resist the truth because it is unpopular with their crowd and unpalatable to carnal hearts.

3. Dr. Fosdick an Example of the "Feigned Words" of Enemies of the Bible

Since Dr. Harry Emerson Fosdick has been for a generation perhaps the best known of the modern or unbelieving churchmen who are the enemies of the Bible, here is a reference to him. Dr. Wilbur M. Smith says:

> **The So-called Contradictions in the Resurrection Narratives.** One of the inexcusably weak and logically unjustified ways that modern rationalists have of getting rid of the whole problem of the Resurrection of our Lord, and the evidence supporting it, is to slurringly speak of what they call the "contradictions" in these narratives, as though just the use of the word "contradiction" is enough to destroy the whole great massive structure built up by the evidence of the Gospels.
>
> This is the way Dr. Harry Emerson Fosdick deals with the subject, in his widely-used and strangely overrated work, **A Guide to Understanding the Bible:** "Certainly if the idea of Jesus' risen life started with any factual elements associated with an empty tomb, that element was never clearly visualized, even in the imagination of the first disciples, and is now confused for us in narratives that contradict each other in every important detail." Now these narratives do not contradict each other "in every important detail." The truth is that in every **important** detail they are in total agreement and when, in spite of this, Dr. Fosdick dares to make the statement we have just quoted, he is saying something that is not true, and because Dr. Fosdick has really been reading and studying the Bible for many years, — well, I leave the sentence unfinished. [2]

"Feigned words," "deceitful words," "wolves in sheep's clothing," the Bible says of such men. The enemies of the Bible are unregenerate men, evil men who deliberately reject the light. Their opinion is not to be trusted about the Bible. They do not have the honesty of heart and the humility of mind to approach with any scientific objective viewpoint the great spiritual truths about the Bible and Christ and the Christian religion.

In the book mentioned above by Dr. Wilbur M. Smith, there

---

2. *Therefore Stand,* pp. 401,402.

is an especially strong chapter of forty-six pages on "Some Reasons for the Unbelief of Men and Their Antagonism to God."

Note the following subtitles in this tremendous chapter by Dr. Smith:

> Man Fallen Away From God Has a Bias Against God
> The Darkness of the Mind of Natural Man
> Early Manifestations of Hatred to God
> Educational Influences That by Their Character Must Create an Attitude of Skepticism[3]

The subtitle of another section is "The Will Not to Believe." Yes, unsaved men have "the will not to believe."

4. Only the Spirit of God Can Make the Wicked Heart Open to the Bible

Bettex says: "The entire theory that science is free from presuppositions rests upon the great, false presupposition that man can be without presuppositions. Only the Holy Ghost can make man free from his presuppositions." [4]

Saint Augustine, the Bishop of Hippo, said, "The dark places in the Bible come from the dark places in our hearts." A heart surrendered to God and penitently, earnestly seeking to please Him is needed if one is to understand the Bible. Bettex says:

> And Luther wrote to Spalatin, who asked him concerning the best method of studying the Bible: "Above all things it is quite certain (**primum id certissimum est**) that one cannot search into the Holy Scriptures by means of study, nor by means of the intellect (**ingenium**). Therefore begin with prayer, that the Lord grant unto you the true understanding of His Word. There is no interpreter of the Word of God, except the Author of the Word, God Himself." (L. Ep. I, p. 88.) In another place he says, "Scripture without any commentary is the sun from which all Doctors receive light."[5]

Those who do not believe the Bible are guilty of a bias, a prejudice, a preference against the Bible and against God.

---

3. *Therefore Stand*
4. *The Bible, the Word of God*, p. 222.
5. *The Bible, the Word of God*, p. 227.

II. ENEMIES OF THE BIBLE ARE WICKED, DECEITFUL MEN

We face a sad fact, stated above, when we consider the pronouncements of unbelievers in the Bible, unbelievers in the virgin birth, the bodily resurrection, the sinless deity of Christ and His blood atonement. Shocking as it may seem, this is one of the clearest teachings of the Bible, and honest men who care about what the Bible says and about what Jesus Christ said must consider this fact.

1. Jesus Warned of False Prophets, Wolves Who Come in Sheep's Clothing

In Matthew 7:15, Jesus says, "Beware of false prophets, which come to you in sheep's clothing, but inwardly they are ravening wolves." He says that we can know these false prophets by their fruits, that is, by their teaching. And in verses 21 to 23 following He plainly says that many of these claiming to prophesy in Christ's name, cast out devils and do good works, will hear the sad words of Jesus, "I never knew you: depart from me, ye that work iniquity." Jesus says that false teachers on these great essentials of the Christian faith are wolves, though they claim to be sheep. And they deceitfully put on sheep's clothing to deceive others.

2. False Teachers Are "Deceitful Workers, Transforming Themselves Into the Apostles of Christ"

In II Corinthians 11:13-15 the Apostle Paul said: "For such are false apostles, deceitful workers, transforming themselves into the apostles of Christ. And no marvel; for Satan himself is transformed into an angel of light. Therefore it is no great thing if his ministers also be transformed as the ministers of righteousness; whose end shall be according to their works."

Note the moral guilt involved here. These are "deceitful workers" who claim to be apostles of Christ when they are not, just as they are ministers of Satan, then. So, those who are enemies of the Bible as the very Word of God, are wicked, deceitful men.

3. Paul Warned Timothy of Such Wicked Unbelief

In I Timothy 4:1 and 2 are these plain words: "Now the Spirit speaketh expressly, that in the latter times some shall depart from the faith, giving heed to seducing spirits, and doctrines of devils; Speaking lies in hypocrisy; having their conscience seared with a hot iron." Notice the sharp denunciation of these that give "heed to seducing spirits, and doctrines of devils; Speaking lies in hypocrisy." Their conscience is seared. This is the state of those who do not believe the Bible and teach against the infallible authority of the Word of God.

And in II Timothy 3:5 Paul warns Timothy again about those "having a form of godliness, but denying the power thereof."

4. Modernists, Liberals "Bring in Damnable Heresies" Privily, Through Covetousness

The Apostle Peter was inspired to write about such false prophets also.

"But there were false prophets also among the people, even as there shall be false teachers among you, who privily shall bring in damnable heresies, even denying the Lord that bought them and bring upon themselves swift destruction. And many shall follow their pernicious ways; by reason of whom the way of truth shall be evil spoken of. And through covetousness shall they with feigned words make merchandise of you: whose judgment now of a long time lingereth not, and their damnation slumbereth not." — II Pet. 2:1-3.

Examine that Scripture again. They "privily . . . bring in damnable heresies." They do not openly, publicly announce their enmity for Christ and the Bible, but they deceive the people, "even denying the Lord that bought them." Why do they do it? They do it "through covetousness." And how? "With feigned words," making merchandise of the people. So liberals in the churches, claiming to be Christians when they are not, claiming to speak as prophets of God when they represent Satan and not God, are enemies of the Bible and are wicked men, deceitful men.

5. Bible Deniers Are "Ungodly Men" Denying the Lord Jesus

The wickedness of unbelieving men is reproved in Jude 3 and 4:

"Beloved, when I gave all diligence to write unto you of the common salvation, it was needful for me to write unto you, and exhort you that ye should earnestly contend for the faith which was once delivered unto the saints. For there are certain men crept in unawares, who were before of old ordained to this condemnation, ungodly men, turning the grace of our God into lasciviousness, and denying the only Lord God, and our Lord Jesus Christ."

Note carefully what God says here: "The faith" is "the faith of the Gospel" of Philippians 1:27, the certain essential doctrines which are in the Gospel and the principal doctrines of Christianity. We must contend for this faith. Why? These men who oppose the faith are "ungodly men, turning the grace of our God into lasciviousness, and denying the only Lord God, and our Lord Jesus Christ." They may say nice words about Jesus, but they do not believe His deity, they do not worship Him as God, they do not trust Him as Saviour.

Many times in the Bible there are references to such unbelieving enemies of the Bible who claim to be Christians. Titus was commanded to 'hold fast the faithful word,' to stop the mouths of vain talkers and deceivers who teach falsely "for filthy lucre's sake" (Titus 1:9-11). In II John 9-11 we are told, "Whosoever transgresseth, and abideth not in the doctrine of Christ, hath not God." Notice, they *transgress* in not accepting the Bible doctrine about Christ in the Bible and such people are not to be received in our houses, not to be bidden Godspeed nor counted as Christians. They 'have not God.'

Those, then, who do not believe the Bible are the enemies of the Bible and tend to deceive. They want to hold positions of leadership and gain in the churches, they wear sheep's clothing, but they are wolves. They intentionally deceive for filthy lucre's sake. They make merchandise of the people for covetousness.

Therefore, we do not count as important the opinions of wicked men, unconverted men, deniers of the Bible, when we study the inspiration of the Bible.

6. Infidels in the Church and Out Are Alike Wicked

Tom Paine wrote the first edition of *The Age of Reason* while he was in prison in France. He plainly admitted that he wrote it without having a copy of the Bible or even a copy of the New Testament at hand, yet he foolishly said that he felt he had proved that the Bible was not reliable, was not the Word of God — a foolish, ignorant boast! Wicked, deceived heart! Why would any intelligent man think that the opinions of a profane, drunken man like Paine were important when he did not study the Bible itself, did not even have at hand a Bible to read when he set out to prove that the Bible was not true! And liberals in the churches, not as honest as Paine, though they are the same kind of infidels privately, are not to be counted good men and their words are not to be counted as wise. Their opinions are not to be regarded. Why? Because they are wicked men, intentionally deceiving, intentionally rejecting the light and trying to blind others to the light.

In a widely published letter, Dr. Harry Emerson Fosdick said: "No, I do not believe in the virgin birth of Christ and I do not know an intelligent man who does."

Had Dr. Fosdick really, honestly investigated this matter and found that no intelligent people believed in the virgin birth and other essentials of the Christian faith? Does he really believe that scholars like Robert Dick Wilson, Machen, Hodge, Warfield, and more recent, Allis of Princeton, all contemporary with him, were not intelligent men? Did he really check and find that R. A. Torrey, C. I. Scofield, William Jennings Bryan, and W. B. Riley, who all lived in his day, and many, many other great, scholarly, Christian men — did he really believe that these were not intelligent men? Winston Churchill openly and in print avowed his belief in all the Bible. But did Dr. Fosdick say that Churchill was not an intelligent man? The answer is

obvious.   Fosdick said what was not true and said it with a
deliberate intention to deceive.   A Christ-rejecting, unconverted
man is an enemy of the Bible and would deceive others.

III. UNCONVERTED MEN CANNOT
UNDERSTAND SPIRITUAL TRUTH

Whose opinion may we value, when we go to study spiritual
truth, for example, on the doctrine of the inspiration of the
Bible?

1. The Natural Man Cannot Receive the
Things of the Spirit of God

In I Corinthians, chapter 2, we have a wonderful revelation
about divine inspiration of the Bible, even the very verbal
inspiration of the Bible.   In verse 14 is this strong statement:
"But the natural man receiveth not the things of the Spirit of
God: for they are foolishness unto him: neither can he know
them, because they are spiritually discerned."

Dr. Carl Henry says about this matter of approaching the
Bible with a wicked bias against God:

> The approach to the Bible, in whole and in part, is ventured
> from only one of two standpoints, that of faith or that of sus-
> pended judgment.   One has either a regard or disregard for its
> authority.   In the one case, its trustworthiness is assumed unless
> conclusive evidence for the contrary appears; in the other, any
> and every passage in the Bible is called in question, and its
> trustworthiness acknowledged only for some other reason than
> that it belongs to the sacred record. [6]

Later on the same page he says:

> The Christian view of inspiration is part and parcel of a
> Christian view of God and the world.   The answer to the ques-
> tion, "Where, in a debatable matter, shall the benefit of the
> doubt go?" will reflect the pattern by which one approaches the
> problem.   Does the benefit fall to the modern view, with its bias

---

6. *Inspiration and Interpretation,* edited by John W. Walvoord, the chapter on
"Divine Revelation of the Bible," by Carl Henry, p. 227.

toward the fallibility of Scripture? Does it fall rather to the side of Biblical authority and reliability? [7]

2. To Give Weight and Respect for Opinions of Bible Enemies Is Wrong

Dr. Edward J. Young takes a fine stand for the verbal inspiration of the Bible. However, he says something in the preface with which I seriously disagree.

> Although I reject most heartily the modern views of the Bible, I have the greatest respect for some of the men who hold these views. The frequent reference to the writings of Otto A. Piper and Alan Richardson, even though so often by way of disagreement, will, I trust, be regarded as an evidence of the respect in which these writers are held. [8]

I do not quote the opinions of unconverted men, enemies of the Bible, except as it becomes necessary to refute those opinions. I do not believe that a man who does not personally accept Christ and love Him, and does not revere the Bible as God's Word, has the sincerity of heart and the humility of heart, the unbiased objective approach, with a good heart which is necessary to understand spiritual truth. I believe that if Tom Paine is to be called an infidel and if Robert Ingersoll is to be called an infidel, then men in the church who take exactly the same attitude toward Christ and the Bible ought to be called infidels, too, because they are exactly that. I believe they ought to be regarded as enemies of Christ and of the Bible, because if they were really friends of Christ and of the Bible they would come to know the truth which God is so willing to reveal to those who seek His face humbly and lovingly. There is room for difference of opinion of Christians on lesser matters but not about the Person of Christ and the authority of the Bible. Men who know Christ as Saviour and love Him and who read and revere and sincerely try to follow the Scriptures are much more likely to understand them, than some other unbelieving man who has a heart set against Christ and the Bible, no matter how many degrees he may have.

---

7. *Inspiration and Interpretation*, edited by John W. Walvoord, the chapter on "Divine Revelation of the Bible," by Carl Henry, p. 277.

8. *Thy Word Is Truth*, p. 7.

3. Disbelievers in the Bible Are Unconverted Men

In II John, verses 9 and 10 we find that the man who does not abide in the Bible doctrine about Jesus Christ "hath not God," that is, he is unconverted. We find that Jesus said that false teachers would come at the judgment to say they had cast out devils, they had prophesied in Christ's name, and He will say to them, "I never knew you: depart from me, ye that work iniquity." And in II Peter, chapter 2, and in Jude, we have a description of the awful wickedness of these men who are unsaved.

So since enemies of the Bible, unbelievers in the Christ of the Bible, are unconverted men and natural men, we learn that "the natural man receiveth not the things of the Spirit of God: for they are foolishness unto him: neither can he know them, because they are spiritually discerned." The unconverted man cannot know the things of God revealed in the Bible.

Oh, if anybody wants to know whether the Bible is true, he must trust in Christ and have his poor, wicked heart changed and have the Holy Spirit of God to live within. Then he can have help and understanding of the Bible.

No unconverted man ought ever be allowed to teach a Sunday school class or fill a pulpit or teach in a Christian college or teach in a theological seminary. No unconverted man who writes on religion ought ever to have his books read or regarded. He does not know and cannot know the best things God reveals until he himself is forgiven and changed.

We do not reject scholarship. We do reject the biased false scholarship of infidels. We are open to all truth but not to the partisan claims of men whose hearts are closed to God's truth.

Bible truth is for saved people and all saved people ought to seek God's truth more and more. But the unconverted man needs first of all to come with a contrite, penitent heart, to be born again.

In a little cow town in West Texas where I lived as a boy, there was the town infidel. He was a crude and uneducated man, a profane, drinking man with a criminal record, though a strong personality. He talked long and loud in his criticism of the Bible to all who would hear. He used the same kind of argument that Paine and Voltaire and Ingersoll used, the same kind of arguments that infidels in the church today use. He used the same kind of arguments that Fosdick and Buttrick and Oxnam used against the inspiration of the Bible, the virgin birth and deity of Christ, and he had the same kind of wicked heart. He was no more intelligent than others, no more scientifically trained; he just had a more wicked, Christ-rejecting heart than many and so he spewed out his infidelity.

Unconverted men cannot understand spiritual truth. They are not good men, they do not have good hearts, they are not to be trusted, and they are not to be regarded as scholars on the matters concerning the Bible.

This is holy ground, to be humbly, reverently approached with a penitent, believing heart and open ears to hear what God says.

Oh, you who read the Bible, I beg you, take the shoes off the feet of your heart as you read.

Dyson Hague has this sweet word here:

> Let me say this one word more. Oh, do not think and do not say, as you have heard men say they think, that we ought to read this Book as we read any other book; we ought to study it and analyze it just as we do any textbook in literature or science. No, no! When you come to this Book, come to it with awe. Read it with reverence. Regard it with a most sacred attention. "Put off thy shoes from off thy feet, for the place whereon thou standest is holy ground." Never, never compare this Book in the terms of human comparisons with other books. Comparison is dangerous. They are of earth. This is from Heaven. And do not think and do not say that this Book only contains the words of God. It is the Word of God. To say the Bible contains the Word of God, instead of saying the Bible is the Word of God, is inadequate and misleading as Saphir declares. Everything that is in Scripture would authenticate itself to us as the Word of God, if we understood it in its right connection with the center. Therefore, think not of it as a good book, or even as a better book, but lift it in heart and mind and faith and love far, far above all, and ever regard it, not as the word of man, but as it is in truth, the Word of God; nay, more, as the living Word of the Living God; supernatural in origin; eternal in duration; inexpressible in value; infinite in scope; divine in authorship; human in penmanship; regenerative in power; infallible in authority; universal in interest; personal in application; and as St. Paul declares, inspired in totality."[9]

_____

9. From "The Wonder of the Book" by Rev. Dyson Hague, D.D., in *Sword Book of Treasures*, p. 47.

CHAPTER III

THE BIBLE CLAIMS TO BE THE INSPIRED
WORD OF GOD

I. SOME BASIC SCRIPTURES CLAIMING DIVINE IN-
SPIRATION

1. The Scriptures Are Breathed Out by God

2. "Every Word" of Scripture "Proceedeth Out of the
Mouth of God"

3. Bible Writers Wrote "As They Were Moved by the
Holy Ghost"

4. Repeatedly Claims That the Holy Ghost Spoke by the
Writers

5. Scriptures Revealed by God's Spirit Miraculously "in
Words Which the Holy Ghost Teacheth"

6. Paul's Gospel Received Not From Men but From God

II. BUT HUNDREDS OF TIMES THE BIBLE CLAIMS
TO SPEAK FOR GOD

1. Literally Hundreds of Times the Bible Says, "The
Word of the Lord Came to Isaiah" or Like Statements

2. The Bible Claims to Describe in Detail Events About
Which No Human Without Direct Information From
God Could Know

3. The Bible Gives Some Amazing Prophecies of the Future

4. The Promises and Warnings of the Bible Enter the
Realm of the Moral Righteousness of God

5. Old Testament Prophets Did Not Understand What
They Wrote

III. THE BIBLE HAS CLAIMS FOR ITS PERFECTION
AND PERMANENCE WHICH ONLY A GOD-GIVEN
BOOK COULD HAVE

1. A Striking Statement About the Indestructible Word Is
   in Isaiah 40:6-8:

2. Jesus Emphatically Taught the Eternal, Perfect Quality
   of Scripture

3. The Scripture Claims Perfection

4. The Scripture Claims to Be Eternal

CHAPTER III

THE BIBLE CLAIMS TO BE THE INSPIRED WORD OF GOD

Nothing any man can say or think about the Bible is as important as what the Bible says about itself. There are many reasons for believing that the Bible is all it claims to be, but the Bible itself is its best witness. And the Bible does clearly, repeatedly, and without any question or limitation, claim to be the very inspired Word of God.

I. SOME BASIC SCRIPTURES CLAIMING DIVINE INSPIRATION

Consider first, there are many express statements that the Bible is inspired or is the Word of God or proceeds from God. Then, in literally hundreds of cases it claims to speak for God. Further, the Bible claims such perfections as could be only true of a God-given Book, and the claim for inspiration includes all parts of the Bible.

1. The Scriptures Are Breathed Out by God

A fundamental statement of Scripture about inspiration is in II Timothy 3:15,16. The Scriptures are breathed out by God. We read:

"And that from a child thou hast known the holy scriptures, which are able to make thee wise unto salvation through faith which is in Christ Jesus. All scripture is given by inspiration of God, and is profitable for doctrine, for reproof, for correction, for instruction in righteousness."

Note this passage speaks of "the holy scriptures" and these writings "are able to make thee wise unto salvation through faith which is in Christ Jesus."

But the express statement in verse 16 is even stronger: "All scripture is given by inspiration of God." And that is why it is so profitable and thoroughly furnishes the man of God, we are told.   Even if you change the order of the words as they are in the American Standard Version of 1901, "Every scripture inspired of God is also profitable for teaching, for reproof, for correction, for instruction which is in righteousness. . . ," it does not change the meaning. A certain group of writings are, all of them, given by inspiration of God.

Webster's New International Dictionary defines inspiration thus:

> **inspiration.** 2. Theol. a A supernatural divine influence on the prophets, apostles, or sacred writers, by which they were qualified to communicate truth without error; a supernatural influence which qualifies men to receive and communicate divine truth.   Various theories as to the degree, extent, and mode of the inspiration of Scripture are held. That of **plenary inspiration** regards the inspiration as extending to all the subjects dealt with; that of **verbal inspiration** extends the inspiration to every word. Some writers identify these two kinds.   The theory of **moral inspiration** limits the inspiration and consequent authoritativeness to the moral and religious instruction the writings contain. As to its mode, inspiration is held by some to be **mechanical,** and the writers to have been simply amanuenses of the Holy Spirit, and by others to be dynamical, and the writers to have been moved by the Holy Spirit operating on and through their natural faculties.

But the word "inspiration" here means a great deal more than the English term usually would imply. Our English word comes from the Latin "inspire," meaning "to breathe in." It is the opposite of the word "expire" or "breathe out." Thus some would take it to mean that God breathed into men's writings and makes them the Word of God, or He breathed on the writings in such a way as to supervise and keep them from error.

But the meaning in the original Greek, *theopneustos,* is much more definite.   It is literally *God-breathed.* All Scripture is "God-breathed," that is, the Scripture itself is breathed out from God.   God is its origin.   The miracle of the Scriptures came directly from God.   A similar terminology is that used when God made Adam "and breathed into his nostrils the breath of life; and man became a living soul" (Gen. 2:7). This is about as strong a statement as human language could make about the inspiration of the Bible. The Scripture was breathed out by God. This is so important, and so often not understood, we stress the point.

Edward J. Young expounds the meaning of II Timothy 3:16, "All scripture is given by inspiration of God. . . ." He wrote:

> The word which for our purpose is of supreme importance is the word **theopneustos,** translated in the English Bible, "inspired of God." It is a compound, consisting of the elements **theo** (God) and **pneustos** (breathed). Now, it is well to note that the word ends in the three letters -tos. In the Greek language, words which 1) end in -tos and 2) are compound with **theo** (God) are generally passive in meaning. An example will make this clear. There is a Greek word **theodidaktos** (many others might also be brought forth), which means "taught of God." As may be clearly seen, it ends in -tos and also contains the element **theo** (God).
>
> Precisely similar is the important word which we are now engaged in considering, namely, **theopneustos.** It likewise is passive in usage, and we should properly translate, "breathed of God." This point is often overlooked, and there have been those who have somewhat vigorously insisted that the meaning is active. They would therefore translate by the phrase "breathing out God," in the sense that the Scriptures breathed forth or were imbued with the Spirit of God. Such, however, as has been noted above, is not the true meaning. The true meaning is passive, "that which is breathed out by God," and it is this strange designation that the Apostle here applies to the Old Testament Scriptures.
>
> What, however, can such a strange designation mean? Why did Paul thus speak of the Scriptures? He thus spoke, we believe, because he wished to make as clear as possible the fact that the Scriptures did not find their origin in man but in God. It was God the Holy Ghost who breathed them forth; they owed their origin to Him; they were the product of the creative breath of God Himself. It is a strong figure, this expression "breathed out by God." A strong figure, however, is needed, in order that Timothy may realize that he is being asked to place his confidence not in writings which merely express the hopes and aspirations of the best of men, but rather in writings which are themselves actually breathed out by God, and consequently of absolute authority. [1]

---

1. *Thy Word Is Truth*, pp. 20,21.

Further, Dr. Young says:

> The Scriptures therefore are writings which found their origin
> in God; they are the very product of His creative breath. It is
> this, then, that we mean when we speak of the inspiration of the
> Bible.   Now the term **inspiration** is, in the humble opinion of
> the present writer, not a happy one.   The word inspiration
> means that which is breathed in. It comes to us from the Latin,
> and in the Latin translation of the Bible, commonly known as
> the Vulgate, is used as a rendering of the Greek **theopneustos**
> (God-breathed).   We are not satisfied with this translation, for
> the English word inspiration, as has just been remarked, means
> a "breathing in," and, as we have seen, that is not at all what
> Paul intends to say.   We must be very explicit on this point.
>   In writing to Timothy, Paul does not wish Timothy to under-
> stand that the Scriptures are a body of human writings into
> which something Divine has been breathed.   That is precisely
> what he does not wish Timothy to understand.   According to
> Paul, the Scriptures are not writings into which something Divine
> has been breathed; they are not even writings which are imbued
> with the Divine Spirit (at least, that is not his emphasis in this
> passage).   The Scriptures, Paul vigorously asserts, are writings
> which came into being because they were breathed out by God
> Himself.   And that is something quite different from what is
> commonly suggested by the word "inspiration." [2]

Benjamin B. Warfield, tremendous scholar that he was, has a
long chapter of fifty-two big pages about "God-Inspired Scripture," dealing entirely with the Greek term used in II Timothy
3:16, *Theopneustos,* quoting many scholars, repelling critics.
He says, "For surely there was no conception more deeply
rooted in the Hebrew mind, at least, than that of the creative
'breath of God'. . ." [3] and he infers that when God breathed
out the Scripture, it was the same kind of perfect creative act
as when He created the world or when He created man—breathed
into his nostrils and he became a living soul.

And he sums up his conclusion thus:

> What is **Theopneustos** is "God-breathed," produced by the
> creative breath of the Almighty. And Scripture is called **Theo-**
> **pneustos** in order to designate it as "God-breathed," the product
> of Divine spiration, the creation of that Spirit who is in all
> spheres of the Divine activity the executive of the Godhead. [4]

W. H. Griffith Thomas misunderstands the statement, "All

---

2. *Thy Word Is Truth,* pp. 21,22.
3. *The Inspiration and Authority of the Bible,* p. 285.
4. *The Inspiration and Authority of the Bible,* p. 296.

scripture is given by inspiration of God...," in II Timothy
3:16. He says, "'...Every writing is God-breathed.' God
somehow or other breathed into these writings, and therefore
we are concerned with the words." [5] But here the good man,
in a great book, is mistaken.

No, the writings did not originate with men and then "God
breathed on them." Rather, God breathed out the very words
and had men write them down!

In his article on inspiration, Warfield says:

> The scriptural conception of the relation of the Divine Spirit to
> the human authors in the production of Scripture is better ex-
> pressed by the figure of "bearing" than by the figure of "in-
> breathing"; and when our Bib. writers speak of the action of
> the Spirit of God in this relation as a breathing, they represent
> it as a "breathing out" of the Scriptures by the Spirit, and not
> a "breathing into" the Scriptures by Him. [6]

Let us make sure that we do not water down this express
statement of Scripture about inspiration. It is not that God
breathed on certain men or that they wrote and God breathed
on the writings. Rather, the very words of Scriptures themselves
are breathed out from God.

The great theologian, Charles Hodge of Princeton, says:

> Inspiration, therefore, is not to be confounded with spiritual
> illumination. They differ, first, as to their subjects. The subjects
> of inspiration are a few selected persons; the subjects of spiritual
> illumination are all true believers. And, secondly, they differ as
> to their design. The design of the former is to render certain
> men infallible as teachers, the design of the latter is to render
> men holy; and of course they differ as to their effects. Inspira-
> tion in itself has no sanctifying influence. Balaam was inspired.
> Saul was among the prophets. Caiaphas uttered a prediction
> which "he spake not of himself." (John xi. 51.) [7]

Note carefully, "Inspiration in itself has no sanctifying influence." Whatever degree of illumination God gave the writers of
the Scripture, it had nothing to do with inspiration itself. They
simply had some of the common heritage of Christians, illumination, but inspiration is a miraculous intervention of God which
does not necessarily involve any spiritual sanctification, any
heightening of natural abilities and faculties, any genius. It

---

5. *God Spake All These Words*, p. 89.
6. *The International Standard Bible Encyclopaedia*, Vol. 3, p. 1480.
7. *Systematic Theology*, Vol. 1, pp. 154,155.

involves the writing down what God gives in God's words, miraculously given.

2. "Every Word" of Scripture "Proceedeth Out of the Mouth of God"

The same meaning is in the statement of Jesus in Matthew 4:4: "It is written, Man shall not live by bread alone, but by every word that proceedeth out of the mouth of God." Here Jesus is quoting from Deuteronomy 8:3 and the same quotation is recorded also in Luke 4:4. So, the Old Testament statement is reinforced by the Lord Jesus who quotes it as authority. Whence came the Scriptures? Every word of them "proceedeth out of the mouth of God." Here the Spirit of God leaps over the details of any human element in the Scriptures, goes beyond the pen and the penman, and any part he may have had in writing the Scriptures, to the original source. The words of the Bible came from the mouth of God. Of course, that means the original autographs.

3. Bible Writers Wrote "As They Were Moved by the Holy Ghost"

Second Peter 1:16-21 makes a very strong assertion about the writings of the prophets:

"For we have not followed cunningly devised fables, when we made known unto you the power and coming of our Lord Jesus Christ, but were eyewitnesses of his majesty. For he received from God the Father honour and glory, when there came such a voice to him from the excellent glory, This is my beloved Son, in whom I am well pleased. And this voice which came from heaven we heard, when we were with him in the holy mount. We have also a more sure word of prophecy; whereunto ye do well that ye take heed, as unto a light that shineth in a dark place, until the day dawn, and the day star arise in your hearts: Knowing this first, that no prophecy of the scripture is of any private interpretation. For the prophecy came not in old time by the will of man: but holy men of God spake as they were moved by the Holy Ghost."

Here Peter uses two arguments to show that the Scriptures he
has believed and preached are not cunningly devised fables.
His teaching about the power and the coming of Christ can be
trusted; first, for the lesser reason that Peter and the other
apostles "were eyewitnesses of his majesty" on the Mount of
Transfiguration. They saw Jesus transfigured with a face like
the sun and His garments as white as the light; they heard the
voice of God attesting, "This is my beloved Son, in whom I am
well pleased." That eyewitness account of the deity of Christ
and thus of the authenticity of the Scriptures about Him, is
good, but there is a better evidence than that! It is the evidence
of the Scriptures themselves.

So Peter was inspired to write, "We have also a more sure
word of prophecy. . . ." That is, prophecy written down in the
Bible is far more sure than the testimony of any eyewitness
not inspired. Peter knew the Lord Jesus, saw His miracles, saw
Him transfigured, heard the voice of God from Heaven approv-
ing Him. But the witness of Peter would be the witness of a
frail man who might have misunderstood some of the implica-
tions or might have failed in some detail of memory or observation. Not so the Scriptures. They are "a more sure word of
prophecy," he said. And why is that? Because ". . . no prophecy of the scripture is of any private interpretation. For the
prophecy came not in old time by the will of man: but holy
men of God spake as they were moved by the Holy Ghost."

We do not here deal with the distinction between revelation
and inspiration. What was revealed was written down, and
there is good evidence, as Warfield shows and as we will mention later, that here the whole plan of the inspiration of the
Bible is involved when God here says "prophecy." The Scripture then came "not. . . by the will of man: but holy men of
God spake as they were moved by the Holy Ghost."

This Scripture is saying that the evidence of the Scriptures
themselves is more sure than any human testimony, even of the
specially fitted and specially favored eyewitnesses who were
closest to Jesus and understood Him best. The eyewitness
accounts of any man are subject to the limitations of the man's
knowledge, memory, understanding and use of language. But
God Himself has no such limitations when He moves men to
write down words of divine prophecy. This is a clear claim to
the inspiration of the Scriptures.

". . .holy men of God spake as they were moved by the Holy

Ghost." The word translated "moved" here is *phero*, "to bear, carry." So actually we must read that in writing the Scriptures "holy men of God were carried along by the Holy Ghost." So the writers were consciously, willingly carried along as God gave the words they were to write. The Scripture is the result of God's action in carrying along men who wrote what He gave them to write. God did not simply follow prophets to correct any mistakes or to intervene if necessary; He carried the prophet along. God was the active source of all Scripture. *God gave; men received.*

4. Repeatedly Claims That the Holy Ghost Spoke by the Writers

We read above in I Peter 1:21, how "holy men of God spake as they were moved by the Holy Ghost." Scriptures repeatedly say even more definitely that the Holy Ghost Himself was speaking in the words which Bible writers wrote down.

The Psalmist David said, "The Spirit of the Lord spake by me, and his word was in my tongue" (II Sam. 23:2). David wrote the words, but it was the Holy Ghost speaking.

And Mark 12:36 quotes David, saying, "For David himself said by the Holy Ghost, The Lord said to my Lord, Sit thou on my right hand, till I make thine enemies thy footstool." David "said by the Holy Ghost."

Peter said in Acts 1:16, "Men and brethren, this scripture must needs have been fulfilled, which the Holy Ghost by the mouth of David spake before concerning Judas, which was guide to them that took Jesus."

It was the mouth of David, but it was the Holy Ghost speaking in Psalm 41:9.

The same explicit statement is given about the prophecy of Isaiah: in Acts 28:25, Paul says, "Well spake the Holy Ghost by Esaias the prophet unto our fathers...."

Men were inspired to write parts of the Bible. It was actually the Holy Ghost speaking. So clearly does God's Word claim divine inspiration.

5. Scriptures Revealed by God's Spirit Miraculously "in Words Which the Holy Ghost Teacheth"

The most detailed teaching about inspiration in a single passage in the Bible is given, we think, in I Corinthians 2:9-14:

"But as it is written, Eye hath not seen, nor ear heard, neither have entered into the heart of man, the things which God hath prepared for them that love him. But God hath revealed them unto us by his Spirit: for the Spirit searcheth all things, yea, the deep things of God. For what man knoweth the things of a man, save the spirit of man which is in him? even so the things of God knoweth no man, but the Spirit of God. Now we have received, not the spirit of the world, but the spirit which is of God; that we might know the things that are freely given to us of God. Which things also we speak, not in the words which man's wisdom teacheth, but which the Holy Ghost teacheth; comparing spiritual things with spiritual. But the natural man receiveth not the things of the Spirit of God: for they are foolishness unto him: neither can he know them, because they are spiritually discerned."

Dr. Hodge says: "There is neither in the Bible nor in the writings of men a simpler or clearer statement of the doctrines of revelation and inspiration" than this. [8]

Here we are told that the revelation from God which Paul wrote down in his epistles (as other Scriptures were written), did not come from what his eye had seen or what his ear had heard or what he had logically come to understand, by study and investigation, in his heart, but it was revealed by God's Spirit. And there we are plainly told that these wonderful things that came by divine revelation could not be known by man unless the Spirit of God revealed them. So the apostle says that he has received "not the spirit of the world, but the spirit which is of God; that we might know the things that are freely given to us of God." And those things are given "not in the words which man's wisdom teacheth, but which the Holy Ghost teacheth; comparing spiritual things with spiritual," that is, Spirit-given ideas or thoughts, in Spirit-given words.

And then verse 14 plainly tells us that the Scripture could not

---

8. *Systematic Theology,* Vol. 1, p. 162.

originate with the natural man. If there were a Scripture without clear divine inspiration, if the Scripture were not directly given from God but only originated with man at his highest and best, it would still have human frailty, weakness and limitations. But here we are told that both the matter and the wording of the Scriptures are given by God's Spirit.

Again, we do not here go into a discussion of the slight difference sometimes between revelation and inspiration. But what was revealed to Paul in "words which the Holy Ghost teacheth" was what he wrote down in the inspired New Testament and it was not just in Paul's heart that the message was given, but it was put into words, words he would give to others.

We dare not neglect what God had Paul so carefully write down for us here about the origin of Scripture. We have not only the positive statement that God's revelation is given in words "which the Holy Ghost teacheth," Spirit-given matter and Spirit-given words, but we are also plainly told that the Bible is "not in the words which man's wisdom teacheth." The Bible was not written as other books are written and the Lord gives even more details in this negative statement of what the Bible is not. The Bible is not "in the words which man's wisdom teacheth," that is, "Eye hath not seen, nor ear heard, neither have entered into the heart of man, the things which God hath prepared for them that love him."

The Bible is not composed of what men have seen, it is not the report of witnesses. The Bible is not what people have heard as they were told by others. Luke did not learn of the virgin birth from Mary. Mark did not learn the facts of his Gospel from Peter. Matthew and Luke did not copy from Mark or from the fictitious "Q" manuscript. Luke did not search out the facts to make his Gospel "certain," nor did Luke get the details for the book of Acts from Paul. Old Testament prophets did not find and copy genealogical records.

No, the Scriptures were given of God, "combining spiritual things with spiritual words" (A.S.V.).

The Bible is not what men reasoned out in their hearts, nor even in the spiritual experiences of good men. It is not a revelation of what "entered into the heart of man." So, we understand that the Bible is "not in words which man's wisdom teacheth, but which the Spirit teacheth; combining spiritual things with spiritual words," as the American Standard Version has it. So, what we have in the Bible came not from what men saw, nor what men got from witnesses, nor what men searched out or investigated, or thought through. Both the matter and the words of the Bible came directly from God, this Scripture says.

6. Paul's Gospel Received Not From Men but From God

Paul affirms in Galatians 1:11 and 12 that the Gospel he preached he did not receive from men. He was not taught it by the other apostles, but he is inspired to write:

"But I certify you, brethren, that the gospel which was preached of me is not after man. For I neither received it of man, neither was I taught it, but by the revelation of Jesus Christ."

Then, following, it tells how he did not consult any of the apostles or others who had known Jesus, about the Gospel he preached, until years after he had been preaching and he found then that God had given him directly from Heaven the same Gospel which the other apostles who had been with Jesus had preached.

He "neither received it of man," he said, "neither was I taught it, but by the revelation of Jesus Christ." Thus we learn clearly that the Gospel, and hence the Bible, originated with God and not with man. It is God's Word.

The Thessalonian Christians and others who were saved on Paul's missionary journeys were taught by Paul, and then received the epistles from Paul, and Paul's preaching and teaching and the epistles he wrote are now part of our Bible. So in I Thessalonians 2:13 Paul writes these Christians:

"For this cause also thank we God without ceasing, because, when ye received the word of God which ye heard of us, ye received it not as the word of men, but as it is in truth, the word of God, which effectually worketh also in you that believe."

What Paul had preached to them and what he wrote in the epistles was "not as the word of men, but as it is in truth, the word of God." And the results of the teaching and preaching of that Word were the results of a supernatural Gospel. The Bible does clearly claim to be the Word of God.

Charles H. Spurgeon in his sermon on "The Bible" says:

First, then, concerning this book; Who is **the author?** The text says that it is God. "I have written to him the great things of my law." Here lies my Bible—who wrote it? I open it, and find it consists of a series of tracts. The first five tracts were written by a man called Moses; I turn on, and I find others. Sometimes I see David is the penman, at other times Solomon. Here I read Micah, then Amos, then Hosea. As I turn further on to the more luminous pages of the New Testament, I see Matthew, Mark, Luke, and John, Paul, Peter, James, and others; but when I shut up the Book, I ask myself, Who is the author of it? Do these men jointly claim the authorship? Are they the compositors of this massive volume? Do they between themselves divide the honor? Our holy religion answers No!

This volume is the writing of the living God: each letter was penned with an Almighty finger; each word in it dropped from the everlasting lips; each sentence was dictated by the Holy Spirit. Albeit, that Moses was employed to write his histories with his fiery pen, God guided that pen. It may be that David touched his harp and let sweet Psalms of melody drop from his fingers; but God moved his hands over the living strings of his golden harp. It may be that Solomon sang canticles of love, or gave forth words of consummate wisdom, but God directed his lips and made the preacher eloquent. If I follow the thundering Nahum, when his horses plough the waters, or Habakkuk, when he sees the tents of Cushan in affliction; if I read Malachi, when the earth is burning like an oven; if I turn to the smooth page of John, who tells of love, or the rugged, fiery chapters of Peter, who speaks of fire devouring God's enemies; if I turn to Jude, who launches forth anathemas upon the foes of God—everywhere I find God speaking. It is God's voice, not man's; the words are God's words, the words of the Eternal, the Invisible, the Almighty, the Jehovah of this earth.

This Bible is God's Bible, and when I see it, I seem to hear a voice springing up from it, saying, "I am the Book of God; man, read me. I am God's writing; open my leaf, for I was penned by God; read it, for He is my author, and you will see Him visible and manifest everywhere. I have written to him the great things of my law."[9]

II. BUT HUNDREDS OF TIMES THE BIBLE CLAIMS TO SPEAK FOR GOD

Besides the basic statements like those given above, that "All

---

9. *A Coffer of Jewels About the Bible*, pp. 45,46.

scripture is given by inspiration of God," there is an authoritative, bold assumption everywhere through the Bible that it is speaking for God and is God's Word.

1. Literally Hundreds of Times the Bible Says, "The Word of the Lord Came to Isaiah..." or Like Statements

Such statements occur again and again, particularly throughout the Old Testament. In perhaps 1800 cases, they claim to give the very word-for-word quotation from God. In reading them, no honest heart can avoid the clear claim that this is the Word of God speaking for God.

2. The Bible Claims to Describe in Detail Events About Which No Human Without Direct Information From God Could Know

That majestic story of the creation in Genesis is a case in point. The report on the events before the flood of which there was left no human records and reports of what God said and what Satan said and what was in the heart of certain people — these matters are so plainly stated that we know the Bible claims to speak infallibly for God.

3. The Bible Gives Some Amazing Prophecies of the Future

That the Bible gives such prophecies, no one surely would deny. And only the most ignorant would deny that many, many of these prophecies have been fulfilled.

For example, it was foretold hundreds of years ahead of time that the Lord Jesus would be born of a virgin, that He would be of the tribe of Judah and of the house and lineage of David, that He would be born in Bethlehem of Judaea. Daniel was even told how long it would be from the decree to rebuild Jerusalem until the coming of the Messiah, the Prince (Dan. 9:25). Then hundreds of details of the life and ministry and death and resurrection of Jesus are foretold. The very day of the month, the day of the passover lamb, was foretold as the day of His crucifixion. The thoughts and sayings of Jesus on the cross were foretold in Psalm 22, and in the Gospels.

I am saying that the Bible is just as explicit in certain future prophecies about Christ's second coming and about the nations and the end of the age, as about His first coming. These bold predictions mean that the Bible is claiming to speak infallibly for God about things that men would not otherwise know.

Sometimes a charlatan fortuneteller or diviner pretends to foretell in some weasel words something that may happen in the future. But the prophecies in the Bible are not shady and indefinite. They claim to speak for God.

4. The Promises and Warnings of the Bible Enter the Realm of the Moral Righteousness of God

Thus we have promises of what God Himself will do if we trust Him, if we bring our offerings, if we keep His commandments. The Bible makes promises that only God would have a right to make and promises that only God could fulfill.

Likewise, the Bible gives warnings about the results of sin, about the wrath of God, about the end of the sinner, about the wages of sin, that only God Himself could cause to come to pass and only God, or someone who speaks with the authority of God, would have the right to say. I am saying that the Bible thus claims to speak for God.

5. Old Testament Prophets Did Not Understand What They Wrote

In I Peter 1:10-12 is a charming and enlightening passage about how the Bible claims to speak from God so that even those who wrote did not understand what they wrote down.

"Of which salvation the prophets have inquired and searched diligently, who prophesied of the grace that should come unto you: Searching what, or what manner of time the Spirit of Christ which was in them did signify, when it testified beforehand the sufferings of Christ, and the glory that should follow. Unto

whom it was revealed, that not unto themselves, but unto us they did minister the things, which are now reported unto you by them that have preached the gospel unto you with the Holy Ghost sent down from heaven; which things the angels desire to look into."

Here we see the amazing picture: Old Testament prophets who had written down some of the Scriptures about the future coming of the Saviour, now sit down and study their own manuscripts and meditate and pray. What do these prophecies mean, these prophecies written by their own pens? And why? Because it was "the Spirit of Christ which was in them" who gave the words foretelling the future sufferings of Christ and the glory that should follow. And they understood that what God gave them to write down was not particularly all for them but "unto us," Peter writes, who live now after Christ has come.

Here we see clearly that the Scripture did not originate in the plan and mind of these men, but it originated with God, and the Spirit of Christ in them had men write down things that they could not fully understand. So the message is God's message, and only secondarily and partially a man's message in any case. Inspiration did not require that they understand what God told them to write.

Dr. A. J. Gordon says:

> Should we see a student who, having taken down the lecture of a profound philosopher, was now studying diligently to comprehend the sense of the discourse which he had written, we should understand simply that he was a pupil and not a master; that he had nothing to do with originating either the thoughts or the words of the lecture, but was rather a disciple whose province it was to understand what he had transcribed, and so be able to communicate it to others.
>
> And who can deny that this is the exact picture of what we have in this passage from Peter? Here were inspired writers studying the meaning of what they themselves had written. With all possible allowance for the human peculiarities of the writers, they must have been reporters of what they heard, rather than formulators of that which they had been made to understand. [10]

On the prophecy of Caiaphas, Dr. James M. Gray well says:

> And Caiaphas also (John 11:49-52), of whom it is expressly said that when he prophesied that one man should die for the

---

10. *The Ministry of the Spirit*, pp. 173, 174.

people, "This spake he not of himself." Who believes that Caiaphas meant or really knew the significance of what he said?[11]

III. THE BIBLE HAS CLAIMS FOR ITS PERFECTIONS AND PERMANENCE WHICH ONLY A GOD-GIVEN BOOK COULD HAVE

1. A Striking Statement About the Indestructible Word Is in Isaiah 40:6-8:

"*The voice said, Cry. And he said, What shall I cry? All flesh is grass, and all the goodliness thereof is as the flower of the field: The grass withereth, the flower fadeth: because the Spirit of the Lord bloweth upon it: surely the people is grass. The grass withereth, the flower fadeth: but the word of our God shall stand for ever.*"

All flesh is grass. Man is fallible, impermanent and limited, and so all human sources wither, "but the word of our God shall stand for ever." That is quoted in I Peter 1:23-25, which says:

"*Being born again, not of corruptible seed, but of incorruptible, by the word of God, which liveth and abideth for ever. For all flesh is as grass, and all the glory of man as the flower of grass. The grass withereth, and the flower thereof falleth away: But the word of the Lord endureth for ever. And this is the word which by the gospel is preached unto you.*"

What kind of a word? An incorruptible word "which liveth and abideth for ever. . . the word of the Lord endureth for ever." That is far beyond any human goodness.

2. Jesus Emphatically Taught the Eternal, Perfect Quality of Scripture

Elsewhere we will discuss more thoroughly the attitude of Jesus toward the Scripture. Here we simply mention that He

---

11. *The Fundamentals for Today,* Vol. 1, p. 136.

continually upheld it as the perfect and eternal Word of God.

In the Olivet discourse Jesus said, "Heaven and earth shall pass away, but my words shall not pass away" (Matt. 24:35; Mark 13:31; Luke 21:33).

Jesus said that not one jot nor tittle of the law should pass away till all be fulfilled (Matt. 5:17,18).

The Lord Jesus said, "The scripture cannot be broken" (John 10:35).

In Luke 9:26 and Mark 8:38 Jesus said, "For whosoever shall be ashamed of me and of my words, of him shall the Son of man be ashamed, when he shall come in his own glory, and in his Father's, and of the holy angels."

Surely this gives a dignity and authority and permanence to the Scriptures which could not be true of any human, fallible man. And we must remember that the attitude of Jesus Christ here expressed in the Scripture is the way the Scripture views itself all the way through.

Some Bibles print the words of Christ in red, but that is misleading. All the words of the Bible are the words of Christ. The Holy Spirit who moves the writing prophets is "the Spirit of Christ" (Rom. 8:9; I Pet. 1:11). He gave the Scripture.

And so Paul could be inspired to write, "Let the word of Christ dwell in you richly" (Col. 3:16). Jesus identified Himself with the Word of God likewise in Luke 9:26 and the companion passage in Mark 8:38. He said, "For whosoever shall be ashamed of me and of my words, of him shall the Son of man be ashamed, when he shall come in his own glory, and in his Father's, and of the holy angels." But this is giving a dignity and authority, a permanence, to the Word of God which could not be true of any human words or book.

3. The Scripture Claims Perfection

Psalm 19:7 says, "The law of the Lord is perfect, converting the soul." "The law" originally meant the Pentateuch, the law of Moses. Eventually the term seemed to refer to all the Bible. And here the claim is not simply that the law is good but that it is perfect and that it works the miraculous change of regeneration in the believing heart.

The purity and perfection of the Word of God is stated wonderfully in Psalm 12:6: "The words of the Lord are pure words: as silver tried in a furnace of earth, purified seven times."

Here the quality of the Scriptures is not described as finite but as infinite. Perfection here is not claimed for simply the thought, the content from God, in the words of men. No, the perfection is in the very words, "pure words." The Scripture is here claiming for itself perfection which could only exist in the very Word of God.

4. The Scripture Claims to Be Eternal

Psalm 119 has several wonderful statements about the Bible.

Verse 89 says, "For ever, O Lord, thy word is settled in heaven."

And verse 144: "The righteousness of thy testimonies is everlasting: give me understanding, and I shall live."

Verse 152 says, "Concerning thy testimonies, I have known of old that thou hast founded them for ever."

Verse 160 says, "Thy word is true from the beginning: and every one of thy righteous judgments endureth for ever."

These marvelous claims are the claims for the perfections, like those of deity, that the Bible is forever settled in Heaven, that the Scriptures are everlasting, that every one of God's righteous judgments there recorded are eternal — that is a claim for no human book, but for the Bible as the very Word of God.

CHAPTER IV

WHAT A PERFECT, GOD-BREATHED BIBLE INVOLVES

I. WE DEFINE INSPIRATION

1. Inspiration Is Claimed for Original Autographs, Not for Translation or Copying
2. An Errorless Record of Good and Bad
3. The Scriptures Are Inspired, Not the Men
4. Scripture Writers Were Still Frail, Sinning Men
5. "It Is the Book, Not the Men," With Which We Deal
6. Warfield Says Prophets Were "Not the Mover but the Moved"
7. Gaussen, Brookes, and Gray Show Not the Writers but the Writings Inspired
8. The Inspired Gospels Differ, but All Are Correct

II. THE SCRIPTURES, THEN, ARE SUPERNATURAL, ARE MIRACULOUSLY GIVEN

1. Necessarily, Christianity Is a Miracle Religion
2. Perfection Has to Be Supernatural and Miraculous
3. Such a Perfect Word of God Must Come From God to Man, Not Originating With Man
4. That Brings Up Serious Problems About the Sources and Methods of the Men Who Were Used to Write the Scriptures

III. THERE ARE, THEN, NO ERRORS IN THE ORIGINAL WORD OF GOD

1. Dr. Orr, Tainted by Critics, Affirmed Errors, Inaccuracies in the Bible

WHAT A PERFECT, GOD-BREATHED BIBLE INVOLVES

The Scriptures are a holy and wondrous thing. We must approach them as such. We are told, "For ever, O Lord, thy word is settled in heaven.... Thy testimonies...thou hast founded them for ever.... Thy word is true from the beginning: and every one of thy righteous judgments endureth for ever" (Ps. 119:89,152,160). We are told that the Word of God is incorruptible, that it lives and abides forever (Isa. 40:7,8; I Pet. 1:23-25). We are told that "every word... proceedeth out of the mouth of God" (Deut. 8:3; Matt. 4:4; Luke 4:4). We are told that the Scriptures are *theopneustos* (God-breathed). With that kind of inspired Scriptures, certain great truths follow necessarily.

I. WE DEFINE INSPIRATION

1. Inspiration Is Claimed for Original Autographs, Not for Translation or Copying

When we say that the Bible is inspired, we do not refer to the translations or copies but to the original autographs, written down under God's direction. It is true that we have so many copies of the original Scriptures that they can be compared and so the actual wording of the translations can now be checked, and we can be sure that in every essential matter we have exactly the Word of God. And since the Scripture plainly claims that it is settled forever in Heaven, that it is everlasting, and Jesus said that "the scripture cannot be broken" (John 10:35), we can be sure that God in loving providence guarantees that we will not lose these Scriptures, the Word of God. But we do not claim for any copy or any translation the absolute, divine perfection that was in the original autographs. Inspiration refers to the original manuscripts.

2. An Errorless Record of Good and Bad

Again, when we say that the Bible is inspired, we do not mean that it never quotes words that are not inspired. For example, Satan told Eve, "Ye shall not surely die" (Gen. 3:4). What Satan said was false, but the Bible record of it is inspired and absolutely accurate.   The Bible reports some things that Job's friends said to him, and what they said was not always true, but the record is exactly correct.

People quote Gamaliel and think they are quoting divinely inspired Scripture; actually, they are only quoting what the divinely inspired Scripture says that Gamaliel said. He said, "Refrain from these men [Peter and John], and let them alone: for if this counsel or this work be of men, it will come to nought: But if it be of God, ye cannot overthrow it; lest haply ye be found even to fight against God" (Acts 5:38,39). God used Gamaliel's testimony to spare Peter and John from death, but the simple truth is that to leave a heresy alone does not mean that it will come to nought. Romanism and all the false cults today prove that that is not true. The Bible is absolutely inspired and accurate when it quotes Gamaliel. But it does not guarantee that what Gamaliel said is true.

So the Bible record is inspired and infallibly correct.

3. The Scriptures Are Inspired, Not the Men

Let us remember that we are speaking of inspired Scriptures, not of inspired men. God spoke through Balaam, a wicked man who spoke against his will in blessing Israel (Num. chaps. 23 and 24). God even spoke through Balaam's ass (Num. 22:28-30). God spoke through Caiaphas, the unconverted priest who led in having Jesus crucified (John 11:49-52). Scriptures are written by Moses and by Peter, but that does not mean that Moses was perfect or that he would not lose his

temper and offend in smiting the rock the second time (Num.
20:8-13).   And Peter compromised and needed to be rebuked
publicly by the Apostle Paul, since Peter had led Barnabas and
others into sin by his compromise (Gal. 2:11-14). We speak
not of infallible men but of the infallible Word of God which
He miraculously gave through men.

Professor James Orr was seriously wrong here. We suppose
that James Orr, who was professor of apologetics and systematic theology in the United Free Church College in Glasgow,
was about the most respected of theologians at the turn of the
century.   His book, *A Christian View of God and the World,*
is widely used as a textbook in Christian colleges, and publishers call him "one of the most profound Bible scholars of the
late nineteenth and early twentieth centuries. His great erudition,
his scientific knowledge, and his philosophical gifts left their
imprint upon the thinking of this age and succeeding generations."   He was the editor-in-chief of the *International Standard
Bible Encyclopaedia,* a monumental work.   But in his book,
Revelation and Inspiration, he makes allowance for the incorporation of all traditions in the Scripture, incorporation of
genealogies and other tables with errors, in the Word of God.
He consents that some of the Scriptures which profess to be
history may be allegorical and mythical, though they teach
truth.

To start with, one must know that Dr. Orr had accepted
evolution as a fact.   He was greatly influenced by the profes-
sions and claims of scientists.   He was postmillennial and
believed that the world was getting better and mankind was
developing more and more.   He believed that the Old Testament
was written "in the childhood of the race," and that inspiration
was "progressive," getting better as the ages passed.   So there
would be some bias favorable to liberals and unbelievers on the
part of this good Christian man.

Orr says:

> A first question arises as to the relation of the **inspired person**
> to the record.   Scripture is spoken of as "God-inspired"; but it
> is important to notice that inspiration belongs primarily to the
> **person,** and to the **book** only as it is the product of the inspired
> person.   There is no inspiration inhering literally in the paper,
> ink, or type, of the sacred volume.   The inspiration was in the
> soul of the writer; the qualities that are communicated to the
> writing had their seat first in the mind or heart of the man who

wrote.   It is on the mind, heart, faculties of the **man** that the Spirit works: the work is inspired as coming from his thought and pen, and as having the power of quickening and awakening a like glow of soul in those who read.   This is seen very clearly in considering the inspiration of **genius,** as it appears, **e.g.,** in the works of a Shakespeare, a Milton, or a Goethe.   The inspiration in these cases is in the souls of the men, and only derivatively in their writings. 1

It is a mistake to illustrate the inspiration of God-breathed Scripture by the expressed human genius of "a Shakespeare, a Milton, or a Goethe" as Orr does.   Shakespeare's writing came from Shakespeare's genius; Moses', David's and Peter's part in Scripture came not from within Moses or David or Peter but from God.   When writing Scripture, they were "moved [or carried along] by the Holy Ghost."   They did not become supermen.

4. Scripture Writers Were Still Frail, Sinning Men

When writing something other than Scripture, they would be liable to mistakes or sin, as other men are.   Moses may disobey God and smite the rock to which he is commanded to speak, and so miss Canaan (Num. 20:12).   When not writing Scripture, David may seduce Bath-sheba, kill Uriah, her husband, with the sword of the Ammonites (II Sam., chap. 11).   Peter, borne along perfectly when writing Scripture, may at other times curse and swear, deny Jesus and quit the ministry.   He may, long after Pentecost, compromise sinfully and be rebuked by Paul (Gal. 2:11-14).   Even the people at Corinth could see that Paul's inspired "letters. . . are weighty and powerful; but his bodily presence is weak, and his speech contemptible" (II Cor. 10:10).

No, it was not *men* inspired but words inspired, or rather, breathed out by God.

It is conclusive proof of this that we read in I Peter 1:10-12 of Old Testament prophets searching their own inspired writings trying to understand some things they could not understand, since some writings were intended for us who were to live later.

---

1. *Revelation and Inspiration,* pp. 162,163.

God gave the words, not always the meaning, of the prophecies they wrote.

Did the prophecy of Caiaphas in John 11:49-51 proceed from his inspired heart? It did not! Did Balaam prophesy out of an enlightened and purified heart when, against his will, he blessed Israel? He did not! Inspiration gives the written message of God. The understanding of the men who wrote was imperfect. When a Moses or a Paul or a John studied the Scriptures they had written, they could have the same kind of illumination that we have when the Holy Spirit helps us understand the Scriptures. But illumination is not inspiration. It is limited, variable and never perfect. The Scriptures are *inspired*. The prophets who were borne along in writing the God-breathed words were, in more or less degree, *illumined*. It is the holy Scriptures that are perfectly breathed out by God. The men are still frail, finite, limited men.

So James Orr is wrong in his view of inspiration, particularly wrong in saying the Scriptures are simply the out-going of what was in the man. That is not so.

5. "It Is the Book, Not the Men," With Which We Deal

Orr says that inspiration "must be held to include the *insight* given by the divine Spirit into the *meaning* of the history, through which holy men are enabled to write it for the instruction of all ages." [2] But that is never taught in the Scriptures.

Dr. Edward Young, one of the most careful and devoted scholars on the matter of the inspiration of the Scriptures, makes a slip here, we believe. He strongly teaches the verbal inspiration of the Scripture but says:

> According to the Bible, inspiration is a superintendence of God the Holy Spirit over the writers of the Scriptures, as a result of which these Scriptures possess Divine authority and trustworthiness and, possessing such Divine authority and trustworthiness, are free from error." [3]

He is right that the Scripture has divine authority and is free from error. I do not think, however, that the term "super-

---

2. *Revelation and Inspiration*, p. 157.
3. *Thy Word Is Truth*, p. 27.

intendence" is the proper word for the work of the Holy Spirit.
The Bible never indicates that the Holy Spirit breathed on men
or superintended men as they wrote. Rather, David said, "The
Spirit of the Lord spake by me" (II Sam. 23:2). And "God
. . . spake in time past unto the fathers by the prophets" (Heb.
1:1). And the men of God who wrote were rather "holy men
of God spake as they were moved by the Holy Ghost" (II
Pet. 1:21), or literally, "as they were borne along by the Holy
Ghost." Superintendence is too weak a word and leaves the
initiative with men, with the Holy Spirit somewhere near and
more or less supervising, checking. But according to the Scriptures, the initiative was with God the Holy Spirit and men are
His instruments in writing the Scriptures.

Drs. Lindsell and Woodbridge say about the Bible writers:

> They retained their own styles, personalities and self-command.
> Their personal powers were not suspended but sharpened. The
> Holy Spirit commanded the operation; but Moses, John and
> Peter remained Moses, John and Peter while writing. Because of
> the close, sustained, continuous, effective supervision of the Holy
> Spirit, the Bible is the inspired Word of God. [4]

Now, the end the good doctors declare is correct. The Bible
is the inspired Word of God. It is true that the writers were not
automata. In some sense they did retain their own style and
personalities and self-command. But the Bible never says that
"their personal powers were. . . sharpened." Whether or not
their powers were sharpened we do not know. The unintended
indication is that here, if men have enough illumination, enough
supervision by the Holy Spirit, they could write the perfect
Word of God. But that is not what the Bible teaches and
surely not what Lindsell and Woodbridge intended to convey.

But Lindsell and Woodbridge correct themselves on the preceding page:

> "Inspiration" is not mere "illumination." The Holy Spirit
> illumines one's soul before he can understand spiritual truth
> (See I Cor. 2:10-12.) But when we speak of the inspiration of
> the Bible, we do not have in mind this sort of spiritual percep-
> tion. We do not mean merely that the intuitive faculties of the
> writers were quickened, or their spiritual insights clarified. Their
> "inspiration" was different, not only in degree but also in kind,
> from the heightened powers of ordinary men, even of men

---

4. *Handbook of Christian Truth,* p. 26.

known for their spiritual genius. The inspiration of the Biblical
authors was unique: it was special, direct, reliable, life-giving,
inerrant. 5

That is better. The Bible does not come from "the heightened
powers of ordinary men, even of men known for their spiritual
genius." If "the intuitive faculties of the writers were quickened,"
the Bible says nothing about it, and it is obviously not necessary
to the kind of inspiration the Bible teaches. There is no evidence
that the "intuitive faculties" of Balaam were quickened when by
inspiration he gave a prophecy he did not want to give nor
that the "intuitive faculties" of Caiaphas the high priest were
quickened when he prophesied that Christ would die for the
people, meaning something else. When God breathed out the
words of the Bible, and the Bible discusses it, it never speaks of
men's "intuitive faculties" being quickened nor of their "heightened powers" nor that "their personal powers were. . .sharp-
ened." I am sure that, without intending to do so and trying
to someway explain the human color and imprint in the Scriptures, good men say about this more than the Bible itself says
here.

Let us say it again: the Scriptures did not come from heightened powers or quickened senses nor by simple illumination of
the Holy Spirit. God Himself gave the Scriptures and inspiration was far more than some superintendence or supervision
of spiritually illumined men with heightened faculties.

6. Warfield Says Prophets Were
"Not the Mover but the Moved"

Dr. Warfield states this matter so clearly and scripturally.
About the prophets, he says:

> . . .they were under the divine control. This control is repre-
> sented as complete and compelling, so that, under it, the prophet
> becomes not the "mover," but the "moved" in the formation of
> his message. The apostle Peter very purely reflects the prophetic
> consciousness in his well-known declaration: "No prophecy of
> scripture comes of private interpretation; for prophecy was never
> brought by the will of man; but it was as borne by the Holy
> Spirit that men spoke from God" (2 Pet. i. 20,21).

---

5. *Handbook of Christian Truth*, p. 25.

What this language of Peter emphasizes — and what is empha-
sized in the whole account which the prophets give of their own
consciousness — is, to speak plainly, the passivity of the prophets
with respect to the revelation given through them. This is the
significance of the phrase: "it was as borne by the Holy Spirit
that men spoke from God." To be "borne" (φέρειν, **phérein**) is
not the same as to be led (ἄγειν, **agein**), much less to be guided
or directed (ὁδηγεῖν, **hodegéin**): he that is "borne" contributes
nothing to the movement induced, but is the object to be moved.
The term "passivity" is, perhaps, however, liable to some mis-
apprehension, and should not be overstrained. It is not intended
to deny that the intelligence of the prophets was active in the
reception of their message; it was by means of their active
intelligence that their message was received: their intelligence
was the instrument of revelation. It is intended to deny only that
their intelligence was active in the production of their message:
that it was creatively as distinguished from receptively active.
For reception itself is a kind of activity. What the prophets
are solicitous that their readers shall understand is that they are
in no sense co-authors with God of their messages. Their messages are given them, given them entire, and given them precisely as they are given out by them. God speaks through them:
they are not merely His messengers, but "His mouth." But at
the same time their intelligence is active in the reception, retention
and announcing of their messages, contributing nothing to them
but presenting fit instruments for the communication of them —
instruments capable of understanding, responding profoundly
to and zealously proclaiming them. 6

Let us say plainly, then, that the Scriptures did not come, in
any degree, from a heightening of men's natural faculties nor
by common illumination to understand spiritual truth. Let us
remember that inspiration refers to the Book, not to the men
who wrote it.

7. Gaussen, Brookes, and Gray Show Not the Writers but the Writings Inspired

On this matter Gaussen says:

And were we, further, called to say at least what the men of
God experienced in their bodily organs, in their will, or in their
understandings, while engaged in tracing the pages of the sacred
book, we should reply, that the powers of inspiration were not

---

6. *The Inspiration and Authority of the Bible*, pp. 90,91.

felt by all to the same degree, and that their experiences were not at all uniform; but we might add, that the knowledge of such a fact bears very little on the interests of our faith, seeing that, as respects that faith, we have to do with the book, and not with the man. It is the book that is inspired, and altogether inspired: to be assured of this ought to satisfy us. 7

Again, on page 116 Gaussen says:

What, then, are we to conclude from this first difference which we have recognized as existing between illumination and inspiration, with respect to the duration of those gifts?

We must conclude from it,

1. That these two operations of the Holy Ghost differ in their essence, and not in their degree only.

2. That the infallibility of the sacred writers depended not on their illumination (which, although raised to an extraordinary measure in the case of some of them, they nevertheless enjoyed in common with all the saints), but solely on their divine inspiration.

3. That divinely-inspired words, having been miraculous, are also all of them the words of God.

4. That as our faith in every part of the Bible rests no longer on the illumination of the writers, but on the inspiration of their writings, it may dispense henceforth with the perplexing study of their internal state, of the degree in which they were enlightened, or of that of their holiness; but must stay itself in all things on God, in nothing on man. 8

W. H. Griffith Thomas wrote:

As Dr. J. H. Brookes used to say about Exodus 4:10-12, it is not "I will be with thy mind and teach thee what thou shalt think," but "I will be with thy mouth and teach thee what thou shalt say," because while it does not so much matter what Moses thought, it **does** matter what he actually said. 9

God inspired the Scriptures, not the men.

Dr. James M. Gray does not make the mistake of Dr. Orr. He says:

When we speak of the Holy Spirit coming upon the men in order to the composition of the books, it should be further understood that **the object is not the inspiration of the men but the books**—not the writers but the **writings**. It terminates upon the record, in other words, and not upon the human instrument who made it.

7. *The Inspiration of the Holy Scriptures*, p. 26.
8. *The Inspiration of the Holy Scriptures*, p. 116.
9. *God Spake All These Words*, p. 93.

To illustrate: Moses, David, Paul, John, were not always and everywhere inspired, for then always and everywhere they would have been infallible and inerrant, which was not the case. They sometimes made mistakes in thought and erred in conduct. But however fallible and errant they may have been as men compassed with infirmity like ourselves, such fallibility or errancy was never under any circumstances communicated to their sacred writings. [10]

8. The Inspired Gospels Differ but All Are Correct

Inspiration of the Bible does not mean that parallel accounts of Christ's life and ministry in the four Gospels must all be exactly alike. The truth is that none of the Gospels tell all that Jesus said or all that happened. Each writer used the part that the Holy Spirit selected for that particular account. And all are true. Some tell what others do not tell. It is so also with the parallel accounts of the history of Israel and the divided nation in the books of Samuel, Kings and Chronicles. No account tells all that could be told but only what God chose to tell in that particular Scripture.

Again, the inspired Bible would not prevent Jesus from quoting an Old Testament passage in His own words, and in translation from the Hebrew to New Testament Greek. The Holy Spirit of God can quote His own statements in slightly different words and give exactly what He means, and be correct. A human paraphrase of the Scripture is not inspired. The Holy Spirit's restatement of Scripture is inspired. The boss can restate his own orders. So God can restate His own Scripture, yet never correct it nor disown it.

II. THE SCRIPTURES, THEN, ARE SUPERNATURAL, ARE MIRACULOUSLY GIVEN

A God-breathed Scripture must come from God. A perfect Scripture, settled forever in Heaven (Ps. 119:89), has a perfection not of men.

---

10. *The Fundamentals for Today*, Vol. 1, pp. 126,127.

1. Necessarily, Christianity Is a Miracle Religion

Yes, Christianity requires a miraculously given, divine Scripture because it is a miracle religion. [11]

The creation of this universe was by the miraculous fiat of God. "God said..." and it was done. Matter did not originate of itself. The galaxies, the suns and planets and moons, did not arrange themselves, start their orbits, establish their own intricate and amazing balance. Plants and animals in their infinite variety did not evolve by inherent resident forces to what they are. Man did not climb upward from the amoeba through fish and reptile and fowl and mammal to man. No; creation was a miraculous act of God. Any other theory of origins is silly, unproven, antichristian.

The coming of the Lord Jesus Christ from God to man, His incarnation, was a miracle. It was the miracle of a virgin birth when the eternal God, the Creator, entered into the womb of a virgin girl and Christ was born. Miracles mark His ministry. His bodily resurrection proved His deity. His second coming, miraculously, wondrously, is assured. There could be no Christ without a miraculous intervention of God.

The regeneration of a soul is a miracle; it is not natural but supernatural. It is not the work of men but of God. It is not a process but a sudden creative act whereby one becomes a child of God, a partaker of the divine nature, a new creature. If you leave out the miracles, you leave out all Christianity.

And so it is with the Bible. It is a miracle Book, a perfect God-breathed Book.

2. Perfection Has to Be Supernatural and Miraculous

If "the law of the Lord is perfect," as Psalm 19:7 says; if the Word is "for ever...settled in heaven," as Psalm 119:89 says; and if the Word of God is incorruptible and can never pass away, as Isaiah 40:8 and I Peter 1:23-25 tell us, then the Bible claims what only God can give.

When Luke was inspired to write the Gospel, he wrote dis-

---

11. See two chapters on miracles in my book, *Prayer — Asking and Receiving*; one chapter on "Is the Age of Miracles Past?" in my book, *Bible Doctrines to Live By*, where detailed discussion is given.

counting the uninspired gospels and accounts that had been written. ". . . having had perfect understanding" *anothen* "from above," he wrote Theophilus, "that thou mightest know the *CERTAINTY* of those things, wherein thou has been instructed" (Luke 1:3,4). But certainty comes "from above."

The Scriptures "cannot be broken," but anything man-made can be broken.   The man who reforms without supernatural rebirth may find that the demons come back to the house to find it empty, swept and garnished, and enter in with more demons.   No letter, no book by purely human authorship endures forever.   The best men who ever lived, still, like the Apostle Paul, have the conflict and the limitations of the old nature and they must say with him, "For that which I do I allow not: for what I would, that do I not; but what I hate, that do I."   And again, "For I know that in me (that is, in my flesh,) dwelleth no good thing: for to will is present with me; but how to perform that which is good I find not. For the good that I would I do not: but the evil which I would not, that I do" (Rom. 7:15,18,19). The best Christian in the world must remember that ". . . the flesh lusteth against the Spirit, and the Spirit against the flesh: and these are contrary the one to the other: so that ye cannot do the things that ye would" (Gal. 5:17). Any saintly, Spirit-filled man of God must still remember, "If we say that we have no sin, we deceive ourselves, and the truth is not in us" (I John 1:8). Just as a frail, sinful, human Saviour would not be enough, so a human, fallible book would not be enough for a perfect revelation from God.

3. Such a Perfect Word of God Must Come From God to Man, Not Originating With Man

Does that seem like a restatement? It is simply another facet of the Bible doctrine of a supernatural revelation written down in human words, an inspired Bible.

It is inherent in perfection that it must come from God, not from sinful men.

The Scripture plainly states that the Scriptures came from God, not from man.

Second Peter 1:21 tells us: "For the prophecy came not in old time by the will of man: but holy men of God spake as

they were moved by the Holy Ghost." In the same passage
Peter tells how he and James and John were "eyewitnesses of
his majesty" when Christ was transfigured before them on the
Mount of Transfiguration and when God the Father spoke
from Heaven, saying, "This is my beloved Son, in whom I am
well pleased." So, says Peter, it was not "cunningly devised
fables" when they preached about the power and coming of
Christ. There were eyewitnesses of His glory, appearing as He
will appear at His second coming.

But Peter tells us there is much better proof. "We have also
a more sure word of prophecy; whereunto ye do well that ye
take heed. . . ," he says in verse 19. The inspired prophecies
in the Bible are "more sure" than any human testimony, even
than that of eyewitnesses, and than the chosen apostles themselves!

Our reliance, then, is not to be principally on eyewitnesses but
on direct revelation in the Bible. "For the prophecy came not
in old time by the will of man: but holy men of God spake as
they were moved by the Holy Ghost." So Paul wrote to the
Christians of Thessalonica, "For this cause also thank we God
without ceasing, because, when ye received the word of God
which ye heard of us, ye received it not as the word of men,
but as it is in truth, the word of God, which effectually worketh
also in you that believe" (I Thess. 2:13).

They heard the Gospel in man's words, but they did not
originate with men; they were from God. As they received the
Word spoken or written by the Apostle Paul, they were to
understand that it did not originate with Paul but with God;
". . .not as the word of men, but as it is in truth, the word
of God. . . ."

In that wonderful passage of I Corinthians 2:9-13, Paul is
inspired to state very plainly that a man could not know the
things of God except as the Holy Spirit revealed them. He
said, "But as it is written, Eye hath not seen, nor ear heard,
neither have entered into the heart of man, the things which
God hath prepared for them that love him. But God hath
revealed them unto us by his Spirit: for the Spirit searcheth all
things, yea, the deep things of God" (vss. 9,10).

When Paul or others wrote part of the Bible, they did not
write what "eye hath seen. . . ." They were not writing simply
from what they saw or knew personally. They did not write
what ear had heard, whether they had interviewed others and

heard the testimony of others or not. Whatever they heard with the ear they did not write down. It was not the basis of revelation. They wrote what the Spirit of God revealed. They did not write what had "entered into the heart of man...," that is, what they had studied out and understood.

In his introduction to the book of Hebrews, the beloved Dr. Scofield says, "We undoubtedly have here the method of Paul's synagogue addresses." We think that is a mistake. Paul may have preached from the book of Hebrews; if so, he would have studied the book of Hebrews, and the Old Testament references, to expound as much as he could of the God-given material in Hebrews. Remember, we speak here not of an inspired man but of inspired writing. Hebrews is not what Paul knew but what God had Paul write down, if Paul wrote that book. By illumination of God's Holy Spirit, Paul would understand much of the Scripture, more than most but never perfectly. The Scripture Paul was inspired to write is perfect and infinite. Paul was limited and finite. In illumination it was only the Lord Jesus to whom the Spirit was given without measure (John 3:34).

Paul had not figured out the great truths of Hebrews; they were revealed to him from God. And I Corinthians 2:13 says they came "...not in the words which man's wisdom teacheth, but which the Holy Ghost teacheth...." So the matter and the content were from God.

4. That Brings Up Serious Problems About the Sources and Methods of the Men Who Were Used to Write the Scriptures

Yes, of course, a miracle always brings up problems when you try to explain it. Foolish and unbelieving men try to explain the destruction of Sodom and Gomorrah by a volcanic eruption. They try to explain the resurrection of Jesus by saying He was not really dead but only in a swoon. They have trouble explaining Jonah being swallowed by a whale (a great fish or sea monster), so they explain that as a fairy tale or a myth or a parable.

Yes, to explain a miracle always is a problem. But whatever the problem, it is still true that the Bible plainly and repeatedly claims to be from God and not from men. It claims miraculous perfection, breathed out from God, which man could not produce.

Sometimes in Paul's letters he no doubt expresses his own preferences, his own burden, his own joy. But we are to understand they were in the mind of God before they were in the mind of Paul. It is true that in addressing his Gospel to Theophilus, Luke said, "It seemed good to me also" to write the Gospel. But we are to understand that it seemed good to God first; and the "perfect understanding" which Luke had was *anothen,* "from above," before he wrote. It seemed good to God before it seemed good to Luke for him to write.

Warfield says:

> And although, throughout its entire duration, God, in fulfill-ment of His promise (Deut. 18:18), put His words in the mouths of His prophets and gave them His commandments to speak, yet it would seem inherent in the very employment of men as instru-ments of revelation that the words of God given through them are spoken by human mouths; and the purity of their super-naturalness may seem so far obscured. And when it is not merely the mouths of men with which God thus serves Himself in the delivery of His messages, but their minds and hearts as well — the play of their religious feelings, or the processes of their logical reasoning, or the tenacity of their memories, as say, in a psalm or in an epistle, or a history — the supernatural element in the communication may easily seem to retire still farther into the background.

> It can scarcely be a matter of surprise, therefore, that question has been raised as to the relation of the natural and the super-natural in such revelations, and, in many current manners of thinking and speaking of them, the completeness of their super-naturalness has been limited and curtailed in the interests of the natural instrumentalities employed. The plausibility of such reasoning renders it the more necessary that we should observe the unvarying emphasis which the Scriptures place upon the absolute supernaturalness of revelation in all its modes alike. In the view of the Scriptures, the completely supernatural character of revelation is in no way lessened by the circumstance that it has been given through the instrumentality of men. They affirm, indeed, with the greatest possible emphasis that the Divine word delivered through men is the pure word of God, diluted with no human admixture whatever. [12]

---

12. *The Inspiration and Authority of the Bible,* pp. 85,86.

The Bible is supernatural, miraculously given, perfect.
Bettex says:

> He who does not believe in miracles does not believe in God,
> but has instead an unreal notion, an impotent, indefinite some-
> thing to which it were senseless and useless to pray, and which
> is more powerless, even, than all the idols of the heathen; for
> the heathen felt that a God without miracles would be a chimera
> that could profit nothing. Such an one, man can neither fear
> nor love. But men do not want to believe in miracles because
> they do not want to believe in God; one follows from the other. [13]

Dr. R. Laird Harris has this to say:

> Of course, it is unscientific to believe that Joshua's day was
> forty-eight hours long, but it is equally absurd to believe that
> an iron axehead could float, or that a virgin could bear a
> child, or that Christ could walk upon the water. All miracles,
> great or small, are impossible with men and are an interruption
> of those regular laws of nature which form the basis of science.
> That is why they are miracles, and that is why God gave them
> to man: to prove that there is a God in heaven more powerful
> than any who is dreamed of in many a Horatio's philosophy.
> But these are not conflicts between science and the Bible. In the
> field of the direct miraculous intervention of God, science cannot
> properly interpose an objection. [14]

There is no way to have any true concept of the Bible as the
Word of God except by simply recognizing its miraculous source
and its miraculous perfection. The Bible is a miracle Book
breathed out from God.

In Acts 15, we have the account of the first great council of
apostles and others in Jerusalem to decide whether Gentiles must
observe the law of Moses. They decided, and sent a message to
the young Christians, "For it seemed good to the Holy Ghost,
and to us, to lay upon you no greater burden than these necessary things. . ." (vs. 28). It seemed good "to the Holy Ghost,
and to us."   That is the way the divine revelation came, the
way the Scriptures were inspired. It "seemed good to the Holy
Ghost" first and then, as He gave men to write or speak, God
made it seem good to them also.

---

13. *The Bible, the Word of God*, p. 191.
14. *Inspiration and Canonicity of the Bible*, p. 31.

III. THERE ARE, THEN, NO ERRORS IN THE ORIGINAL WORD OF GOD

We think now not of translations and copies but of the original autographs.   Of them we are told that ". . . every word. . . proceedeth out of the mouth of God" (Matt. 4:4).   So all must be true.   If the Scriptures are God-breathed, *theopneustos,* as II Timothy 3:16 says, then God did not breathe out errors and mistakes.

It seems strange and sad that we would have to argue that there are no errors in the Word of God.   But, sadly, there is a flood of material by scholars and even by those who love the Lord and claim to believe the Bible, who cast doubt on the absolute accuracy of the Word of God.

1. Dr. Orr, Tainted by Critics, Affirmed Errors, Inaccuracies in the Bible

Orr says:

> The same remark applies to the tendency to make "inerrancy" — i. e. hard and fast literality in minute matters of historical, geographical, and scientific detail — a point in the essence of the doctrine of inspiration. The subject will come up later, but at present it may be observed that, at best, such "inerrancy" can never be demonstrated with a cogency which entitles it to rank as the foundation of a belief in inspiration. [15]

Orr does not believe, with the liberals, that the first chapters in Genesis "are based on Babylonian myths," but he says:

> It is truer to regard them as the embodiments of the earliest and most precious traditions of the race, in the purer form in which they descended through the ancestors of the Hebrew people. They may, however, be ancient, and yet bear traces of transmission in a more or less allegorical or symbolical form. Few, e. g., will be disposed to take literally the account of the making of Eve out of the rib taken from Adam's side while he slept. The story of the Fall, again, may well be the account of an actual historical catastrophe in the commencement of the race, in its cradle in the region of the Tigris and Euphrates. Truths of eternal moment may be enshrined, it is believed are, in its

---

15. *Revelation and Inspiration,* p. 199.

simple narrative. Yet, with many of the most devout expounders of the story, we can hardly err in seeing symbolical elements, or an allegorical dress, in the features of the serpent, the trees, the cherubim. [16]

Orr thinks that the only part God had, when a Bible writer quoted "traditions, monuments, state records, genealogies, etc., as well as written narratives," is some providential circumstances.   He says that *"an important extension"* of the idea of revelation must be made; that is, that inspiration may include things revealed from God and may include other things not revealed from God but provided providentially, without correcting the errors involved. [17]   He says:

> Here again the principle of the co-operation of divine providence with revelation for the subserving of the ends of the latter finds application.   To providence must be entrusted the securing and preserving of such materials as are necessary for a proper presentation of the history.   These materials need not be the work of inspired men, but may come through the ordinary channels of information — may consist of traditions, monuments, state records, genealogies, etc., as well as written narratives. Inspiration is seen in the use made of these materials, not in the providing of them. [18]

Orr says:

> Very commonly it is argued by upholders of this doctrine that "inerrancy" in every minute particular is involved in the very idea of a book given by inspiration of God.   This might be held to be true on a theory of verbal dictation, but it can scarcely be maintained on a just view of the actual historical genesis of the Bible. [19]

Orr again says:

> Theories of dictation of historical matter, or of communication of facts that could be ascertained by ordinary methods, are now universally surrendered. [20]

Of course we now know Orr is mistaken here.

Orr further says: "The dispensational imperfections of the Old Testament are fully recognized."   So he says Jesus "took

---

16. *Revelation and Inspiration,* p. 166.
17. *Revelation and Inspiration,* p. 156.
18. *Revelation and Inspiration,* p. 157.
19. *Revelation and Inspiration,* p. 213.
20. *Revelation and Inspiration,* p. 212.

up, therefore, as Son of Man, a lordly and discretionary attitude towards its letter, laws, and institutions." [21]　　We are reminded here of the infidel accusations of Buttrick and Georgia Harkness. In fact, Orr says the strange and shocking thing: "Inspiration does not in any case create the fact-materials it works with.　It works with the materials it has received," [22] that is, traditions, genealogies, records by fallible men.

Bernard Ramm, no more orthodox than Orr and less theologically reliable, says that the Bible has minor errors of fact. His book is reviewed in great detail in our book, *Earnestly Contending for the Faith,* chapter 9, "Shall We Appease Unbelieving Scholars?"　Ramm says, "In that inspiration came through the mold of the Hebrew culture, the hyperorthodox is wrong." [23]　By the hyperorthodox people he means those of us who believe in verbal or plenary inspiration.

"If God spoke through the Hebrew and Greek languages, He also spoke *in terms of the cultures in which these languages were embedded.*　The eternal truths of the Hebrew-Christian religion are clothed and garbed not only in the Hebrew and Greek languages but also in the cultural molds of the times of the composition of the Bible." [24]　He says that "being inspired of God, the writers were restrained from error." [25]　But he thinks the writers' restraint "from error" was limited, saying, "Because the Scriptures are inspired, the truth of God is there in the cultural, but not obviously so.　The truth under the cultural partakes of the binding character of inspiration, not the cultural vehicle.　Therefore our guide in such matters are those passages of Scripture which are clearly didactic, theological, and hence, transcultural." [26]

So, Ramm professes he can simply ignore errors that he finds in matters where the Hebrew culture was uninformed, and claims that the general thought is inspired, and so that one gets his teaching from other Scriptures.

Ramm says about the great flood of Genesis:

> A third view, and the one which we hold, is that the **entire record** must be interpreted phenomenally.　If the flood is local

21. *Revelation and Inspiration,* p. 184.
22. *Revelation and Inspiration,* p. 163.
23. *The Christian View of Science and Scripture,* p. 71.
24. *The Christian View of Science and Scripture,* p. 71.
25. *The Christian View of Science and Scripture,* p. 71.
26. *The Christian View of Science and Scripture,* p. 79.

though spoken of in universal terms, so the destruction of man is local though spoken of in universal terms. The record neither affirms nor denies that man existed beyond the Mesopotamian valley. Noah certainly was not a preacher of righteousness to the peoples of Africa, of India, of China or of America — places where there is evidence for the existence of man many thousands of years before the flood (10,000 to 15,000 years in America). The emphasis in Genesis is upon that group of cultures from which Abraham eventually came. [27]

Ramm gives many reasons telling why he thinks there could not have been the kind of universal flood which the Bible describes. [28]

Ramm writes, of course, with a bias against fundamental Bible believers whom he calls "hyperorthodox," and with a bias in favor of unbelieving scientists and an eagerness to please them.   But his view that the Bible has errors is too widely held.

2. Hodge Says "Inspiration" Is Not Confined to Moral and Religious Truths, but Extends to the Statements of Facts, Whether Scientific, Historical, or Geographical

Charles Hodge of Princeton, greatest of the Calvinistic theologians, has a subhead which says, "Inspiration extends equally to all parts of Scripture." Then he says:

This is the fourth element of the Church doctrine on this subject.   It means, first, that all the books of Scripture are equally inspired. All alike are infallible in what they teach. And secondly, that inspiration extends to all the contents of these several books. It is not confined to moral and religious truths, but extends to the statements of facts, whether scientific, historical, or geographical. It is not confined to those facts the importance of which is obvious, or which are involved in matters of doctrine. It extends to everything which any sacred writer asserts to be true. [29]

If the Bible is true, it is all true.   If it is really God speaking, then what God says about incidental or geographical or histori-

27. *The Christian View of Science and Scripture*, pp. 239,240.
28. *The Christian View of Science and Scripture*, pp. 243-246.
29. *Systematic Theology*, Vol. 1, p. 163.

cal or scientific matters is just as true as what God says about anything else.

3. The Bible Still Claims to Be Without Error

We are face to face with clear statements in the Word of God like: "Every word of God is pure" (Prov. 30:5), and, "Man shall not live by bread alone, but by every word that proceedeth out of the mouth of God" (from the Lord Jesus in Matt. 4:4), and "All scripture is God-breathed" (the literal translation of II Tim. 3:16). We must face the fact that Jesus said, "the scripture cannot be broken" (John 10:35); that God's "word is settled for ever in heaven" (Ps. 119:89); that the Word is "true from the beginning" (Ps. 119:160). So we must not take the words of men with a bias against the Bible and a bias in favor of unbelieving critics, but must take the plain statement of the Scriptures about themselves. The original autographs of the Scriptures were infallibly correct. "Every word of God is pure" (Prov. 30:5). If one has problems in explaining everything in the Bible, one would have far more problems explaining Christ and Christianity and the Word of God itself mixed with human errors and unreliable statements. No, the Bible does not simply in some places "contain the Word of God"; the Bible *is* the Word of God.

Ussher's chronology has some errors, just as any other man-made exposition of the Scripture. But where the Bible speaks, it tells the truth. And the genealogies may have some gaps but they are intentional gaps and for a divine purpose, and genealogies in the Bible are to be trusted implicitly, just as other Scriptures.

The Bible is not necessarily a book of science in the sense of modern terminology and modern theories; it is, however, absolutely correct when it speaks on matters of history or geography.

As Jesus Christ, "THE WORD," was sinless, so the Bible, the written Word, must be errorless; and it is.

Always, if he seeks for it, one may find some bias, some preference, some contrary influence in every man who sets out to find errors in the Bible.

CHAPTER V

THE INSPIRATION OF THE BIBLE IS CLAIMED
ALIKE FOR ALL ITS PARTS

I. THE BIBLE ITSELF AFFIRMS INSPIRATION FOR
ALL SCRIPTURE

1. The Claim of II Timothy 3:16 Is, "All Scripture Is
Given by Inspiration of God"

2. The Lord Jesus Certainly Regarded the Law of Moses,
the Pentateuch, As Inspired

3. When the Resurrected Saviour Met the Two on the
Road to Emmaus He "Expounded...All the Scriptures"

4. The Apostle Peter Was Inspired to List the Writings of
the Apostle Paul Along With Other Scriptures

5. The Gospel of Luke Is Quoted As Scripture Also by the
Apostle Paul

II. GAUSSEN AND WARFIELD SHOW HOW UNSCRIP-
TURAL AND ILLOGICAL IS PARTIAL INSPIRA-
TION

1. Some Propose Only Part of Bible Fully Inspired

2. Such Teaching "Is Fantastic," Not Authorized by Scriptures, Unknown to Early Christians

3. A Partially Inspired Bible Never Accepted by Creed or
People

III. NO DEGREES IN INSPIRATION

1. Orr Confuses the Degree of Knowledge of the Bible
Writer With Degree of Inspiration — a Serious Error

2. Mistaken Teaching of "Progressive Inspiration"

THE INSPIRATION OF THE BIBLE
IS CLAIMED ALIKE FOR
ALL ITS PARTS

We will not deal in great detail here with the question of the canon of Scriptures. We accept the books of the Bible as we have them, as all being the very Word of God, and we believe the claim for inspiration covers all the Scriptures.

I. THE BIBLE ITSELF AFFIRMS INSPIRATION
FOR ALL SCRIPTURE

With what detail the Scripture claims inspiration for various parts!

1. The Claim of II Timothy 3:16 Is, "ALL Scripture
Is Given by Inspiration of God"

Surely that means that all the writings, then accepted by Jews as the Word of God and which now comprise our Old Testament, are counted as inspired of God.

2. The Lord Jesus Certainly Regarded the Law
of Moses, the Pentateuch, As Inspired

He says in Matthew 5:17 and 18, "Think not that I am come to destroy the law, or the prophets: I am not come to destroy, but to fulfill. For verily I say unto you, Till heaven and earth pass, one jot or one tittle shall in no wise pass from the law, till all be fulfilled."

3. When the Resurrected Saviour Met the Two Men on the Road to Emmaus He "Expounded...All the Scriptures"

"*Then he said unto them, O fools, and slow of heart to believe all that the prophets have spoken: Ought not Christ to have suffered these things, and to enter into his glory? And beginning at Moses and all the prophets, he expounded unto them in all the scriptures the things concerning himself.*" — Luke 24:25-27.

The Saviour is saying that the things foretold in the Old Testament naturally ought to be expected to come to pass since that is the Word of God. And "beginning at Moses and all the prophets, he expounded unto them in all the scriptures the things concerning himself." What a lesson on Christ in the Old Testament, including Moses, all the prophets, all the Scriptures, and when the disciples told of it, they said, "Did not our heart burn within us, while he talked with us by the way, and while he opened to us the scriptures?" Clearly He included all the Old Testament.

Then in the same chapter He appeared to the rest of the disciples in Jerusalem and He said unto them, "These are the words which I spake unto you, while I was yet with you, that all things must be fulfilled, which were written in the law of Moses, and in the prophets, and in the psalms, concerning me" (Luke 24:44). Here He expressly included the Psalms as well as the law of Moses and the prophets. He included the whole Old Testament as the Scriptures that ought to be believed because they foretold with divine authority His own death, sufferings, and resurrection.

4. The Apostle Peter Was Inspired to List the Writings of the Apostle Paul Along With Other Scriptures

In II Peter 3:15,16 we read:

"*And account that the long-suffering of our Lord is salvation; even as our beloved brother Paul also according to the wisdom given unto him hath written unto you; As also in all his epistles, speaking in them of these things; in which are some things hard to be understood, which they that are unlearned and unstable wrest, as they do also the other scriptures, unto their own destruction."*

And some people would wrest the writings of Paul "as they do also the other scriptures."

And the claim of Paul in I Corinthians 2:9-13 and in Galatians 1:11 and 12 certainly means that he claimed for his own writings the same perfection and inspiration that were claimed for the Old Testament. And as many have said, hardly anyone who admits the inspiration of the Old Testament would deny the inspiration of the New Testament, too. All the Bible is the inspired Word of God.

5. The Gospel of Luke Is Quoted As Scripture Also by the Apostle Paul

He says, "For the scripture saith, Thou shalt not muzzle the ox that treadeth out the corn. And, The labourer is worthy of his reward" (I Tim. 5:18). The first part of that Scripture which Paul quotes is from Deuteronomy 25:4. But the second part is from Luke 10:7, "The labourer is worthy of his hire." So when Paul says, "The scripture saith," he refers to the Gospel of Luke. And Paul boldly called his own teaching to the Thessalonians "the word of God," not the word of men (I Thess. 2:13).

We may be sure then that New Testament Christians regarded all the Old Testament the Word of God as the Jews had done before, and they regarded all the New Testament as the Word of God, too, as it plainly claims to be.

We hold, then, the consistent position of fundamental, Bible-believing Christians through all the ages that all of the Scriptures, as we know them, are the very Word of God and inspired alike.

II. GAUSSEN AND WARFIELD SHOW HOW UNSCRIPTURAL AND ILLOGICAL IS PARTIAL INSPIRATION

Gaussen discusses in detail this matter of the total inspiration of the Bible in all parts alike.   He says that there are "three descriptions of men, in these late times, without disavowing the divinity of Christianity, and without venturing to decline the authority of the Scriptures, have thought themselves authorized to reject this doctrine,"[1] that is, the doctrine of complete and plenary inspiration of all the Scriptures.

1. Some Propose Only Part of Bible Fully Inspired

He says, "Some of these have disowned the very *existence* of this action of the Holy Ghost; others have denied its *universality*; others, again, its *plenitude.*"[2]

Some say that none of the Bible is supernaturally and miraculously inspired, though they think it has a message from God. Some say that part of the Bible is inspired and part of it is not. And others think that the inspiration varies in degrees.   Of that he says,

> Many of these, particularly in England, have gone so far as to distinguish four degrees of divine inspiration: the inspiration of **superintendence**, they have said, in virtue of which the sacred writers have been constantly preserved from serious error in all that relates to faith and life; the inspiration of **elevation**, by which the Holy Ghost, further, by carrying up the thoughts of the men of God into the purest regions of truth, must have indirectly stamped the same characters of holiness and grandeur on their words; the inspiration of **direction**, under the more powerful action of which the sacred writers were under God's guidance in regard to what they said and abstained from saying; finally, the inspiration of **suggestion**.   Here, they say, all the thoughts, and even the words, have been given by God, by means of a still more energetic and direct operation of his Spirit.

> "The Theopneustia," says M. Twesten, "extends unquestionably even to words, but only when the choice or the employment of them is connected with the religious life of the soul; for one ought, in this respect," he adds, "to distinguish between the Old and New Testament, between the Law and the Gospel, between history and prophecy, between narratives and doctrines, between the apostles and their apostolical assistants."[3]

---

1. *Theopneustia, The Plenary Inspiration of the Holy Scriptures*, p. 26.
2. *Theopneustia, The Plenary Inspiration of the Holy Scriptures*, p. 26.
3. *Theopneustia, The Plenary Inspiration of the Holy Scriptures*, pp. 27,28.

2. Such Teaching "Is Fantastic," Not Authorized by Scriptures, Unknown to Early Christians

Gaussen answers these foolish ideas as follows:

> To our mind these are all fantastic distinctions; the Bible has not authorized them; the Church of the first eight centuries of the Christian era knew nothing of them; and we believe them to be erroneous in themselves, and deplorable in their results.

> Our design then, in this book, in opposition to these three systems, is to prove the existence, the universality, and the plenitude of the divine inspiration of the Bible.

> First of all, it concerns us to know if there has been a divine and miraculous inspiration for the Scriptures. We say that there has. Next, we have to know if the parts of Scripture that are divinely inspired are equally and entirely so; or, in other terms, if God have provided, in a certain though mysterious manner, that the very words of his holy book should always be what they ought to be, and that it should contain no error. This, too, we affirm to be the case. Finally, we have to know whether what is thus inspired by God in the Scriptures, be a part of the Scriptures, or the whole of the Scriptures. We say that it is the whole Scriptures; — the historical books as well as the prophecies; the Gospels as well as the Song of Solomon; the Gospels of Mark and Luke, as well as those of John and Matthew; the history of the shipwreck of St. Paul in the waters of the Adriatic, as well as that of the shipwreck of the old world in the waters of the flood; the scenes of Mamre beneath the tents of Abraham, as well as those of the day of Christ in the eternal tabernacles; the prophetic prayers in which the Messiah, a thousand years before his first advent, cries in the Psalms, "My God, my God, why hast thou forsaken me? — they have pierced my hands and my feet — they have cast lots upon my vesture — they look and stare at me" — as well as the narratives of them by St. John, St. Mark, St. Luke, or St. Matthew.

> In other words, it has been our object to establish by the Word of God that the Scripture is from God, that the Scripture is throughout from God, and that the Scripture throughout is entirely from God. 4

That is the historic Christian position and the clear position which the Bible itself claims. All the Bible is inspired alike, and is God-breathed, infallibly correct, every part alike.

---

4. *Theopneustia, The Plenary Inspiration of the Holy Scriptures*, pp. 28, 29.

3. A Partially Inspired Bible Never
Accepted by Creed or People

Warfield says that despite the evil influence of rationalism
". . . it has failed to supplant in either the creeds of the church
or the hearts of the people the church doctrine of the plenary
inspiration of the Bible, i.e., the doctrine that the Bible is inspired not *in part* but *fully* in all its elements alike, —things
discoverable by reason as well as mysteries, matters of history
and science as well as of faith and practice, words as well as
thoughts."[5] And so we agree.

III. NO DEGREES IN INSPIRATION

The perfect Word of God is all perfect. It is all the Word of
God. All of it is settled forever in Heaven (Ps. 119:89). All of
it is incorruptible and cannot be broken (I Pet. 1:23; John
10:35).

That does not mean that all Scripture is as important in
some particular situation as some particular part is. It does
not mean that John 3:16, for example, is not to be treasured
more than some narrative verse in a minor prophet. But it
means that every bit of the Word of God is inspired perfectly
and alike. There are no degrees of inspiration. Many evangelicals have been misled on this matter.

1. Orr Confuses the Degree of Knowledge of the Bible
Writer With Degree of Inspiration—a Serious Error

James Orr says, ". . . it may serve a useful purpose to glance
briefly at the highest and most perfect forms in which revelation
is presented in the Bible—those, viz., in *Moses* and in *Christ*."[6]
Notice the terms, "the highest and most perfect forms." Revelation, Orr thinks, is relative and varying, in differing matter
in the Bible. Again Orr says, "Now it is worthy of observation
that it is an *approach* to this higher mode of revelation [he

---

5. *The Inspiration and Authority of the Bible,* p. 113.
6. *Revelation and Inspiration,* p. 74.

means that of Christ Himself]—though necessarily on an immensely lower level—which is attributed to Moses, the founder
of the old dispensation, as Christ is of the new.''[7]   Orr thought
what Moses wrote in the Bible is ''on an immensely lower level''
than the revelation through Christ.   In other words, he said,
the revelation (and the inspired Word written by Moses) was
imperfect!

Then Orr says, ''It is in any case to be remarked that the
higher prophetic consciousness of a later age never attained
to the altitude here assigned to Moses. . . .   In this respect the
superiority of the New Testament revelation stands out in bold
relief.''[8]   But the scholarly Orr here confuses two entirely
different things.   How much other Old Testament prophets
understood what God inspired them to write as compared to
how much Moses understood what he was inspired to write, is
not the issue.   How much the apostles understood the divine
revelation they were called to speak and write as compared
with less that Moses understood, is not the question at all.
When we speak of *inspiration* we do not speak about how
much *illumination* men had from God in *understanding* the
Scriptures.   We speak of what God Himself committed to men,
breathed out from God, and had men write down.

2. Mistaken Teaching of "Progressive Inspiration"

In the chapter on ''Inspiration—the Scriptural Claims,'' Orr
says, ''The limitations attaching to inspiration arise from the
causes already specified—the *progressiveness* of revelation, the
varying *degrees* of inspiration, and the *fragmentariness* or
other defects of the materials with which inspiration deals.'' [9]
See the three limits which Orr places on inspiration.   But progressiveness here necessarily involves degrees in inspiration.
He says the writings of Moses are on a lower plane than those
of the New Testament. And the writings of other Old Testament
prophets are on a lower plane than those of Moses, says Dr.
Orr.

Again Orr says, ''It is implied, as already said, in any true

---

7. *Revelation and Inspiration*, p. 76.
8. *Revelation and Inspiration*, p. 77.
9. *Revelation and Inspiration*, p. 175.

doctrine of inspiration, that the record of revelation must emanate
from one possessed in a special degree of the Spirit of revelation,
qualifying him for his task; but it does not follow that all
inspired persons possess the Spirit in a *like* eminent degree.
Inspiration in Scripture is of different kinds, and for different
ends." [10]   But Dr. Orr's mistakes here are more than one.   He
implies that certain men are spiritually qualified to write the
Bible, and some more qualified than others, and that the inspiration is in the man himself.   But that is certainly *not* what the
Bible teaches.

Orr lists: "The Mosaic stage of revelation," which, he says,
"did not clearly condemn polygamy or slavery. . . ."   He
says, "The Song of Deborah is an inspired production. . . but
parts are on the lower key of the rude age of the Judges."
He says, "There are portions of the Psalms—prayers for the
destruction of enemies and imprecatory psalms, which no
Christian congregation could now sing, or use in any form
without excessive spiritualisation."   And there again Orr shows
his misconception about inspiration when he says, "We find
in the New Testament that inspired apostles themselves grew
in knowledge with regard to circumcision, and the obligation
of the law on the Gentiles, and to the end some had wider and
some narrower views." [11]

But the differing perception of spiritual truth by the apostles
or others is not the same problem as the problem of inspiration.
When John wrote something, we cannot find how much John
knew; he wrote what God had him write.   Yes, Peter for a time
resisted the command to go preach to the Gentiles, and he
compromised to please the Judaizing leaders in Jerusalem, but
that is not apparent in Peter's divinely inspired writing.   What
Peter may have felt or said is one thing; what God Himself said
in the inspired, God-breathed words He had Peter write down
is another.   When we speak of inspiration we are not talking
about genius or Christian character or growth in grace; we
are speaking of God's wonderfully, miraculously given revelation put down by divine inspiration in our Scriptures.

We insist that the imprecatory Psalms were inspired just like
the other Psalms.   It is God whom men criticize when they pass
judgment on their morality.   The Old Testament Scriptures

10. *Revelation and Inspiration*, p. 177.
11. *Revelation and Inspiration*, p. 176.

were inspired just like the New Testament Scriptures. There are no degrees, no progress in the nature of inspiration.

The only progress in divine inspiration was that God added to what He had previously said. He never set a different moral standard nor gave a different interpretation of facts, never changed the picture of the coming Saviour nor proclaimed a different plan of salvation! No wonder that Peter was inspired to say about Jesus in Acts 10:43, "To him give all the prophets witness, that through his name whosoever believeth in him shall receive remission of sins."   This theme never varied among the prophets.

No, the Bible does not claim to have differing degrees of inspiration.   It does not allow that Scriptures in the Old Testament are imperfect or that any part of the Bible is only partially true, only partially the Word of God.

3. Dr. Carl Henry Answers Orr's Mistake

Dr. Carl F. H. Henry says, "No distinction of this inspiration exists between parts of the Bible. All are inspired, although not for the same immediate purposes." [12]   Again Dr. Henry says, "An examination of the biblical texts from which a Scriptural doctrine of inspiration may be derived indicates as their common element the recognition of the divine authorship and quality of Scripture.   Nowhere is any hint to be found of the compatibility of inspiration with error or that some parts of Scripture are to be segregated from others as more, or less, trustworthy." [13]   He says further, contradicting Orr, as quoted above, "The scriptural emphasis falls on the reliability of the end product, of the Word as written, and not on the detailed *modus operandi* of inspiration." [14]

Those who take the Word of God at simple face value, and believe it, accept the fact that the God-breathed Scripture, the perfect Scripture, is settled forever in Heaven, a book where "Every word of God is pure. . ." (Prov. 30:5). We accept the Bible which claims: "The words of the Lord are pure words: as silver tried in a furnace of earth, purified seven times" (Ps.

---

12. *Inspiration and Interpretation*, p. 257.
13. *Inspiration and Interpretation*, p. 275.
14. *Inspiration and Interpretation*, p. 275.

12:6). We claim that these holy Scriptures are entirely, in every part, inspired and infallible. There are no degrees of inspiration; there is no progress from a lesser to a greater degree of inspiration and accuracy.

It is inherent in God-breathed Scriptures that there are no degrees and no parts of the original Scriptures with lesser accuracy or lesser authority.

IV. SOME WOULD CLAIM PARTS OF THE BIBLE ARE UNINSPIRED

Some people claim that the Bible contains errors and therefore in those parts could not be infallibly inspired of God. It is said that the writers of the Bible contradict each other. About these alleged discrepancies Charles Hodge says (*Systematic Theology,* Vol. 1, page 169):

> All that can be expected here is a few general remarks: (1) These apparent discrepancies, although numerous, are for the most part trivial; relating in most cases to numbers or dates. (2) The great majority of them are only apparent, and yield to careful examination. (3) Many of them may fairly be ascribed to errors of transcribers. (4) The marvel and the miracle is that there are so few of any real importance. [15]

On the following page, Hodge says:

> Admitting that the Scriptures do contain, in a few instances, discrepancies which with our present means of knowledge, we are unable satisfactorily to explain, they furnish no rational ground for denying their infallibility. "The Scripture cannot be broken." (John x. 35.) This is the whole doctrine of plenary inspiration, taught by the lips of Christ himself. [16]

Then concerning the historical and scientific objections, Hodge says:

> The second great objection to the plenary inspiration of the Scripture is that it teaches what is inconsistent with historical and scientific truth.
> Here again it is to be remarked, (1) That we must distinguish between what the sacred writers themselves thought or believed, and what they teach. They may have believed that the sun

---

15. *Systematic Theology,* Vol. 1, p. 169.
16. *Systematic Theology,* Vol. 1, p. 170.

moves around the earth, but they do not so teach. (2) The language of the Bible is the language of common life; and the language of common life is founded on apparent, and not upon scientific truth. It would be ridiculous to refuse to speak of the sun rising and setting, because we know that it is not a satellite of our planet. (3) There is a great distinction between theories and facts. Theories are of men. Facts are of God. The Bible often contradicts the former, never the latter. (4) There is also a distinction to be made between the Bible and our interpretation. The latter may come into competition with settled facts; and then it must yield. [17]

There is neither the space nor the need for detailed discussion of every objection, every supposed inaccuracy. We need not explain nor justify every verse which some may not think is inspired. But there are logical and proper answers to every objection, if we were only wise enough to know the answers.

Dr. R. A. Torrey states [18] the following solid principles to observe about so-called difficulties.

1. From the very nature of the case, difficulties are to be expected in the infinite wealth in the Word of God. It is beyond any shallow and easy understanding of everything in it.

2. A grave objection to a doctrine does not, in any wise, prove the doctrine to be untrue.

3. There are much greater difficulties in believing that the Bible is of human origin and fallible than to believe the Bible is of divine origin and infallible. How explain the Bible unless it is God's Word?

4. If you cannot solve a difficulty, that does not prove it cannot be solved. If you cannot answer an objection, that does not prove it cannot be answered by someone with more knowledge or more light.

5. The supposed difficulties and seeming defects in the Bible are exceedingly insignificant in comparison with its many marvelous excellencies.

6. These so-called difficulties have far more weight with superficial readers than profound students.

7. Dr. Torrey said that difficulties in the Bible rapidly disappear among careful and prayerful study. He found, as many of us have found, that the more he studies the Bible with prayerful and believing heart, the more the difficulties disappear.

17. *Systematic Theology*, Vol. 1, pp. 170,171.
18. See book, *Difficulties in the Bible*, pp. 1-16.

Since perhaps a thousand supposed difficulties once plagued me, and now I might find only ten or fifteen, would it not be sensible to suppose that with more light, if I knew all the facts, the other difficulties would disappear, too, as have hundreds of others before prayerful study?

Dr. Robert Dick Wilson, Princeton Seminary, was probably the most erudite Semitic scholar in America. He was familiar with forty-five languages. He said: "In conclusion, let me reiterate my conviction that no one knows enough to show that the true text of the Old Testament in its true interpretation is not true." [19]

He also said, "The evidence in our possession has convinced me. . .that the Old Testament in Hebrew 'being immediately inspired by God' has 'by his singular care and providence been kept pure in all ages.' " [20]

So we do not seek to answer all the objections and difficulties, but to mention a few principal Scriptures which some people think indicates part of the Scriptures are not inspired and infallible.

1. It Is Claimed That Paul Admitted Some of His Writing Was Not From God

In I Corinthians 7, verses 10 to 12, we read:

"And unto the married I command, yet not I, but the Lord, Let not the wife depart from her husband: But and if she depart, let her remain unmarried, or be reconciled to her husband: and let not the husband put away his wife. But to the rest speak I, not the Lord: If any brother hath a wife that believeth not, and she be pleased to dwell with him, let him not put her away."

In verse 10 Paul gives instructions and says, "Yet not I, but the Lord." But in verse 12 he says, "But to the rest speak I, not the Lord." Does not that mean that the statement in verse 10 and 11 is inspired and verse 12 is not? No, it does not mean that at all. In verse 10 Paul is simply saying that the Lord Jesus, as recorded in the Gospels, has already plainly

---

19. *A Scientific Investigation of the Old Testament*, p. 13.
20. *A Scientific Investigation of the Old Testament*, p. 13.

taught that a marriage ought not to be broken, that the wife
should not leave her husband. He refers evidently to the statements of Jesus in Matthew 5:31,32 and in Matthew 19:9.   But
in verse 12 Paul is not quoting from the recorded words of
Jesus in the Gospels.   He is giving what God has inspired
him to give.   It is just as certainly the perfect Word of God as
if Jesus had said it and if it were written down in the Gospels
and so quoted by Paul.   In verse 10 Paul refers to a statement
of Jesus in the Gospels.   In verse 12 he says he has no statement from the Gospels, recorded in the words of Jesus on the
matter, but he has nevertheless a statement inspired of God
which is equally authoritative.   Paul would claim here, as in
I Thessalonians 2:13 that his word was "not as the word of
men, but as it is in truth, the word of God."

2. Orr, Carnell and Others Say Old Testament Moral
Standards Are Not Inspired Equally With
Teaching of New Testament Standards

Tom Paine and Robert Ingersoll scoffed at the moral standards in the Old Testament.   It is a little shocking to find Orr,
Carnell, and others who believe that the Bible is in some degree
the Word of God, joining with them in such matters.

Orr teaches "degrees of inspiration" and that inspiration was
"progressive," first accommodating itself to primitive moral
standards and knowledge to be "corrected" by later revelation. [21]

Dr. Edward John Carnell quoted Orr extensively, agreeing
with him that "the concept of 'progressive revelation' is the key
to biblical hermeneutics."[22]   Carnell quotes Orr to prove his
stand for "defective forms" of some earlier Scriptures and the
New Testament "abrogation of whatever was imperfect in the
earlier stages," as Orr states it.

The "imprecatory Psalms" are disdained.   Orr says, "There
are portions of the Psalms—prayers for the destruction of
enemies and imprecatory psalms, which no Christian congregation could now sing, or use in any form without excessive
spiritualisation."[23]

---

21. See *Revelation and Inspiration*, pp. 102,103,175-177.
22. *The Case for Orthodox Theology*, p. 52.
23. *Revelation and Inspiration*, p. 176.

Let us examine two of these cases in the Psalms which are criticised.

Psalm 109:6-12:

"Set thou a wicked man over him: and let Satan stand at his right hand. When he shall be judged, let him be condemned: and let his prayer become sin. Let his days be few; and let another take his office. Let his children be fatherless, and his wife a widow. Let his children be continually vagabonds, and beg: let them seek their bread also out of their desolate places. Let the extortioner catch all that he hath; and let the strangers spoil his labour. Let there be none to extend mercy unto him: neither let there be any to favour his fatherless children."

In Psalm 137:7-9 we read:

"Remember, O Lord, the children of Edom in the day of Jerusalem; who said, Rase it, rase it, even to the foundation thereof. O daughter of Babylon, who art to be destroyed; happy shall he be, that rewardeth thee as thou hast served us. Happy shall he be, that taketh and dasheth thy little ones against the stones."

But why should any Christian congregation now sing, praying for the destruction of Edom and of Babylon? They have already been destroyed. The prayer of the psalmist was answered.

And why should any Christian make his own prayer about just anybody and everybody, the prayer of David about particular enemies? David did not sing that prayer on every occasion and about everybody: why should anybody else do that? In a particular case God Himself inspired David to write a certain Psalm about particular people. They hated and fought against David without a cause. He had loved them and yet they rewarded him evil for good and hatred for his love. Now David, God's anointed man, is inspired to write this Psalm about them.

There are two things to be said about such Psalms. First, they are inspired of God. It was God who wanted these particular men destroyed or punished. David doubtless entered into God's desire, too, but we cannot avoid the fact that God Himself often does decree the death of His enemies and the death of wicked men. And who are Orr or Carnell, any more than infidels Ingersoll and Paine, to sit in judgment on the righteousness of God?

Again, it is fair to say that some good Hebrew scholars think that in the Hebrew text the same form was used for the imperative (let it be done) and the simple future (it shall be done). So the psalmist may have been simply quoting a prophecy that God had put in his heart about what would happen. No matter what David thought or did not think, the Psalm is from God and who is wise enough to say that God was wrong in these particular cases?

Those who do not like the prayer in Psalm 137 against Edom and Babylon are put in the place of criticising God because He did really destroy Babylon and did destroy Edom.

The accounts of execution of Agag by Samuel and of the prophets of Baal by Elijah are held morally inadequate by some critics and thus not perfectly inspired.

In I Samuel 16:33 it is quite clear that God approved Samuel when he "hewed Agag in pieces before the Lord." God had decreed the destruction of Agag and his people. In a public spectacle, the prophet showed before King Saul the deadly importance of carrying out God's command to the letter.

Also it is clear that the Lord approved the Prophet Elijah when he beheaded the 450 prophets of Baal after God's wonderful answers to his prayer on Mount Carmel (I Kings 18:40).

But you who criticise are criticising God. And you criticise the New Testament as well as the Old. Did not Ananias and Sapphira fall dead at the inspired word of the Apostle Peter in the New Testament (Acts 5:5-10), and did not God strike Elymas the sorcerer blind at the word of Paul in Acts 13:11? And does not the New Testament clearly teach in Romans 13:1-7 that the ruler is the minister of God and that he bears the sword for the Lord to punish with death when need be? And in Luke 13:1-5, does not the dear Lord Jesus Himself teach that the destruction of the wicked — whether by authority of the government or by "acts of God" in nature — is really the work of God? Does not God have the power of life and death and does He not execute that power as much in the New Testament as in the Old? And so with the destruction of the Amalakite nation, Canaanites and others, who had gone into the vilest idolatry and would most certainly lead Israel into sin if left unhindered. "O man, who art thou that repliest against God?" (Rom. 9:20).

Orr and Carnell and others mention that the Old Testament allowed polygamy and slavery. Well, the Old Testament is not specially different from the New Testament in that matter. Paul sent the slave Onesimus, after he was converted, back to his master Philemon. The word slave is not used in the King James Bible but one time, in Revelation 18:13, where it is really the word for "a body, a person." The word generally translated "servant" is *doulos*, which Young's Analytical Concordance says means "a servant, slave."

In I Timothy 6:1 and 2 the Apostle Paul is inspired to say, "Let as many servants as are under the yoke count their own masters worthy of all honour, that the name of God and his doctrine be not blasphemed. And they that have believing masters, let them not despise them, because they are brethren; but rather do them service, because they are faithful and beloved, partakers of the benefit. These things teach and exhort."

Ephesians 6:5 and 6 commands, "Servants, be obedient to them that are your masters according to the flesh, with fear and trembling, in singleness of your heart, as unto Christ; Not with eyeservice, as menpleasers; but as the servants of Christ, doing the will of God from the heart."

Then Colossians 3:22 commands, "Servants, obey in all things your masters according to the flesh; not with eyeservice, as menpleasers; but in singleness of heart, fearing God."

Titus 2:9 and 10 says, "Exhort servants to be obedient unto their own masters, and to please them well in all things; not answering again; Not purloining, but shewing all good fidelity; that they may adorn the doctrine of God our Saviour in all things."

So there is no particular difference in the Old Testament teaching and the New Testament about slavery. However, as sensible people all know, there is in the Scripture such clear teaching about acting in love, seeking the welfare of others, doing unto others as you would they should do unto you, that eventually in any country where Christian sentiment prevails, slavery disappears.

It is significant that in the Bible, regularly the same word is used for servant, meaning simply a helper or assistant, and a slave. As a father has command over his children, and should have — and that is good and not bad — so in many cases, no doubt, it were better for people to have somebody else manage their affairs, if it were done lovingly and unselfishly as the

Bible commands. I am not saying that slavery is right but in some cases slavery would not be as unhappy as to be under the heel of a loan shark or enslaved by drink, or with the dope habit, or in a government under a dictator.

Nor does the New Testament teach necessarily differently from the Old Testament on the matter of polygamy. The one difference is that when the Scripture speaks of a bishop or pastor it is required that he be "the husband of one wife" (I Tim. 3:2 and Titus 1:6). It seems clear that people with plural wives were saved and taken into the church and were expected to care for the wives they had married and the children they had begotten. But it is also understood that the best way and the proper way is for a man to have only one wife, and so the leaders in the churches were so required.

And it is only fair to say that in the Old Testament when God instituted marriage in Genesis 2:24 and said, "Therefore shall a man leave his father and his mother, and shall cleave unto his wife: and they shall be one flesh," and in the New Testament where Jesus quoted that passage in Matthew 19:4-6, the plain teaching is that a marriage of one man and one woman is the proper and intended plan.

We may plainly say that in the New Testament God added to revelation which had been given before but did not break it nor discredit it, just as Paul in I Corinthians 7:10 repeats the commandment Christ made about divorce and then adds another inspired instruction in verse 12. But the earlier inspiration is exactly as much from God as the later revelation.

3. Critics Are Skeptical About Certain Miracles of the Bible

But once you honestly face the fact of miraculous creation and a miracle-working God, then all the miracles related in the Bible are believable and suitable. As Dr. Blanchard, long-time president of Wheaton College, said, "If there be a God, He must act like God." A God who could make this world and this universe could control it. Colossians 1:16 and 17 says, "For by him were all things created, that are in heaven, and that are in earth, visible and invisible, whether they be thrones, or dominions, or principalities, or powers: all things were created by him, and for him: And he is before all things, and by him all things consist." It is Christ who made all things, and made them for Himself. He is the One by whom "all things consist," or hold together. So is the plain statement of Scripture.

People complain that some miracles of the Bible are "contrary to the laws of nature," but what people call the "laws of nature" are no more than the usual way that God works. There is no moral authority in what some call "laws of nature." In countless cases people who by no laws of nature seem certain to die, have lived. In countless cases men have been cured of the dope habit, the liquor habit, the tobacco habit, with none of the known and usually inevitable withdrawal struggles and adjustment in recovery. I prayed for a woman dying with TB. After two years in a state sanitarium she was sent home to have her last hemorrhage and die. Her children had already been given away, the home was already sold, to take effect at her death. But she was healed immediately; in two weeks she was doing all her own housework. More than thirty years later I found she was still well and strong.

I would rarely expect such a miraculous intervention of God. Certainly that is not God's customary way of healing tuberculosis. But God is Creator, Sustainer, and Master of His own universe. He did not break any laws. He can work miracles and can do things out of His customary way, when He chooses.

We read in Joshua 10:13-15 that the sun stood still at Joshua's command.

"And the sun stood still, and the moon stayed, until the people had avenged themselves upon their enemies. Is not this written in the book of Jasher? So the sun stood still in the midst of heaven, and hasted not to go down about a whole day. And there was no day like that before it or after it, that the Lord hearkened unto the voice of a man: for the Lord fought for Israel."

It would appear either that the earth ceased to revolve, or at least that the revolution was slowed down about the space of a day.

Critics say to us that if the earth should cease to revolve or drastically slow its speed, the whole surface of the earth would be devastated by ocean tides, buildings would fall, civilization would be destroyed. But how do they know? The earth revolves at about 1,040 miles per hour at the equator, and much less in the temperate zone. Jet planes travel twice that fast, then land and come to a stop in a few minutes with no harm or discomfort. Astronauts circle the earth at 18,000 miles an hour, yet decelerate and splash down with no harm. And why could not God, if He stopped the revolution of the earth, stop the revolution of the water in the seas and the rivers, too? If He should see fit to do it, is God short on energy or wisdom for such a miracle? Any miracle is incredible unless you believe in a miracle-working God. A great miracle is not hard to believe if you have a great enough God who says He worked such a miracle.

Dr. L. R. Scarborough, president of Southwestern Seminary, told us students how his six-year-old son came back from Sunday school one day saying, "Dad, they taught us something in Sunday school today that I don't believe." He was shocked to find infidelity in one so young!

"What was it that you can't believe?" Dr. Scarborough asked.

The lad answered that it was the story about Jonah and the whale that swallowed him—how could a man be swallowed by a whale and stay alive three days and then come out to preach?

But Dr. Scarborough explained to his son that if there is a God who could make a whale and make a man, why could He not have the whale swallow the man and keep the man alive for His own purpose?

"Oh!" said the boy, "if you are going to put God into it I can believe it, too." So can I, if you put God into it!

The universal flood is denied by Ramm, by Carnell, and by others anxious to accept the opinion of some scientists. The flood is not only plainly described in Genesis, but Jesus Christ authenticated that account and said, "But as the days of Noe were, so shall also the coming of the Son of man be. For as in the days that were before the flood they were eating and drinking, marrying and giving in marriage, until the day that Noe entered into the ark, And knew not until the flood came, and took them all away; so shall also the coming of the Son of man be" (Matt. 24:37-39). The flood was as sudden and as worldwide in its impact evidently as the second coming of Christ to which it is likened here. If you believe Jesus Christ, you believe the Bible.

Second Peter 3:3-6 tells us:

"Knowing this first, that there shall come in the last days

scoffers, walking after their own lusts, And saying, Where is the promise of his coming? for since the fathers fell asleep, all things continue as they were from the beginning of the creation. For this they willingly are ignorant of, that by the word of God the heavens were of old, and the earth standing out of the water and in the water: Whereby the world that then was, being overflowed with water, perished."

Scoffers do not believe the Bible. Christians do, surely. And by the flood "the world that then was, being overflowed with water, perished," says the Word of God. And that is in the New Testament, too. So the Old Testament is to be believed as the inspired Word of God just as the New Testament.

Until about one hundred years ago, or a little more, nearly all scientists believed in the universal flood as recorded in the Bible and that that flood produced the strata in the ground, the coal beds, the fossils, which we now find. But as unbelief everywhere increased, the fancy of many unbelieving scientists turned to natural causes and so they try to explain a universe without God either to create it or to sustain it, and without an inspired Bible to tell of it. However, those who want millions of ages in order to make room for the evolution they want to believe, go on opinion and speculation, not on scientific proof.

An example of scientific dissent is the book, *Earth in Upheaval,* by Immanuel Velikovsky. And Dr. Velikovsky is one of the most learned men of the centuries. As a youthful scholar he edited *"The Scripta Universitatis,"* a collective work out of which the Hebrew University at Jerusalem grew. He was an intimate friend of Professor Einstein. He lectured in the graduate school of Princeton University. Dr. Robert H. Peiffer of Harvard University says, "If Dr. Velikovsky is right, this volume is the greatest contribution to the investigation of ancient time ever written." Velikovsky, a Jew, is not a fundamentalist, does not believe the Bible is inspired, and is an evolutionist. But he believes that the Old Testament is historically accurate in the matter of the flood, of the sun standing still, of the plagues in Exodus, etc. His books published by Doubleday have created a profound scientific impression. I mention him only to show that the supposed millions of years of the earth and the denial of the accuracy of the Scripture is not universally accepted among the most learned scientific men in the world.

It is not ignorance, it is not foolish to believe the Bible.

We are saying that all the Word of God is inspired alike and infallibly correct.

CHAPTER VI

THE TESTIMONY OF JESUS CHRIST ABOUT THE WORD OF GOD

I. WHAT JESUS TAUGHT ABOUT THE SCRIPTURES

1. Jesus Quoted and Made His Own the Statement From Deuteronomy 8:3, "Man Shall Not Live by Bread Alone, but by Every Word That Proceedeth Out of the Mouth of God" (Matt. 4:4 and Luke 4:4)

2. And Jesus Plainly Said Not a Jot Nor Tittle of the Law Should Pass Away Till All Be Fulfilled

3. Jesus Plainly Said That "Scripture Cannot Be Broken"

4. Jesus Said in the Olivet Discourse, "Heaven and Earth Shall Pass Away, but My Words Shall Not Pass Away" (Matt. 24:35; Mark 13:31; Luke 21:33)

5. Rejectors Will Be Judged by the Word of God and Their Attitude Toward That Word

II. JESUS OFTEN QUOTED THE WORD OF GOD AS FINAL AUTHORITY

1. Jesus Quoted the Genesis Account of Creation As True and the Very Word of God

2. Jesus Verified the Genesis Account of a Universal Flood

3. Jesus Believed and Approved the Bible Story of Jonah and Nineveh

4. Jesus Quoted From Isaiah, Calling the Prophet by Name Again and Again As Writer of the Whole Book

5. The Lord Jesus Accepted All the Old Testament As the Word of God

THE TESTIMONY OF JESUS CHRIST
ABOUT THE WORD OF GOD

Jesus Christ affirmed the Bible to be exactly what it claims to be—the very eternal Word of God. His testimony is so exactly and so often stated, His daily dependence upon the Bible, His quotations from the Bible, so that Jesus Christ Himself stands or falls with the Bible.

Jesus Christ, the eternal, sinless, virgin-born Son of God, and the Bible, the eternal, God-breathed, perfect Word of God, go together. But for the Bible to be unreliable and not actually the perfect Word of God would mean to have a Christ who was Himself ignorant and deceived or deliberately false and a charlatan, a fraud. If Jesus Christ was mistaken about the Bible, then all of us are mistaken who call Him the Son of God, the Saviour of the world.

I. WHAT JESUS TAUGHT ABOUT THE SCRIPTURES

1. Jesus Quoted and Made His Own the Statement From Deuteronomy 8:3, "Man Shall Not Live by Bread Alone, but by Every Word That Proceedeth Out of the Mouth of God" (Matt. 4:4 and Luke 4:4)

Jesus was being tempted of Satan. He had spent forty days without food, and everything good for man and God is now at stake. If Jesus should fail now and succumb to Satan, this world would be all gone to Hell, the human race ruined, without any possible salvation. Christ Himself would have been dishonored and His whole idea of redemption would have failed. So, when He was tempted to make bread out of stones, He said, "It is written, Man shall not live by bread alone, but by every word that proceedeth out of the mouth of God." He was not speaking to men who might be deceived but to the prince of devils himself, that fallen archangel, the god of this world, the prince of darkness. And Jesus knew that Satan himself knew the Scriptures as the Word of God. The spirits knew Jesus and called Him by name: "I know thee who thou art; the Holy One of God" (Luke 4:34). "Devils also believe, and tremble" (James 2:19). And speaking to that awful head of principalities and powers of evil, Jesus relied on the Word of God and quoted it. And He said that men ought to live day by day and feed day by day not only on the bread of this world but on the Word of God. "...every word...proceedeth out of the mouth of God." What higher testimony could men or angels or God Himself give about the Bible? It is no time for foolish dodging or subterfuge. Jesus defeated Satan here with the Word of God of which Jesus said, "...every word ...proceedeth out of the mouth of God," as the Old Testament Scriptures themselves had said.

2. And Jesus Plainly Said Not a Jot Nor Tittle of the Law Should Pass Away Till All Be Fulfilled

How striking is the statement of Christ in Matthew 5:17,18:

" Think not that I am come to destroy the law, or the prophets: I am not come to destroy, but to fulfil. For verily I say unto you, Till heaven and earth pass, one jot or one tittle shall in no wise pass from the law, till all be fulfilled."

Jesus knew that the time for offering passover lambs would be gone when He, God's Passover Lamb, should die. Jesus knew that those ceremonies which are "a shadow of things to come," would be fulfilled, "but the body is of Christ" (Col. 2:16,17). But the Scripture — all of it — is guaranteed to never pass away till all be fulfilled.

How perfect is the law of God, the Bible? Christ here guarantees every jot and tittle. The jot is the *yod,* the smallest character in the Hebrew alphabet. The tittle is the little curl or tail-like thing, smaller than a comma, which is a part of and distinguishes certain of the Hebrew consonants. Jesus is saying that not only the words but the very spelling of the original Hebrew manuscript is of God and unchangeable. Despite some mistakes copyists or translations might make, God has guaranteed that in the last the Word of God will be perfectly preserved "until all be fulfilled."

He speaks here not of the words of men but of the words of God where true integrity cannot be questioned.

3. Jesus Plainly Said That "Scripture Cannot Be Broken"

What a powerful statement that is which Jesus seems to say very casually in John 10:35. Let us read verses 34 to 36:

"Jesus answered them, Is it not written in your law, I said, Ye are gods? If he called them gods, unto whom the word of God came, and the scripture cannot be broken; Say ye of him, whom the Father hath sanctified, and sent into the world, Thou blasphemest; because I said, I am the Son of God?"

Jesus is quoting from Psalm 82:6, "Ye are gods," and uses that to show how foolish it is to deny that Jesus is God when the Bible teaches that men are made somewhat after the pattern of God and in the image of God. To deny it is to deny that Jesus, "whom the Father hath sanctified, and sent into the world," is the Son of God as He said. How could Jesus be blaspheming to make such a claim? And in the midst of that argument He says almost incidentally, "and the scripture cannot be broken." He did not argue the point. It needed no argument. He knew, and those who heard Him would agree, as sensible, reverent people now agree and accept at face value, that "the scripture cannot be broken."

That must mean, first, that the Word of God is eternal. It must mean also that it is, as elsewhere claimed, incorruptible. That must mean that the words of God are pure words, that they are forever settled in Heaven. They are pure like silver refined seven times, as the Scripture claims. And surely every honest reader will have to say that Jesus meant that the Scriptures are the eternal Word of God.

4. Jesus Said in the Olivet Discourse, "Heaven and Earth Shall Pass Away, but My Words Shall Not Pass Away" (Matt. 24:35; Mark 13:31; Luke 21:33)

We may be sure that when Jesus said, "My words shall not pass away," He meant the Scriptures. Jesus never made a distinction between the value of words He Himself spoke as distinct from other words of Scripture. The words of Christ are the Word of God and all the words in the Scriptures are the words of Christ. In Colossians 3:16 we are admonished to "let the word of Christ dwell in you richly." But does not that mean the Word of God, the Bible, the Scriptures?

In John 5:24 Jesus said, "Verily, verily, I say unto you, He that heareth my word, and believeth on him that sent me, hath everlasting life, and shall not come into condemnation; but is passed from death unto life." Does that mean that one could not be saved by trusting in the Gospel as witnessed in the Bible, or must one find salvation only in the recorded spoken words of Jesus in the Gospels? Of course not. We know that sinners can be saved through preaching the truth in Isaiah 53, about the atoning Saviour who bore our sins. I won sixty-six lost people in one summer on Isaiah 55:6 and 7, "Seek ye the Lord while he may be found, call ye upon him while he is near: Let the wicked forsake his way, and the unrighteous man his thoughts: and let him return unto the Lord, and he will have mercy upon him; and to our God, for he will abundantly pardon."

Many have been saved through the preaching of the Gospel as given in Acts 16:31, "Believe on the Lord Jesus Christ, and thou shalt be saved." So when Jesus said in John 5:24, "He that heareth my word, and believeth on him that sent me," He referred to any one who heard the words of the Gospel through the Scriptures and believed on Christ. You see, the Bible, all the Scriptures, are the words of Christ.

God created the heavens and earth, but it is Christ, the second Person of the Trinity, who did the creating. So the Word of God is the Word of Christ. He said, "I and my Father are one." And that is true about the Bible.

Jesus is saying, then, that the Scriptures cannot pass away.

He did not mean that you could go through a printing of the Bible which has all the words of Christ in red, and He would guarantee that the part printed in red would never pass away, though the rest might fail! No! No! He is saying that the Scriptures themselves will never pass away. Heaven and earth shall pass away in their present form, but God's Word, never!

Heaven and earth shall pass away. That means that one of these days the earth will melt with fervent heat. God will purge this old earth by fire as it was purged once before by water (II Pet. 3:10). And Revelation 6:13,14 tells us of a time yet to come but revealed here: "And the stars of heaven fell unto the earth, even as a fig tree casteth her untimely figs, when she is shaken of a mighty wind. And the heaven departed as a scroll when it is rolled together; and every mountain and island were moved out of their places." But when the heaven is rolled up as a scroll and this earth is melted with fervent heat and everything that fire can destroy is destroyed so that God can make of earth a new Garden of Eden and have a new heaven and a new earth—in that time the Word of God will still abide the perfect and eternal Word of God! So Jesus Christ said.

If Jesus Christ is the perfect Son of God, the Bible will last forever.

5. Rejectors Will Be Judged by the Word of God and Their Attitude Toward That Word

The Lord Jesus held the Word of God in an awesome reverence. He inferred that to be true to Christ was to be true to the Bible, the Word of God. And to be ashamed of the Word of God would be to be ashamed of Christ.

In Mark 8:38 Jesus said, "Whosoever therefore shall be ashamed of me and of my words in this adulterous and sinful generation; of him also shall the Son of man be ashamed, when he cometh in the glory of his Father with the holy angels." The same statement of Christ is quoted in part, in Luke 9:26.

Let us face it honestly: to be ashamed of the Scriptures is to be ashamed of Christ. And to be ashamed of the Scriptures means that when the Lord Jesus shall return, He, in all the glory of the Father and the holy angels, will be ashamed of that person.

So, in John 12:47 and 48 Jesus said, "And if any man hear my words, and believe not, I judge him not: for I came not to judge the world, but to save the world. He that rejecteth me, and receiveth not my words, hath one that judgeth him: the word that I have spoken, the same shall judge him in the last day."

People who reject Jesus Christ and die unsaved will go to Hell and at the great judgment time bodies will be brought out of the grave and out of the sea and souls out of Hell, to face Jesus Christ and to face *the Scriptures!* That is what Jesus Christ said. That is how He valued the Scriptures. They were to Christ plainly the eternal, unchangeable Word of God, concerning which God would hold every person to account.

Jesus is the sinless and infallible Son of God and the Bible is the infallible Word of God.

II. JESUS OFTEN QUOTED THE WORD OF GOD AS FINAL AUTHORITY

1. Jesus Quoted the Genesis Account of Creation As True and the Very Word of God

Jesus verified the Genesis account of creation of man in Matthew 19:4-6:

"And he answered and said unto them, Have ye not read, that he which made them at the beginning made them male and female, And said, For this cause shall a man leave father and mother, and shall cleave to his wife: and they twain shall be one flesh? Wherefore they are no more twain, but one flesh. What therefore God hath joined together, let not man put asunder."

So, Jesus accepts what Genesis says about direct creation of Adam and Eve. And based on that, He said, "What therefore God hath joined together, let not man put asunder."

2. Jesus Verified the Genesis Account of a Universal Flood

Jesus clearly believed and quoted as the very Word of God

the account of the flood in the days of Noah. In Matthew 24:37-39 Jesus said:

"But as the days of Noe-were, so shall also the coming of the Son of man be. For as in the days that were before the flood they were eating and drinking, marrying and giving in marriage, until the day that Noe entered into the ark, And knew not until the flood came, and took them all away; so shall also the coming of the Son of man be."

The flood is also mentioned by the Lord Jesus in Mark 13:28,29 and in Luke 21:29-31.

Genesis is reliable in speaking of the universal flood, with Noah and his wife and his three sons and their wives left to populate the earth, and the rest of the whole former huge population swept away. Jesus regarded all the Mosaic Law as reliable, of course. We have seen how He quoted and authenticated Deuteronomy 8:3 and He said, "For had ye believed Moses, ye would have believed me: for he wrote of me" (John 5:46). Jesus plainly names Moses as the writer of the Pentateuch. "Moses therefore gave unto you circumcision; (not because it is of Moses, but of the fathers;). . ." (John 7:22).

Again, "If a man on the sabbath day receive circumcision, that the law of Moses should not be broken; are ye angry at me, because I have made a man every whit whole on the sabbath day?"

Jesus gave abundant evidence that Moses wrote the Pentateuch, the law. I have just counted, in the Gospels, twenty-four times He mentioned Moses as writer of the law, sixteen times that He quoted Moses. In John 7:19 Jesus said plainly, "Did not Moses give you the law, and yet none of you keepeth the law?"

They are not friends of Jesus Christ who would foolishly, in wicked unbelief, say that the Pentateuch was not written till long after the day of Moses or that Moses could not write or that it is the patchwork, a fraud, prepared by a lying "redactor" or editor, and they slander Him. He is their opponent. Jesus Christ believed it and authenticated that Moses was the instrument of God writing the Law.

3. Jesus Believed and Approved the Bible Story of Jonah and Nineveh

In Matthew 12:40,41 Jesus said, "For as Jonas was three days and three nights in the whale's belly; so shall the Son of man be three days and three nights in the heart of the earth. The men of Nineveh shall rise in judgment with this generation, and shall condemn it: because they repented at the preaching of Jonas; and, behold, a greater than Jonas is here." Notice here that Jesus plainly says that Jonah was three days and three nights in the whale's belly (or in the sea monster's belly). That is a type of His own three days and nights in the grave before His future bodily resurrection. The miraculous deliverance of Jonah from the whale was true, Jesus said. And He said that the men of Nineveh repented; so they will stand in judgment against those who do not repent.

4. Jesus Quoted From Isaiah, Calling the Prophet by Name Again and Again As Writer of the Whole Book

Unbelieving scholars feel so superior to the Bible that they freely sit in judgment on it. Such men have decided that there was a real Isaiah who wrote the first thirty-nine chapters of the book by his name, but that chapters 40 to 66 were written by others and inserted later, "the last half of the fifth century B. C."[1]

That blasphemous commentary says:

> Is the book of Isaiah the work of a single writer, the prophet Isaiah, whose prophetic oracles appear in chs. 1-39? This view has been held until relatively modern times. In the twelfth century, however, Ibn Ezra in somewhat guarded language expressed his doubts that chs. 40-66 were written by Isaiah. The hypothesis that they originated with a later poet was first formulated and defended by Johann Christoph Doderlein in 1775, popularized by Johann Gottfried Eichhorn in 1780-83, and is now widely accepted. The arguments for this position are based upon (a) the historical background reflected in the book; (b) the language, literary style, and form; and (c) the theological ideas. [2]

1. *The Interpreter's Bible.*
2. *The Interpreter's Bible,* Vol. 5, p. 382.

These enemies of the Bible call chapters 1 to 39 of the prophecy, "Isaiah," and chapters 40 to 66, "Second Isaiah" or "Deutero Isaiah."

The Lord Jesus made no such division.   He quoted both parts alike, calling it all the work of Isaiah.

In Matthew 13:14,15, He quoted Isaiah 6:9,10 and called it "the prophecy of Isaiah."

In Mark 7:6, Jesus quoted Isaiah 29:13 and said, "Well hath Esaias prophesied of you hypocrites. . . ."

But in John 12:38-41 Jesus quotes from three places in Isaiah: in 53:1, 6:10, and 6:1. He introduces these quotations thus: "That the saying of Esaias the prophet might be fulfilled, which he spake" and, "Esaias said again" and, "These things said Esaias, when he saw his glory, and spake of him."

So on the authority of the Lord Jesus the whole book of Isaiah was written, as it claims to be, by the Prophet Isaiah.

5. The Lord Jesus Accepted All the Old Testament As the Word of God

The canon of Old Testament Scripture was already settled before the time of Christ, and had been translated from Hebrew into Greek by a group of seventy devout and learned Jews. That translation is called the Septuagint. Jesus often quoted from it, and accepted that Old Testament, exactly the same books we and all Protestants have today, as the Word of God.

When Jesus after His resurrection came upon the two disheartened disciples on the road to Emmaus, here is what He said and did:

" Then he said unto them, O fools, and slow of heart to believe all that the prophets have spoken: Ought not Christ to have suffered these things, and to enter into his glory? And beginning at Moses and all the prophets, he expounded unto them in all the scriptures the things concerning himself." — Luke 24:25-27.

Note the phrase "all the scriptures." All the writings were then accepted among the Jews as inspired Scripture! Jesus verified them all as the authoritative, prophetic Word of God.

Then, appearing to the assembled disciples in Jerusalem, the resurrected Christ "... said unto them, These are the words which I spake unto you, while I was yet with you, that all things must be fulfilled, which were written in the law of Moses, and in the prophets, and in the psalms, concerning me" (Luke 24:44). So to Jesus, the Law of Moses, the prophets and the Psalms — all the Old Testament — was the infallible Word of God.

Those who deny the inspiration and authority of the Old Testament thus rebel against the authority and deity of the Lord Jesus.

III. JESUS WAS SO SATURATED IN HEART BY THE SCRIPTURES THAT HE QUOTED AND REFERRED TO THEM CONTINUALLY

How can I show the overwhelming use Jesus made of the Scriptures, how He was full of them, revered them as absolute authority, the very voice of God?

1. Saphir Shows Beautifully How Jesus Quoted and Referred to Scripture

Adolf Saphir sums it up well:

> Jesus, in His teaching, constantly alludes to the writings of Moses and the prophets. He refers to almost every period of the history recorded in Scripture. He speaks of the creation of man, the institution of marriage, the death of Abel, the days of Noe, the destruction of Sodom, the history of Abraham, the appearance of God in the burning bush, the manna in the wilderness, the miracle of the brazen serpent, the wanderings of David, the glory of Solomon, the ministry of Elijah and Elisha, the sign of Jonah, the martyrdom of Zechariah; events which embrace the whole range of the Jewish record. And not merely do we meet with these direct references. The allusions to Scripture are almost innumerable; and every careful reader of Christ's discourses, who possesses a knowledge of the so-called Old Testament, must feel convinced that Jesus knew the Scripture from a child; and that His mind, His memory, His imagination, His whole inner man, was filled with the treasures of the written Word.
>
> Consider Christ in His relation to the people in general, and to their teachers and spiritual rulers. In teaching them and arguing with them, the Lord invariably refers to the Scriptures

as the authority which cannot be gainsayed; the standard which is infallible, and against which there is no appeal. He teaches according to Scripture: His doctrine, His works, His aim, His life are to fulfil that which is written. When He entered the synagogue of Nazareth, and the eyes of all were fixed on Him, He called for the roll of the prophecy of Isaiah, and in the words of the prophet (Isa. lxi.) announced to them the object of His mission as the Saviour of sinners. "How readest thou? What is written in the law?" is His frequent reply to the questions addressed to Him. He reminds the cities which heard of Him, of Tyre and Sidon and Sodom. He speaks of the sign of Jonah to the Pharisees who demand a miracle. He explains to the messengers of John, in the words of the prophet Isaiah, the works which prove that He is the promised Messiah.

To the Jews who followed Him in the wilderness, He speaks of the manna; to Nicodemus, of the brazen serpent; and frequently He shows that Moses wrote of Him, and that the Scripture is the only and all-sufficient message of God; leaving men without excuse, and proving their unbelief, which even the apparition of one rising from the dead would not conquer (Luke xvi). The conduct of the children singing His praise He defends by the words of the eighth Psalm: "Out of the mouth of babes and sucklings Thou hast ordained strength." He proves His Divine dignity by quoting the Spirit-given words of David, "The Lord said unto my Lord." When accused by the Jews of blasphemy, because He made Himself equal with God, He shows from the expression in the Psalms, "Ye are gods," that He whom the Father hath sealed was high above those to whom the Word of God had come; and He fortifies His argument by reminding the Jews of what they all admitted, that the Scripture cannot be broken.   Every link of the chain is perfect;—not one can be taken away, even as every one of them is reliable and solid.   When He speaks of His rejection and the future of the nation, He views it as the fulfilment of prophecy, of what is written in the 118th Psalm about the stone rejected by the builders, and in Daniel of the stone which should crush the ungodly.   In arguing with the Sadducees, Christ proves the resurrection by the spiritual exposition of a single expression which God had used, and which is recorded by the Holy Spirit in the book of Exodus.   And on this occasion He shows the source of error.   If we know not the power of God and the Scripture, we err. These two go together. An outward knowledge of the letter of Scripture without an inward experience of the power of God is without avail; the spiritual experience of God's power is always accompanied with the knowledge and love of Scripture.

These direct references to Moses and the prophets—so numerous, so striking, so solemn, and so comprehensive—must be taken in connection with the more concealed allusions to Scripture thoughts and teaching, with which Christ's discourses are replete. In His sermon on the mount, in the discourses recorded in the Gospel of John, in His conversation with His disciples, in the parables, there is scarcely a thought which is not in some manner connected with the Scripture. All Christ's thoughts and expressions have been moulded in that wonderful school of the testimony which God had given to His chosen people. [3]

2. Infidels Falsely Say Jesus Corrected Mistakes in the Old Testament

Instead of humbly seeking the mind of the Lord, those scorners who would sit as arrogant judges of the Scriptures would put Jesus as correcting the Old Testament Scriptures, thus dishonoring them.

They say that in Matthew 5:24-46 these statements of Jesus, "Ye have heard that it hath been said. . . But I say unto you . . ." show that Jesus now brings better word than the Scriptures. As the blasphemous *Interpreter's Bible* commentary puts it, "This artisan from Galilee weighed the sacred law in his balances and found it wanting." [4]

How could one be so blind to the most emphatic statement of Jesus in verses 17 and 18 of the same chapter, that "I am not come to destroy, but to fulfil. For verily I say unto you, Till heaven and earth pass, one jot or one tittle shall in no wise pass from the law, till all be fulfilled" (Matt. 5:17,18).

No, in these passages Jesus simply gives added emphasis and interpretation to the law. Not only murder but hate; not only adultery but lust; not only limits on divorce but stronger limits; not only not to break an oath but not to make one; not only restitution but double, if necessary, to satisfy. And the foolish teaching of rabbis to "love thy neighbour, and hate thine enemy" (not in the law, of course) He corrected as the law itself would have done (Lev. 19:17,18). Only an unscriptural and unbelieving heart would put Jesus as correcting or cancelling His own law as written in the Scriptures. In the author's commentary on Matthew we have dealt more in detail with this matter.

J. I. Packer of England calls attention to a quotation of

---

3. *Christ and the Scriptures*, pp. 12-14.
4. *The Interpreter's Bible*, Vol. 7, p. 294.

R. V. G. Tasker in *The Old Testament in the New Testament,*
page 32: "Our Lord came into conflict with the Pharisees not
because He was opposed to the written word of the law, to which
both He and they appealed, but because in His judgment the
formalism and the casuistry of the legal system which the
Pharisees had superimposed upon the Law rendered them in-
sensitive to the living word of God;... What roused His
antagonism were such things as the casuistry which justified
the practice of Corban; the false deduction that the command to
love one's neighbour implied that one should hate one's enemies;
the limiting of the divine prohibition of murder and adultery
to the specific acts of murder and adultery; the assumption that
the only oaths which need be taken seriously were those made
by the actual use of the divine name; and the extension of the
exception clause in the law of divorce so as to permit divorce
'for any cause' whatever."[5]

We rejoice in the words of Adolph Saphir:

> And when Jesus began to preach, and to show forth His
> Divine mission, His words and His acts, as well as His method
> and manner, proceeded from a heart in which God's Word was
> hid, from One who had completely and fully identified His
> spiritual life with the Scripture. [6]

3. In Temptation, Jesus Relied Upon the Scripture

Baptized and filled with the Spirit, and now to begin His
ministry as the perfect Son of man, the dear Saviour went into
the wilderness to be tempted of Satan.   He must be tempted
in all points like as we are, yet without sin (Heb. 4:15).   Then
He would be a fit Substitute for us, a race of tempted, sinning
men.   And there Jesus, Pattern for all who have been saved by
His blood, turned to the Scriptures for strength, for wisdom, for
answer to the tempter.

"It is written...," Jesus said, quoting Deuteronomy 8:3.   The
Scripture gave an answer to His hunger and to Satan's assault (Matt. 4:4).

"It is written again," He said, in answer to the temptation to
show His power, "Thou shalt not tempt the Lord thy God"
(Matt. 4:7).   His heart turned to Deuteronomy 6:16 and He

---

5. *"Fundamentalism" and the Word of God,* p. 56.
6. *Christ and the Scriptures,* p. 21.

then could not be misled by Satan's false use of Scripture.

Oh, but Satan promised he would give Christ Jesus all the nations of the world, that He would have a crown with no cross, a throne without crucifixion, if He would but bow down and worship Satan. Many a preacher, deceived into honoring infidels, would be saved that sin if they revered and lived in Scripture as did Jesus. But Jesus was impelled by Deuteronomy 10:20 and knew not only the letter but the spirit of it, which included "only." Matthew 4:10 tells us, "Then saith Jesus unto him, Get thee hence Satan: for it is written, Thou shalt worship the Lord thy God, and him only shalt thou serve."

In His secret heart, with no one near but the Heavenly Father and that awful Enemy of souls, Jesus loved, relied upon, had wisdom, strength, and victory through the Scriptures. They were to Him, as to us, the infallible, living Word of God.

4. See the Constant Concern of Jesus "That the Scripture Might Be Fulfilled"

In Luke 18:31-33 Jesus said, "Behold, we go up to Jerusalem, and all things that are written by the prophets concerning the Son of man shall be accomplished. For he shall be delivered unto the Gentiles, and shall be mocked, and spitefully entreated, and spitted on: And they shall scourge him, and put him to death: and the third day he shall rise again."

In Luke 22:37 He said, "For I say unto you, that this that is written must yet be accomplished in me, And he was reckoned among the transgressors: for the things concerning me have an end."

When Peter would have defended Jesus with a sword, Jesus said, "Thinkest thou that I cannot now pray to my Father, and he shall presently give me more than twelve legions of angels? But how then shall the scriptures be fulfilled, that thus it must be?" (Matt. 26:53,54).

When Jesus hung upon the cross, He was so conscious that every Scripture must be fulfilled that He cried out the prophesied lament of Psalm 22:1, "My God, my God, why hast thou forsaken me?" (Matt. 27:46). He was so one with the Scriptures that He, the incarnate Word, must fulfill the written Word.

But before He could die on the cross, one Scripture must yet be fulfilled! Psalm 69:21 had foretold, "They gave me also gall for my meat; and in my thirst they gave me vinegar to drink." Just before they had spiked the unresisting Body to the cross, Matthew 27:34 says, "They gave him vinegar to drink mingled with gall: and when he had tasted thereof, he would not drink."

He did not drink before—now it must be fulfilled, so John 19:28-30 tells us, "After this, Jesus knowing that all things were now accomplished, that the scripture might be fulfilled, saith, I thirst. Now there was set a vessel full of vinegar: and they filled a spunge with vinegar, and put it upon hyssop, and put it to his mouth. When Jesus therefore had received the vinegar, he said, It is finished: and he bowed his head, and gave up the ghost."

Oh, what a peaceful sense that the awful payment is made in full. That the Scriptures about His atoning death are now fulfilled to the letter comforts the heart of the suffering Saviour! Now He can again call God "Father" and commend to Him His tortured spirit (Luke 23:46). So He cries out, "It is finished!" and gives up His spirit!

IV. CHRIST AND CHRISTIANITY STAND OR FALL WITH THE BIBLE

Jesus believed and quoted and relied upon the Bible as the very infallible Word of God which could not be broken, which would stand forever. If Christ was mistaken about the Bible, then He was subject to human error and therefore subject to sin, and could not be the virgin-born Son of God, the pre-existent and perfect Substitute which God would offer as a sacrifice for the sins of the world. If the Bible is not God's own infallible Word, Jesus is not God. So if you lose the Bible you lose Christianity and salvation. Again we say, Christ and the Bible stand or fall together.

Dr. Clark H. Pinnock, associate professor of theology in New Orleans Baptist Theological Seminary had his Ph.D. degree in New Testament studies from the University of Manchester, England. Then he was the assistant lecturer in New Testament at the University of Manchester serving under Professor F. F. Bruce. Dr. Pinnock has been a guest lecturer at Cambridge and Harvard Universities. In his lecture "Sola Scriptura," before the Southern Baptist Pastors' Conference, Houston, Texas, 1968, Dr. Pinnock says the following:

> As a matter of fact, however, though the discussion be complex, the issue remains as simple as it always was. It is a matter of Christology—who do you think Christ is, and how do you rate his teaching? Liberals profess him as Lord and Master (Mt. 23:10) but often fail to continue in his word (Jn. 8:31). There can be no honest doubt as to Christ's doctrine of Scripture. It cannot be broken (Jn. 10:35). "It is easier for heaven and earth to pass away, than for one dot of the law to become void." (Luke 16:17). While it is likely for a Southern Baptist liberal to deny this because he cannot face the alternative of denying Christ's divine authority (at least not publicly), the real critics have openly admitted it.
>
> H. J. Cadbury, Harvard professor and New Testament critic of radical stripe, once stated that he was more sure as a mere historical fact that Jesus held to the common Jewish view of an infallible Bible than that Jesus believed in his own Messiahship. Adolf Harnack, John Knox, and F. C. Grant, all concur on this point, that Jesus regarded Scripture to be infallible and inerrant in all that it teaches. Liberal scholars of highest rank freely admit the conservative's point about Jesus' high view of inspiration.
> The question obviously boils down to one of Christology. If we accept Christ as divine Lord, it is consistent to accept his teaching about the Bible. But to profess his Lordship and to deny plenary inspiration is quite inconsistent, and bespeaks a confusion in mind which is dangerous and mistaken. Southern Baptist evangelicals honour the Bible as the infallible Word of God out of simple obedience to Christ. It was our Lord, not we ourselves, who constituted Christianity a religion of Biblical authority. It is his doctrine we seek to honour. He bowed to Scripture; so much the more must we. Scripture was at the root of his concept of authority; so shall it be at the foundation of ours. It was fundamental to his message; so shall it be to our own. To affirm Christ and reject infallibility is an act of intellectual impenitence and schizophrenia.
>
> Evangelicals learn their doctrines from Christ, and make a plea for consistency and fidelity among the leaders of our denomination. John Calvin wrote, "A dog barks when his master is attacked. I would be a coward if I saw that God's truth is attacked and yet would remain silent, without giving any sound." [7]

Again we say, to deny the inspiration of the Bible and its perfect accuracy is to deny the clear statements of Jesus Christ

---

7. *A New Reformation*, pamphlet, p. 9.

and thus to make Him a frail, deceived man or a wicked charlatan deceiving others. Christ and the Bible stand or fall together.

Let the Bible believer rejoice that Jesus knew the Bible was the infallible Word of God, settled forever in Heaven, that it could not be broken (Ps. 119:89; John 10:35). Let the doubter, the scorner of a Scripture breathed out from God, mourn; for when you give up an infallible Bible, you leave also the Saviour whose deity and atonement are bound up with it!

CHAPTER VII

THE HUMAN ELEMENT IN WRITING INSPIRED SCRIPTURE

I. BIBLE WRITERS TELL THEIR OWN DESIRES, THEIR OWN EXPERIENCES, SEND THEIR OWN GREETINGS

    1. The Writers Used the First Person and Tell of Their Own Experiences

    2. The Problem of Style and Vocabulary

II. MANY SCHOLARS HAVE OVEREMPHASIZED THE HUMAN ELEMENT IN WRITING THE BIBLE

    1. Here Is the Folly of the Graff-Wellhausen Theory in Passing Judgment on the Word of God

    2. Critics Have Manufactured Documentary Hypotheses, Explain Synoptic Gospels on Human Grounds

    3. Luke and Paul Both Insisted Human Sources Were Not Enough; Why Seek Them?

    4. Packer Says That Critical Emphasis "on the Human Side of Scripture...Has Blurred the Church's Awareness of the Divine Character of Scriptural Teaching..."

III. THE DOCTRINE OF VARYING HUMAN STYLES AND VOCABULARIES WITH DIFFERENT AUTHORS HAS DEFINITE LIMITATIONS

    1. Divine Revelation Sometimes Came From the Voice of God in Heaven

    2. Balaam's Ass Spoke to Balaam and the Conversation Is Recorded (Num. 22:28-30)

THE HUMAN ELEMENT IN WRITING
INSPIRED SCRIPTURE

The Bible is the Word of God but it is written by men. God breathed out the Scriptures but men wrote them down, and in some degree the Scripture has the color and flavor of the writers. In some degree but how much? Did men write as influenced by their own experience? Did the human penmen of the Bible see the truth and then select out of their own vocabulary the words in which to tell it? How much, if any, did the human element enter into the actual wording of the Scriptures?

I. BIBLE WRITERS TELL THEIR OWN DESIRES, THEIR OWN EXPERIENCES, SEND THEIR OWN GREETINGS

1. The Writers Use the First Person and Tell of Their Own Experiences

Isaiah writes, "In the year that king Uzziah died I saw also the Lord sitting upon a throne, high and lifted up. . ." (Isa. 6:1). And he tells of the experience of his call.

The book of Jeremiah is plainly labeled, "The words of Jeremiah the son of Hilkiah, of the priests that were in Anathoth in the land of Benjamin: To whom the word of the Lord came . . ." (Jer. 1:1,2). It is the Word of the Lord but in some sense "the words of Jeremiah." They are at least the words which he wrote down or which he had his amanuensis write down. In Jeremiah 15:16 he writes, "Thy words were found, and I did eat them; and thy word was unto me the joy and rejoicing of mine heart: for I am called by thy name, O Lord God of hosts." And in Jeremiah 20:9 Jeremiah tells us how he decided not to preach any more, but the Word of God was like a burning fire shut up in his bones and he could not forbear. In Jeremiah 37:18-20 Jeremiah tells us how he pleaded with King Zedekiah not to put him back in prison. These brief samples simply show there was a human element in the book of Jeremiah.

What a rich, personal element appears in the Psalms. The psalmist could say, "This poor man cried, and the Lord heard him, and saved him out of all his troubles" (Ps. 34:6). He could say, "I have been young, and now am old; yet have I not seen the righteous forsaken, nor his seed begging bread" (Ps. 37:25).

So Luke could write, "It seemed good to me also, having had perfect understanding of all things from the very first [rather *anothen*, from above], to write unto thee in order, most excellent Theophilus" (Luke 1:3). But Luke considered and chose to write the book of Luke, although doubtless he was personally controlled by the Holy Spirit. Luke saw the need and intended to write the Gospel. So though it was inspired and proceeded from the mouth of God, Luke participated in it as he wrote it down.

So writing to Timothy, Paul could plead with him, "Be not thou therefore ashamed of the testimony of our Lord, nor of me his prisoner...." (II Tim. 1:8). We believe that although Paul wrote "not in the words which man's wisdom teacheth, but which the Holy Ghost teacheth; comparing spiritual things with spiritual" (I Cor. 2:13), yet Paul's heart entered into the matter and it was a personal letter as well as a divinely given letter. And so Paul could put in this personal word, "The cloke that I left at Troas with Carpus, when thou comest, bring with thee, and the books, but especially the parchments" (II Tim. 4:13).

Even in the mysteries and symbolic language of the book of Revelation, John participated in writing the book. He said, "John to the seven churches which are in Asia... " (Rev. 1:4). So it was from God, but it was from John. And he tells them in verses 9 and 10, "I John, who also am your brother, and companion in tribulation, and in the kingdom and patience of Jesus Christ, was in the isle that is called Patmos, for the word of God, and for the testimony of Jesus Christ. I was in the Spirit on the Lord's day, and heard behind me a great voice, as of a trumpet...."

Surely, then, all are agreed that men of God who wrote down the Word of God were often, nay, usually, if not always, participating themselves in what they wrote and they usually felt deeply about it whether or not they understood all they said.

So the Scriptures tell what God wants to tell, but also, in telling what God wants to tell, the penmen may, as God chooses, tell what they want also. Peter tells how he witnessed the glory of Christ at the transfiguration (II Pet. 1:16-21). Even there Peter tells us that we have now "a more sure word of prophecy" in the inspired, written Scriptures, but he gave his witness of a personal experience.

And in I John 1:1 the beloved John wrote in his epistle about the One "which we have heard, which we have seen with our eyes, which we have looked upon, and our hands have handled, of the Word of life." How many sweet memories must have run through the mind of John as he was inspired to write down the epistle and refer to his experience with Christ.

And John knew the reason for some of the things he wrote down, although the reason was from God. God's motivation and John's motivation must have been the same, God's preceding John's, when he said, "I write unto you, little children, because..." and "I write unto you, fathers, because...," etc. In some degree the Bible is the word of men although it is not primarily the word of men, and the Word does not originate with men but was breathed out from God. God made His eternal Word in the words of men.

2. The Problem of Style and Vocabulary

The Bible has a great variety of literary form. There is history; there are genealogies; there are long, rather prosaic lists of requirements of the ceremonial law; there is the poetry of the Psalms, the Song of Solomon and Ecclesiastes, perhaps, and other small parts. And there is the deep devotional content in the Psalms. Not only because of its wonderful predictions about the coming Saviour, but because of the warmth and beauty of its language, the book of Isaiah is sometimes called the Gospel in the Old Testament. In the Gospels, we are told by the best students of the Greek language that the book of Luke exceeds the other three Gospels in the beauty of language, and that Luke and Acts exceed the Pauline Epistles and other epistles in the New Testament in literary form.

A little study can show that the work of certain writers has a tendency to use certain words and that that tendency differs with different penmen of the Bible. At least there are distinct differences in style and vocabulary. We do not have other uninspired writings by Bible authors so we cannot say just how much the styles used are distinctive of the writers, but we believe God prepared the individuals so that their style, vocabulary and viewpoints, as much as they are included in the Scriptures, are exactly in God's plan.

II. MANY SCHOLARS HAVE OVEREMPHASIZED THE HUMAN ELEMENT IN WRITING THE BIBLE

All of us see that men wrote the Bible and in some secondary sense, we see that the Bible is a book from men. Of course, it is primarily and originally the Word of God and not of men. Because they put the emphasis on man's part, many, many scholars, particularly unbelieving men, have had very limited theories about the inspiration of the Bible.

1. Here Is the Folly of the Graff-Wellhausen Theory in Passing Judgment on the Word of God

Higher criticism tends to sit in judgment on the Bible and let poor, sinning, frail, ignorant, mortal men pass judgment on the Word of God. Now, good Christians are not afraid of any honest and reverent investigation of facts. All truth is of God and the more truth one knows about the Bible, the more he will know about God. But no unconverted man, with a bias against the supernatural and with a proud opinion of his own wisdom, is fit to study the Word of God. Because such men do not have the humility, the objective spirit, and the eagerness for the right that true science must have, they invent and propound wild theories about the Bible.

Dr. Astruc of France, companion of harlots and medical specialist on venereal disease, wrote some suppositions about the Mosaic authorship of the Pentateuch, suggesting that by judging the style and the use of certain words, one could go through the Pentateuch and find it was the product of a number of men. Eichhorn, Graff and Wellhausen and others took up the theory and so concluded that the Pentateuch was assembled from three or four different manuscripts, with a bit here and a bit there collected into one manuscript by some fraudulent editor who put it out in the name of Moses but centuries after Moses died!   Parts of it he ascribed to a certain writer who used the word "Jehovah" for God.   Other parts were ascribed to some unknown writer who used "Elohim" for God.   Certain parts they said came from priestly sources.   We need not now go into great detail on this foolish and extravagant doctrine.

The work of Dr. Robert Dick Wilson of Princeton, the great work of Dr. Allis of Princeton on *The Five Books of Moses* and other scholarly works, have demolished the Graff-Wellhausen theory.   For a Bible-believer it does not need to be demolished. That is simply an example of wicked and arrogant men who try to settle the problem of sources in the Bible on a purely human and natural plane, denying divine inspiration.   If you intentionally leave God out of the origin of the Bible, then you must make fantastic guesses about how it came to be.

2. Critics Have Manufactured Documentary Hypotheses, Explain Synoptic Gospels on Human Grounds

The three Gospels by Matthew, Mark and Luke follow much the same general outline of events in the life of Christ and so they are called the synoptic Gospels.   The natural, human tendency has been to try to find some mundane human explanation for the similarities without accepting the fact that God Himself simply gave these Gospels through three different men in these three similar forms.

Dr. Merrill C. Tenney, head of Wheaton College Graduate School, expresses this matter for many, when he says:

THE LITERARY SOURCES OF THE GOSPELS

As historical documents the Gospels had some sources. Up to this point the source of oral tradition has been assumed. A story like that of Jesus which purports to speak of a living personality seldom appears in literature without first being passed from one person to another by word of mouth. It may be that a documentary tradition underlies these Gospels also; for the strong verbal resemblances existing between Matthew,

Mark, and Luke call for some relationship which is not merely
accidental. [1]

Now, of course, all will admit that "the strong verbal resemblances existing between Matthew, Mark, and Luke call for
some relationship which is not merely accidental." Now men,
without divine inspiration, would not make them often word-for-
word the same, and following the same general outline, throughout, except by some acquaintance with a common source or with
each other.   But could not God give His own very words
through the three men and follow the same correct outline?

Speaking of the agreements and differences in the synoptic
Gospels Dr. Tenney says:

> From phenomena such as these arises the so-called Synoptic
> problem.   If the three Gospels of Matthew, Mark, and Luke are
> completely independent in origin, how can one account for the
> striking and minute verbal resemblances which exist between
> them?   If they are interdependent, or if they are substantially
> the same account drawn from a common source, how can one
> explain their dissimilarities? The problem is to account for the
> similarities and dissimilarities by the same theory.
>   Many hypotheses have been propounded to answer this prob-
> lem.   A historic survey of them at this point would be both
> tedious and fruitless, since the main purpose of these lectures is
> to discuss the genius of the Gospels rather than to review the
> history of Gospel criticism.   The chief theory that holds the
> field today, even with such conservative scholars as A. T. Rob-
> ertson and W. Graham Scroggie is the Two-document Hypothesis.
> It maintains that the bulk of the Synoptic material has two chief
> sources: the Gospel of Mark, and a document called "Q" (abbre-
> viated from the German **Quelle**, "source"), which contained
> principally a collection of sayings of Jesus and which survives
> only as it may have been incorporated in Matthew and in Luke. [2]

The simple fact is that no one ever saw manuscript "Q."
This fictitious legend is simply manufactured by critics who
want to find some explanation rather than immediate word-for-
word inspiration of the Gospels, to explain them as resulting
from human literary sources.   And the church father who had
suggested that Mark wrote at the dictation of Peter or from
facts the Apostle Peter gave him, and that Luke wrote speaking
for Paul, whose companion he long was, and from whom he
was supposed to have gotten much of his information, are, on

---

1. *The Genius of the Gospels*, p. 24.
2. *The Genius of the Gospels*, pp. 27,28.

this matter, wholly unreliable. An opinion of a church father living after the time of Christ would be simply a matter of human opinion. And the testimony of Papias, church father, quoted by another father, that there was an Aramaic language original from which the Gospel of Matthew in Greek was copied, has no weight for those who simply rely on divine inspiration as the one great explanation of the Scriptures. We have Bible explanations of the origin of Scriptures, which reverent believers must accept concerning God's divine revelation given to Paul in the words of Scripture. We read, "But as it is written, Eye hath not seen, nor ear heard, neither have entered into the heart of man, the things which God hath prepared for them that love him. But God hath revealed them unto us by his Spirit." And, "Which things also we speak, not in the words which man's wisdom teacheth, but which the Holy Ghost teacheth; comparing spiritual things with spiritual" (I Cor. 2:9,10, 13). Even the Lord Jesus could say, "...and the word which ye hear is not mine, but the Father's which sent me" (John 14:24). And again Jesus said, "For I have given unto them the words which thou gavest me; and they have received them..." (John 17:18). Why should not Matthew, Mark, and Luke claim the same thing—"For I have given unto them the words which thou gavest me..."? Why would men rather have some hazy, oral tradition, some legendary "Q" manuscript, some Aramaic copy of the book of Matthew from which someone (unbelieving scholars say not Matthew) translated the Greek Gospel of Matthew, which we have?

3. Luke and Paul Both Insisted Human Sources Were Not Enough; Why Seek Them?

In Galatians 1:11 and 12, the Apostle Paul said, "But I certify you, brethren, that the gospel which was preached of me is not after man. For I neither received it of man, neither was I taught it, but by the revelation of Jesus Christ." Then he tells us that when he was called to preach, "...immediately I conferred not with flesh and blood: Neither went I up to Jerusalem to them which were apostles before me; but I went into Arabia, and returned again unto Damascus." He is insisting that the apostles gave him nothing of his Gospel (Gal. 1:16,17).

Three years later he went up to Jerusalem and saw Peter and James for a few days. And then after fourteen years he went up to Jerusalem to check on his Gospel to see if it was exactly the same as the other apostles had. And so we read in Galatians 2:9, "And when James, Cephas, and John, who seemed to be pillars, perceived the grace that was given unto me, they gave to me and Barnabas the right hands of fellowship; that we should go unto the heathen, and they unto the circumcision." Paul is explaining that his Gospel came not from consulting with others; it was received by direct revelation from God.

In chapter 13 I will give an elaborate discussion correcting current misapprehensions about where Luke got his materials. He says that he got them "*anothen,*" that is, "from above." But here I call particular attention to the fact that Luke 1:1 and 2 tells that "many have taken in hand to set forth in order a declaration of those things which are most surely believed among us," which they got from eyewitnesses and preachers. But "in order...that thou mightest know the certainty of those things, wherein thou hast been instructed," Luke writes his Gospel "having had perfect understanding of all things *anothen* [from above]." If all those many apocryphal gospels, written by those who checked with all the eyewitnesses and talked with all the preachers and apostles involved — if these accounts were insufficient, unreliable, why should Matthew, Mark, and Luke have the same sources for their Gospels? They would be equally unreliable.

4. Packer Says That Critical Emphasis "on the Human Side of Scripture...Has Blurred the Church's Awareness of the Divine Character of Scriptural Teaching..."

J. I. Packer of England calls attention to the fact that emphasis on the human side of Scripture, on so-called human sources, has often detracted from the understanding of the Bible and dependence on it as the Word of God.

> A century of criticism has certainly thrown some light on the human side of the Bible — its style, language, composition, history and culture; but whether it has brought the Church a better understanding of its divine message than Evangelicals of two, three and four hundred years ago possessed is more than doubtful. It is not at all clear that we today comprehend the plan of

salvation, the doctrines of sin, election, atonement, justification, new birth and sanctification, the life of faith, the duties of church-manship and the meaning of Church history, more clearly than did the Reformers, or the Puritans, or the leaders of the eight-eenth-century revival. When it is claimed that modern criticism has greatly advanced our understanding of the Bible, the reply must be that it depends upon what is meant by the Bible; criti-cism has thrown much light on the human features of Scripture, but it has not greatly furthered our knowledge of the Word of God. Indeed, it seems truer to say that its effect to date has been rather to foster ignorance of the Word of God; for by concentrating on the human side of Scripture it has blurred the Church's awareness of the divine character of scriptural teaching, and by questioning biblical statements in the name of scholarship it has shaken confidence in the value of personal Bible study. [3]

Certainly we admit gladly that there is a "human side of the Bible — its style, language, composition, history and culture." God used men to write the Bible. But the Bible never puts the emphasis on Scripture as coming from men, and neither should we. The Scriptures are fundamentally the Word of God, not the word of men, except in some incidental and controlled and limited sense. And that human side is wholly secondary, and is treated as incidental when the Bible speaks of itself, its origin and authority.

III. THE DOCTRINE OF VARYING HUMAN STYLES AND VOCABULARIES WITH DIFFERENT AUTHORS HAS DEFINITE LIMITATIONS

We know that there are differences in style and in vocabulary in different parts of the Bible and we take for granted (the Bible nowhere expressly says so) that these variations in style and vocabulary represent the various cultural backgrounds, viewpoints, manner of thinking and of style, of the men who were inspired to write the different parts of the Bible.

However, there are certain clear limitations which we must consider.

---

3. *"Fundamentalism" and the Word of God*, pp. 112,113.

1. Divine Revelation Sometimes Came From the Voice of God in Heaven

For example, in Exodus 20:1 we read, "And God spake all these words," referring to the Ten Commandments. Then in Exodus 31:18 we are told that God gave Moses "two tables of testimony, tables of stone, written with the finger of God." Thus the Ten Commandments were not only spoken aloud from Heaven, with the comments that are recorded in Exodus 20, but those Ten Commandments were written with the finger of God on stone. Hence, there could be no human question of style or vocabulary there.

Again, when God spoke at the baptism of Jesus, and again on the Mount of Transfiguration, and when Jesus spoke from Heaven to Paul the apostle on the road to Damascus, the inspired words came from God and could not have had any color of human variation and style. The style was God's style and the vocabulary was God's vocabulary.

Now, if we believe, and I do, that these were accurately recorded in the Bible, then inspiration does not necessarily involve a human style.

And I think we could say the same for the many times the angels spoke to men throughout the Bible.

2. Balaam's Ass Spoke to Balaam and the Conversation Is Recorded (Num. 22:28-30)

Now, was the language that the donkey spoke in the donkey's customary style? Of course not. Then divine inspiration is not limited to human style. That means that God could have used the usual form of speech, the vocabulary, of men who wrote the Bible but that *it is not necessary that He do so!* If there are variations in the style of different books in the Bible, then that is by God's choice and under His control and because He selected those variations in style.

3. The Style of Paul's Epistles: Was It His Customary, Natural Style?

Were the epistles written by the Apostle Paul formed in the matrix of his own customary manner of speech? Is the style in the epistles distinctively Paul's usual style? There is reason to doubt it. Christians at Corinth did not think that the inspired letters were compatible with his usual manner of speech. In II Corinthians 10:10 Paul reports what they said: "For his letters, say they, are weighty and powerful; but his bodily presence is weak, and his speech contemptible."

The divinely inspired letters of Paul were acknowledged as obviously "weighty and powerful" instead of the contemptible speech, halting, perhaps, and blundering. We judge from this statement that at least it is possible that there is a distinct difference in even the style and vocabulary and manner of speech of Paul when he was ordinarily preaching, differing from his inspired letters which were so weighty and powerful.

Of course we know that the inspired Word of God is always weighty and powerful, whatever the literary style. But in view of this statement, we dare not be too dogmatic in insisting that all the *regular* style and vocabulary of the varying penmen was reproduced in their *inspired* writings.

It is only fair to infer, then, that God used any particular style He wished to use, and that probably He often used the style of speech and vocabulary which His penmen ordinarily used and to which they were accustomed. However, the style then is God's style. And He would choose to use any varying and particular style He wished.

4. The Folly of Making Too Much of Variations in Style Is Illustrated by the Now Greatly Discredited Graff-Wellhausen Theory

Further research and the scholarship of great men of God like Dr. Robert Dick Wilson of Princeton, Dr. Melvin Grove Kyle of Xenia Seminary (now Pittsburg), Professor Allis of Princeton in his *The Five Books of Moses*, and others, have shown the folly of that oversimplification. No, one cannot judge authorship by style, which they claimed to do. In the book of Luke and in the book of Acts are a few terms called "medical terms." Actually there are only a few and they are terms that any cultivated man of the age might have used and probably did use. They are counted very distinctive marks of "Luke the physician" in his writings. Critics make violent arguments on the one side or the other. One should not jump to too radical a conclusion in one's judgment of style.

5. Would It Be Difficult for God to Write in Different Styles?

I was greatly surprised to learn years ago that the Christmas poem for children, beginning,

> 'Twas the night before Christmas,
> And all through the house
> Not a creature was stirring
> Not even a mouse,

and all about St. Nicholas and his gifts and reindeers, was written by a prominent theologian whose ponderous tomes on theology have long since passed out of usage. The rollicking, colorful style of the poem for children had nothing to indicate that it was from the same pen as the dry, metaphysical, and theological discussions in the man's other works.

You see, a man's style is not as limited and as individual as one might hastily judge.

I have written many words, some of them doubtless very poorly, carrying the holy message I intended. But you may be sure that there is a great deal of difference in the style of the half-a-hundred song poems or hymns I have written and in the casual, chatty "Editor's Notes" each week in *The Sword of the Lord* magazine, and my polemic arguments and defense of the faith against heresy.

A greatly respected missionary, who is familiar with much of my writings, was astonished when he read my introduction to that charming volume of sermons, *Bread From Bellevue Oven*, from the wizard with words, Dr. R. G. Lee. He was first disbelieving and then astonished that my words of introduction were colored by the subject and the style of a man whose book I introduced.

Dr. Lewis Sperry Chafer says:

> THE MECHANICAL OR DICTATION THEORY. Had
> God dictated the Scriptures to men, the style and writing would
> be uniform.   It would be the diction and vocabulary of the
> divine Author, and free from the idiosyncrasies of men. [4]

He says in the same paragraph:

> The result is as complete as dictation could make it; but the
> method, though not lacking in that mystery which always
> accompanies the supernatural, is more in harmony with God's
> ways of dealing with men, in which He **uses**, rather than **annuls**,
> their wills.[5]

It is unfortunate that this devoted advocate of the Bible here
did not think through the issue.   First, to assume that if God
dictated the words it would be mechanical is *non sequitur*, that
is, does not follow.   When God dictated the words of the Ten
Commandments to Moses and the words written on plaster
walls to Belshazzar, did God then "annul their wills," as in the
same paragraph He says it would?

Why could not God cause men to gladly be moved to think
what God wanted them to think, receiving what God gave, with
the fullest activity of a receiving heart?

Good men, Bible believers, are not wise, we think, to thus
give credence to the slanders of unbelievers by using their false
terminology by which unbelievers caricature verbal inspiration.
No sensible believer claims that dictation was mechanical and
that God annulled men's wills when He had them write Scripture.

But how would Dr. Chafer know how limited is God's vocabulary, how irrelevant His language would be to men?   Since
God called Isaiah "from the womb," named him, made his
"mouth like a sharp sword," made him "a polished shaft"
hidden in God's quiver, formed him "from the womb to be his
servant" (Isa. 49:1-5), did Isaiah have a more eloquent tongue
than God?   God said to Moses, "Who hath made man's mouth?
or who maketh the dumb, or deaf, or the seeing, or the blind?
have not I the Lord?" (Exod. 4:11).   Could God then not
talk with as much human color and variety as Moses?   Would
Luke's diction be more clear than God's?   Could Paul better
communicate on human terms than He who "sent forth his Son,

---

4. *Systematic Theology*, Vol. 1, p. 68.
5. *Systematic Theology*, Vol. 1, p. 68.

made of a woman, made under the law" (Gal. 4:4)?

In fact, God did speak in human language. God made the men and God made the language. God prepared the circumstances. Then God gave the words in the Bible. God could thus use the men He made to be the willing penmen, writing in language and vocabulary which God had given them, the words that He now would give.

It is not proper, we think, to say God's diction would not be as good or as relevant to human hearts and needs as man's unaided, uncontrolled diction. And if you admit God's absolute control, that God gave the words, then you must say that the diction is God's diction completely and only secondarily as God gave it man's diction.

Dr. James M. Gray, late president of Moody Bible Institute, says wisely on this matter:

> **There is the variety in style.** Some think that if all the writers were alike inspired and the inspiration extended to their words, they must all possess the same style—as if the Holy Spirit had but one style!
> Literary style is a method of selecting words and putting sentences together which stamps an author's work with the influence of his habits, his condition in society, his education, his reasoning, his experience, his imagination and his genius. These give his mental and moral physiognomy and make up his style.
> But is not God free to act with or without these fixed laws? There are no circumstances which tinge His views or reasonings, and He has no idiosyncrasies of speech, and no mother tongue through which He expresses His character, or leaves the finger mark of genius upon His literary fabrics.
> It is a great fallacy then, as Dr. Thomas Armitage once said, to suppose that uniformity of verbal style must have marked God's authorship in the Bible, had He selected its words. As the Author of all styles, rather does He use them all at His pleasure. He bestows all the powers of mental individuality upon His instruments for using the Scriptures, and then uses their powers as He will to express His mind by them.
> Indeed, the variety of style is a necessary proof of the freedom of the human writers, and it is this which among other things convinces us that, however controlled by the Holy Spirit, they were not mere machines in what they wrote. [6]

Dr. Gray, an old-time fundamentalist, and not ashamed of the reproach of Christ, was wiser than the "new evangelicals," was

---

6. *The Fundamentals*, Vol. 2, p. 51.

not so easily persuaded or so easily bluffed by modernists. He says the words of the Bible are God's words, the style is God's style as well as man's, yea, God gave and then used each man's style.

6. "And God Spake All These Words..."

W. H. Griffith Thomas wrote a book under the title, *God Spake All These Words,* quoting, doubtless, from Exodus 20:1, given above. His book was about "How We Got Our Bible and Why We Believe It Is God's Word." It was published by Moody Press.

At the first look, one sees that the Scripture here speaks directly of the giving of the Ten Commandments in the first seventeen verses of Exodus 20. The Scripture means certainly that God spake aloud from Heaven. And following that, we read in verses 18 and 19:

"And all the people saw the thunderings, and the lightnings, and the noise of the trumpet, and the mountain smoking: and when the people saw it, they removed, and stood afar off. And they said unto Moses, Speak thou with us, and we will hear: but let not God speak with us, lest we die."

Moses recounts the matter again in Deuteronomy 5. There, after repeating the Ten Commandments, he said:

"These words the Lord spake unto all your assembly in the mount out of the midst of the fire, of the cloud, and of the thick darkness, with a great voice: and he added no more. And he wrote them in two tables of stone, and delivered them unto me. And it came to pass, when ye heard the voice out of the midst of the darkness, (for the mountain did burn with fire,) that ye came near unto me, even all the heads of your tribes, and your elders; And ye said, Behold, the Lord our God hath shewed us his glory and his greatness, and we have heard his voice out of the midst of the fire: we have seen this day that God doth talk with man, and he liveth. Now therefore why should we die? for this great fire will consume us: if we hear the voice of the Lord our God any more, then we shall die. For who is there of all flesh, that hath heard the voice of the living God speaking out of the midst of the fire, as we have,

and lived? Go thou near, and hear all that the Lord our God shall say: and speak thou unto us all that the Lord our God shall speak unto thee; and we will hear it, and do it. And the Lord heard the voice of your words, when ye spake unto me; and the Lord said unto me, I have heard the voice of the words of this people, which they have spoken unto thee: they have well said all that they have spoken. O that there were such an heart in them, that they would fear me, and keep all my commandments always, that it might be well with them, and with their children for ever! Go say to them, Get you into your tents again. But as for thee, stand thou here by me, and I will speak unto thee all the commandments, and the statutes, and the judgments, which thou shalt teach them, that they may do them in the land which I give them to possess it." — Deut. 5:22-31).

Oh, it was terrifying when God spake person-to-person, speaking aloud from Mount Sinai to the people. Two days ahead of time, all the people must wash their clothes and be ready. Bounds were set about Mount Sinai so that any person who touched it should be put to death, and even a beast should be shot through or stoned. The trumpet sounded long (Exod. 19:13). The psalmist tells us that "the mountains skipped like rams, and the little hills like lambs" (Ps. 114:4). Moses himself said, "I exceedingly fear and quake" (Heb. 12:21). We can understand how the people trembled as the fire of God blazed in the mountain and a voice like thunder spoke the words of God to them. They pleaded that God would speak through men, and God agreed.

Note carefully: God did not change His plan, even the words He would speak. The very words of the Ten Commandments He wrote on tables of stone, and Moses brought them down. Afterward, with trembling, people besought God not to speak to them directly but to speak to Moses and let him bring the words of God. Afterwards Moses wrote God's revelation. We read in Exodus 24:3 and 4:

"And Moses came and told the people all the words of the Lord, and all the judgments and all the people answered with one voice, and said, All the words which the Lord hath said will we do. And Moses wrote all the words of the Lord, and rose up early in the morning, and builded an altar under the hill, and twelve pillars, according to the twelve tribes of Israel."

So we can see why the eternal words of God, already settled in Heaven, must come to us through men. Men felt they would surely die if God — a holy, infinite, terrible God — spoke to them directly. So He spoke to Moses. He spoke the same words to Moses and had Moses write down the same words He had spoken to the people, and further words. The fact that God put some of these words on tables of stone indicated that they were a part of the eternal Word of God which would never pass away even though they were in man's words.

The truth is still God's truth, and the words of Scripture are still as truly God's words as when God spake them from Heaven. In God's mercy, they are given to men so men could hear them, believe them, teach and preach them, memorize them, delight in them, live by them. But God did not dilute His Word. Inspiration is not less perfect because God gave it through men.

Is it not so about the coming of the Saviour into the stream of mankind, through the womb of the virgin Mary? The eternal Jehovah God, the I AM, the Creator and Sustainer and Heir of all things, became a man. God's seeking, yearning, weeping, atoning, forgiving love became manifest in the flesh. Jesus is no less God than when He created the worlds. That He is born of Mary, of the seed of David, of the seed of Abraham, that He is the Son of man, does not limit His perfect deity. So the words of Scripture, given not only through the pens of human writers, but involving somewhat human hearts and personalities and testimonies, is no less directly and absolutely and perfectly breathed out from God.

If God, speaking from Heaven, at Sinai, gave the very words from God, without changing the color of them or weakening the impact of them a particle by any limitation, just as certainly the same kind of inspiration is that which we have in the Bible. It is given through human words but it is still the same kind, the perfect revelation from God, perfectly recorded, as were those words spoken from Mount Sinai. So in some proper sense W. H. Griffith Thomas could call his book about the Bible, *God Spake All These Words*. He did speak "all these words"; all the words in the Bible in the original autographs were verily breathed out from God. The human element is there by God's plan and mercy, but the words are still God's words.

Yes, there are variations in style and language and the human element enters largely into the things we find written in the Bible. But the Bible makes no issue about that as if it would in any wise limit the clear, oftstated principle that, "Which things also we speak, not in the words which man's wisdom teacheth, but which the Holy Ghost teacheth" (I Cor. 2:13). The Bible is still the Word of God and not the word of men except in some incidental way that God Himself chose to put Scripture in the style of some man He had prepared to write it.

CHAPTER VIII

WHERE DID LUKE GET HIS FACTS?

I. MANY FOLLOWED HARNACK AND SIR WILLIAM RAMSAY

  1. Ramsay Says Luke Followed Oral Tradition, Learned From Witnesses

  2. Theologians Eagerly Followed Ramsay, the Great Scholar

II. LUKE'S GOSPEL CONTRASTED WITH THE MANY APOCRYPHAL GOSPELS

  1. Many Uninspired Accounts of the Gospel Had Been Written Which Were Untrustworthy, Fallible, Inexact

  2. Luke Claims an Accuracy, a Certainty These Others Who Relied on Eyewitnesses Could Not Give

III. DID LUKE TRACE OUT ACCURATELY AND INVESTIGATE SOURCES IN WRITING HIS GOSPEL?

  1. Do Not Follow Unbelieving Critics

  2. It Would Be Ridiculous for Luke to Claim Perfection, Certainty, in All Things by Human Investigation

  3. The Greek Word in Luke 1:3, *Parakoloutheo*, Does Not Mean "Traced Out"

IV. LUKE DID NOT CLAIM TO HAVE HAD UNDERSTANDING OF ALL THINGS "FROM THE VERY FIRST" BUT LITERALLY "FROM ABOVE"

  1. The Greek Word *Anothen* Certainly Means "From Above"

  2. Matthew Henry, B. H. Carroll, Scofield, Gaussen, Light-

WHERE DID LUKE GET HIS FACTS?

Luke tells us, in the first four verses of his Gospel something of the source of his Gospel.

"Forasmuch as many have taken in hand to set forth in order a declaration of those things which are most surely believed among us, Even as they delivered them unto us, which from the beginning were eyewitnesses, and ministers of the word; It seemed good to me also, having had perfect understanding of all things from the very first, to write unto thee in order, most excellent Theophilus, That thou mightest know the certainty of those things, wherein thou hast been instructed." — Luke 1:1-4.

Two important factors have led to a customarily believed doctrine of human sources used in Scripture, particularly as to the sources for the books of Luke and Acts. That teaching I believe to be clearly wrong.

One factor which led to the customary concept of sources in Luke's Gospel is a poor and inadequate translation of Luke 1:3. Instead of Luke's saying, "Having had perfect understanding of all things *from the very first*," was the reason for his writing, proper translation shows that Luke said, "Having had perfect understanding of all things *from above....*" I will endeavor to show that this is the correct translation by reference to the Greek itself and to many of the best scholars, a little further on.

This inadequate and weak translation gave strength to the second factor leading to this usually held teaching about human sources for Luke's Gospel.

The second very influential factor in the position so widely accepted about human sources was the higher criticism which sought a human explanation for the content of the Scriptures instead of a miraculous divine source, by verbal, infallible inspiration.

How did this conception of German rationalists become current among even Bible-believing expositors and commentators?

I. MANY FOLLOWED HARNACK AND
SIR WILLIAM RAMSAY

The German rationalists attacked the validity of the New Testament records, particularly in the book of Acts. Harnack, the most eminent of German scholars, said that Luke was unreliable and untrustworthy as a historian and he made a very greatly detailed study of the evidence in this matter. Good Christians were not so much interested in Harnack, because he was obviously an enemy of the Bible and the historic Christian faith.

But to answer and correct a lot of the mistakes of Harnack and the German rationalists, Sir William Ramsay came on the scene. He was not a theologian but an archaeologist. He spent long years in study of archaeology in the lands of the Roman Empire, particularly the lands of Paul's missionary journeys. He wrote *St. Paul the Traveller and Roman Citizen,* and *The Cities of St. Paul.* He wrote *The Church in the Roman Empire* and *The Bearing of Recent Discovery on the Trustworthiness of the New Testament.* There Ramsay himself frankly admits that he grew to have a profound respect for the trustworthiness of Bible accounts, the historical exactness with which Luke described people and cities, as the facts were uncovered and proven by his studies in Bible lands, and particularly in Turkey, where much of Paul's missionary work was done.

In 1908, Hodder and Stoughton published Ramsay's book, *Luke the Physician.* Only 65 pages are given to Luke, and the other chapters are "other studies in the history of religion." But the book made a profound impression, for Ramsay had collected such an amazing amount of proof that the book of Acts was reliable historically, he was counted as a friend of the Christian religion. The tremendous impact which archaeology has made, compelling modernists to retreat from their attacks on many portions of the Bible, was just then well beginning. Theologians took great heart in the reassurance that the Bible

was generally accurate and trustworthy in historical and geographical matters. So Ramsay's positions concerning Luke and
the authorship and sources of the Gospel According to Luke and
the book of Acts were regarded as profound. They were so influential as to color the thinking of Christian leaders and theologians on both sides of the Atlantic, and Ramsay himself was
so popular that he was knighted by the English government.

Ramsay's article on "Luke the Physician" is principally an
answer to Harnack, showing that Harnack was wrong in supposing Luke's writing to be inaccurate. He called attention to
Hobart's and Hawkins's books on the medical language of
Luke. Ramsay insists on "the perfect unity of authorship
throughout the whole of the Third Gospel and the Acts....The
writer is the same throughout."

1. Ramsay Says Luke Followed Oral
Tradition, Learned From Witnesses

Ramsay did not say that Luke was divinely inspired and infallible. He says, "What was the truth? How far was Luke
right? I cannot say." [1] He thinks that Luke was limited because of his Hellenic background. He says, "Luke had been a
Hellenic pagan, and could not fully comprehend either Judaism
or Christianity." [2] Ramsay did not believe that Luke was
perfectly correct. He said, "I do not at all deny that there are
in his Gospel (as there are in the other Gospels) traces of the
age and the thoughts amid which they were respectively composed; but these are recognized because they are inharmonious
with the picture as a whole. They are stains, and not parts of
the original picture." [3] Yet he insisted that by all human standards, Luke was a very accurate and trustworthy historian and
so Ramsay's opinion had great weight. It is rather pitiful that
if Ramsay or even an infidel says he thinks Jesus was a good
man, or that some of the Bible is true, we want to herald it to
the whole world as a great victory!

Ramsay was very precise in what he thought were the sources
of Luke's Gospel and of Acts. He said, "The picture was

---

1. *Luke the Physician*, p. 10.
2. *Luke the Physician*, p. 12.
3. *Luke the Physician*, p. 14.

given to, and not made by, Luke; and the Author himself shows plainly how it was given him. He had intimate relations with some of those who had known Jesus, and from that, more than from the early written accounts to which he also had access, he derived his conception."[4]

Ramsay says that, like Harnack, he thinks "that the story in Luke 1., 2., is dependent on an oral not a written report; but unlike him, I think that this report comes from Mary herself. Like Professor Sanday, I should conjecture that it came through one of the women named by Luke elsewhere."[5]

So after Ramsay all the theologians so anxious to be thought scholarly began to adopt and teach that the sources of Luke's Gospel were oral traditions, testimonies of eyewitnesses, and perhaps some copying from other written records or Gospels. We were told that Luke probably talked to Mary herself or to someone who had talked to Mary, and that the reliability of the story of the virgin birth depended on a second- or third-hand account, put down as exactly as a good man of his period could do it, by Luke!

In the Sunday school lesson series of various great publishing houses this teaching of human sources was widely taught.

2. Theologians Eagerly Followed Ramsay, the Great Scholar

Dr. Hodge of Princeton says, "The evangelist Luke does not refer his knowledge of the events which he records to revelation, but says he derived it from those 'which from the beginning were eyewitnesses, and ministers of the word' (Luke 1:2)."[6]

But here the theologian mistakenly takes at face value the comments of somebody else on that passage without examining it carefully himself. He would ascribe to Luke the sources which Luke plainly says were those of other men. Luke 1:1 and 2 says, "Forasmuch as many have taken in hand to set forth in order a declaration of those things which are most surely believed among us, Even as they delivered them unto us, which from the beginning were eyewitnesses, and ministers of

---

4. *Luke the Physician*, p. 14.
5. *Luke the Physician*, p. 13.
6. *Systematic Theology*, Vol. 1, p. 155.

the word." The sources thus were mentioned of the many apocryphal gospels that were written, but which must be corrected by Luke's writing and Luke says, "It seemed good to me also, having had perfect understanding of all things *anothen* [literally from above]," to write his Gospel. Luke certainly does not claim simply to use hearsay evidence without divine revelation, and what he ascribes to the human, uninspired gospels ought not to be credited to Luke, since he makes no such claim.

G. Campbell Morgan, in his commentary on Luke, 1931, says concerning Luke's introduction:

> Then he gives us the sources of his information. He tells us that many had taken in hand to write a narrative. The reference may include the story Mark had written, and the story which Matthew had written; but it includes many more. He said many had taken in hand to write. Thus we first see him collecting every such story he could find. But there was another source of information. "Those who from the beginning were eyewitnesses and ministers of the Word" — those who had actually seen Jesus, and served Him in the days of His flesh. To them he talked. His word for these people is arresting: "eyewitnesses".... 7

We must remind the reader that we should not be guilty of oversimplification here. I use Sir William Ramsay because he was the most popular spokesman for the higher critics, making his plea more acceptable to Bible believers. I quote Dr. G. Campbell Morgan not to indicate a direct connection between his teachings and those of Sir William Ramsay. Dr. Morgan believed the Bible and nobly expounded it. Whether Morgan was influenced directly by Ramsay or by Harnack, or whether indirectly through others, I do not pretend to know. I only use Dr. Morgan as a popular example, showing that Bible believers have, I think thoughtlessly and unworthily but honestly, taken up the position of higher critics, that Luke got his Gospel from oral tradition, from eyewitnesses whom he may have consulted, from written records, and from other human sources.

Thus, strangely, by a mistranslation and by the heavy influence of higher criticism along with the natural carnal tendency of all of us to try to find a human and natural reason for

---

7. *The Gospel According to Luke*, p. 12.

things instead of the supernatural and miraculous, good men
have taught that Luke got the materials for his Gospel from
human sources.

At any rate, the subject is worthy of more detailed study.

II. LUKE'S GOSPEL CONTRASTED WITH
THE MANY APOCRYPHAL GOSPELS

Examine Luke 1:1,2 and one must see Luke's Gospel claims
to provide a certainty others did not give.

1. Many Uninspired Accounts of the Gospel Had Been
Written Which Were Untrustworthy, Fallible, Inexact

To understand the need for Luke's inspired Gospel we are
told that "many have taken in hand to set forth in order a
declaration of those things which are most surely believed
among us, Even as they delivered them unto us, which from
the beginning were eyewitnesses, and ministers of the word"
(Luke 1:1,2).

It was but natural that eyewitnesses of the miracles Jesus
wrought, and those who remembered hearing Him preach,
possibly even including the apostles themselves, had written
accounts of the birth, life, death, and resurrection of Jesus.

Matthew Henry says:

> That there were **many who had undertaken to publish** narra-
> tives of the **life of Christ,** many well-meaning people, who **de-
> signed** well and **did** well, and what they published had **done
> good,** though not done by divine inspiration, nor so well done
> as might be, nor intended for perpetuity. [8]

The International Standard Bible Encyclopaedia says:

> The introduction to the third canonical Gospel shows that in
> the days of the writer, when the apostles of the Lord were still
> living, it was a common practice to write and publish accounts
> of the acts and words of Jesus. It has even been maintained
> (S. Baring-Gould, **Lost and Hostile Gospels,** xxiii, London,
> 1874) that at the close of the 1st cent., almost every church had

8. *Matthew Henry's* Comment on Luke 1:1,2.

its own gospel with which alone it was acquainted. These were probably derived, or professed to be derived, from the oral reports of those who had seen, heard, and, it may be, conversed with our Lord. It was dissatisfaction with these compositions that moved Luke to write his Gospel.

It is possible that the Gospels of Mark and Matthew had been written before this time, but Luke does not refer to them. Two Gospels are not "many." No, he has in mind uninspired accounts, written as carefully as men knew to do with human judgment, quoting others, oral tradition, and eyewitnesses, or thirdhand reports.

The International Standard Bible Encyclopaedia says, "It was dissatisfaction with these compositions that moved Luke to write his Gospel." At least Luke gives that dissatisfaction as a reason for the need of his Gospel, although we believe the motivation of Luke's Gospel and of all Scripture was the direct moving of the Holy Spirit.

Note the contrast between the reliability claimed for Luke's Gospel as compared with these other accounts. Others had undertaken (not necessarily accomplishing it accurately) "a declaration of those things which are most surely believed among us." So at best they had to judge from oral traditions and the mass of testimonies about things that had happened. In the nature of the case, these other writings would not be wholly reliable.

2. Luke Claims an Accuracy, a Certainty These Others Who Relied on Eyewitnesses Could Not Give

And notice that on the contrary, Luke claims for himself, "having had perfect understanding of all things." It is important to see that Luke does not set out to do just what others had already done so unsatisfactorily. He does not rely on oral traditions. He does not have to judge between conflicting reports and testimonies. He "had perfect understanding of all things," he says. In other words, Luke is claiming for himself a supernatural accuracy which was denied the uninspired accounts. If words mean anything, then "perfect understanding of all things" is a claim of infallibility, of absolute correctness, which is not possible in a human document, but possible only by clear revelation and inspiration from God.

And why is the Gospel of Luke written? "That thou mightest know the *certainty* of those things, wherein thou hast been instructed."

The man Theophilus to whom Luke addressed the Gospel, and all other lovers of God represented by him, had heard already traditions, oral accounts, testimonies, and preaching about Christ — His life, His death, His miracles, His wonderful resurrection, His sayings.   But no two people could tell so many things exactly alike.   They would not see them alike. How could one know by reading the uninspired accounts of the life of Christ what was exactly so and what was not true?   The only way is for somebody to write by divine inspiration so that "thou mightest know the certainty of those things, wherein thou hast been instructed."

So Luke is inspired to write his Gospel as an infallible standard by which the things they had heard might be judged.   Mistakes that others had made would be rectified.   Uncertainty would become "certainty" by Luke's Gospel.

One cannot avoid the meaning here: What Luke wrote is claimed to be perfect and certain.   What others had written before, in uninspired accounts, had been drawn from eyewitnesses and oral reports and perhaps copied from others.   But what Luke was writing was out of "perfect understanding of all things," and with the assurance that those who read might "know the certainty of those things, wherein thou hast been instructed."

The difference between the common uninspired accounts of the life of Christ and Luke's Gospel is the difference between human and divine writing, between tradition and inspiration.   It was the difference between human investigation and judgment and human frailty in expression as contrasted with the perfection of divine inspiration.

Who was it that used eyewitness accounts and oral tradition as a basis for their writings?   It was these uninspired accounts which others had written.   Luke does not even hint here that he talked with Mary the mother of Jesus, or with somebody else who had talked with Mary, to find out about the virgin birth. He does not say that his Gospel was written, like these unreliable accounts were written, from oral tradition and from eyewitnesses, from hearsay, and from copied documents.

No, the sources of these other uninspired and unreliable gospels are not the same as Luke's.   Theirs are human; his is divine. Theirs are unreliable; his is perfect and accurate and certain. So here, by divine inspiration, Luke claims and so Bible believers should believe.

There is no way to understand Luke's introduction to his Gospel unless we understand that he is clearly here professing that his Gospel is different in origin and different in reliability from the other accounts to which he refers.

III. DID LUKE TRACE OUT ACCURATELY AND INVESTIGATE SOURCES IN WRITING HIS GOSPEL?

Here good men have been led astray by scholars.

1. Do Not Follow Unbelieving Critics

Sir William Ramsay says:

> He was, of course, dependent on information gained from others: the Author [Ramsay refers here to Harnack but approves] is disposed to allow considerable scope to oral information in addition to the various certain or probable written sources; but Luke treated his written authorities with considerable freedom as regards style and even choice of details, and impressed his own personality distinctly even on those parts in which he most closely follows a written source. 9

Here Ramsay, following Harnack, says that Luke quoted "oral information in addition to the various certain or probable written sources," and that Luke even then felt free to change material as he chose!

Now when you read that kind of talk from a modern commentator, remember it started with unbelieving higher critics. Harnack did not believe even in the miracles of the Bible. Ramsay believed in some of the miracles but did not believe in the infallible inspiration of the Bible. The idea of Luke's having oral tradition, eyewitness reports, and copied documents as sources for the Gospel, came from unbelievers. It is not in

---

9. *Luke the Physician*, p. 7.

Luke's own introduction to his Gospel, and there is no scriptural evidence for these suggested sources.

Luke plainly indicates that his Gospel, unlike the common uninspired accounts which had been written before, is certain and accurate in detail.

Dr. C. I. Scofield was an ardent fundamentalist. The editors of the Scofield Reference Bible were devoted believers and reverent scholars. And Dr. Scofield calls attention to the mistranslation of the Greek word *anothen*, and says that it should definitely be translated "from above." But then, strangely enough, Dr. Scofield says:

> The use by Luke of **anothen** is an affirmation that his knowledge of these things, derived from those who had been eyewitnesses from the beginning (Lk. 1. 2), was confirmed by revelation. In like manner Paul had doubtless heard from the eleven the story of the institution of the Lord's Supper, but he also had it by revelation from the Lord (cf. 1 Cor. 11. 23), and his writing, like Luke's "**anothen**" knowledge, thus became firsthand, not traditional, merely. [10]

But here, alas, Dr. Scofield reads into the passage what Luke did not say. Luke did not give "an affirmation that his knowledge of these things, derived from those who had been eyewitnesses from the beginning, was confirmed by revelation." Rather, he plainly states that he *received* these things by revelation. Luke knew naturally only what everybody else knew, "those things which are most surely believed among us." He did not claim to have any human sources of knowledge more than everybody else had, and he did not claim to have written as a result of those sources at all. What Luke wrote was not "confirmed by revelation." It was actually *given* by revelation.

And then Dr. Scofield says, "In like manner Paul had doubtless heard.... " How does Dr. Scofield know? Paul did not say so. On the contrary, speaking about his contact with the other apostles he said, "But I certify you, brethren, that the gospel which was preached of me is not after man. For I neither received it of man, neither was I taught it, but by the revelation of Jesus Christ" (Gal. 1:11,12). Then in verses 15 to 17 Paul says that when God called him to preach, "immediately I conferred not with flesh and blood: neither went I up to Jerusalem to them which were apostles before me; but I went

---

10. *Scofield Reference Bible,* p. 1070.

into Arabia, and returned again unto Damascus." Paul did not go to Jerusalem till three years later to see Peter, and was with Peter fifteen days. Then fourteen years later he went up to Jerusalem to confer with the apostles. Paul is expressly disavowing any idea that he got his preaching and doctrines and teaching from the other apostles.

So it is only guesswork and supposition to say that "Paul had doubtless heard from the eleven the story of the institution of the Lord's Supper." Paul got his revelation directly from God. If he had heard other things, he disregarded them. Hearsay evidence is never infallibly correct enough to be included in a supernatural Word of God. Inspiration does not "confirm" rumors and oral tradition. Inspiration breathes out words from God.

But someone says that the Greek word *parakoloutheo*, here translated "perfect understanding," means "traced carefully." The Scofield Reference Bible is by all odds the greatest in the world, but in this matter the author of the notes was misled by a current fallacy, in our humble judgment.

Ellicott's Commentary says, "Having had perfect understanding of all things. — Better, *having traced (or investigated) all things from their source.* The verb used is one which implies following the course of events step by step."[11] But this description of the Greek word, I think, is prejudiced by the mistranslation which Ellicott did not notice. He thought Luke was claiming to know perfectly all things even from the very first of the Gospel by natural means and by human sources. And so he read into the Greek word translated "perfect understanding" the idea of tracing things from their source.

2. It Would Be Ridiculous for Luke to Claim Perfection, Certainty, in All Things by Human Investigation

In the first place, it would be a ridiculous claim for Luke to say that he, by purely human means, going by oral tradition, had "traced" or "investigated" enough to have had a perfect understanding of those things written in his Gospel. As far as we know, John the Baptist, Zacharias, and Elisabeth were all

---

11. *Ellicott's Commentary*, p. 243.

dead long before Luke was converted. He did not secure his facts from them. The Bible never hints that he ever met Mary, and if he had talked to Mary about what the angel said to her and what she said to the angel it would be only hearsay and subject to human errors of memory and understanding. There was no human way that Luke could have perfectly learned about the message of the angels to the shepherds and the coming of the shepherds to see the Baby Jesus. The idea "perfect understanding" is simply not attained by investigation, by going through oral traditions, copying a few scattered manuscripts, talking to unreliable people, accepting hearsay evidence. It is impossible that Luke should have perfect understanding of all the things he wrote about, and that those who read the Gospel would "know the certainty" of all things written here if Luke followed only human sources and searched them out.

3. The Greek Word in Luke 1:3, *Parakoloutheo,* Does Not Mean "Traced Out"

The word *parakoloutheo* used in Luke 1:3, translated "perfect understanding," does not here mean "traced out," could not mean that because it would not make sense. Since the Bible never speaks of men being perfect or having perfect understanding or perfect memory or being infallibly correct in reporting, we may be sure that that is not what it is saying here.

Let us look again at the word *parakoloutheo*, here translated "perfect understanding." The Greek word is used four times in the New Testament: Mark 16:17; I Timothy 4:6; II Timothy 3:10; and here in Luke 1:3. If we consider how the Holy Spirit used the word the only three other times it is used in the New Testament we should get a good idea of its meaning here.

In Mark 16:17, "And these signs shall follow them that believe," *parakoloutheo* is translated "follow."

It does not mean investigate, trace, or search out. It means simply to follow accurately.

First Timothy 4:6 reads, "If thou put the brethren in remembrance of these things, thou shalt be a good minister of Jesus Christ, nourished up in the words of faith and of good doctrine, whereunto thou hast attained." Here *parakoloutheo* is translated "hast attained." Timothy had attained "the words of faith and of good doctrine." The word itself does not tell us how Timothy had attained the words of faith and good doctrine. If it was by searching out, by private investigation, by consulting eye-witnesses, that is not discussed in the verse here. The word simply means here "hast attained." Williams' translation says, "They were feeding your own soul on the truth of the faith and of the fine teaching which you have followed."

Second Timothy 3:10 reads, "But thou hast fully known my doctrine, manner of life, purpose, faith, longsuffering, charity, patience." And here the Greek word *parakoloutheo* is translated "hast fully known."

Summing up, then, the word here translated in Luke 1:3 as "had perfect understanding" means just that. Luke had known, or attained, or in his mind perfectly followed certain things given him of God. No one has a right to say what the Bible does not say, that Luke had searched out, consulted witnesses, consulted other documents, carefully compared oral tradition, and thus from human sources received a matter written in his Gospel. That is not what he said. That is the reasonings of men, but it is not exposition of the Scriptures. Luke "had perfect understanding," that is, detailed and accurate understanding, following the truth accurately, as given by divine inspiration. And so he tells us in his introduction to his Gospel.

IV. LUKE DID NOT CLAIM TO HAVE HAD UNDERSTANDING OF ALL THINGS "FROM THE VERY FIRST" BUT LITERALLY "FROM ABOVE"

The King James Version of Luke 1:3 is, unfortunately, inaccurate, and this inaccurate translation has followed in nearly all versions. Yet the mistake is fairly obvious upon detailed study.

1. The Greek Word *Anothen* Certainly Means "From Above"

Here Luke 1:3 says, "It seemed good to me also, having had perfect understanding of all things from the very first, to write

unto thee in order, most excellent Theophilus." And the note
in the Scofield Bible properly says, "'From the very first':
Gr. *anothen,* 'from above.' So translated in John 3:31; 19:11;
James 1:17; 3:15,17. In no other place is *anothen* translated
'from the very first.'" [12]

The meaning of the Greek word *anothen* is clear when we
study how the term is used elsewhere in the Bible. In John
3:31 the Scripture says, "He that cometh from above is above
all...." It refers to Jesus, and the term "from above" is a
translation of *anothen.*

In John 19:11 Jesus speaks to Pilate saying, "Thou couldest
have no power at all against me, except it were given thee from
above...." The term "from above" is a translation of *anothen.*
It obviously means from above.

James 1:17 says, "Every good gift and every perfect gift is
from above, and cometh down from the Father of lights...."
And the term "from above" is a translation of *anothen.* It
really means from above.

James 3:15 says, "This wisdom descendeth not from above,
but is earthly, sensual, devilish." And the term "from above"
here also is a translation of *anothen.*

The second verse below, James 3:17, says, "But the wisdom
that is from above is first pure, then peaceable...." And the
term "from above" is a translation of the Greek word *anothen.*

The word *anothen* is once translated "again." In John 3:3
we read that Jesus told Nicodemus, "Verily, verily, I say unto
thee, Except a man be born again, he cannot see the kingdom
of God." But the word "again" is a translation of the Greek
word *anothen,* and it properly means that one must be born
"from above."

In John 3:7 Jesus said, "Marvel not that I said unto thee, Ye
must be born again." And the word "again" is a translation
of the same Greek word *anothen,* and means that Nicodemus
must be born from above. The word does not refer to natural
knowledge from the beginning of a matter, but supernatural
knowledge from above. So Luke received his Gospel by revelation from above.

Only once, that is in Acts 26:5, is *anothen* translated as if it
might mean "from the very first." There it is translated "from
the beginning." But even the translations "from the very first"

---

12. *Scofield Reference Bible,* p. 1070.

and "from the beginning" might be legitimate if we refer to a first cause, to the origin or source of things, that is, to God Himself. And that seems to be involved in the word *anothen.*

If Luke had meant "from the very first" he would have used *arche* as he did in the preceding verse (Luke 1:2) for "from the beginning."

Actually Luke declared that he "having had perfect understanding of all things" from above was writing Theophilus "that thou mightest know the certainty of those things, wherein thou hast been instructed."

The terms used, "perfect understanding," and "the certainty of those things, wherein thou hast been instructed," involve a perfection that could come only from above. And that is what Luke here claims for the Gospel which God inspired him to write. He received it from above. He did not trace it out from oral tradition nor copy it from other manuscripts nor get it from eyewitnesses nor thirdhand witnesses. He got it from above.

2. Matthew Henry, B. H. Carroll, Scofield, Gaussen, Lightfoot, Erasmus, Trapp, and Many Other Scholars Say *Anothen* Must Mean "From Above"

What other authorities understand Luke to here claim that he received his Gospel "from above" and not "from the very first"?

We have mentioned Dr. Scofield and the editors of the Scofield Bible, and the statement which he clearly makes, that the Greek word *anothen* here means "from above."

Matthew Henry, while he follows the customary line in supposing that Luke depended upon the testimony of eyewitnesses and apostles, yet quotes Luke 1:3 as saying, "'It seemed good to me, having attained to the exact knowledge of all things, *anothen*—from above;' so I think it should be rendered; for if he meant the same with *from the beginning* (v. 2), as our translation intimates, he would have used the same word."[13] So Matthew Henry says *anothen* means from above.

Dr. B. H. Carroll, founder of the Southwestern Baptist Theo-

---

13. *Matthew Henry's* Comment on Luke 1:1,2.

logical Seminary, the greatest theologian Southern Baptists have ever had, says:

> Some questions have been raised which I wish to answer. One of these is relative to the scholarly support of my position on the first part of Luke, in which I set forth in a former chapter a possible translation justifiable — a translation that would make Luke claim inspiration for everything he wrote. Those who are familiar with the Greek will understand the explanation better than those who are not. It depends upon the translation of a single word. Luke says that he had perfect understanding of all things, and now comes in the modifying word **anothen**. That word primarily means "from above." It is so translated in the third chapter of John: "Except a man be born **anothen;**" it is so translated in the letter of James: "The wisdom that cometh **anothen**," and in an overwhelming majority of cases in the New Testament it has that translation. So that if you translate that word, "Having had perfect understanding of all things from above," it makes his claim to inspiration refer to his entire record.
>
> Now the question is as to whether that translation has any real scholarly support. I stated that John Gill favored that translation, and he was a great scholar of the early English Baptists. But the question now is, "What other scholarship supports it?"
>
> I answer: Matthew Henry, in his **Commentary;** Erasmus, the prince of the Greek scholars; Gomarus, another distinguished Greek scholar; Lightfoot, another distinguished exegete — all these men adopt that rendering, together with Galson, the great French scholar, who not only adopts it but makes an elaborate argument in support of it. These are all very distinguished men." [14]

(We believe that Carroll's secretary mispelled Carroll's pronunciation of Gaussen, and should have used that word instead of Galson.)

Again Dr. Carroll says:

> A distinguished lawyer once heard me preach on inspiration, and he came to me with this case:

> "I want to know how this squares with what I heard you preach," he said. "Luke 1:1-4 says, 'Forasmuch as many have taken in hand to draw up a narrative concerning those matters which have been fulfilled among us, even as they delivered them unto us, who from the beginning were eyewitnesses and ministers of the word, it seemed good to me also, having traced the course of all things accurately from the first, to write unto

---

14. *Inspiration of the Bible,* pp. 74,75.

thee in order, most excellent Theophilus, that thou mightest know the certainty concerning the things wherein thou wast instructed.' "Now," he went on, "evidently, from the face of that, Luke gathered his information just like any other historian — no evident inspiration about it; that he traced out everything from the first."

"Didn't those other writers that Luke tells about try to do the same thing?' I answered. "Then why was it necessary for Luke to write an account? Those other writers didn't make things certain; Luke makes them certain. He says, 'I am going to write you an account that you may know the things which are certain.' If he were writing to give a mere history to the world, it would not make things certain. What has become of all the memoirs or histories of Christ? Luke says that a number wrote them. Why have these accounts survived — Matthew, Mark, Luke, John and Paul?"

"Well," replied my interrogator, "I think you are putting too much emphasis on that."

I handed him a Greek concordance (I knew he was a Greek scholar) and a Greek Testament.

"What is the Greek word for 'from the first'?" I asked him.

"**Anothen,**" he answered.

"Now," I said, "look through the Greek concordance and tell me what that word means."

"Well," he replied, "in many cases in the Bible it means 'from above.' "A man must be born," says Christ — 'anothen' — born "from above."

"Very good," I added. "Now let me read the Greek to you and translate it in this passage of Luke: 'Having been instructed in all things accurately — anothen — from above.' Why not translate anothen that way here, since you do translate it that way in other cases in the New Testament? A good many scholars deny that anothen should be translated 'from above,'" I went on. "I have studied what they say, and it seems to me they make out a poor case of it."

My friend replied that he did not know that that word was there. Now note the object was that Luke was to write to produce absolute certainty. He had heard a good many things on this problem. Luke says, "Having been instructed in all things **from above**, I will write you so you may know the certainty of the things that are believed among us."

This staggered my lawyer.

"Anyway, whether you accept that position or not," I said, "you see the need; that when one goes to write a history of Christ he must write about Christ's boyhood; that, Luke knew nothing about. He learned this from God, who told Moses many things and who told Paul about the Lord's Supper. Paul says, 'Jesus told me Himself.' There is no record of Mary telling Luke, as some believe. How did Luke find out just exactly what Elisabeth, the mother of John the Baptist, said when Mary visited her? How did he find out just exactly what Mary said when she sang the Magnificat? 'Now,' says Luke, 'if you would know the certainty of these things you must know them from above.' "15

This passage by Dr. B. H. Carroll was sent to Dr. A. T. Robertson, famous Greek scholar. Dr. Cranfill, the editor of Carroll's book, put this footnote:

> With the desire to secure the opinion of Dr. A. T. Robertson, of Southern Baptist Theological Seminary and perhaps the greatest Greek scholar in America, I submitted to him some pages from this chapter in which the author discusses at some length the critical meaning of the word **anothen** and asked Dr. Robertson to give me his view on Dr. Carroll's interpretation of this Greek word. Replying to my query, he said: "The literal meaning of **anothen** is 'from above,' and the context in Luke's Gospel will make good sense with Dr. Carroll's translation of it." — The Editor.16

So Scofield, Carroll, Matthew Henry, Erasmus, Gomarus, Lightfoot, Gaussen, and A. T. Robertson agree to the meaning of *anothen*. It means "from above," and Luke got his material not from human sources but "from above."

Probably the most important book ever written on the inspiration of the Scriptures is *Theopneustia*, (*The Plenary Inspiration of the Holy Scriptures*) by L. Gaussen a hundred years ago. His book, greatly loved by Spurgeon, was brought to America by Dr. James M. Gray, Moody Bible Institute, published by Moody Press.

Gaussen says:

> And therefore, adds St. Luke, **it seemed good to ME also, having had perfect understanding of all things** FROM ABOVE, **to write of them unto thee in order.**
>
> St. Luke had obtained this knowledge FROM ABOVE: that is to say, by the wisdom which comes from above, "and which had been given him." It is very true that the meaning ordinarily attached to this last expression, in this passage, is **from the very first,** as if instead of the word **anothen** (from above), there were here the same words **ap arche (from the commencement),** which we find in verse second. But it appears to us that the opinion of Erasmus, of Gomarus, of Henry, of Lightfoot, and other commentators, ought to be preferred as more natural, and that we must take the word **anothen** here in the sense in which St. John

---

15. *Inspiration of the Bible,* pp. 49-51.
16. *Inspiration of the Bible,* p. 51.

and St. James have used it, when they say: "Every perfect gift cometh **from above**" (James 1:17)—"Thou couldst have no power against me, except it were given thee **from above**" (John 19:11—"Except a man be born **from above**, he cannot see the kingdom of God" (John 3:3)—"The wisdom that cometh from above is first pure."—(James 3:15,17).

The prophet Luke, then, "had obtained from above a perfect understanding of all things that Jesus began both to do and teach, until the day in which he was taken up." [17]

3. Many Others of the Best Scholars Say Luke Got Perfect Understanding "From Above"

Bishop J. C. Ryle, in his marvelous *Expository Thoughts on the Gospels,* commenting on Luke 1:3 says:

> (**From the very first.**) The Greek word so translated, means literally, "from above." It is so rendered in John 3:31, 19:11, James 1:17, 3:15, 3:17. Gomarus and Lightfoot think that it should be taken in this sense, and that it is an assertion of Luke's inspiration. The expression would then signify, "having accurately traced up all things under Divine inspiration, or teaching, from above." [18]

Dr. Ryle admits that "the majority of commentators agree with our translators." However, the following passage concerning the inspiration of the Gospel of Luke here is important.

> It would be mere waste of time to inquire from what source St. Luke obtained the information which he has given us in his Gospel. We have no good reason for supposing that he saw our Lord work miracles, or heard Him teach. To say that he obtained his information from the Virgin Mary, or any of the apostles, is mere conjecture and speculation. Enough for us to know that St. Luke wrote by inspiration of God. Unquestionably he did not neglect the ordinary means of getting knowledge. But the Holy Ghost guided him, no less than all other writers of the Bible, in his choice of matter. The Holy Ghost supplied him with thoughts, arrangement, sentences, and even words. And the result is, that what St. Luke wrote is not to be read as the "word of man," but the "word of God." (I Thess. 2:13.)

> Let us carefully hold fast the great doctrine of the plenary inspiration of every word of the Bible. Let us never allow that

---

17. *Theopneustia, The Plenary Inspiration of the Holy Scriptures,* pp. 86,87.
18. *Expository Thoughts on the Gospels,* p. 6.

any writer of the Old or New Testament could make even the slightest verbal mistake or error, when writing as he was "moved by the Holy Ghost" (II Peter 1:21).[19]

Commenting further Bishop Ryle said:

> There is no encouragement here for those who place confidence in unwritten traditions, and the voice of the church. St. Luke knew well the weakness of man's memory, and the readiness with which a history alters its shape both by additions and alterations, when it depends only on word of mouth and report. What therefore does he do? He takes care to "write."[20]

Trapp's *Commentary on the New Testament* is regarded very highly "in some respects...the best of the Puritan commentaries." Charles H. Spurgeon once said of Trapp, "He who shall excel Trapp had need to rise very early in the morning. Trapp is my especial companion and treasure."

Trapp says, on Luke 1:3:

> Ver. 3. **Having had perfect understanding**] Or, following them close at heels, and (as we say) hot-foot, **parakoloutheo.**
> **From the very first**] Or, from above, **anothen**, as inspired from heaven.[21]

Here we have an imposing array of devout Bible scholars who say that the Greek word *anothen* in Luke 1:3 means "from above," and that Luke got his material, not from careful investigation but by direct revelation from above. That the word *anothen* literally means "from above" and should be translated so was clearly stated by Dr. C. I. Scofield, by Matthew Henry, by B. H. Carroll, by Erasmus, Gomarus, Lightfoot, Gaussen, by Trapp and Bishop Ryle. Dr. A. T. Robertson said, "The literal meaning of *anothen* is 'from above,' and the context in Luke's Gospel makes good sense with Dr. Carroll's translation of it."[22]

And since the Greek word *anothen* is translated "from above" in John 3:31; in John 19:11; James 1:17; James 3:15 and 17; and since the term "born again" in John 3:3 and John 3:7 is literally "born *anothen*" or "born from above," the unbiased, believing scholar ought certainly to conclude that "from above" is the proper translation of *anothen* in Luke 1:3 and that

19. *Expository Thoughts on the Gospels*, pp. 3,4.
20. *Expository Thoughts on the Gospels*, pp. 4,5.
21. *Trapp's Commentary on the New Testament*, p. 304.
22. *Inspiration of the Bible*, p. 51.

Luke got his facts "from above," and not from eyewitnesses, not from investigation, and that, therefore, one who reads the book of Luke may "know the certainty" of these things written "with perfect understanding from above" by Luke.

V. DID DIVINE INSPIRATION HAVE BIBLE WRITERS QUOTE FROM ORAL TRADITION, COPY FROM ANCIENT MANUSCRIPTS, OR RELY ON THEIR OWN INTELLIGENCE OR MEMORY IN WRITING SCRIPTURES?

There is a widely held teaching, even by Bible believers, that the Holy Spirit "supervised" the writing of the Bible in such a fashion as simply to keep people from mistakes, as they thought out what they would write or copied from manuscripts or talked with witnesses. However, that is not what the Bible itself teaches about inspiration.

1. The Man-Made Theory of a Bible Written by Human Wisdom Is Unscriptural

If the Bible should tell us plainly that God told a man to go copy from a certain manuscript and that he did and that God had verified its correctness or had corrected any mistakes, of course we could believe it. But the Bible says nothing like that. That whole idea of human sources as the beginning of the Bible or of any part of the Bible is a man-made theory which originated with rationalists and has been sometimes accepted by noble, good men. But as I say, it is not taught in the Bible.

Again is it necessary and fitting that divine inspiration should require the help of Babylonian manuscripts for the writing of Genesis, and oral tradition handed down for the writing of the historical books of the Old Testament, and some "Q" manuscript from which the Synoptic Gospels would be largely patterned? And does the plan require or make room for the account of the virgin birth to be depending on Mary's own testimony, for example?

In other words, is God able and does God usually choose to go utterly beyond human wisdom and human sources in His divine revelation? I think that a thoughtful answer must be that God does in divine revelation go beyond the wisdom of men and that in the nature of the case divine revelation being perfect, eternal, supernatural, does not need to depend on oral tradition, other manuscripts, or eyewitnesses.

What eyewitness was present when God created the heavens and the earth? No possible human source could be reliable for Genesis 1 and 2. What eyewitness saw God and Moses alone when Moses died and was buried on the mount?

I believe that the whole idea of Luke depending on human sources cheapens and lowers the standard of perfection which divine inspiration requires. If Mark wrote down what Peter told him to write, as a church father, Papias, thought, we have a word from Peter instead of from God. If Matthew and Luke copied, on their own initiative, from Mark, then we have in those Gospels a report from some other human sources, not from God. If the Gospel of Luke depended partly on hearsay evidence, thirdhand perhaps, from Mary about the virgin birth, then that precious doctrine has scant authority. If the scientific accuracy of Genesis depends only on what Moses copied from some ancient Babylonian records, then Genesis is myth and legend and not the very Word of God.

I agree with beloved Dr. Henry C. Thiessen, long chairman of the department of Bible, theology, and philosophy in Wheaton College, who said:

> We feel that Matthew and Luke are not mere human adaptations of the materials in Mark, together with some more or less reliable supplementary materials derived from other sources; but that they are equally inspired with Mark, divinely originated to give specific pictures of the wonderful life and work of our Lord. [23]

On the next page Dr. Thiessen says:

> In the absence of all historical proof that Matthew and Luke were thus dependent upon Mark; in view of the possibility of explaining this phenomenon of agreements in the Synoptics in another way (see under **A Proposed Solution,** below); in the light of Lightfoot's declaration as to the doctrinal sacrifice necessary to the development of the theory; and because of our firm belief in the full and equal inspiration of all the Gospels, we are obliged to reject the Two-Document theory. [24]

---

23. *Introduction to the New Testament,* p. 117.
24. *Introduction to the New Testament,* p. 118.

2. The Scripture Plainly Disclaims Eyewitness, Hearsay, and Thought-Out Sources

But more important than argument is the teaching of Scripture on the nature of inspiration. In I Corinthians 2:9 and 10 we are told this great principle of divine revelation:

"But as it is written, Eye hath not seen, nor ear heard, neither have entered into the heart of man, the things which God hath prepared for them that love him. But God hath revealed them unto us by his Spirit: for the Spirit searcheth all things, yea, the deep things of God."

Paul is talking about divine revelation here. Some have supposed verse 9 to refer to the glories of Heaven unrevealed, but it does not. Paul is talking about the matter of divine revelation which Paul gave to the people, particularly his inspired letters. Did Paul write from his personal experience what he had seen? No, he said, "Eye hath not seen, nor ear heard, neither have entered into the heart of man, the things which God hath prepared for them that love him." What Paul wrote down he wrote not on the authority of his own seeing or his own hearing or his own thinking. He wrote on the absolute authority that God had revealed them to him by His Spirit.

And in verse 13 below he said, "Which things also we speak, not in the words which man's wisdom teacheth, but which the Holy Ghost teacheth...." So divine inspiration is not based upon what Paul or Luke saw or heard or thought. It is not based upon human sources. As we have shown before, Paul in Galatians 1:11 and 12 says, "But I certify you, brethren, that the gospel which was preached of me is not after man. For I neither received it of man, neither was I taught it, but by the revelation of Jesus Christ."

Paul did not write what some witness told him. He did not write what he was taught by men. The Gospel he preached was not after men. He received it "by the revelation of Jesus Christ." And later when Paul, after preaching many years, went to see the apostles in Jerusalem, he said, "For they who seemed to be somewhat in conference added nothing to me" (Gal. 2:6). The apostles who had been with Jesus three and one-half years added nothing to what Paul knew by divine inspiration and what he preached!

So divine inspiration, we are told, "is not after man." It does not come by human sight or hearing or human experience or knowledge. It comes by divine revelation.

And is not the same principle of divine revelation told us in II Peter 1:21? There we are told, "For the prophecy came not in old time by the will of man: but holy men of God spake as they were moved by the Holy Ghost."

The Scripture, or prophecy, "came not in old time by the will of man: but holy men of God spake as they were moved by the Holy Ghost."

Divine inspiration does not require, and in fact does not allow for, any authority or human sources for the Bible.

3. The Inspired Writer Luke Gladly Joined With God in Writing the Gospel

God used men to write the Bible. God used human language, the same words that men used in their dealings with one another, in writing the Bible.

We are told that Luke uses medical terms in his Gospel and in the book of Acts which are not generally used in other parts of the New Testament. And Luke is called "the beloved physician" (Col. 4:14). Did God inspire Luke to use some medical terms which God might not have given a man without medical experience to use? He may have done so.

We are told also that Luke's Gospel and the book of Acts are beautifully written, that there is a cultured finish, a beauty in the writing which is not present in all parts of the Greek New Testament. Does that mean that God may have inspired Luke with a different vocabulary than He inspired other Bible writers? We believe that is true. We believe there is some difference in style in the writings of different parts of the New Testament.

Here we enter into the tremendous problem of the union of deity and humanity. Always that is miraculous, always somewhat beyond human understanding. Jesus Christ is both man and God. The Gospel of Luke is both God's Word and Luke's Gospel. God graciously allowed Luke to have part in writing this supernaturally perfect Gospel as He allowed Mary to have part in bringing into this world the supernaturally perfect Son of God, the God-man Jesus Christ. Jesus may have had in His features some likeness to Mary His mother. But if so, that was by the choice of God, not the choice of Mary. God selected Mary, prepared Mary, and used Mary. Mary gladly believed and offered herself for God's plan. But Mary did not initiate the birth of Christ. God did that.

Just so Luke gladly acceded to the mind of God in writing his Gospel. He says, "It seemed good to me also" to write the Gospel. But we are not to suppose that the Gospel originated with Luke. God planned it and Luke was glad to enter into the plan. It was God who inspired Luke to write it and inspired him to believe that it would be good to write.

God who has infinite wisdom could write in any style He wished. Why would He not choose to use any style suitable to the instrument used, the man who was writing down the words? So we believe God chose to use a style that would fit Luke in telling Luke what to write. Luke had perfect knowledge of all things from above. He had a glad understanding of the need for his Gospel, also from above. God who may have made Jesus look like Mary, may have made the style of the Gospel of Luke look like Luke. But in each case the written Word and the incarnate Word came from God. And Luke, like Mary, was the glad partner, the passive and trusting partner in God's plan.

CHAPTER IX

ETERNAL WORD OF GOD SETTLED IN HEAVEN BEFORE IT WAS WRITTEN DOWN BY MEN GOD PREPARED

I. THE SCRIPTURES CLAIM ETERNAL, PREVIOUS EXISTENCE

   1. The Scriptures Are Settled Forever in Heaven

   2. Scriptures Already Founded Forever Before Written

   3. The Scriptures and the Earth Alike Established of Old

II. KNOWN UNTO GOD ARE ALL HIS WORKS FROM THE BEGINNING OF THE WORLD

   1. The Creation of All Things Was Known of God Before He Made All Things

   2. Israel Was Known Ahead of Time

   3. The Moral Law Is Part of God's Eternal Character

   4. Man's Sin Was Known

   5. God Foreknew Who Would Trust Christ and Be Saved

III. THUS THE SCRIPTURES ARE NOT FROM HUMAN SOURCES

   1. "Prophecy Came Not...by the Will of Man"

   2. "Not as the Word of Men, but as It Is in Truth, the Word of God"

   3. "Not in the Words Which Man's Wisdom Teacheth, but Which the Holy Ghost Teacheth"

   4. Does This Mean That the Bible Is Given by "Mechanical Dictation"?

IV. AND THIS TRUTH OF THE ETERNAL PERFECTION
   OF SCRIPTURE PROVES TWO THINGS

   1. In All the Copies and Translations, God Still Keeps
      His Word
   2. Whatever the Difficulty, the Words Are Still God's Words

ETERNAL WORD OF GOD SETTLED IN HEAVEN BEFORE IT WAS WRITTEN DOWN BY MEN GOD PREPARED

The Bible doctrine of inspiration will be greatly clarified if we find that the perfect Word of God was settled in Heaven before God's Holy Spirit revealed it to men and they wrote it down. If before God breathed out the words of the Scripture they were already in the mind and plan of God, that puts certain definite boundaries around the Bible doctrine of the method and quality of divine inspiration of the Scriptures.

That would mean that men did not select the words. They were God's words prepared ahead of time. It will not be hard to believe what the Bible expressly claims, that God gave the very words if they were in the mind and plan of God ahead of time.

That would help to settle the questions about style, vocabulary, personalities expressed as men wrote down the Scriptures. God prepared the men ahead of time, just as He had in His own heart and mind the Scriptures eternally before they were written.

Then the Scriptures are not the result of human investigation, as many people think Luke searched out the details written in His Gospel. The Scripture did not depend on eyewitness accounts.

There would need to be no copying of faulty records, no relying on oral traditions, if the Scriptures were all determined in Heaven and settled forever before they were written down.

I. THE SCRIPTURES CLAIM ETERNAL, PREVIOUS EXISTENCE

As Christ, the Incarnate Word, was with God in the beginning, before He became man, why could not the Scriptures, which are also the Word of God, God's eternal and perfect revelation to man, have been in God's mind and plan before He gave the words to men to write down? If Christ was God before He became Man, why not the infinite Word of God also before it was put in finite, human words? We believe the Bible clearly teaches this: the eternal Word of God was settled in Heaven before it was written down by men.

1. The Scriptures Are Settled Forever in Heaven

What a strange statement that is! Psalm 119:89 says, "For ever, O Lord, thy word is settled in heaven." The meaning of this plain statement is that the Word of God, the Scriptures, originated in Heaven, not on earth.

The Scriptures are eternal, will never pass away, as Isaiah 40:8, I Peter 1:23 and 25, and the words of Jesus in Matthew 24:35 and the synoptic passages in Mark and Luke say. This truth is repeated in Psalm 119 several times. So we are told that the Scriptures are settled forever, they are incorruptible, they abide forever, they will never pass away. In Psalm 119:152 we read, "Concerning thy testimonies, I have known of old that thou hast founded them for ever." In the same chapter, verse 160 says, "Thy word is true from the beginning: and every one of thy righteous judgments endureth for ever."

Now we are glad to see that the Word of God will never pass away, cannot be broken, is incorruptible. And twelve times at least the Scripture speaks of "the everlasting covenant," referring to God's promises. So, in the future, surely the Scriptures will abide through eternity. They are so perfect, they so represent God and perhaps we might even say they are so much a part of the character of God that they cannot pass away.

But what about the past? Was the Word of God settled in the eternal past also, before it was ever given to men? Note, the text in Psalm 119:89 talks of a finished matter. Long before much of the Bible was written, we read, "For ever, O Lord, thy word is settled in heaven." Already settled before it was all written? That seems to be the plain meaning of the Scripture here. When John or Paul or Luke writes in the New Testament, they will be writing down something that was already settled in Heaven.

2. Scriptures Already Founded Forever Before Written

Notice also the statement in Psalm 119:152, "Concerning thy testimonies, I have known of old that thou hast founded them for ever." Not that they would *eventually* be founded forever but that they were *already* in existence, already founded forever!

And verse 160 says, "Thy word is true from the beginning: and every one of thy righteous judgments endureth for ever." Not simply the part of Scripture already written when this Psalm was put down, but "every one of thy righteous judgments," the psalmist says, "endureth for ever." And notice, "Thy word is true from the beginning." Does that mean from the beginning of the world, the beginning of creation? I think that is implied. Not only that the Word of God would be true when it was written down in human words, but it was already true from the beginning. It is as eternal as God is. It was already settled in Heaven.

3. The Scriptures and the Earth Alike Established of Old

In Psalm 19:7 we find that "the law of the Lord is perfect...." And the Hebrew word for "perfect" there is *tamin*, which Young defines as "perfect, plain, whole, complete." Then was the Word of God already whole, already complete, when Psalm 19:7 was written?

It is also suggestive that the testimony of God through nature and the testimony through the Word of God are both mentioned together. In Psalm 19 we find that "the heavens declare the glory of God," but "the law of the Lord is perfect, converting the soul." Nature, accursed for man's sin, is not perfect, but the law of the Lord is perfect. But does God mean to imply that the law of the Lord is as old as the earth?

And in Psalm 119 God illustrates the law by the creation. Read verses 89 to 91 together: "For ever, O Lord, thy word is settled in heaven. Thy faithfulness is unto all generations: thou hast established the earth, and it abideth. They continue this day according to thine ordinances: for all are thy servants."

Does not the Lord here mean that the Word of God and the abiding earth alike picture God's faithfulness and alike they "continue this day according to thine ordinances: for all are thy servants." It seems the Word of God and the creation of God are alike signs of God's faithfulness and that both alike continue forever.

The least we can say about these passages is that the Scriptures are clearly declared to be eternal, looking in the future, and, as we understand, clearly stated that they were all settled in Heaven before they were given to men.

II. KNOWN UNTO GOD ARE ALL HIS WORKS FROM THE BEGINNING OF THE WORLD

An all-inclusive statement is that of Acts 15:18, "Known unto God are all his works from the beginning of the world."

All of the works of God were known of Him and planned by Him before the beginning of the world. Surely that must include the Scriptures as well as creation of the earth and its foreordained history and final restoration as the Paradise of God. Surely that must include man's fall, his wickedness and need for a Saviour.   It does certainly include the Lord Jesus and His coming as a Man to live a perfect life, die an atoning death and to save sinners. It includes the plan of salvation, of course. It includes Israel and their final restoration of a remnant, with Christ sitting on David's throne. It involves certainly the moral law, the righteousness of God.

Known unto God are all His works — meaning that He knows ahead of time who will trust Him for salvation and those whom He foreknows He predestines to be conformed to the image of His Son.   So God knows ahead of time His prophets who would preach and who would write the Scriptures. How can anyone believe that "known unto God are all his works from the beginning of the world," without including the Scriptures as known of God from the beginning of the world?

1. The Creation of All Things Was Known of God Before He Made All Things

Creation was planned ahead of time, and all the innumerable details of the history of this planet, the curse of sin, and finally that God will purge the earth with fire, will make new heavens about us and make this earth new.

2. Israel Was Known Ahead of Time

When God called Abraham, He already had the plan made out. Abraham should be the father of many and through him should come blessing to all the earth through Christ. Before Jacob was born, he, not Esau, was selected to head the nation Israel, and Esau, the firstborn, was rejected. We do not mean rejected for salvation. I understand that there is no evidence in the Bible that God ever coerces men in moral judgments and decisions. God offers forgiveness and salvation to every sinner and we do not know whether Esau was saved or not. We do know he could have been saved. He could not be the head of the nation Israel. That was predetermined. We know that the time in Israel was foretold and planned ahead of time and even Pharaoh was raised up and God, knowing his wicked rejection of the truth and the despising of God's warnings, planned to make him an example of judgment (Exod. 9:16; Rom. 9:17). It was foretold, and so we know God had it planned ahead of time that Christ would be crucified among Jews, that the Gospel would go to all the world.

3. The Moral Law Is Part of God's Eternal Character

Was God's moral law already known to God before the world began? Obviously. The righteousness of God is a part of His eternal character. When the Ten Commandments were given from Mount Sinai and written down with the finger of God, then recorded in Exodus 20, they were not new. They were as old as God. The righteousness of God is somewhat revealed in those commandments. And even the Sabbath commandment, which is ceremonial, is a picture of the truth that if one were righteous and did all his work, he could earn Heaven. So the law, to men who sinned, as all do, was a schoolmaster to turn people to Christ.

Who would say that at Mount Sinai God first thought about a command against murder or against adultery or against stealing or false witness or against covetousness? The moral law is eternal, as much from the beginning as on into the eternal future.

4. Man's Sin Was Known

Yes, and the plan of salvation was all planned ahead of time. When God told Eve that the Seed of the woman should bruise the Serpent's head and he should bruise His heel (Gen. 3:15), God already knew about the sinfulness of man, his need to be born again, the atoning death of Christ. When Abel offered his first sacrifice by faith, God had planned all about salvation. And so Christ was "the Lamb slain from the foundation of the world," Revelation 13:8 tells us.

Then, surely, Isaiah 53 was in the heart and mind of God from the beginning. Surely the 22nd Psalm, picturing the agony and the torment of Jesus Christ on the cross, was known of God before it was written down.

Why, even the ceremonial laws pointing to Christ were already planned ahead of time. The Tabernacle in the wilderness was to be patterned after one that was already in Heaven which Moses saw, and he was commanded, "And look that thou make them after their pattern, which was shewed thee in the mount" (Exod. 25:40). And all the priests only pictured that One Priest, Jesus Christ, who would be "a minister of the sanctuary, and of the true tabernacle, which the Lord pitched, and not man" (Heb. 8:2). And all the priests served "unto the example and shadow of heavenly things, as Moses was admonished of God when he was about to make the tabernacle: For, See, saith he, that thou make all things according to the pattern shewed to thee in the mount" (Heb. 8:5). Yes, the ceremonial law was known of God and planned in Heaven and the Tabernacle was in Heaven before it was on earth.

5. God Foreknew Who Would Trust Christ and Be Saved

Every single person to be saved is known ahead of time by the Lord before they are born. The Lord who knows the hearts of all men knows ahead of time who will trust Him for salvation and love Him and serve Him, after they hear the Gospel. So Peter could write to those who were "elect according to the foreknowledge of God the Father, through sanctification of the Spirit, unto obedience and sprinkling of the blood of Jesus Christ..." (I Pet. 1:2). And so Romans 8:29,30 tells us:

"For whom he did foreknow, he also did predestinate to be conformed to the image of his Son, that he might be the first-born among many brethren. Moreover whom he did predestinate, them he also called: and whom he called, them he also justified: and whom he justified, them he also glorified."

Mark, God does not usurp the will of man. No man is ever compelled to do wrong. Any man could be saved because he is commanded to repent and God "is not willing that any should perish" (Acts 17:30,31 and II Pet. 3:9). So, based on God's foreknowledge, He predestinates everyone whom He foreknows will be saved and plans that they will be called by the Spirit, that they will be justified when they trust Christ and that they will be glorified at the resurrection.

Can one imagine that every detail of the preaching of the Gospel and the salvation of particular sinners, millions of individuals, is all planned, and yet that God did not know ahead of time His Gospel, His truth, His Word, before it was written down? Were the Scriptures an afterthought?

No, we have the plain statement of the Word of God, "Known unto God are all his works from the beginning of the world." And among "all his works" surely is the wonderful, revealed Word of God, inspired and written down in the Scriptures. Before God breathed out the words of Scripture, He knew them from the beginning of the world.

Do we deny that there is an expression of human thought, style, color, characteristics, experiences and feelings in the Scriptures? Not at all. We see them and rejoice that they are there. Paul wrote but rejoices that the Thessalonians "received it not as the word of men, but as it is in truth, the word of God" (I Thess. 2:13). In II Samuel 23:1 and 2 we read, "Now these be the last words of David. David the Son of Jesse said, and the man who was raised up on high, the anointed of the God of Jacob, and the sweet psalmist of Israel, said, The Spirit of the Lord spake by me, and his word was in my tongue." What a statement! These are the words of David and yet David said, "The Spirit of the Lord spake by me, and his word was in my tongue." David spake but the words were God's words! David wrote personal experiences, prayers, praises, and said, "God spake by my tongue." How reconcile these two truths, that every word of Scripture in the original autographs was "God-breathed" (II Tim. 3:16), and "proceedeth out of the mouth of God" (Matt. 4:4), yet that they are colored by men, by men's experiences, circumstances, men's thinking, their style of language?

Here is the simple, scriptural answer: God formed the eternal Word settled in Heaven "from the beginning," then He prepared the men, the circumstances, the feelings, the experiences, so that as men would write if they wrote the very words God had planned. Did God control the men? More than that, He made them. Did He allow them to express their thoughts? Yes, but more than that, He made the thoughts! And that we will discuss more fully in the next chapter.

III. THUS THE SCRIPTURES ARE NOT FROM HUMAN SOURCES

The Scriptures are not of man but of God. They were only from men as God selected the men and prepared the men and told the men what to write. They are written in the style and vocabulary of particular men only as God prepared those styles and vocabularies and selected them. If the words are such as Paul or Moses would ordinarily use, it was still God who selected them. It is time surely to carefully consider now positive statements of God's Word, that the Scriptures are from God in all their sources and are only from men as God chose to give it through men.

1. "Prophecy Came Not...by the Will of Man"

In II Peter 1:21 we have the clear statement, "For the prophecy came not in old time by the will of man: but holy men of God spake as they were moved by the Holy Ghost."

Dr. Warfield clearly shows that the word "prophecy" here refers to all the Scriptures as they were revealed from God and written down. And here we are told that prophecy "came not in old time by the will of man." Men did not decide what to write. Men did not decide what words to use. God so mastered the men in the moment of writing that they wrote what God willed and not what men willed. If the prophecy came "not... by the will of man," then man did not make the choices and the decisions. He simply participated little or much in God's choices and God's decisions.

2. "Not As the Word of Men, but As It Is in Truth the Word of God"

In I Thessalonians 2:13, we have this word written down by the Apostle Paul: "For this cause also thank we God without ceasing, because, when ye received the word of God which ye heard of us, ye received it not as the word of men, but as it is in truth, the word of God, which effectually worketh also in you that believe."

Even in this very verse Paul participates and tells how he thanks God without ceasing and then paradoxically in the same verse we find that he is praising God, "because, when ye received the word of God which ye heard of us, ye received it not as the word of men, but as it is in truth, the word of God...."
In the same breath in which Paul tells about his own heart gratitude, he is saying that even his preaching of the truth among the Thessalonians was not the word of men but the word of God. And Paul was grateful because God was grateful and put gratitude in his heart and put the words in his pen when he wrote them down!

3. "Not in the Words Which Man's Wisdom Teacheth, but Which the Holy Ghost Teacheth"

But one of the most detailed statements on this question in the Bible is in I Corinthians 2:9-13. It could not be stronger than II Timothy 3:16 which says, "All scripture is *theopneustos* [God-breathed]." It could not be stronger, we think, than Deuteronomy 8:3 which Jesus quoted in Matthew 4:4 and Luke 4:4, that, "Man shall not live by bread alone, but by every word that proceedeth out of the mouth of God." But at least this passage in I Corinthians 2 is more detailed.

Let us read that passage again:

"But as it is written, Eye hath not seen, nor ear heard, neither have entered into the heart of man, the things which God hath prepared for them that love him. But God hath revealed them unto us by his Spirit: for the Spirit searcheth all things, yea, the deep things of God. For what man knoweth the things of a man, save the spirit of man which is in him? even so the things of God knoweth no man, but the Spirit of God. Now we have received, not the spirit of the world, but the spirit which is of God; that we might know the things that are freely given to us of God. Which things also we speak, not in the words which man's wisdom teacheth, but which the Holy Ghost teacheth; comparing spiritual things with spiritual."

Note what verses 9 and 10 say about the wonderful things which God has prepared for His people — not Heaven but the things revealed in the Bible!

Incidentally, here again it seems clear that God prepared ahead of time the Scriptures that are now revealed in Spirit-given words.

But where did matter, which is now revealed to us by the Spirit, originate? Did human eyes see it and so men write down what they saw? Did human ears hear and report the words they heard? Did men most carefully consider the wonderful dealings of God and figure out for themselves the wonderful things God has for us? For example, did the Apostle Paul study the œremonial law, the sacrifices, the priesthood, then out of the wonderfully illumined logical mind write us the book of Hebrews? No, no!

The things that are written to us in the Bible were not written as by eyewitnesses — "Eye hath not seen" these things. What is written in the inspired Word is not what human ears heard from human sources. What we have written here was not figured out in the enlightened heart of men who followed what leads and made what investigation they could know. The wonderful things here are revealed by the Spirit and they did not come from human sources. "Eye hath not seen, nor ear heard, neither have entered into the heart of men, the things which God hath prepared for them that love him. But God hath revealed them unto us by his Spirit."

And verse 11 tells us plainly that no human wisdom or industry or spirituality could ever reach the plane to understand God except as it is revealed by the Spirit of God.

And so now Paul tells us that not only the matter but the very words of the revelation are given by God. "Now we have received, not the spirit of the world but the spirit which is of God; that we might know the things that are freely given to us of God. Which things also we speak, not in the words which man's wisdom teacheth, but which the Holy Ghost teacheth; comparing spiritual things with spiritual." Or as the American Standard Version gives it: "...combining spiritual things with spiritual words."

So, if one did not know that the Greek word in Luke 1:3 is *anothen,* "from above," and that Luke had a perfect understanding of all things "from above," not by investigation, he could certainly know it by this Scripture. Human investigation did not furnish the source of material for the Bible.

How did Luke know about the virgin birth? Not believing that the Bible is infallibly inspired, Sir William Ramsay said that Luke probably talked to Mary herself and learned the facts. But such hearsay evidence is not even received in the courts of the land, and every reader of the newspapers knows how biased and inexact are different men's reports of the same events. No! No! The word about the virgin birth came not from men but from God. God gave Luke the truth and gave him the very words in which he expressed it, "from above."

Papias, one of the early church fathers, is quoted as saying that Peter told Mark the things of the Gospel and Mark wrote them down. But Papias was mistaken. He knew no more about it from actual experience than anybody knows today, and he did not know as much about it as you and I may know, because he did not take to heart the plain word of Scripture as we are taking it here in these pages.

Mark's Gospel came from God, not from Peter. Not only the thought but the words came from God. The Gospel was written "not in the words which man's wisdom teacheth, but which the Holy Ghost teacheth." Some have said that Luke wrote down what he learned from Paul. Luke was with Paul in many of his travels, including Rome. This is obvious from the "we" passages in the book of Acts and from Paul's own references to Luke. And some would like to give Luke apostolic authority by having him write down what Paul told him to write. But, no, that is not the way the Bible came into being. Not what eye saw nor ear heard nor what entered into the heart of man but which the Holy Ghost revealed, is what we have in the Bible and it is given, not in Paul's words that Luke wrote but words "which the Holy Ghost teacheth."

4. Does This Mean That the Bible Is Given by "Mechanical Dictation"?

Let us say again a plain word here that greatly needs to be said. I do not know any reputable scholar of the past or present who could be properly accused of believing in "mechanical dictation," that is, that the writers of the Bible were only machines and that their feelings and emotions and their minds were not "in gear" when they were inspired to write down parts of the Bible. I say, no intelligent defender of the faith, in all my knowledge, has taught that. Among six thousand volumes in my library, I have many on inspiration — the works of Bettex, Urquhart, Bannerman, Warfield, Robert Dick Wilson, Allis, Kyle, Engelder, Gaussen, Collett, Carroll, Scofield, Torrey, Wilbur Smith, Laird Harris, Coder, Griffith Thomas, and others. I have commentaries by Matthew Henry, Spurgeon; Jamieson, Fausset and Brown; Gray, Lange, Ellison, Simeon, Ryle, Broadus, Ellicott, Ironside, Darby and others.

Dr. Laird Harris in *Inspiration and Canonicity of the Bible* calls attention to the fact that those who rush to defend against the doctrine of "mechanical dictation" are simply setting up a straw man, that they may knock down their own creation. Thus, those who argue against mechanical dictation are either foolishly quoting somebody else, hoping to gain favor by appearing to be scholarly, or they are themselves unbelievers who dishonestly try to attack verbal inspiration by calling it mechanical dictation.

Disclaiming mechanical dictation and trying not to offend, Warfield said that some may have taught that. But Dr. Warfield, you are too modest and too apologetic.

Dictation? Yes, if you simply mean that God gave the words. So He did! The Bible explicitly says that, from the mouth of Jesus (Matt. 4:4; Luke 4:4; and in I Cor. 2:13 and many other Scriptures). Mechanical? Certainly not.

Mary joyfully surrendered to the will of God that she might become the mother of the Saviour through a virgin birth, and she said, "Be it unto me according to thy word." Every detail here was determined by God, not by Mary, and yet *it was not mechanical!*

When a soul is born again, it is God who does all the miracle of regeneration. It is "not by works of righteousness which we have done, but according to his mercy he saved us, by the washing of regeneration, and renewing of the Holy Ghost" (Titus 3:5).

"For by grace are ye saved through faith; and that not of yourselves: it is the gift of God: Not of works, lest any man should boast" (Eph. 2:8,9). And yet who would say that re-generation is mechanical? I do not say that no emotion or no decision of the will or no glad opening of the heart's door to Jesus takes place. I simply say that God works the miracle, that man is a participant, gladly receiving what God Himself gives. No, the Bible is given by verbal inspiration but not by mechanical dictation.

But, like it or not, those who believe the Bible must accept it as a plainly stated fact—the Scriptures are from God, not from men, though the Scriptures came through men and though God sometimes had men to incorporate and write down their own thoughts and feelings and experiences as He breathed out the Scriptures. So honest and scholarly men, let us have no more silly talk about mechanical dictation. It is the ruse of unbelievers who would like to discredit what the Bible clearly teaches about word-for-word inspiration, verbal inspiration, plenary inspiration.

IV. AND THIS TRUTH OF THE ETERNAL PERFECTION OF SCRIPTURE PROVES TWO THINGS

The Scriptures "shall not pass away," they "abide for ever" as we are plainly told in Isaiah 40:8 and I Peter 1:21-23. A later chapter will be given to this, but brief mention is proper here.

1. In All the Copies and Translations, God Still Keeps His Word

One copying scribe may make an error. But others will not make the same error, and eventually that error will be discovered by those who love and search the Word. One honest preacher may misinterpret some passage, but the Holy Spirit will yet use the perfect Word of God imperfectly preached and take it to hearts of people and do His work in them.

A translator may miss part of the meaning, either with wicked, unbelieving bias, as liberals have sometimes done, or ignorantly, as reverent, good men sometimes do, but other translations will correct the error. And in the thousands of manuscripts available, the perfect Word of God is eternally preserved and we may be sure that it always will be preserved.

Dr. John Clifford likened the Bible to an anvil which wears out the hammers of the scorners who beat upon it, but itself lasts forever:

Last eve I paused beside the blacksmith's door,
And heard the anvil ring the vesper chime;
Then looking in, I saw upon the floor,
Old hammers worn with beating years of time.

"How many anvils have you had," said I,
"To wear and batter all these hammers so?"
"Just one," said he, and then with twinkling eye,
"The anvil wears the hammers out, you know."

"And so," I thought, "The Anvil of God's Word
For ages sceptic blows have beat upon,
Yet, though the noise of falling blows was heard,
The Anvil is unharmed, the hammers gone."

2. Whatever the Difficulty, the Words Are Still God's Words

Make no mistake about it—the Bible is written originally

"not in the words which man's wisdom teacheth, but which the Holy Ghost teacheth."

Do you find some difficulty in believing that the Scriptures were all in the mind of God before they were written down? Do you hesitate to accept it as truth that all the details in the life and character, ancestry and circumstances of each writer of the Scripture was so carefully planned and formed by God that the language was God's language, the vocabulary was God's vocabulary, the feelings and thoughts were God's thoughts, even though God made them also the thoughts and words and feelings sometimes of the men who wrote them? Well, you are still going to have to deal with the plain truth so emphatically stated in the Bible. It is God's Word, not man's. The words themselves are "not...the words which man's wisdom teacheth, but which the Holy Ghost teacheth." In the Scriptures, Jesus Christ said, "Every word...proceedeth out of the mouth of God" (Matt. 4:4). No Christian has a right to make any concession limiting the absolute perfect quality of the Scriptures as word for word given from God.

CHAPTER X

GOD PUT HIS STYLE INTO THE PROPHETS

I. BUT BIBLE PENMEN WERE CALLED LONG BE-
FORE THEY WERE BORN

  1. We Find That God Regularly Prepared From Birth,
     and Before, the Men He Would Use

  2. The Selection of a Moses or a Paul to Write Scripture
     Was No Afterthought

  3. God Declares That He Called, Ordained and Prepared
     Isaiah, Jeremiah and Paul Before They Were Born, to
     Write Scripture

II. BENJAMIN B. WARFIELD WROTE EXTENSIVELY
ON THIS MATTER

  1. God's "Physical, Intellectual, Spiritual" Preparation of
     Bible Writers "Attended Them," Even "Their Remote
     Ancestors," Says Dr. Warfield

  2. So God Put in the Writers the Qualities He Wanted in
     Scripture

  3. God Controlled History, Prepared the Matters of Which
     the Bible Would Speak

III. HOW EASY IT IS TO SEE, THEN, THAT THE
VARYING STYLE AND LANGUAGE AND TESTI-
MONIES OF THE MEN WHO WROTE THE BIBLE
WERE SO PREPARED THAT THEY ARE DEFI-
NITELY GOD'S FIRST AND MEN'S SECONDARILY

IV. THIS TRUTH SETTLES MANY DIFFICULTIES

  1. The Paradox of Men's Words Being Really God's
     Words Is Solved

GOD PUT HIS STYLE INTO
THE PROPHETS

Since God knew ahead of time every individual who would trust Him when they hear the Gospel and planned the details of their being called and justified and glorified, it is not surprising that He would select and prepare His prophets long ahead of time. And so we learn He did.

I think surely we can all agree that the infinite God is capable of infinite variety in style and language. We should not be surprised to find that God Himself formulated the style, the viewpoint, the vocabulary, and even the situations involved, in the writing of the Bible.

I. BUT BIBLE PENMEN WERE CALLED
LONG BEFORE THEY WERE BORN

It is rather foolish and shortsighted to suppose that, wanting to make a revelation, God suddenly looked around and seized upon some man and so of necessity limited Himself by the vocabulary and style of that man He happened to select. That ignores the far ahead predestination that God had selected certain men and that He would plan them for His work.

1. We Find That God Regularly Prepared From Birth,
and Before, the Men He Would Use

Think how God prepared Samuel: given in answer to prayer to a devoted and godly mother, reared in the Temple and miraculously protected from going, under Eli, into the wildness and sin of Eli's children, becoming a mighty prophet of God. Did not God prepare every detail of Samuel's life?

And did He not so plan the life of Samson, announcing the child's birth before he was born to Samson's mother and father, telling how the child must be reared?

Did God not plan every detail of the life of John the Baptist, from the angelic announcement of his birth, his life as a separated Nazarite, and his foreordained and prophesied ministry as a forerunner of the Saviour? Did not God so prepare Moses, select his environment, make the man?

Is it surprising that Isaiah was called by name before he was born, polished like a shaft in God's quiver?

That should not surprise us because God had the same Isaiah mention by name the emperor Cyrus in Isaiah 44:28 and Isaiah 45:1 some two hundred years before he was born. And in I Kings 13:2 King Josiah was mentioned by name three hundred years before his birth.

To the glory of God, may I humbly say that I consider, moved by a thousand evidences, that God had His hand on me before I was born. My father and my mother prayed that God would make me a preacher. My mother died before I was six, and nineteen years later I read one of her letters to her sister in which she called me her "preacher boy." God deepened my heart during my motherless years and gave me compassion. He matured me by poverty and hard work. He built in character in my rearing by a godly and strict father. As discipline He put about me wild horses, college football, the army, college teaching and coaching, voice and speech training. In uncounted ways God was molding me — my attitudes, my vocabulary, my experiences. Through strange channels God put a few remarkable books in my hands which molded my life. A few remarkable people influenced me. God was answering the prayer of my father and my mother and was preparing me to be the preacher, the evangelist, the Bible prophet He wanted me to be.

Did God do less than this for any man that He set apart to write part of the Bible from before his birth? God notes the fall of every sparrow. He clothes every wild flower in beauty.

His angels camp round about His own day and night.

2. The Selection of a Moses or a Paul to Write Scripture Was No Afterthought

If God foreknew everyone who would trust Him for salvation and determine that that one should be called, then justified and later glorified, did God give no attention to the formation of character and language and personality of those who would write the Bible? Bible writers used the style God had created in them to write the words He gave, had planned long before. When the word, already settled forever in Heaven, was written down, the words of God in the style God had planned for them became written Scripture.

Dr. Loraine Boettner, Reformed theologian, says:

And back of that we are to remember that throughout the entire life of the prophet the providential control of God had been preparing him with the particular talents, education and experience which would be needed for the message which he was to give. This providential preparation of the prophets, which gave them the proper spiritual, intellectual and physical background, must, indeed have had its beginning in their remote ancestors. The result was that the right men were brought to the right places at the right times, and wrote the particular books or gave the particular messages which were designed for them. When God wanted to give His people a history of their early beginnings, He prepared a Moses to write it. When He wanted to give them the lofty and worshipful poetry of the psalms, He prepared a David with poetic imagination. And since Christianity in its very nature would demand logical statement, He prepared a Paul, giving him a logical mind and the appropriate religious background which would enable him to set it forth in that manner. In this natural way God so prepared the various writers of Scripture that with the appropriate assistance of His directing and illuminating Spirit they freely and spontaneously wrote what He wished as He wished and when He wished. Thus the prophet was fitted to the message, and the message was suited to the prophet. Thus also the distinctive literary style of each writer was preserved, and each writer did a work which no one else was equipped to do. [1]

---

1. *The Inspiration of the Scriptures,* pp. 40,41.

3. God Declares That He Called, Ordained and Prepared Isaiah, Jeremiah, and Paul Before They Were Born, to Write Scripture

Does Isaiah have exalted imagery, a deep-moving language with heights of eloquence and sharpness of rebuke? Isaiah said, "The Lord hath called me from the womb; from the bowels of my mother hath he made mention of my name. And he hath made my mouth like a sharp sword; in the shadow of his hand hath he hid me, and made me a polished shaft; in his quiver hath he hid me" (Isa. 49:1,2). Again he said, "And now, saith the Lord that formed me from the womb to be his servant, to bring Jacob again to him, Though Israel be not gathered, yet shall I be glorious in the eyes of the Lord, and my God shall be my strength" (Isa. 49:5).

It was God who made the mouth of Isaiah like a sharp sword and made his words like a polished shaft of an arrow in the quiver of God. Yes, Isaiah was hid in the quiver of God, was formed and prepared in the womb to be God's servant, to bring the seed of Jacob to Him. If God made Isaiah, He made his language, his viewpoints, his vocabulary.

Not only Isaiah but from before his birth Jeremiah was prepared for his prophetic ministry and to be a penman of God. Jeremiah 1:4 and 5 says: "Then the word of the Lord came unto me, saying, Before I formed thee in the belly I knew thee; and before thou camest forth out of the womb I sanctified thee, and I ordained thee a prophet unto the nations." He was set apart and ordained to the job before he was born! It is not out of character, then, that in verse 9 of the same chapter we read, "Then the Lord put forth his hand, and touched my mouth. And the Lord said unto me, Behold, I have put my words in thy mouth."

Suppose Jeremiah had a style. It was God's style, built in him through the preparing hand of God in all his years from before he was born! Ah, that seems to have been God's plan always with His prophets. In Galatians 1:15 and 16 the Apostle Paul is inspired to say, "But when it pleased God, who separated me from my mother's womb, and called me by his grace, To reveal his Son in me, that I might preach him among the heathen; immediately I conferred not with flesh and blood."

In view of other similar Scriptures, do we not understand this

Scripture to mean that at the birth of the baby who was to become the Apostle Paul, God had already planned Paul's ministry of preaching and writing the Word? We are certain that
Paul was under God's hand long before his call to preach! And
we may be sure that the entire ministry of Paul was carefully
planned out by the Lord ahead of time. So the Lord could
tell Ananias about Paul, "...for he is a chosen vessel unto me,
to bear my name before the Gentiles, and kings, and the children
of Israel: For I will shew him how great things he must suffer
for my name's sake" (Acts 9:15,16).

Can you not see that the character, the experiences, the emotions, the viewpoint and vocabulary of the men who wrote the
Bible were formed by the hand of God in detail to fit them to
write down the words He would give them?

II. BENJAMIN B. WARFIELD WROTE EXTENSIVELY ON THIS MATTER

In Warfield's book, *The Inspiration and Authority of the
Bible*, he mentions this truth, that God formed the men Himself
with their peculiarities and put them in their circumstances in
which they would write what He gave them to write, and so that
it would represent men but would originate with God. Although
the words and often the thoughts would partially fit the men,
they would be always wholly God's thoughts and God's words.
We give several quotations here.

1. God's "Physical, Intellectual, Spiritual" Preparation of Bible Writers "Attended Them," Even "Their Re- mote Ancestors," Says Dr. Warfield

Warfield says:

> And there is the preparation of the men to write these books to
> be considered, a preparation physical, intellectual, spiritual,
> which must have attended them throughout their whole lives,
> and, indeed, must have had its beginning in their remote an-
> cestors, and the effect of which was to bring the right men to
> the right places at the right times, with the right endowments,
> impulses, acquirements, to write just the books which were
> designed for them. When "inspiration," technically so called, is

superinduced on lines of preparation like these, it takes on quite a different aspect from that which it bears when it is thought of as an isolated action of the Divine Spirit operating out of all relation to historical processes.[2]

The above statement by Warfield is also given verbatim in the *International Standard Bible Encyclopaedia*, page 1480, on the topic of inspiration and there he continues in the same paragraph:

> Representations are sometimes made as if, when God wished to produce sacred books which would incorporate His will — a series of letters like those of Paul, for example — He was reduced to the necessity of going down to earth and painfully scrutinizing the men He found there, seeking anxiously for the one who, on the whole, promised best for His purpose; and then violently forcing the material He wished expressed through him, against his natural bent, and with as little loss from his recalcitrant characteristics as possible. Of course, nothing of the sort took place. If God wished to give His people a series of letters like Paul's, He prepared a Paul to write them, and the Paul He brought to the task was a Paul who spontaneously would write just such letters.[3]

2. So God Put in the Writers the Qualities He Wanted in Scripture

Back to Warfield's book again:

> As light that passes through the colored glass of a cathedral window, we are told, is light from heaven, but is stained by the tints of the glass through which it passes; so any word of God which is passed through the mind and soul of a man must come out discolored by the personality through which it is given, and just to that degree ceases to be the pure word of God. But what if this personality has itself been formed by God into precisely the personality it is, for the express purpose of communicating to the word given through it just the coloring which it gives it? What if the colors of the stained-glass window have been designed by the architect for the express purpose of giving to the light that floods the cathedral precisely the tone and quality it receives from them? What if the word of God that comes to His people is framed by God into the word of God it

---

2. *The Inspiration and Authority of the Bible*, p. 155.
3. *The International Standard Bible Encyclopaedia*, Vol. 3, p. 1480.

is, precisely by means of the qualities of the men formed by Him for the purpose, through which it is given?[4]

We know that "the prophecy came not in old time by the will of man: but holy men of God spake as they were moved by the Holy Ghost." So the writers were not the *means* of forming the Scriptures in the sense of origin, but they were the *channels* through which God breathed out the Scriptures. And Warfield, wise and devoted scholar that he was, saw that God prepared the men, the channels. He says again:

> Or consider how a psalmist would be prepared to put into moving verse a piece of normative religious experience: how he would be born with just the right quality of religious sensibility, of parents through whom he should receive just the right hereditary bent, and from whom he should get precisely the right religious example and training, in circumstances of life in which his religious tendencies should be developed precisely on right lines; how he would be brought through just the right experiences to quicken in him the precise emotions he would be called upon to express, and finally would be placed in precisely the exigencies which would call out their expression. [5]

3. God Controlled History, Prepared the Matters of Which the Bible Would Speak

And Warfield calls attention to the fact also that God controlled history and thus prepared the matters about which God's Word given through these men would speak. He reminds us about God's dealing with Israel and, "Now all these things happened unto them for ensamples: and they are written for our admonition" (I Cor. 10:11).

Warfield reminds us that God controlled the conditions around the Apostle Paul to fit in with the Scriptures he would write. And Paul wrote in II Corinthians 1:4-6 of God:

"Who comforteth us in all our tribulation, that we may be able to comfort them which are in any trouble, by the comfort wherewith we ourselves are comforted of God.   For as the sufferings of Christ abound in us, so our consolation also aboundeth by Christ. And whether we be afflicted, it is for your

---

4. *The Inspiration and Authority of the Bible*, pp. 155,156.
5. *The Inspiration and Authority of the Bible*, p. 157.

consolation and salvation, which is effectual in the enduring of the same sufferings which we also suffer: or whether we be comforted, it is for your consolation and salvation. "

God prepared Paul's experiences so He could have Paul write of them.

Dr. Lewis Sperry Chafer goes along with Warfield on this matter very wisely. Chafer tells us how God prepared ahead of time even the languages in which the Scripture would be written.

> It is reasonable to believe that those languages in which the Oracles of God were written, were, by divine supervision, being developed through the natural processes by which all languages emerge, certain words were divinely introduced and their meaning determined and preserved with a view to the all-important service which they would render and the precise truth they would convey in the written Word of God. It is equally conceivable that certain words would need to be immediately coined which would indicate aspects of supernatural relationships and undertakings that could have had little or no occasion of expression before and at such times when the language in question was serving only as the enunciation of mundane things and that which is born of mere human speculation. The word θεόπνευστος appears but the once in the New Testament, and probably not at all in profane Greek. On the surface of the problem, it is presumable that nothing exactly similar to the idea of God-breathed, written Oracles had arisen among the Hellenistic peoples which called for expression. It is a fair assumption that this crucial word is of divine origin being fashioned by God with a view to the elucidation of a conception which is not only foreign to the range of things human, but supreme in the range of things divine. Thus the New Testament writers found a goodly number of words divinely prepared and introduced which were capable of expansion in their meaning in order to convey truths which had been heretofore unrevealed. The student will do well to note at this point the many compounds with Θεός, Χριστός, and Πνεῦμα, which his vocabulary affords.[6]

The Scriptures were already written in Heaven, settled forever: God controlled the course of history, prepared the nations in which Scripture should be written, prepared the languages in which they would be written, prepared the prophets who would write them and then, in a certain fullness of time, He had these prepared men write in the prepared language, the Scriptures which had existed from before the world began!

---

6. *Systematic Theology*, Vol. 1, pp. 77,78.

Speaking of plenary inspiration, Hodge says:

> This doctrine involves nothing out of analogy with the ordinary operations of God. We believe that He is everywhere present in the material world, and controls the operations of natural causes. We know that He causes the grass to grow, and gives rain and fruitful seasons. We believe that He exercises a like control over the minds of men, turning them as the rivers of water are turned. All religion, natural and revealed, is founded on the assumption of this providential government of God. Besides this, we believe in the gracious operations of his Spirit, by which He works in the hearts of his people to will and to do; we believe that faith, repentance, and holy living are due to the ever-present influence of the Holy Spirit. If, then, this wonder-working God everywhere operates in nature and in grace, why should it be deemed incredible that holy men should speak as they were moved by the Holy Ghost, so that they should say just what He would have them say, so that their words should be his words. [7]

Thus we can see that since God prepared men, their environment, their natures, He could have them write His words which He gave through their own consciousness and personality.

And so again we quote from Warfield:

> It lies equally on the face of the New Testament allusions to the subject that its writers understood that the preparation of men to become vehicles of God's message to man was not of yesterday, but had its beginnings in the very origin of their being. The call by which Paul, for example, was made an apostle of Jesus Christ was sudden and apparently without antecedents; but it is precisely this Paul who reckons this call as only one step in a long process, the beginnings of which antedated his own existence: "But when it was the good pleasure of God, who separated me, even from my mother's womb, and called me through his grace, to reveal his Son in me" (Gal. 1. 15. 16; cf. Jer. 1. 5; Isa. 49. 1.5). The recognition by the writers of the New Testament of the experiences of God's grace, which had been vouchsafed to them as an integral element in their fitting to be the bearers of His gospel to others, finds such pervasive expression that the only difficulty is to select from the mass the most illustrative passages. [8]

---

7. *Systematic Theology*, Vol. 1, p. 167.
8. *The Inspiration and Authority of the Bible*, p. 159.

III. HOW EASY IT IS TO SEE, THEN, THAT THE VARYING STYLE AND LANGUAGE AND TESTIMONIES OF THE MEN WHO WROTE THE BIBLE WERE SO PREPARED THAT THEY ARE DEFINITELY GOD'S FIRST AND MEN'S SECONDARILY

So in time of trial, God would have David call on the Lord and find deliverance and then have David write, "This poor man cried, and the Lord heard him, and saved him out of all his troubles" (Ps. 34:6). God would prepare Luke and all the surrounding circumstances and his own heart that Luke would set out to write the Gospel, saying, "It seemed good to me also..." (Luke 1:3), because it seemed good to God first, and God prepared Luke's heart for the understanding of all these things "from above" (*anothen*).

God arranged the imprisonment of Paul in, we suppose, the Mamertine Prison at Rome and had Paul write to Timothy, "Demas hath forsaken me, having loved this present world" (II Tim. 4:10). Oh, but God meant to press upon millions of readers the loneliness and reproach that properly comes in serving God with all one's heart and that those who pay such a price to serve God could expect to lose friends and loved ones less full of zeal and sacrificial devotion than Paul. And God arranged that Paul would remember and need "the cloke that I left at Troas with Carpus...and the books, but especially the parchments," and would ask Timothy to bring them (II Tim. 4:13).

The circumstances of the Bible writers? God prepared them. The heart-attitude and emotions of the writers? God arranged that, too. And the vocabularies, the style, the idiosyncrasies of various writers? Yes, God planned all that so that each one was chosen before he was born and fitted to be the instrument God wanted to use. The varying styles are all God's styles in the Bible. God made the men and made the styles, and used them according to plan.

IV. THIS TRUTH SETTLES MANY DIFFICULTIES

If we understand that the Scriptures are part of God's works, of which it is said, "Known unto God are all his works from the beginning of the world" (Acts 15:18), and that the Scriptures were all known to God before they were breathed out to be written down by God's penmen: if we understand that God prepared these writers long ahead of time, every detail of their lives and personalities so that the variations in style and language and conditions are from God, it will solve many perplexities about the underlying inspiration of the Scriptures.

1. The Paradox of Men's Words Being Really God's Words Is Solved

Where then is that troublesome paradox that the Scriptures claim to be the very words of God in the original autographs, but they are in the words of men also?   Since God prepared the men, the vocabularies, the feelings, the circumstances, then it was no afterthought of God to select men and be obliged to let them pick their own words.   No, no.   Both the men and the circumstances and the language of Scriptures are all prepared ahead of time by the Lord.

Now, why not simply believe that God gave the very words of Scriptures, as the Bible so plainly and repeatedly says?   Why not accept the full import of the Bible statements that the words of Scripture were breathed out by God and that the Scripture is given "not in words which man's wisdom teacheth, but which the Holy Ghost teacheth" (I Cor. 2:13)?

2. No Need, Then, to Compromise, to Explain Human Element

Certainly this truth that the Word of God was all settled in Heaven and that men who wrote the Scriptures were planned for and prepared from the time before their birth, answers all the compromises of evangelicals who are timid and would concede so much to please unbelieving liberals.   One says the creation account is a beautiful myth, not necessarily true in historical detail.   One says that it is figurative and allegorical to impress in poetic language that God in some way created things, possibly by evolution! One says that the virgin birth is not necessarily literally true; it was just a primitive and poetic way of teaching the incarnation!   One says that the Bible thus is true morally and religiously but not necessarily true in science or historical facts.   One may say, like Ramm, that the Bible writers simply tell of God's dealings but that what they wrote was limited by the culture of their times, etc.[9]

Or, one may say, as did Orr, that genealogical lists and records may have been copied into the Bible, mistakes and all, as Bible writers found them.[10]

All these really are saying that the Bible is not perfect, is not errorless, is not word-for-word from God in the original autographs.   And because people do not see that the Word of God was settled forever in Heaven before it was written down and they do not see that all the details in the lives of the men who wrote the Scriptures were prepared by God, then they feel that they must give some human explanation of the human color in the Scriptures, that they must allow the men to select their own words under some kind of divine supervision.   But that is not what the Bible says.

Whatever variance in style and vocabulary you find in the great books of the Bible, they are all the style of God, the vocabulary of God which God Himself formed in His prophets for the purpose intended.   Whatever words they wrote they were "not in the words which man's wisdom teacheth, but which the Holy Ghost teacheth" (I Cor. 2:13).

3. God's Instruments Express Themselves Little or Much but Wrote God's Words Perfectly

Men had some part, but always it was the part God Himself gave.   However, man's part was less than God's part and subject to God's part.

If men used their own vocabulary and style, it was because God selected that vocabulary and style. What men wrote, they understood little or much but never perfectly.   The inspiration was in an inspired word, not in inspired men.

We conclude, then, that in every case, whatever the vocabulary or style of language in which men of God wrote as they were moved by the Holy Ghost, it was God's language, God's style,

9. *The Christian View of Science and Scripture*, p. 71.
10. *Revelation and Inspiration*, pp. 163,164,165.

God's vocabulary. Isaiah's words might have been his own words, but they were God's words first. The flowing language of the Gospel according to Luke may be in Luke's words, but they were in God's words first. God formed the prophets and God formed their language and vocabulary. God gave the very words which He had already determined to use and had put in their own language.

So Luke could say, "It seemed good to me also" to write the account of things that he understood perfectly "from above." But it seemed good to God first and then good to Luke. So Paul wanted his cloke against the winter chill of the Mamertine Dungeon in that second imprisonment just before he was beheaded. God, who put the words in his mouth, wanted not simply that cloke, but He wanted millions of readers to know what it means to serve God at any cost.

God put His style in the men, then gave the Scriptures through the men He had prepared in the historical setting He made.

CHAPTER XI

SOME AMAZING CASES ILLUSTRATING INSPIRATION:
WHAT THEY SHOW

I. CONSIDER IN PARTICULAR CASES THE DIVINE
   REVELATION AND INSPIRATION

   1. In Some Cases No Human Element Intervened in God's
      Revelation
   2. Consider the Words of God Through Balaam's Ass
   3. Consider the Prophet Balaam, a False Prophet Speaking
      God's Words
   4. Consider Caiaphas, the Unconverted High Priest Who
      Worked to Have Jesus Crucified
   5. Consider the Old Testament Prophets Who Did Not
      Understand What They Had Written
   6. Consider the Apostle Paul

II. WHAT THESE CASES OF INSPIRATION SHOW

   1. Human Authorship Is Not Always "Present Without
      Impairment" or Limitation in Scripture
   2. Bible Writers Did Not Always Understand What They
      Wrote by Inspiration
   3. The Bible Writers Only Partly Represent Their Own
      Feelings and Thoughts
   4. There Is Only One Kind of Divine Inspiration — All
      Scripture Is Inspired to the Same Perfect Degree and
      Quality

SOME AMAZING CASES ILLUSTRATING INSPIRATION: WHAT THEY SHOW

I. CONSIDER IN PARTICULAR CASES THE DIVINE REVELATION AND INSPIRATION

In studying what part men had in writing the Scriptures, it is fair and proper to study particular cases of divine revelation which, being written down, we will call revelation.

The Scriptures plainly claim complete or plenary inspiration of all its parts. There are no differing degrees in the inspiration of various parts of the Bible. All parts are said to be "true from the beginning," and "every word of God is pure," and "For ever, O Lord, thy word is settled in heaven." And the Word of God is "incorruptible," it "liveth and abideth for ever." And whatever particular cases we study of how God's Word came through some agency will surely fit this pattern which God Himself has set. It will have the same perfect quality of inspiration, infallibility. In every case, it will be the Word of God. We must conclude that all the inspired Scripture is as perfectly, completely God's words with a prophet's participation or without it.

And it will be "in the words which the Holy Ghost teacheth."

1. In Some Cases No Human Element Intervened in God's Revelation

In Exodus 20:1 we read, "And God spake all these words," and then follows the Ten Commandments spoken aloud from Heaven. There were wonderful manifestations. The astonished people were overpowered with awe and fear. And in Exodus

20:18,19, following the quotation of the words God spoke in Heaven, we read, "And all the people saw the thunderings, and the lightnings, and the noise of the trumpet, and the mountain smoking: and when the people saw it, they removed, and stood afar off. And they said unto Moses, Speak thou with us, and we will hear: but let not God speak with us, lest we die."

In this case, God did not speak to Moses in particular to have him write down the commandments. They were spoken aloud from Heaven so that a nation of people heard them and trembled and they were accompanied with evidences of how awful and authoritative and eternal was this Word of God revealed to them.

Again in Exodus 31:18 we read that God "gave unto Moses, when he had made an end of communing with him upon mount Sinai, two tables of testimony, tables of stone, written with the finger of God."

Now, taking for granted that when a Scripture here claims to give the exact words of the Ten Commandments, spoken by God, the same commandments written on tables of stone and with the finger of God — let us say then that there was no human color, no human characteristics, no human penmen between God and the people when God gave them His Word.

Again, when Belshazzar, the king in Babylon with a thousand of his lords and wives and concubines, were at a drunken feast, "in the same hour came forth fingers of a man's hand, and wrote over against the candlestick upon the plaister of the wall of the king's palace: and the king saw the part of the hand that wrote" (Dan. 5:5). And Daniel read the words to the king, "And this is the writing that was written, MENE, MENE, TEKEL, UPHARSIN." Here was verbal inspiration, plenary inspiration. The word was God's word, not man's. But is not that exactly what is claimed for all Scripture? It seems obvious, then, that in perfect and complete inspiration, there may be no human element at all.

That seems to be true about the case when God spoke from Heaven at the baptism of Jesus and again on the mount of transfiguration, for example. Would that not be true in the words spoken by Jesus to Saul, converted on the way to Damascus?

Would it not be true in the messages that angels brought to men whether to Joshua, or to the mother of Samson, or to

Jacob who wrestled with the angel at the Brook Jabbok? Would not the human element be lacking entirely when the angel spoke to Paul on shipboard in the storm at sea? Or when at Corinth he was comforted and promised that no one should lay hands on him there (Acts 18:10)? Is it not true also about the words of the angel to Joseph, or to Mary and to the angels at Bethlehem? Granting that the Bible gives, as it claims to give, the exact words of angels and the exact words of God when He spoke in these cases, it seems we must say that God can give perfect revelation, and sometimes did, without any human participation except to hear it or to read it. And did not God speak directly to Hagar, Sarah's servant?

2. Consider the Words of God Through Balaam's Ass

In Numbers 22:28 we read, "And the Lord opened the mouth of the ass, and she said unto Balaam, What have I done unto thee, that thou hast smitten me these three times?"

Again in verse 30, "And the ass said unto Balaam, Am not I thine ass, upon which thou hast ridden ever since I was thine unto this day? was I ever wont to do so unto thee? And he said, Nay."

"The Lord opened the mouth of the ass." So I understand that God arranged what the donkey would say. The words were God's words, though they came through the mouth of the ass.

I think they represented the ass, too. The donkey said what a donkey might say if she could talk. She protested the beating which she did not deserve. Why should she be beaten because she stopped before an angel? Didn't Balaam know that there was something miraculous there? Had she, the donkey, ever acted so before? So, the words represented the donkey but they represented God and they originated with God. They were on the initiative of God, not on the initiative of the donkey.

No one could say that the donkey chose the words and that they were in the donkey's regular style of speech and colored by the donkey's state of mind or devotion or viewpoint. The words were the donkey's words, but they were God's words first. They were breathed out from God.

So, then, revelation from God, when written down as inspiration, is simply breathed out from God. The thought is

God's and the words are God's words, no matter whether He uses a donkey or man.

Now the inspiration of this donkey was complete, perfect. It was *plenary* inspiration. It was *verbal* inspiration. But was the donkey any more inspired than the Apostle Paul or Moses when they wrote what God gave them to write in the Bible?

3. Consider the Prophet Balaam, a False Prophet Speaking God's Words

Balak the king offered him great riches and honor if he would pronounce a curse against the children of Israel. Balaam may have been a saved man, and at any rate he was certainly a prophet of God and God had put words in his mouth before. Balak sent word to Balaam, "...for I wot that he whom thou blessest is blessed, and he whom thou cursest is cursed" (Num. 22:6). Numbers 22:18 says, "And Balaam answered and said unto the servants of Balak, If Balak would give me his house full of silver and gold, I cannot go beyond the word of the Lord my God, to do less or more." Later, when Balaam wickedly kept trying to go, verse 35 tells us, "And the angel of the Lord said unto Balaam, Go with the men: but only the word that I shall speak unto thee, that thou shalt speak." And in verse 38, "Balaam said unto Balak, Lo, I am come unto thee: have I now any power at all to say any thing? the word that God putteth in my mouth, that shall I speak."

After there were built seven altars and on them Balaam had offered seven rams and seven lambs, he went to curse Israel but instead God put blessing in his mouth for His people who had come out of Egypt.

Next, King Balak again built seven altars and Balaam offered seven bullocks and seven rams. And again, when he would have cursed Israel, God blessed them through his mouth. The words were God's words. And so it happened the third time. Then Balaam pronounced great blessing on Israel, as we see in Numbers 24:15-24. Here he foretold the future. He foretold the coming of Christ, the "Star out of Jacob, and a Sceptre shall rise out of Israel." And he told of the reign of Christ on earth and destruction of Moab.

Now consider this divine revelation given through the mouth

of a man who did not want to give it, a man who had compromised with evil and was not allowed to say what he wanted to say for gain.

His prophecy did not involve any of Balaam's own desires. It covered matters about which he could not have known, and no investigation or no eyewitnesses could have given him the material.

So, in Numbers 23:16 we read, "And the Lord met Balaam, and put a word in his mouth, and said, Go again unto Balak, and say thus." Detailed dictation of what Balaam should say was given him by the Lord.

But remember all Scripture is inspired alike. All of it is settled forever in Heaven. All of it is incorruptible. It was of all the Scripture that Jesus said, "The scripture cannot be broken." So there are no degrees in inspiration. Balaam was perfectly inspired just as his ass was perfectly inspired. The words were God's words. But is God more particular and careful in breathing out His words through Balaam than through the Apostle Paul or Moses? Surely not.

4. Consider Caiaphas, the Unconverted High Priest Who Worked to Have Jesus Crucified

The chief priests and Pharisees had a council as to what they would do with Jesus, who had worked so many miracles, and they said:

"*If we let him thus alone, all men will believe on him: and the Romans shall come and take away both our place and nation. And one of them, named Caiaphas, being the high priest that same year, said unto them, Ye know nothing at all, Nor consider that it is expedient for us, that one man should die for the people, and that the whole nation perish not. And this spake he not of himself: but being high priest that year, he prophesied that Jesus should die for that nation. . . .*" — John 11:48-51.

Here Caiaphas, because he was high priest and ought to be able to speak for God, was given a prophecy. He prophesied the substitutionary death of Jesus Christ as an atonement for all the people. That was not what he meant. He meant to save Israel from subjugation by the Romans, but God meant that Christ would be an atoning substitute for the sins of the world. Here an unsaved man, a wicked man with a murderous heart, foretold the atoning death of Christ. In the principal meaning, it did not represent his viewpoint. He entered not at all into the blessing of it. Yet it was perfect inspiration, and meaning something else, he spoke this prophecy!

Here is a case again of divine inspiration where human wisdom, or devotion, or investigation, or even human preference had no part in the wonderful prophecy given. It was God's Word, given in God's words, though in Caiaphas' words, too. So inspiration may have much or little of man's mind and heart.

5. Consider the Old Testament Prophets Who Did Not Understand What They Had Written

In I Peter 1:10-12, we have a wonderful account of Old Testament prophets searching diligently and pondering over the Scriptures they themselves had written down, trying to find the meaning and realizing that the message was not just for them but for a later generation.

"Of which salvation the prophets have inquired and searched diligently, who prophesied of the grace that should come unto you: Searching what, or what manner of time the Spirit of Christ which was in them did signify, when it testified beforehand the sufferings of Christ, and the glory that should follow. Unto whom it was revealed, that not unto themselves, but unto us they did minister the things, which are now reported unto you by them that have preached the gospel unto you with the Holy Ghost sent down from heaven; which things the angels desire to look into."

Make sure you see in this passage the difference between illumination and inspiration.

The Word of God is all breathed out from God, but the human penmen's understanding of the Scripture is only partial — sometimes more, sometimes less, but never perfect. They wrote what they did not understand. So any illumination of their hearts and minds was only partial and incidental. God inspired the words.

6. Consider the Apostle Paul

Paul wrote thirteen of the books of the New Testament, four-teen if we count Hebrews from Paul, as I think we should. It seems probable that Moses who met God face to face, may have understood spiritual things better than anybody else in the Old Testament and that Paul, having been taken up into the third Heaven and seen things that were not lawful to utter, may have understood God better and represented God better than anybody else in the New Testament.

Now, how were the letters of Paul inspired? The answer is they were inspired just like all the other parts of the Bible. They were perfect, breathed out from God; they were settled for-ever in Heaven; were revealed "not in the words which man's wisdom teacheth, but which the Holy Ghost teacheth," as he himself was inspired to write in I Corinthians 2:13.

Consider Paul's letter to the Romans. In Romans 1:9, Paul tells how he prays continually for these people in Rome, "Mak-ing request, if by any means now at length I might have a prosperous journey by the will of God to come unto you." He was expected to come to Rome, but he did not foresee all the trouble involved.

In Romans 15:23,24 he says, "But now having no more place in these parts, and having a great desire these many years to come unto you; Whensoever I take my journey into Spain, I will come to you: for I trust to see you in my journey, and to be brought on my way thitherward by you, if first I be somewhat filled with your company."

"Whensoever I take my journey into Spain!" Did Paul ever go to Spain? I think he did. I believe that this is the very Word of God and that Paul did go to Spain. But not in the way he expected.

Paul did not foresee what God had in mind in his coming to Rome, that he would be arrested, imprisoned, spend two years in Caesarea in prison and at last be brought as a prisoner, be shipwrecked on the island of Malta, and then to Rome, con-fined.

Now he says, "Whensoever I take my journey into Spain." When will that be? Evidently God has a second imprisonment in mind. I think that after two years in his own hired house, Paul was probably freed from prison. He wrote Philemon,

"But withal prepare me also a lodging: for I trust that through your prayers I shall be given unto you" (Philem. 22). And from prison in Rome, Paul wrote the Philippians, "Nevertheless to abide in the flesh is more needful for you. And having this confidence, I know that I shall abide and continue with you all for your furtherance and joy of faith." So, we believe Paul was released and visited Philemon and the Philippians as he had promised and made his journey to Spain. On his voyage the second time to Rome, he left Trophimus at Miletum sick (II Tim. 4:20).

So, by devious ways, Paul came to Rome first and went by them later to Spain. But he did not foresee and did not understand further all that God had in those short verses that God had inspired him to write. He participated but only in the degree that God Himself uttered the words that were, in part, the revelation of Paul's heart thoughts. And his part was secondary. All the meaning of the Scriptures was in the mind of God and God had Paul write them down. God put some of them in the words that would represent Paul as well as God. But Paul's part was incidental and secondary, never original. And so Paul could say, "Which things also we speak, not in the words which man's wisdom teacheth, but which the Holy Ghost teacheth; comparing spiritual things with spiritual" (I Cor. 2:13).

If the Apostle Paul were here on earth today preaching the Gospel, would he already know all that the Scriptures mean in those thirteen or fourteen epistles which he wrote? No, he would not! He would have divine illumination to understand enough of the Scriptures for his present need and more and more as he studied and prayed and as he had God's favor, just as we may have. But illumination is relative, partial, imperfect. To know what they meant, Paul would have to study the Scriptures he himself wrote. And even then he would have less than the infinite perfection of understanding which God Himself has in those Scriptures.

So Paul, chosen from his mother's womb to be a prophet and apostle of God, and 'counted worthy' to be in God's ministry (I Tim. 1:12), was used to write inspired Scripture. But it represented Paul only as God put Paul into the matter and as God provided Paul the words, feeling and viewpoint. But always the eternal Word of God came from God to men and through men to men.

II. WHAT THESE CASES OF INSPIRATION SHOW

The cases mentioned above are simply examples of the way God inspired men to speak His words or to write His words. Dr. Lewis Sperry Chafer writes in detail under the heading "DUAL AUTHORSHIP," saying there are four primary opinions about inspiration: "(a) The Bible is divine authorship almost exclusively; (b) The Bible is human authorship almost exclusively; (c) The Bible is in some parts almost exclusively divine and in other parts almost exclusively human; and (d) The divine and human authorship are both without impairment to either, wholly present in every word from the first to the last." [1]

Note carefully "(d)" that we emphasize because he does: "*The divine and human authorship are both without impairment to either, wholly present in every word from the first to the last.*"   And then he says, "The final of these four classifications is here declared to be the true representation of the fact of inspiration." No, that is a mistake.

1. Human Authorship Is Not Always "Wholly Present," "Without Impairment" or Limitation in Scripture

There is often present in Scriptures both divine and human authorship but not always.   So to say that "without impairment" the human authorship is "wholly present in every word from the first to the last" is simply not true. The human authorship was not present in the Ten Commandments which God spoke from Heaven (Exod. 20:1), then recorded on tables of stone (Exod. 31:18).   Human authorship was not wholly present in the writings of the fingers of a man's hand on the walls of Belshazzar's palace (Dan. 5:5).   And certainly the human authorship was impaired or limited in some strange way in the case of the prophecies of Balaam and the prophecies of Caiaphas.   And I think that we would have to say that every time any man of God wrote as Scripture some of the things which he did not understand, in that degree the human authorship was impaired or limited.

---

1. *Systematic Theology*, Vol. 1, pp. 72 ff.

To put the human element and the divine element on such an equal basis is not what the Bible claims for itself. There is always some limitations and control of the human authorship and in some cases the Scriptures do not represent men at all, and in other places only in some limited degree so that Paul was inspired to say to the Thessalonians that "when ye received the word of God which ye heard of us, ye received it not as the word of men, but as it is in truth, the word of God" (I Thess. 2:13). Thus Peter was inspired likewise to say, "For the prophecy came not in old time by the will of man: but holy men of God spake as they were moved by the Holy Ghost" (II Pet. 1:21). God makes it very clear that He usually used men in writing the Scriptures. He also makes it clear that it was not according to their own will, and that sometimes He could communicate in words and ways where they could not color the Scriptures at all.

2. Bible Writers Did Not Always Understand What They Wrote by Inspiration

We are told particularly in I Peter 1:10-12 that Old Testament prophets who foretold the sufferings of Christ "inquired and searched diligently" trying to understand their own prophecies about the coming death of Christ but could not. So inspiration does not necessarily mean that the writers understand what they write.

How much did Caiaphas, that wicked high priest, understand of the substitutionary death of Christ which he himself foretold (John 11:49-52)? It is certain from the examples given that even Paul and Moses did not always understand the things God inspired them to write. Let us say, then, that inspiration does not require that the writer understand much, or little, or any, of what he wrote.

3. The Bible Writers Only Partly Represent Their Own Feelings and Thoughts

So Luke could say in Luke 1:3, "It seemed good to me also" to write a Gospel. And we are sure that he wrote gladly and with a high degree of participation and understanding but not with perfect understanding, and it is certain that he wrote down things that did not represent his own feelings or thoughts. So in his writings Paul could tell of his own burden for Israel, or his love for his people at Philippi, but we can be sure that Paul did not fathom the depth of the love and concern which God Himself had when He had these things written in Scripture. Certainly Balaam did not write what he wished when he wrote of the blessings God would bring to Israel. Balaam wanted to prophesy the opposite and he did entice Israel to sin with the Midianites and brought a curse upon them and then Balaam died with the enemies of God. So those wonderful prophecies of Balaam represented God but did not represent Balaam. Thus the Scripture was only in part and that a variable part, more or less or none, representing the thoughts and feelings of those who wrote.

4. There Is Only One Kind of Divine Inspiration— All Scripture Is Inspired to the Same Perfect Degree and Quality

Then what wicked Balaam said and what unbelieving Caiaphas said under inspiration was inspired exactly like what God gave Paul or John to write.

In other words, all Scriptures are equally inspired and perfect. Thus inspiration is always alike entirely from God and He chose and prepared men to understand much or little and to participate more or less as He chose in writing down what God gave them to write.

CHAPTER XII

THREE DIVINE-HUMAN THINGS: CHRIST, REGENERATION AND THE SCRIPTURES

I. DIVINE-HUMAN UNION ALIKE IN JESUS CHRIST AND IN SCRIPTURE

II. THERE IS A LIKENESS IN THE WAY GOD MIRACULOUSLY REGENERATES A HUMAN SOUL AND THE WAY HE USED MEN TO WRITE THE BIBLE

III. THESE THREE ARE ALIKE "FROM ABOVE"

1. Christ Came From Above
2. The New Birth Is "From Above"
3. But the Scriptures Are Also "From Above"

IV. ALL THREE OF THESE ARE FROM GOD

1. We Know That Jesus Is Called "the Only Begotten Son of God" in John 3:16
2. But the New Birth, When a Christian Is Born Again, Is From God Also
3. But That Is Just What the Bible Says About the Bible, the Scriptures

V. ALL THESE: CHRIST, THE NEW BIRTH AND THE SCRIPTURES, ARE THE WORK OF THE HOLY SPIRIT THROUGH HUMAN FLESH

1. Christ Conceived as the Holy Christ
2. Christians Are "Born of the Spirit" Too
3. Scriptures Given by "The Spirit of Christ" Also

VI. ALL THESE THREE ARE ALIKE ETERNAL

1. We Learn That Christ Was "in the Beginning...With God" (John 1:1)
2. Likewise, the Born-Again Christian Has Eternal Life
3. But the Word of God Is Eternal Also

VII. CONSIDER HOW THE HUMAN-DIVINE CHRIST ILLUSTRATES THE HUMAN-DIVINE BIBLE

1. Both Are Called the Word of God
2. Both Christ and the Word of God Have a Part in Saving the Sinner
3. Christ and the Word Are Put Together in the Judgment
4. In Incarnation and Inspiration, the Human Only Received What God Gave
5. Whatever Jesus Inherited of a Likeness to Mary, It Was Wholly of God
6. The Body in Which Jesus Appeared Sometimes in the Old Testament Was Probably After the Pattern of the Body God Would Prepare for Jesus for His Incarnation

THREE DIVINE-HUMAN THINGS: CHRIST, REGENERATION AND THE SCRIPTURES

1. In the virgin birth of Christ, He became the God-Man, both man and God.

2. By being "born of the Spirit," the penitent sinner becomes the child of God as well as the child of Adam.

3. When God breathed out (*theopneustos*) the Word of God and had men write it down, the Scriptures thus became the Word of God in the words of men.

By studying these analogies we trust we can better see that as Christ was wholly perfect deity, without sin or fault or limitation, though in human form, so the Word of God is infallibly correct, with even the words from God, though through human penmen.

We should better understand that though a sinner must choose to receive Christ and be saved, yet the miracle of regeneration is God's own work. The trusting sinner becomes a partaker of the divine nature — God's "seed remaineth in him: and he cannot sin" (the new nature, not the old) and that new nature is everlasting. So is the Word of God. Men *receive* the miracle of the new birth, they do not work it, and the product is God's product.

I. DIVINE-HUMAN UNION ALIKE IN JESUS CHRIST AND IN SCRIPTURE

Many years ago Bible-believing people worked out and came to understand and to agree to the theology that Jesus Christ is both man and God, without making Him sinful or limiting Him more than He limited Himself. No Bible believer writes books about Jesus as the result of His human mother and environment. But the kindred truth, that the Bible is through men and the writers somewhat participated in it, yet the Scripture is wholly God-breathed and perfect even to the words in the original autographs and not colored or formed by any human sources, ought to have been worked out and have become solidly known and affirmed long ago. For the Scripture is as clear on the word-for-word perfection of the Scriptures as it is on the perfection of Christ. God was as active and the human element controlled as completely in one case as in the other. Jesus had a human mother, lived in a human environment, but these human factors were all planned of God, and any human or environmental influence was God's influence, planned and controlled of God.

God enlisted the body, the love, the trust, the character of the virgin Mary in bringing His pre-existent Son into this world, yet the humanity of Christ brought no taint, no failure, no lack to the perfect, sinless, eternal Son of God. So God enlisted the personalities, some more and some less, and the thoughts and hopes and fears and opinions and experiences of men through whom He gave the very words of the Scripture, and yet the color of humanity so wonderfully incorporated in the Bible involves no human weakness nor lack nor limitation. As Christ was miraculously perfect and wholly from God, born through a woman and in circumstances which He Himself had planned and prepared long ago, even so the blessed Word of God, the Scriptures, were written by the pen of men and under circumstances and involving emotions, ways of speech and vocabularies which God Himself had planned and prepared long before. Christ is God's own Son. The Bible is God-breathed Scripture.

Dr. Warfield says:

> It has been customary among a certain school of writers to speak of the Scriptures, because thus "inspired," as a Divine-human book, and to appeal to the analogy of Our Lord's Divine-human personality to explain their peculiar qualities as such. The expression calls attention to an important fact, and the analogy holds good a certain distance. There are human and Divine sides to Scripture, and, as we cursorily examine it,

we may perceive in it, alternately, traits which suggest now the one, now the other factor in its origin. [1]

Dr. Lewis Sperry Chafer calls attention to Christ, "the Word," and the Scriptures, "the Word." He says:

> The term Λόγος (**Logos** — 'Word') is used in the New Testament about two hundred times to indicate God's Word written, and seven times to indicate the Son of God—the Living Word of God (John 1:1,14; I John 1:1; 5:7; Rev. 19:13); and it is important to recognize that in either of these forms of the **Logos** both the divine and human elements appear in supernatural union.   These two forms of the **Logos** are subject to various comparisons: They are, alike, the **Truth** (John 14:6; 17:17); **everlasting** (Ps. 119:89; Matt. 24:34,35; I Pet. 1:25); **life** (John 11:25; 14:6; I Pet. 1:23; I John 1:1); **saving** (Acts 16:31; I Cor. 15:2); **purifying** (Titus 2:14; I Pet. 1:22); **sanctifying** (John 17: 17; Heb. 10:14); **beget life** (I Pet. 1:23; James 1:18); **judge** (John 5:26,27; 12:48); **glorified** (Rom. 15:9; Acts 13:48).   While theology is the θεολογία (**theologia**, or 'ology of God'), the Λόγος of God is the expression of God—whether it be in Living or Written form.
>
> Basing its confidence on such Scriptures as Luke 1:35 which reports the angel's word to Mary—"That holy thing which shall be born of thee shall be called the Son of God"—, and Hebrews 4:15 where it is said that Christ, the perfect High Priest, was in all points tempted like as we are—sin apart, that is, apart from temptations which arise from a sin nature—, the church has with full justification believed that Christ, the Living Logos, was not only free from the **practice** of sin, but was also free from the sin nature, and that the perfection of His Deity was in no way injured by its union with His humanity.   In like manner and with the same justification, the church has believed that the perfection of God's Word has been preserved, even though written by human authors. [2]

The humanity of Jesus is as obvious as the human element in the Scriptures, but the human element in both was planned and prepared of God long before. As Jesus is the God-man but wholly God, so the Scriptures are wholly divine even in human words and using the personality of men.

In his famous classic, *The Plenary Inspiration of the Holy Scriptures,* Gaussen says:

> It will thus be seen, that this question is of immense importance in its bearing upon the vitality of our faith; and we are entitled

---

1. *The Inspiration and Authority of the Bible,* p. 162.
2. *Systematic Theology,* Vol. 1, pp. 72,73.

to say, that between the two answers that may be made to it, there lies the same great gulf that must have separated two Israelites who might both have seen Jesus Christ in the flesh, and both equally owned him as a prophet; but one of whom looking to his carpenter's dress, his poor fare, his hands inured to labour, and his rustic retinue, believed further, that he was not exempt from error and sin, as an ordinary prophet; whilst the other recognised in him Immanuel, the Lamb of God, the everlasting God, our Righteousness, the King of kings, the Lord of lords. [3]

Did Jesus have eyes like Mary? or a dimple like hers? or her smile or mannerisms? If so, God made it so, not Mary. God made it so in Mary; may have used Mary to make it so in Jesus. As a boy, did Jesus learn from Mary as He "grew in favor with God and man"? God arranged it so, decreed it before the foundation of the world. God could have Jesus look or act or think like His mother Mary without Mary deciding that at all. Just so, God could call Jeremiah or Moses or Isaiah or Paul before they were born and plan the color and individual characteristics which He would have them use when He would give them the words of God-breathed Scripture.

II. THERE IS A LIKENESS IN THE WAY GOD MIRACULOUSLY REGENERATES A HUMAN SOUL AND THE WAY HE USED MEN TO WRITE THE BIBLE

Gaussen calls attention to this likeness between the work of the Holy Spirit in causing the Scriptures to be written and in converting a soul.

> In fact, it is with divine inspiration as with efficacious grace. In the operations of the Holy Ghost while causing the sacred books to be written, and in those of the same divine agent while converting a soul, and causing it to advance in the ways of sanctification, man is in different respects entirely active and entirely passive. God does all there; man does all there; and it may be said for both of these works what St. Paul said of one of them to the Philippians, "It is God that worketh in you to will and to do." Thus you will see that in the Scriptures the same operations are attributed alternately to God and to man. God converts, and it is man that converts himself. God circum-

---

3. *Theopneustia, The Plenary Inspiration of the Holy Scriptures*, p. 12.

cises the heart, God gives a new heart; and it is man that should circumcise his heart, and make himself a new heart. "Not only because, in order to obtain such or such an effect, we ought to employ the means to obtain such or such an effect," says the famous President Edwards in his admirable remarks against the errors of the Arminians, "but because this effect itself is our act, as it is our duty; **God producing all, and we acting all.**"

Such, then, is the Word of God. It is God speaking in man, God speaking by man, God speaking as man, God speaking for man! This is what we have asserted, and must now proceed to prove. Possibly, however, it will be as well that we should first give a more precise definition of this doctrine.[4]

Let us consider then the very combination of divine and human factors in the incarnation of Christ, and the divine and human factors in regenerating a soul and see what light they give us on the inspiration of the Scriptures through human penmen.

We reverently study, then, how the Bible deals alike with these three divine-human wonders, Jesus Christ, regeneration, and the Scriptures.

It would do well to note how clearly the Bible uses the same terminology or similar terminology about these three matters in which the human and divine combine, always with the divine dominating completely but always using the human. God gives, man receives. So it was with Mary about the birth of Christ. So it is with every sinner who receives Christ and gets born of the Spirit. So it is with the blessed Word of God; the eternal Word comes from God, is breathed out from God but is written down by human penmen in human words.

III. THESE THREE ARE ALIKE "FROM ABOVE"

The miracles of Christ's incarnation, of the sinner's regeneration, and the inspiration of the Scriptures through men, are all described alike as "from above," using the same Greek word *anothen.*

---

4. *The Inspiration of the Holy Scriptures,* p. 32.

1. Christ Came From Above

That is the plain statement of John 3:31. Here the inspired
words of John the Baptist are written down by the inspired
Apostle John:

"*He that cometh from above is above all: he that is of the
earth is earthly, and speaketh of the earth: he that cometh from
heaven is above all.*"

Now note the words "from above." That is a translation of
the Greek word "*anothen*," meaning "from above." So it is
translated in John 19:11, in James 1:17, James 3:15-17, and,
of course, it is properly translated here, for Jesus Christ is
literally "from above." The same verse speaks of Him as "he
that cometh from heaven." In John 6:33 Jesus calls Himself
"the bread of God. . .which cometh down from heaven." And in
verse 51 He says, "I am the living bread which came down
from heaven." Yes, Jesus Christ is "from above," *anothen.*

2. The New Birth Is "From Above"

In John 3:3 we find that Jesus told Nicodemus, "Except a
man be born again, he cannot see the kingdom of God." But
the word translated "*again*" is the same Greek word *anothen*
which is translated in other places "from above." And in
John 3:7 Jesus used the same word again, "Marvel not that I
said unto thee, Ye must be born again," or specifically, "from
above," for the word here translated "again" is the Greek
word *anothen*, elsewhere translated "from above."

So the regeneration of a soul is "from above," just as Jesus
is "from above."

3. But the Scriptures Are Also "From Above"

In Luke 1:3 we read in the prologue to the Gospel of Luke
that Luke writes, "It seemed good to me also, having had
perfect understanding of all things from the very first, to write
unto thee in order, most excellent Theophilus." But as I show
in the chapter, "Where Luke Got His Facts," the best scholars

say that the term, "From the very first," ought to be translated "from above," for that phrase is a translation of the same Greek word *anothen*, other places translated "from above." The Scriptures are "from above." So say Gaussen, Lightfoot, Gomarus, Matthew Henry, B. H. Carroll, Spurgeon, James M. Gray, C. I. Scofield, and many others. As Christ is "from above" in John 3:31, and just as when one is born again he is born "from above," so the Word of God is given "from above." And God uses the same word about all three in the Greek New Testament. Note then that the divine dominates the human alike in the three matters of Christ, regeneration and the Scriptures.

IV. ALL THREE OF THESE ARE FROM GOD

1. We Know That Jesus Is Called "the Only Begotten Son of God" in John 3:16

Jesus praised Peter for saying, "Thou art Christ the Son of the living God." Many, many Scriptures clearly say that Jesus is from God.

2. But the New Birth, When a Christian Is Born Again, Is From God Also

In John 1:12,13 we read:

"But as many as received him, to them gave he power to become the sons of God, even to them that believe on his name: Which were born, not of blood, nor of the will of the flesh, nor of the will of man, but of God."

Oh, when one is born again, it is "not of blood, nor of the will of the flesh, nor of the will of man, but of God."

3. But That Is Just What the Bible Says About the Bible, the Scriptures

Isaiah 40:7,8 and I Peter 1:23 say that *the Word of God* is "incorruptible," "*the word of God,* which liveth and abideth for ever." And again we read that "*the word of God* is quick, and powerful, and sharper than any twoedged sword..." (Heb. 4:12).

And Paul praises those in Thessalonica that they received his word "not as the word of men, but as it is in truth, the word of God" (I Thess. 2:13). So these three miraculous works, in which God Himself used human beings, are all alike "from God." And the divine dominates, controls perfectly the miracle in each case alike.

V. ALL THESE: CHRIST, THE NEW BIRTH AND THE SCRIPTURES, ARE THE WORK OF THE HOLY SPIRIT THROUGH HUMAN FLESH

1. Christ Conceived as the Holy Christ

Mary was privileged to bear the Saviour, and so the eternal Christ who was in the beginning with the Father entered into a human body but the angel told Joseph, "That which is conceived in her is of the Holy Ghost" (Matt. 1:20).

2. Christians Are "Born of the Spirit" Too

Now all of us were conceived physically by human fathers and our birth was natural. But in the second birth, we, too, were "born...of the Spirit," as John 3:5 says. The Holy Spirit created in us the new nature just as the Holy Spirit in the womb of Mary conceived the human body of the Lord Jesus.

3. Scriptures Given by "The Spirit of Christ" Also

The Scriptures, too, came as the work of the Holy Spirit. We are told that Old Testament prophets, who did not understand the Scriptures they had penned, inquired, "searching what, or what manner of time the Spirit of Christ which was in them did signify, when it testified beforehand the sufferings of Christ, and the glory that should follow" (I Pet. 1:11). The Scriptures are given by "the Spirit of Christ," that is, the Holy Spirit.

And so we read in I Corinthians 2:10 that the things that God hath prepared for us were not discovered by human eyes nor ears nor thoughts, "But God hath revealed them unto us by his Spirit."   And again in verse 13, "Which things also we speak, not in words which man's wisdom teacheth, but which the Spirit teacheth; combining spiritual things with spiritual words" (ASV).   So we see that the Holy Spirit worked through human personality, as David said, by divine inspiration, in II Samuel 23:2, "The Spirit of the Lord spake by me, and his word was in my tongue."

Jesus was physically conceived in the womb of the virgin Mary by the Holy Spirit.   All of us who are saved have been born of the Spirit in a second birth.   The Word of God was revealed by His Spirit, written down as holy men were moved by the Holy Ghost.

It is suggested that the word for "breath" and the word for "spirit" have the same root word, and when God breathed out the Scriptures (*theopneustos*), it reminds us of how He breathed into the form of Adam and he became a living soul (Gen. 2:7). How alike are these three: the divine-human Saviour, the new birth, and the Word of God.

VI. ALL THESE THREE ARE ALIKE ETERNAL

1. We Learn That Christ Was "in the Beginning... With God" (John 1:1)

Isaiah 9:6 prophesies Jesus as "The everlasting Father." And Hebrews 13:8 tells us, "Jesus Christ the same yesterday, and to day, and for ever." Christ is eternal.

2. Likewise, the Born-Again Christian Has Eternal Life

So says John 3:15, Luke 18:30; has "everlasting life," as mentioned in John 3:16; John 3:36; John 5:24; John 6:47. As Jesus told Martha, "Whosoever liveth and believeth in me shall never die" (John 11:26).

3. But the Word of God Is Eternal Also

"For ever, O Lord, thy word is settled in heaven" (Ps. 119: 89). And "every one of thy righteous judgments endureth for ever" (Ps. 119:160). And Psalm 119:152 says, "Concerning thy testimonies, I have known of old that thou hast founded them for ever."

So, we see that Christ and the new-born Christian and the Word of God all are alike, eternal.

VII. CONSIDER HOW THE HUMAN-DIVINE CHRIST ILLUSTRATES THE HUMAN-DIVINE BIBLE

The Bible treats Christ and the inspired Word very much the same.

1. Both Are Called the Word of God

In John 1:1 we read, "In the beginning was the Word, and the Word was with God, and the Word was God." Verse 14 in the same chapter says, "The Word was made flesh, and dwelt among us."

Christ is to return riding a white horse, crowned with many crowns, leading the armies of Heaven, when He comes back to fight the battle of Armageddon, cut down all the enemies and set up His kingdom on earth. We read that "his name is called The Word of God" (Rev. 19:13).

But how many times the Scriptures are called "the Word of God," in the Old Testament and in the New: for example, Isaiah 40:7 and I Peter 1:23, and many other places.

Christ and the Scriptures are alike a revelation from God called The Word.

2. Both Christ and the Word of God Have a Part in Saving the Sinner

It is through the merits of Christ's atoning death that a sinner can be saved but he cannot be saved without hearing the Gospel.

So, "The law of the Lord is perfect, converting the soul" (Ps. 19:7). So, "Being born again, not of corruptible seed, but of incorruptible, by the word of God, which liveth and abideth for ever" (I Pet. 1:23). I believe that "born of water and of the Spirit" in John 3:5 means the planting of the Word of God, the Gospel, and the work of the Holy Spirit, as the two are combined—the work of the Spirit and the Word—in the salvation of a sinner. Christ is an atoning Saviour and the Scripture has the saving Gospel.

When the Word is preached it is like seeds sown, and when the seed sprouts it becomes "Christ in you, the hope of glory."

3. Christ and the Word Are Put Together in the Judgment

Jesus said, "For whosoever shall be ashamed of me and of my words, of him shall the Son of man be ashamed, when he shall come in his own glory, and in his Father's, and of the holy angels" (Luke 9:26). See also Mark 8:38. One who is ashamed of Christ will be ashamed of His words, that is, of the Bible. And Christ Himself will be ashamed of everyone who is ashamed of the Word of God and of Christ, we are told.

4. In Incarnation and Inspiration, the Human Only Received What God Gave

In both cases, that is, of the incarnation and the inspiring of the Word of God, the human agent received the miracle but was not the author of it.

When the announcement was made to Mary that she was to be the mother of the Saviour, she said, "Be it unto me according to thy word." It was not "mechanical" but it was "dictation." God said it and it was done. Mary did not a thing to create "that holy thing" in her womb. And so, the human writers of the Bible did not originate the Scriptures. It came from God to them and through them. In some cases, certainly God used their feelings, their thoughts, their wishes, and had the Scriptures thus to represent their human writers. But the Scriptures came from God, and the human writers received them. So Paul said about his Gospel, "But I certify you, brethren, that the gospel which was preached of me is not after man.   For I neither received it of man, neither was I taught it, but by the revelation of Jesus Christ" (Gal. 1:11,12).   Neither the Christ who was born of Mary nor the Bible, given through human penmen, was the product of human effort, but rather God chose to give the Lord Jesus to mankind through woman.   God chose to give the Scriptures through men.   The men who wrote the Bible were no more the authors of it, literally, than Mary was the creator of the Lord Jesus.

5. Whatever Jesus Inherited of a Likeness to Mary, It Was Wholly of God

Let us consider it again: Did Jesus look like Mary?   Did He from Mary inherit a tendency to be tall or short, fair or dark?   Was His smile like Mary's?   Were His teeth, or the shape of His nose?   Did His hair curl a little like Mary's, colored like hers?   I do not know.   He was the Son of Adam, of Abraham, of David, and Son of man, so possibly He was physically a composite of all that was noble in the appearance and strength of a man's body and face.   But perhaps He looked like Mary.   Perhaps He had eyes like her or a smile.   If so, Mary did not plan or effect that.   She had no choice in the matter.

The truth is that God chose Mary ahead of time, prepared her features and all her individual personality, and if God put some of these same traits in Jesus that would remind one of Mary, it was God who selected the details of His features, personality, and appearance before the world began and then whatever He liked He put in Mary and, through Mary, could put in His Son, or not do, as He chose.

Since Jesus was with the Father in the beginning and His death on the cross was a settled fact before the world began, it is clear that the body of Jesus was already planned long before Mary knew anything about it.

In Hebrews 10:5 we have a strange Scripture about Jesus, a quotation from Psalm 40:6:   "Wherefore when he cometh into the world, he saith, Sacrifice and offering thou wouldest not, but a body hast thou prepared me."

I understand this to mean that the body of Jesus was prepared according to God's own specifications.   God had already prepared Mary's body. If He wanted to include some of the details of Mary's personality and body — her color, her eyes, features, her hair — He could have done so and may have done so, and then the Lord Jesus may have gotten through Mary what God had already prepared. I do not know all the details. I simply know that Mary was a trusting recipient of the blessing of God and she did not create the Lord Jesus nor have any choice in the details of what He looked like, what were His features, in any personal, distinctive characteristics. God prepared the body. Jesus was wholly from God. Mary did not create Jesus but she received Him who had already been "in the beginning...with God."

6. The Body in Which Jesus Appeared Sometimes in the Old Testament Was Probably After the Pattern of the Body God Would Prepare for Jesus for His Incarnation

Devout Bible scholars generally agree that Christ sometimes appeared in the Old Testament. When in anger King Nebuchadnezzar had the three Hebrew children cast in the fiery furnace because they would not bow down to his idol, it seems that Christ went into the fiery furnace and walked with them. Read Daniel 3:24,25:

"*Then Nebuchadnezzar the king was astonied, and rose up in haste, and spake, and said unto his counsellors, Did not we cast three men bound into the midst of the fire? They answered and said unto the king, True, O king. He answered and said, Lo, I see four men loose, walking in the midst of the fire, and they have no hurt; and the form of the fourth is like the Son of God.*"

The Man in the fiery furnace was one who appeared even to the heathen king "like the Son of God." We believe he was correct and that Christ Himself came to His faithful servants in that hour and delivered them. If so, the Lord Jesus appeared in a visible, tangible, human form. Then did the body appear like the body which God would prepare for Jesus in His incarnation, after He was born of the virgin Mary?

In Genesis, chapter 32, at the Brook Jabbok, Jacob met an angel of God and wrestled with him until the breaking of day but Jacob came to know that this was not one of many angels;

he had met Deity! So he said, "I have seen God face to face, and my life is preserved" (Gen. 32:30). Now Jacob wrestled with a Man with a human body and a human voice. Was that body of the same size; were the features the same; were the tones of the voice the same as that which God had prepared to give Jesus when He was to be born in a human family? I think so.

When Israel was about to encompass Jericho and take the city, we read of a strange happening in Joshua 5:13-15:

"And it came to pass, when Joshua was by Jericho, that he lifted up his eyes and looked, and, behold, there stood a man over against him with his sword drawn in his hand: and Joshua went unto him, and said unto him, Art thou for us, or for our adversaries? And he said, Nay; but as captain of the host of the Lord am I now come. And Joshua fell on his face to the earth, and did worship, and said unto him, What saith my lord unto his servant? And the captain of the Lord's host said unto Joshua, Loose thy shoe from off thy foot; for the place whereon thou standest is holy. And Joshua did so."

I believe that the "man" Joshua saw was the Lord Jesus. He was then and is now "captain of the Lord's host," even as Jesus will come with the armies of Heaven following Him to fight the battle of Armageddon. Now, did the "man" Joshua saw, Christ appearing in the Old Testament, look as He looked in New Testament times? Was His voice like the voice Jesus would later have?

Let us put it this way: When the three Hebrew children met the ascended Saviour in a human body, was He strange to them and different from the one they had seen before and known before? Or was He the same Christ, visibly the same? And when Jacob and Joshua saw the ascended Christ come back to Heaven in a human body, was He the same Christ, in what might appear to be the same body, with the same voice, the same visible characteristics as He had had when they met Him before? Why not? Of course in the Old Testament appearances of Christ the body He used was temporary. But would it not be like Christ's body?

Do you think God had one plan as to what Christ would look like when He appeared in the Old Testament and then change His mind and change the specifications of the human body He would prepare? A person's body represents and fits his spirit, his characteristics, his character. Would not the temporary body of Jesus, appearing in the Old Testament, need to represent the same qualities as His New Testament body?

What I am saying is that even as the body of Christ was planned ahead of time and was wholly of God though it came through the body of the virgin Mary, so the Scriptures were settled in Heaven forever before they were written down, and whatever style Isaiah or David or John or Paul would write the Scriptures in was already planned in Heaven, already in fact a part of the eternal Word of God, already settled there in the mind and plan of God.

So men who wrote the Bible received it. They did not make it. Paul said of his Gospel, "But I certify you, brethren, that the gospel which was preached of me is not after man. For I neither received it of man, neither was I taught it, but by the revelation of Jesus Christ" (Gal. 1:11,12).

And Jude, verse 3, tells us, "Ye should earnestly contend for the faith which was ONCE DELIVERED unto the saints."

If Jesus, with Mary for a mother, yet was holy, divine, sinless, perfect, without any limitations which Mary could give, then surely the Word of God is not limited by the human penmen but is the infallible, plenary, verbally inspired Scripture from God, "God-breathed." The human writers of the Bible received but they did not create the miracle of God-breathed words.

Does the ignorant, powerless sinner create his new nature? Not at all. He becomes a "partaker of the divine nature" by the miracle of regeneration which God does, and it is "not of works" lest any man should boast. It is wholly of grace.

But the inspiration of the Bible, using men to write down what God said, is also wholly of grace and not of works. No human research nor investigation nor talking with witnesses nor meditating and planning can account for the miraculous Word of God, like the miraculous birth of Jesus, God's perfect Son. And like the miraculously given new heart in the new convert, so the miraculous Word of God coming through men is still from God and is the Word of God and not the word of men, except as God chose to let His words represent them also.

CHAPTER XIII

WORD-FOR-WORD INSPIRATION

I. THE DOCTRINE IS STRESSED FOR ALL SCRIPTURE

1. First Corinthians 2:9-13 Clearly Expresses This Doctrine:

2. In Deuteronomy 8:3 Is a Remarkable Verse in Which It Seems, Almost Incidentally, the Doctrine of Word-for-Word Inspiration Is Given:

3. Matthew 24:35 and Mark 13:31 Have the Same Identical Statement:

4. Another Passage That Teaches Inspiration of the Words Is II Peter 1:20,21:

5. Again, in John 8:47 the Lord Jesus Rebukes the Pharisees, Saying:

6. In Deuteronomy 18 We Have Two Promises About a Prophet God Would Raise Up

7. But Does Not Reason Tell Us That if God Is to Reveal Things to Men, and if That Is to Be a Perfect and Eternal Revelation in a Certain Body of Truth, Should It Not Be in God's Words?

II. SOME MARVELOUS EXAMPLES OF WHERE, BEYOND CONTROVERSY, GOD GAVE THE WORDS

1. The Ten Commandments Were Spoken Aloud by God on Mount Sinai

2. Another Express Example of When God Gave Exact Words Is Daniel 5:5

3. In Numbers 23:28 We Read About Balaam's Ass Who Spoke the Words of God

4. We Have Repeated Instances of When God Spoke Aloud From Heaven

5. There Is the Striking Case of Caiaphas

6. Another Case That Indicates the Verbal Inspiration Is That of Balaam

7. Hundreds of Times the Bible Says "The Lord Spake Unto Moses, Saying," and Similar Statements

III. LET US CONSIDER, THEN, HOW PARTICULAR BOOKS OF THE BIBLE ARE CLAIMED TO BE VERBALLY INSPIRED

1. In Exodus 24:3-8 We Are Told How Moses Wrote Down the Books Ascribed to Him in the WORDS of the Lord:

2. Isaiah Wrote Also the Very Words of God

3. Jeremiah Tells Us That God Promised Him Word-for-Word Inspiration for His Prophecies

4. Ezekiel, Too, Was Given Word-for-Word Inspiration

5. The Psalms of David Were Written by Word-for-Word Inspiration Also

IV. HOW JEALOUSLY GOD GUARDS THE WORDS OF SCRIPTURE!

1. The Lord Jesus Said That the Jots and Tittles of the Scripture Would Never Pass Away Till All Be Fulfilled

2. In the Original Scriptures, the Distinctions of Singular and Plural Are Divinely Inspired and Accurately Recorded

3. A Curse Is Pronounced on Those Who Take From the Words or Add to the Words of Scripture

WORD-FOR-WORD INSPIRATION

We believe in the inspiration of the Bible. What do we mean by inspiration? Some speak of *dynamic* inspiration, by which they mean God simply sharpens the natural abilities of men to proclaim divine truth, not necessarily without error. To some, inspiration means *moral* inspiration, or simply that in moral and spiritual matters the Bible is inspired and reliable, not necessarily the science and history and genealogies and narratives. Some speak of *thought* inspiration, by which they mean that God gives the thought and lets men put it in their own words.

But what the Bible teaches is *word* inspiration, that is, that God gave the words in which the original Scriptures were written down. That is called verbal inspiration from the Latin word *verbum*, meaning "word." So we say a man is "verbose" if he uses many words. The inspiration is verbal, that is, it is an inspiration of the words in the original manuscripts.

We are not now discussing the translations. Translators are not inspired, and there can be mistakes in translation although these mistakes are largely overcome by having translations checked and double checked by numerous godly scholars. There may be mistakes in copying, though such mistakes can usually be found by comparing manuscripts with manuscripts since there are hundreds of manuscripts of the New Testament available and many of the Old Testament. But when we speak of inspiration, we speak of the original autographs written down in the Old Testament in Hebrew, except for a small part of the book of Daniel which is in Chaldaic, and the New Testament, which is in koine Greek.

The Bible claims that God gave the very words.

I. THE DOCTRINE IS STRESSED FOR ALL SCRIPTURE

The Bible does clearly teach the doctrine of word-for-word inspiration of all the Scriptures.

There are a number of Scriptures that are very plain and explicit referring to the whole matter of divine revelation, written down by inspiration.

1. First Corinthians 2:9-13 Clearly Expresses This Doctrine:

"*But as it is written, Eye hath not seen, nor ear heard, neither have entered into the heart of man, the things which God hath prepared for them that love him. But God hath revealed them unto us by his Spirit: for the Spirit searcheth all things, yea, the deep things of God. For what man knoweth the things of a man, save the spirit of man which is in him? even so the things of God knoweth no man, but the Spirit of God. Now we have received, not the spirit of the world, but the spirit which is of God; that we might know the things that are freely given to us of God. Which things also we speak, not in THE WORDS WHICH MAN'S WISDOM TEACHETH, BUT WHICH THE HOLY GHOST TEACHETH; comparing spiritual things with spiritual.*"

Now consider what is taught here.

First, "the things which God hath prepared for them that love him" is a general term for Scripture truth. It refers not only to what Paul had revealed to him but to all the matters God would have men know. God has revealed them by His Spirit.

Second, the things that were being written into the Scriptures were already "*prepared*" of God before they were revealed to men; in the case of the eternal Scriptures, they were in the mind of God before they were ever written down.

Third, "the things of God" could not possibly be known by human faculties alone, by what people see, what they hear, what they think—these are not the origin of the Word of God. It is true that the man who writes part of the Scriptures may mention what he saw or what he heard, but his real source is from God; and the correctness and perfection of what he writes in such case is guaranteed by God and not by his own faculties.   Men do not see correctly what their eyes look upon.   Men do not remember exactly what they see.   Human reason does not always come out with the right answer.   The only way to know the divine truth discussed here is that God's Holy Spirit is to give it to men.

Fourth, what "God hath prepared for them that love him" is revealed "not in the words which man's wisdom teacheth, but which the Holy Ghost teacheth; comparing spiritual things with spiritual" or, as in the American Standard Version, "...combining spiritual things with spiritual words."   The matter is God-given and the words in which it is put down are God-given also.

And we are compelled to believe that since here God is discussing the whole matter of divine truth as given to men, He most surely includes the written Word of God.   It comes in words, Spirit-given words.   Inspiration is in the very words of God.   That is word-for-word inspiration.

2. In Deuteronomy 8:3 Is a Remarkable Verse in Which It Seems, Almost Incidentally, the Doctrine of Word-for-Word Inspiration Is Given:

"*And he humbled thee, and suffered thee to hunger, and fed thee with manna, which thou knewest not, neither did thy fathers know; that he might make thee know that man doth not live by bread only, but by EVERY WORD that proceedeth out of the mouth of the Lord doth man live.*" — Deut. 8:3.

God dealt wonderfully well with the children of Israel, giving them manna from Heaven; but that was to make them know "that man doth not live by bread only, but by every word that proceedeth out of the mouth of the Lord doth man live."

And that is so important that Jesus, tempted of Satan to make bread of stones, said:

"*Man shall not live by bread alone, but by EVERY WORD that proceedeth out of the mouth of God.*" — Matt. 4:4.

The same quotation is repeated in Luke 4:4.

So, on the authority of the Bible, reinforced by the endorsement and quotation of Jesus Christ Himself, we learn of the Scriptures, that every word "proceedeth out of the mouth of God." The Lord speaks here not primarily of doctrines, not primarily of commandments, not primarily of teachings or any other such general terms; but God speaks of "every word that proceedeth out of the mouth of God." Where do the Scriptures come from? If we ask Jesus Christ, He answers, "every word ...proceedeth out of the mouth of God." That is word-for-word inspiration.

3. Matthew 24:35 and Mark 13:31 Have the Same Identical Statement

"*Heaven and earth shall pass away, but MY WORDS shall not pass away.*" — Matt. 24:35.

The Lord Jesus speaks not of the Word in a general sense but of the "words." Jesus did not mean that the thought would never pass away, or the general substance of what He said, but that the very words would not pass away. They are eternal and therefore must be God's words.

And the Bible is called "the word of Christ" (Col. 3:16). The Holy Spirit who gave the words to the penmen who wrote the Scriptures is "the Spirit of Christ" (Rom. 8:9; I Pet. 1:11). So all the Bible is the Word of Christ, and the words of the Bible are the words of Christ.

There is no way to take such a statement at honest face value without acknowledging that the very words as originally given in the Scriptures are the words of God.

4. Another Passage That Teaches Inspiration of the Words Is II Peter 1:20,21:

"*Knowing this first, that no prophecy of the scripture is of any private interpretation. For the prophecy came not in old time by the will of man: but holy men of God spake as they were moved by the Holy Ghost.*"

"Prophecy" is used here for what is spoken by the Holy Spirit. "To prophesy" in the Bible is to speak for God with God's Spirit. But in the Scripture, as mentioned here, "the prophecy came not...by the will of man," but the Scriptures came as "holy men of God *spake* as they were moved by the Holy Ghost." Not that they *thought* as "moved by the Holy Ghost"; the emphasis is not on the thought but on the words. If men had simply been moved or supervised by the Holy Spirit so that their thoughts were directed a certain way, then their thinking might be by the Holy Ghost but the words would not necessarily be God's words. But that is not what the Bible claims here; it claims that men spake, and the words were God's words.

And since the Bible here speaks expressly of Scripture, then it is the written words which God has given.

5. Again, in John 8:47 the Lord Jesus Rebukes the Pharisees, Saying:

"*He that is of God heareth GOD'S WORDS: ye therefore hear them not, because ye are not of God.*"

In this passage Jesus is speaking of His own words in that conversation, but He makes no distinction between the words He spoke in that conversation and other words of God in the Bible. It is noticeable that elsewhere in the same dialogue the Lord Jesus spoke of "my word," as in verse 31, referring to the whole body of revealed truth. But in verse 47 He refers to "God's words." What is the Scripture? It is made up of God's words. That is verbal inspiration, word-for-word inspiration.

6. In Deuteronomy 18 We Have Two Promises About a Prophet God Would Raise Up

Deuteronomy 18:15 says, "The Lord thy God will raise up unto thee a Prophet from the midst of thee, of thy brethren, like unto me; unto him ye shall hearken." Surely this refers to "that prophet" of John 1:25. But in verses 16 to 19 of Deuteronomy 18, the Lord tells us more. He refers to the time when they heard the voice of God from Heaven and the people were frightened. They wanted Moses to speak for God to them, and God said, 'That plan is good,' and so then He said, in verses 18 and 19:

"*I will raise them up a Prophet from among their brethren, like unto thee, and will put MY WORDS in his mouth; and he shall speak unto them all that I shall command him. And it shall come to pass, that whosoever will not hearken unto my words which he shall speak in my name, I will require it of him.*"

Note carefully, God first refers to His own words spoken aloud in the Ten Commandments from Mount Sinai, and then promises that He will raise up from among their brethren and "will put my words in his mouth," and then that "whosoever will not hearken unto my words which he shall speak in my name, I will require it of him." Note this: As the words of the Ten Commandments, spoken aloud by the Lord from Mount Sinai were God's words, just so He puts His words in the mouth of His prophets, and they speak for Him God's words. And they will give account to God for God's words. This is word-for-word inspiration.

In some sense this passage teaches the inspiration of all the Old Testament and gives God's wholesale plan of inspiration. God gave through prophets in Israel the very words of God. And so Romans 9:4 and 5 tells us:

"*Who are Israelites; to whom pertaineth the adoption, and the glory, and the covenants, and the giving of the law, and the service of God, and the promises; Whose are the fathers, and of whom as concerning the flesh Christ came, who is over all, God blessed for ever. Amen.*"

The covenants, the law, the promises were given through prophets of Israel; and of Israel, Christ came. But note now, Deuteronomy 18:18 is a promise that God puts the very words in the mouth of those prophets of Israel who wrote the Scriptures.

7. But Does Not Reason Tell Us That if God Is to Reveal Things to Men, and if That Is to Be a Perfect and Eternal Revelation in a Certain Body of Truth, Should It Not Be in God's Words?

If the Lord Jesus Christ, to be a Saviour, must become a man, if God's thoughts and plans are to be revealed to man, they must be put down in man's words but God's perfect words, just as Christ is God's perfect Son.

There is no transmission of thought without words. In fact, we have learned that children have to learn words before they learn to express thoughts.

There can be no written music without notes, no written thought without words, no written arithmetic without numbers. If inspiration is to carry through to make perfect Scriptures, it must give the words from God. What God breathed out was not thoughts without words, but words perfectly expressing God's thoughts.

The frailty, the weakness, the limitations of every human writer is such that unless God Himself gave the words, we could never be sure about what God wanted us to know. In the best Christians "the flesh lusteth against the Spirit, and the Spirit against the flesh" (Gal. 5:17). The wisest and greatest Christian in the New Testament must say, as must all of us, "The good that I would I do not: but the evil which I would not, that I do....I find then a law, that, when I would do good, evil is present with me" (Rom. 7:19,21).

Wesley and Whitefield, noblest of men, read the Scriptures and came out with one following Arminius and one following Calvin. Two of the most devoted and godly men I know were Dr. H. A. Ironside, for eighteen years pastor of Moody Church in Chicago, and Dr. George W. Truett, for over forty years pastor of the First Baptist Church of Dallas, Texas. Truett, loving the Bible and believing it, comes out a postmillennialist. Ironside, loving the Bible and believing it, comes out a premillennialist. Would you blame Truett that he was influenced by B. H. Carroll, or blame Ironside that he was influenced by Darby? I am simply showing that no man in this world is wise enough, or well balanced enough, or so perfectly attuned to God, that he could express exactly what God wanted him to say if he had only the thought and not God's words.

At the trial of a drunken man who had run headlong across the highway into an oncoming car, killing the driver, I was asked to witness as to the color of the car in which my friend was killed. On the witness stand I said, "It was a 1938 two-door Buick sedan. The color was black."

The prosecuting attorney said, "Are you sure?"

I answered, "Of course I am sure. The car sat in my driveway two weeks. I rode in it. I drove it. The car was black."

In the same trial, the deputy sheriff, who witnessed the accident and had the car towed in to a garage, witnessed that the car was green.

When I learned of that testimony, I went to the district attorney and assured him that the deputy sheriff was certainly wrong. He said, "You must both go see the car. It is stored in a garage nearby." We went. Neither I nor the deputy sheriff were correct. The car was not black; it was not green; it was dark blue! Both of us were as honest as we knew how to be, but human frailty being what it is, nobody can be trusted to tell the exact truth about things that he sees.

Oh, what kind of a Bible would we have if God had left it to men to put into their own words His truth? He did not do that. God gave the words.

How could I know that the psalms of David were exactly what God said, when I know that David had fallen into grievous sin, committed adultery and murder? I could not trust David. I could trust only God when He put words in David's mouth.

How could I read the epistles of Peter and trust him, knowing that Peter, after he was saved, had cursed and sworn and denied Jesus Christ, and quit the ministry? Oh, as Peter himself said, we need "a more sure word of prophecy" than his testimony (II Pet. 1:19). How could I trust the proverbs of Solomon if I knew that that wisest man in all the world had married so many heathen women and then, in his old age, had been led away into idolatry? No, I could not trust Solomon's righteousness nor his memory nor his understanding. What we need is not words by the wisest men; we need words which God Himself puts in the mouths of men. They may be "unlearned and ignorant men" (Acts 4:13) as were Peter and John and the other apostles, but if God gives the words, I can trust the Scriptures. Those who look for perfection in men always must be disillusioned. If the Bible is God's Word, it must be in God's words.

II. SOME MARVELOUS EXAMPLES OF WHERE, BEYOND CONTROVERSY, GOD GAVE THE WORDS

We may not only have the clear doctrine that in the Scripture we have words from the mouth of God, but we have many examples where all must agree they came from God.

1. The Ten Commandments Were Spoken Aloud by God on Mount Sinai

So we see in Exodus 20:1, "And God spake all these words." The astonished people besought Moses, "Speak thou with us, and we will hear: but let not God speak with us, lest we die" (Exod. 20:19). Then the Ten Commandments were written on tables of stone with the "finger of God" (Exod. 31:18). Here we have, beyond controversy, the very words of God.

2. Another Express Example of When God Gave Exact Words Is Daniel 5:5

There we read, "In the same hour came forth fingers of a man's hand, and wrote over against the candlestick upon the plaister of the wall of the king's palace: and the king saw the part of the hand that wrote." Verse 25 reads to us that writing on the wall: "And this is the writing that was written, MENE, MENE, TEKEL, UPHARSIN." There is no question here of human style or personal investigation or research or copying or quoting oral tradition. These are the words of God.

3. In Numbers 23:28 We Read About Balaam's Ass Who Spoke the Words of God

The Scripture says, "And the Lord opened the mouth of the ass, and she said unto Balaam, What have I done unto thee, that thou hast smitten me these three times?" And, again, in verse 30: "And the ass said unto Balaam, Am not I thine ass, upon which thou hast ridden ever since I was thine unto this day? was I ever wont to do so unto thee? And he said, Nay."

A donkey has no vocabulary, no idiosyncracies of style in speaking or writing! In this case, the inspired message was in the very words God gave the donkey.

It is true that the donkey spoke what she may have felt and just as, we suppose, a donkey might wish to talk if she could talk, but the words were God's words, not simply God's thoughts. They were the donkey's thoughts, we suppose, but certainly God put the unaccustomed words in the mouth of the donkey.

4. We Have Repeated Instances of When God Spoke Aloud From Heaven

So He did when Abraham was offering Isaac on the altar; so it was when God spoke to Jesus at His baptism and on the Mount of Transfiguration; so it was when God talked to Saul of Tarsus on the road to Damascus.

And like that are the cases when "the angel of the Lord" spoke again and again to Jacob, to the mother and father of Samson, to Zachariah, Mary, Joseph, the wise men, to Peter and John in prison, to Paul on shipboard, to Philip the evangelist, and others. In these cases certainly God gave particular words. The message was not only in thought, but the words were God's words.

5. There Is the Striking Case of Caiaphas

He was the wicked, unconverted high priest who hated Jesus Christ and wanted Him killed for his own wicked purposes. We read about it in John 11:47-52:

"Then gathered the chief priests and the Pharisees a council, and said, What do we? for this man doeth many miracles. If we let him thus alone, all men will believe on him: and the Romans shall come and take away both our place and nation. And one of them, named Caiaphas, being the high priest that same year, said unto them, Ye know nothing at all, Nor consider that it is expedient for us, that one man should die for the people, and that the whole nation perish not. And this spake he not of himself: but being high priest that year, he prophesied

that Jesus should die for that nation; And not for that nation only, but that also he should gather together in one the children of God that were scattered abroad."

Lest the priests should lose their place of leadership and the Romans should take over in detail the government which they had now left largely to the priests, Caiaphas wanted Jesus killed. But God had Caiaphas as the high priest prophesy the atoning death of Jesus Christ: "...that Jesus should die for that nation; And not for that nation only...." " Now the sentiment which Caiaphas intended was one thing; the sentiment God intended was another. Only God could so manipulate Caiaphas, the high priest, that he unwittingly, and no doubt unwillingly announced the atoning death of Jesus Christ. God used the mouth of Caiaphas, and it expressed his wicked will, but it also expressed perfectly the good will of God miraculously. The words surely must have been God's words. Do you think that God could not use words that were both man's and God's?

6. Another Case That Indicates the Verbal Inspiration Is That of Balaam

He was the false prophet who tried so persistently to bring a curse upon Israel, but God would not allow it and, instead, had him pronounce again and again blessings. The story is told in Numbers, chapters 22-24. In Numbers 22:38 we read, "And Balaam said unto Balak, Lo, I am come unto thee: have I now any power at all to say any thing? the word that God putteth in my mouth, that shall I speak." Balaam did not think the thoughts of God. His own thoughts were far different. He simply pronounced the words of God. So in Numbers 23:5 we read, "And the Lord put a word in Balaam's mouth...." In verse 12 Balaam said, "Must I not take heed to speak that which the Lord hath put in my mouth?" Again, in Numbers 23:16 we read: "And the Lord met Balaam, and put a word in his mouth." And in another promise of great blessing Balaam tells us, "He hath said, which heard the words of God, which saw the vision of the Almighty, falling into a trance, but having his eyes open..." (Num. 24:4).

Here we are told more than once that the words were God's words. Balaam did not agree to them, would gladly have pronounced different words, but God would not allow it. He "heard the words of God" (Num. 24:16) and said them. Can anyone say that this was less than word-for-word inspiration?

7. Hundreds of Times the Bible Says, "The Lord Spake Unto Moses, Saying," and Similar Statements

But the evidence becomes overwhelming when we see in literally hundreds of cases through the Bible that "the Lord spake unto Moses, saying...," or "the word of the Lord came unto Jeremiah, saying...," or similar statements. In literally countless cases, the Bible proclaims and gives exact quotations from God. Are those quotations, then, not in the words of God?

These are instances of the word-for-word inspiration which is so clearly claimed for all the Scriptures.

III. LET US CONSIDER, THEN, HOW PARTICULAR BOOKS OF THE BIBLE ARE CLAIMED TO BE VERBALLY INSPIRED

Jesus plainly taught that all the Old Testament was inspired of God, and He quoted many, many times from the Pentateuch, from the Psalms and the Prophets. He said, "Moses...wrote of me" (John 5:46). After Jesus had risen from the dead He talked to two on the road to Emmaus, and "beginning at Moses and all the prophets, he expounded unto them in all the scriptures the things concerning himself" (Luke 24:27). And in the same chapter He announced the miraculous fulfillment of prophecies "which were written in the law of Moses, and in the prophets, and in the psalms, concerning me" (vs. 44). Now let us consider how these books of the Bible were inspired word for word.

1. In Exodus 24:3-8 We Are Told How Moses Wrote Down the Books Ascribed to Him in the WORDS of the Lord:

"And Moses came and told the people ALL THE WORDS OF THE LORD, and all the judgments: and all the people answered with one voice, and said, ALL THE WORDS WHICH THE LORD

HATH SAID WILL WE DO. And MOSES WROTE ALL THE WORDS OF THE LORD, and rose up early in the morning, and builded an altar under the hill, and twelve pillars, according to the twelve tribes of Israel. And he sent young men of the children of Israel, which offered burnt-offerings, and sacrificed peace-offerings of oxen unto the Lord. And Moses took half of the blood, and put it in basins; and half of the blood he sprinkled on the altar. And he took the book of the covenant, and read in the audience of the people: and they said, Moses took the blood, and sprinkled it on the people, and said, Behold the blood of the covenant, which the Lord hath made with you concerning ALL THESE WORDS."

Will you note carefully the following things stated here.

First, Moses "told the people all the WORDS of the Lord" (vs. 3).

Second, the people said, "All that the Lord hath said will we do" (vs. 3).

Third, "And Moses wrote all the WORDS of the Lord" (vs. 4).

Fourth, then Moses reminded them: "Behold the blood of the covenant, which the Lord hath made with you concerning all THESE WORDS" (vs. 8).

So the Pentateuch, written by Moses, was written in the very words which God gave, and Moses wrote them in a book.

2. Isaiah Wrote Also the Very Words of God

In Isaiah 51:16 we read: "And I have put my words in thy mouth, and I have covered thee in the shadow of mine hand, that I may plant the heavens, and lay the foundations of the earth, and say unto Zion, Thou art my people."

I think we may say that God put words in the mouth of Isaiah. The same thing is borne out in Isaiah 49:1 and 2. God made Isaiah's mouth "like a sharp sword." God made Isaiah "a polished shaft." And how exalted and beautiful is his language! And how marvelous his portrayal of the Gospel and the Saviour in the Old Testament! But surely God here is speaking of Isaiah's mouth, not Isaiah's mind. He is speaking about the words He gave Isaiah and not only the thoughts.

"I have put my words in thy mouth" would refer to Isaiah.

But does it not also refer to other prophets of God through Israel? The fifty-first chapter of Isaiah seems to be addressed to Israel. So God is saying that the oracles of God will come through Israel and through Israel's prophets. And these revelations will be written down in God's words which He will put in the mouth of His Prophet Isaiah and in the mouths of other prophets.

I remember how years ago I received with joy a letter from the late I. M. Haldeman, then pastor of the First Baptist Church of New York City. 'Yes,' he wrote with trembling, aged fingers, 'he believed in the verbal inspiration of the Bible,' and he quoted: "I have put my words in thy mouth" (Isa. 51:16).

3. Jeremiah Tells Us That God Promised Him Word-for-Word Inspiration for His Prophecies

In Jeremiah 1:9 we read: "Then the Lord put forth his hand, and touched my mouth. And the Lord said unto me, Behold, I have put my words in thy mouth."

And it was the same about the prophecies which Jeremiah wrote down in the book.

Jeremiah 30:1,2 says: "The word that came to Jeremiah from the Lord, saying, Thus speaketh the Lord God of Israel, saying, Write thee all the words that I have spoken unto thee in a book."

Then in verse 4, following, we read: "And these are the words that the Lord spake concerning Israel and concerning Judah." Jeremiah wrote down the very words of God, in the book of Jeremiah.

Again, in Jeremiah 36:2, Jeremiah was commanded: "Take thee a roll of a book, and write therein all the words that I have spoken unto thee against Israel, and against Judah, and against all the nations, from the day I spake unto thee, from the days of Josiah, even unto this day."

In verse 4 we read: "Then Jeremiah called Baruch the son of Neriah: and Baruch wrote from the mouth of Jeremiah all the words of the Lord, which he had spoken unto him, upon a roll of a book."

In verse 6 Jeremiah called this roll which he had written, "the words of the Lord."

Ah, but the wicked Jehoiakim and his lords were displeased with the prophecies of doom in that manuscript, and so Jehoiakim cut it with a penknife and burned it in the fire, as we read in Jeremiah 36:21,23. But in verse 32 we are told: "Then took Jeremiah another roll, and gave it to Baruch the scribe, the son of Neriah; who wrote therein from the mouth of Jeremiah all the words of the book which Jehoiakim king of Judah had burned in the fire: and there were added besides unto them many like words."

There can be no doubt that if the Bible is the truth, if God's Word means what it says, then the very words written down in the book of Jeremiah are the words of God. It was word-for-word inspiration.

4. Ezekiel, Too, Was Given Word-for-Word Inspiration

God said to Ezekiel: "And thou shalt speak my words unto them, whether they will hear, or whether they will forbear: for they are most rebellious" (Ezek. 2:7). Ezekiel was timid and feared the people, but God gave him, word for word, what he should tell them. As a symbol of direct verbal inspiration, God gave Ezekiel the roll of a book wherein was written "lamentations and mourning and woe," and he was commanded to eat the roll; and he did so. Thus Ezekiel symbolized that the words which he should speak and write were literally the words of God dictated by the Holy Spirit. God then assured Ezekiel, "But when I speak with thee, I will open thy mouth, and thou shalt say unto them, Thus saith the Lord God; He that heareth, let him hear; and he that forbeareth, let him forbear: for they are a rebellious house" (Ezek. 3:27).

5. The Psalms of David Were Written by Word-for-Word Inspiration Also

In Acts 1:16 we read that Peter was inspired to stand up and speak, saying, "Men and brethren, this scripture must needs have been fulfilled, which the Holy Ghost by the mouth of

David spake before concerning Judas." The mouth was David's mouth; the speaking was God's speaking.

In II Samuel 23:2 we have "the last words of David" (vs. 1), and there we read: "The Spirit of the Lord spake by me, and his word was in my tongue." God's Word was in David's tongue. That explains the Psalms; they were given word for word from God. The words were God's words.

IV. HOW JEALOUSLY GOD GUARDS THE WORDS OF SCRIPTURE

We have already noted how Jesus said, "Heaven and earth shall pass away, but my words shall not pass away" (Matt. 24:35; Mark 13:31). We have already noted that the words of God are eternal words, settled forever in Heaven (Ps. 119:89). But it is wonderful what detailed concern God Himself shows about the words of the Scripture.

1. The Lord Jesus Said That the Jots and Tittles of the Scripture Would Never Pass Away Till All Be Fulfilled

In Matthew 5:17,18 we have the words of the Saviour:

"Think not that I am come to destroy the law, or the prophets: I am not come to destroy, but to fulfill. For verily I say unto you, Till heaven and earth pass, one jot or one tittle shall in no wise pass from the law, till all be fulfilled."

We understand that certain ceremonial matters like the animal sacrifices, the earthly priesthood, the Temple in Jerusalem, would be fulfilled and pass away in the coming sacrificial death and high-priestly ministry of Jesus Christ; so in the sense of being binding commands to Christians, their authority would expire. But Jesus is saying that the law and the prophets, here representing all the Old Testament, jealously guarded and enforced, cannot be altered or left out.

The jot is the smallest Hebrew letter. The tittle is a little, tiny extension, somewhat like the serifs on a printed alphabet, but in Hebrew it is used on some letters of the alphabet to distinguish one letter from the others — like our "Q" has a little tail to distinguish it from the "O." And Jesus said that these two smallest features of the Hebrew spelling of the words of Scripture would never pass away till all be fulfilled!

Do you mean that even the spelling was inspired? Yes, the words were inspired and the spelling was inspired in the original autographs.

2. In the Original Scriptures, the Distinctions of Singular and Plural Are Divinely Inspired and Accurately Recorded

In Galatians 3:16 Paul makes an argument that a certain Hebrew word is given in the singular and so must refer to Christ, the special seed of Abraham, instead of the plural, referring to other descendants of Abraham. We read:

"Now to Abraham and his seed were the promises made. He saith not, And to seeds, as of many; but as of one, And to thy seed, which is Christ."

How careful was God to guarantee the absolute accuracy of His Word! God gave the words, and so He had men to write down just the form of the word which expressed His divine thought. God thus had Moses to write down in Genesis 13:15 the promise of God to Abraham, had Moses write what he could not have known without divine revelation: that the Seed of Abraham was the promised Messiah, our Saviour. God cared for the very spelling of the words.

3. A Curse Is Pronounced on Those Who Take From the Words or Add to the Words of Scripture

In Revelation 22:18,19, God gave some concluding words for the book of Revelation but also a conclusion to the whole Bible. He said:

"For I testify unto every man that heareth the words of the prophecy of this book, If any man shall add unto these things, God shall add unto him the plagues that are written in this book: And if any man shall take away from the words of the book of this prophecy, God shall take away his part out of the

book of life, and out of the holy city, and from the things which are written in this book."

It is not only the thoughts and principles and doctrines of the book of Revelation that God here so jealously guards; it is "the words of the prophecy of this book." And so there is a double plague:

First, to anyone who adds to "the words of the prophecy," God will add to him "the plagues that are written in this book." And that is for all who add doctrines and teachings not in the Bible. Then there is a curse on any who "take away from the words of the book of this prophecy." He loses the Heaven which is offered him. One cannot be saved and go to Heaven without believing essentially the Bible. The saving Gospel is that "Christ died for our sins ACCORDING TO THE SCRIPTURES; And that he was buried, and that he rose again the third day ACCORDING TO THE SCRIPTURES" (I Cor. 15: 3,4). Such is the teaching also of II John, verses 9 and 10.

But here the emphasis is on the words. The words themselves are from God. And great plagues are on those who discount the words or add to the words of the Scripture.

But surely there is a sense here in which God speaks not only of the book of Revelation but of the whole canon of Scripture. God is here closing the canon of Scripture. No one is to add to what has been written, counting it with the same authority as the Word of God. Other men may have illumination and may witness for Christ, but no one now can write out God-breathed words to become a part of the Bible.

In conclusion, let us simply state it again: We have available the things which God prepared for those who love Him, since they are revealed by His Spirit, and Paul says, "Which things also we speak, not in the words which man's wisdom teacheth, but which the Holy Ghost teacheth; comparing spiritual things with spiritual" (I Cor. 2:13). The words are God's words.

CHAPTER XIV

VERBAL INSPIRATION: IS IT "MECHANICAL DICTATION"?

I. LIBERALS AND INFIDELS HATE VERBAL INSPIRATION AND MOCK AT IT

 1. Nels F. S. Ferre Is an Example of These Wolves in Sheep's Clothing
 2. Fosdick Mocks at "Mechanical Inerrancy"
 3. Brunner Denies Verbal Inspiration, Calling It "Mechanical"
 4. Infidel Buttrick Denies Bible "Is God's Message Dictated by Him"
 5. Karl Barth Slanderously and Falsely Infers That the Doctrine of Verbal Inspiration Was Invented After the Reformation

II. BUT THIS CHARGE OF "MECHANICAL DICTATION" AGAINST FUNDAMENTAL BIBLE BELIEVERS IS DISHONEST PRETENSE

III. HOW GAUSSEN GLORIES IN THE WAY GOD USED MEN TO WRITE HIS WORD!

IV. CONSERVATIVES HAVE BEEN FAR TOO SENSITIVE ABOUT THE TERM "MECHANICAL DICTATION"

 1. Orr Says "All Intelligent" Believers "Repudiate Dictation"
 2. Urquhart, English Editor and Scholar, Although Much More Faithful to the Scriptures Than Orr, Falls Into the Same Error of Language
 3. Henry Thinks Divine Dictation Erroneous

VERBAL INSPIRATION: IS IT "MECHANICAL DICTATION"?

We have found, beyond any possible cavil or denial, that the Bible teaches that the very words of the original Scriptures proceeded from God. Of the Scriptures, Jesus says, quoting Deuteronomy, "every word...proceedeth out of the mouth of God" (Matt. 4:4). God, through the Apostle Paul, says that divine revelation and inspiration are "not in the words which man's wisdom teacheth, but which the Holy Ghost teacheth" (I Cor. 2:13). God put His words in the mouth of His prophets, we are told repeatedly. So the Bible is verbally inspired.

Remember, too, that verbal inspiration means word-for-word inspiration, from the Latin *verbum*, meaning word. Now, whether people like it or not, the Bible claims verbal inspiration. Let no one obscure this vital truth upon which the Scriptures so insist. The words of the Bible in the original autographs are God's words.

I. LIBERALS AND INFIDELS HATE VERBAL INSPIRATION AND MOCK AT IT

Any real, God-breathed Scripture is going to be attacked, slandered and misrepresented by the enemies of Christ and the Bible. And when such false teachers wear sheep's clothing, when the infidels in bishop's robes or with the professor's cap and gown, pretend to be Christians while they deny this essential of the Christian faith, they will twist the Christian position in order to ridicule it. Not willing to openly avow that they are infidels, enemies of the God-inspired Bible and of the Christ it represents, they will pretend to some kind of inspiration but will specially slander word-for-word inspiration of the Bible.

1. Nels F. S. Ferré Is an Example of These Wolves in Sheep's Clothing

Ferre says, "The use of the Bible as a final authority for Christian truth is idolatry."[1] To accept the Bible as inspired is idolatry, says Ferre!

It was Ferre who said that to worship Jesus as God is idolatry, that Jesus was only human, that He was sinful, that Jesus may have been the bastard son of harlot Mary and of a blond Roman soldier. Yet his publishers speak of "Ferre's commitment to evangelical Christianity." Northern Baptists sponsor him as professor at Andover-Newton; Methodists kept him some years teaching in Vanderbilt University; Southern Baptist Seminary at Louisville had him for his infidel lectures. But do not expect from Ferre or from any defender of Ferre an honest defense of the Scriptures.

2. Fosdick Mocks At "Mechanical Inerrancy"

Dr. Harry Emerson Fosdick said, "From naive acceptance of the Bible as of equal credibility in all its parts because mechanically inerrant, I passed years ago to the shocking conviction that such traditional bibliolatry is false in fact and perilous in result."[2] But before you are influenced by such sly unbelief, remember Fosdick is the one who wrote the sermon on "The Peril of Worshiping Jesus," saying Jesus never intended to be worshiped, never claimed to be God, and that Jesus was divine only in the sense that Fosdick's mother was divine.[3]

Now note Fosdick's statement. He says he had accepted the Bible "as of equal credibility in all its parts," but he says that attitude was naive or ignorant. But since it is the prophesied course of such enemies of Christ and the Bible, that "through covetousness shall they with feigned words make merchandise of you" (II Pet. 2:3), and that these who deny the faith will be "giving heed to seducing spirits, and doctrines of devils; Speaking lies in hypocrisy; having their conscience seared with a hot

---

1. *The Sun and the Umbrella*, p. 39.
2. *The Modern Use of the Bible*, p. 273.
3. *The Hope of the World*, p. 104.

iron," (I Tim. 4:1,2) we need not expect an honest, straight-forward statement by Dr. Fosdick.

The Lord Jesus said such wolves would wear sheep's clothing. So Fosdick equates acceptance of the Bible as believable with being "mechanically inerrant." Note that term "mechanically." We will come to that again in a moment. But he also must sneer at old-fashioned, Bible-believing Christians, calling them idolaters, guilty of "bibliolatry." One who hates the Bible and cannot meet its honest claims, thus perverts it and slanders those who defend it.

3. Brunner Denies Verbal Inspiration, Calling It "Mechanical"

So Emil Brunner says that the churches "are still suffering from the incubus of the old mechanical theory of inspiration." [4] Here Brunner speaks as if the old-time view of inspiration, held by all Christians for seventeen hundred years, the claim of the apostles and the claim of the Bible itself, that it was given of God, verbally inspired, is "the old mechanical theory of inspiration." Instead of facing the fact that the Bible itself claims to be verbally inspired, Brunner slanders it by calling that doctrine "the old mechanical theory of inspiration."

4. Infidel Buttrick Denies Bible "Is God's Message Dictated by Him"

George A. Buttrick says about the Bible: "The theory, not without warrant in experience, was: this is God's message, dictated by Him, and written as His Hand guided the hand that held the pen...."[5] And on page 157 he says about old-time Christians:

> Then people believed the Bible. It was their daily bread, God's direct and explicit word of truth. They may not have regarded it as instantaneously celestial like the Mormon Bible, which, according to the fable, was found just as it had fallen from heaven—clamped in gold, and, resting on its covers, a pair of supernatural spectacles to guarantee the infallibility of

4. *The Mediator*, p. 183.
5. *The Christian Fact and Modern Doubt*, p. 159.

the reader; but our forefathers were sure that the Bible had as little human adulteration.   Its writers were "not so much the 'pen-men' as the 'pen' of the Holy Spirit." Every verse equally with every other was God's perfect utterance.[6]

Buttrick does not use the term "mechanical dictation," but his words mean that.   He says that the historic position about the Bible—"Its writers were 'not so much the "pen-men" as the "pen" of the Holy Spirit.'" That is, he claims that the dictation was mechanical.

Yet you must remember that it is Buttrick who tells how he walked out of a service because the minister preached on the blood atonement.   And he said of the God who required a substitute for sinful man, "That God is my Devil."[7]   He says, "But that sermon came of bibliolatry—the worship of a man-made idol called 'the inerrancy of the Scriptures.'"   And you should remember that this Buttrick, editor of the *Interpreter's Bible* commentary, darling of the seminaries, particularly Methodists and Southern Baptists, denies the deity of Christ, the inspiration of the Bible, the virgin birth, the blood atonement—every essential of the Christian faith.   Do not expect him to have Christian morals and to face the truth honestly.   Wolves wear sheep's clothing when they pretend to be sheep.   They come with "feigned words" because they are covetous for the things one can get as a professor.

But in his book, in the chapter on "The Authority of the Bible," Buttrick says, "Something has happened to the Bible." He says, "First, there was a collision with science...," then "the discovery of contradictions in the Bible." Then, "It is no use our evading or trying to hide Bible inconsistencies." He further says, "Literal infallibility of Scripture is a fortress impossible to defend: there is treason in the camp.   Probably few people who claim to 'believe every word of the Bible' really mean it." And he continues in the same paragraph: "They do not believe that the earth is flat, nor that the sky is a rain-filled plaque whose underside is studded with brilliants; nor do they expect to find at the earth's edge 'the pillars of heaven.'"

Now, of course, all honest men know that fundamental Christians all over the world know that the Bible does not teach "that the earth is flat, nor that the sky is a rain-filled plaque whose

---

6. *The Christian Fact and Modern Doubt,* p. 157.
7. *The Christian Fact and Modern Doubt,* p. 174.

underside is studded with brilliants," etc. But the truth would be much harder to answer than to state a lie, a slander, to make the infidel look wise and the Christian look silly.

Then Buttrick says, "Thirdly, the Bible was called to task for low ethical and spiritual standards."[8]

So, before you are much impressed with Buttrick's misrepresentation of the theory of verbal inspiration, remember that he is an infidel, an enemy of the Bible.

5. Karl Barth Slanderously and Falsely Infers That the Doctrine of Verbal Inspiration Was Invented After the Reformation

Barth says, "The historic conception of the Bible with its cult of heroes and the mechanical doctrine of verbal inspiration are the products of the same age and the same period."[9] Note Barth's dishonest term, "the mechanical doctrine of verbal inspiration."

II. BUT THIS CHARGE OF "MECHANICAL DICTATION" AGAINST FUNDAMENTAL BIBLE BELIEVERS IS DISHONEST PRETENSE

The Bible never teaches that it was mechanically dictated, that is, that those who put down the words of Scripture were unconscious, that their own minds and hearts were never involved, as if God did not use men at all in writing the Bible. I say, the Bible does not teach that and as far as I know, no intelligent Christian in the world believes anything of the kind.

It has been my privilege to have some contact with the great defenders of the faith, popular preachers, famous Bible teachers and evangelists. I have known fairly well W. B. Riley, H. A. Ironside, Gipsy Smith, Billy Sunday, Bob Jones, Sr., Paul Rader, James M. Gray, T. T. Shields, Wilbur Smith, George W. Truett, L. R. Scarborough and Bob Shuler. None of them have held any such doctrine. I am well familiar with the writings of

---

8. *The Christian Fact and Modern Doubt,* pp. 158-163.
9. Quoted by Pfieffer in his *Introduction to the Old Testament,* p. 170.

Charles G. Finney, Spurgeon, D. L. Moody, Sam Jones, R. A. Torrey, J. Wilbur Chapman, I. M. Haldeman, C. I. Scofield, Gaebelein, Machen, Robert Dick Wilson, Allis, Melvin Grove Kyle and Talmage. I have on my desk just now works on inspiration by Engelder, Urquhart, Laird Harris, Gaussen, B. H. Carroll, Edward J. Young, Carl W. Henry, Arthur T. Pierson, Saphir, Bettex, W. H. Griffith Thomas, Bannerman and Hodge. None of them teach a "mechanical dictation theory," meaning the writers were somnolent, or unconscious, or uninvolved in writing the Bible. Neither did the great reformers, nor Luther nor Calvin, nor the church fathers.

Dr. Hodge says, "The Church has never held what has been stigmatized as the mechanical theory of inspiration. The sacred writers were not machines. Their self-consciousness was not suspended; nor were their intellectual powers superseded. Holy men spake as they were moved by the Holy Ghost." [10]

You see, instead of saying plainly "the Bible is a lie; it claims to be inspired of God, but it is not," these wolves in sheep's clothing profess to believe that the Bible is in some sense the Word of God or at least that it contains the Word of God, but that they cannot agree with ignorant Christians that it was given by "mechanical dictation." Such a slanderous charge is a pretense, is unchristian and is intentionally deceitful.

Laird Harris writes:

> It should be unnecessary, but may perhaps be wise, to insert a protest against the equation of verbal inspiration and mechanical dictation. The protest of Machen is still worth reprinting: "The Spirit, it is said, is represented in this doctrine as dictating the Bible to writers who were really little more than stenographers. But of course all such caricatures are without basis in fact, and it is rather surprising that intelligent men should be so blinded by prejudice about this matter as not even to examine for themselves the perfectly accessible treatises in which the doctrine of plenary inspiration is set forth. It is usually considered good practice to examine a thing for one's self before echoing the vulgar ridicule of it. But in connection with the Bible, such scholarly restraints are somehow regarded as out of place. It is so much easier to content one's self with a few opprobrious adjectives such as 'mechanical,' or the like. Why engage in serious criticism when the people prefer ridicule? Why attack a real opponent when it is easier to knock down a man of straw?" Engelder quotes A. H. Strong, T. A. Kantonen, E. E. Flack, A.

---

10. *Systematic Theology*, p. 157.

Deissmann, G. T. Ladd, W. Sanday, and others who make this fatal confusion (he could also have cited Karl Barth). He also quotes Quenstedt of the Lutheran Reformation, Epiphanius and other ancients, Graebner, F. Pieper, Warfield, and other moderns as definitely not holding a mechanical theory, but advocating verbal inspiration none the less. Warfield enters a protest like Machen's against the caricature. [11]

Edward J. Young says:

> Since the writers of the Scriptures were under the influence of the Holy Spirit, it might be argued that they were nothing more than mere passive instruments through whom He spake. In speaking from God they were utterly passive, mere automata, who simply repeated the message that had been given to them. Their human characteristics were in a state of suspended animation, and they, in reality, amounted to no more than dictaphones. Hence the cry is constantly raised: "We want no mechanical dictation theory of inspiration." About this cry against "mechanical dictation," he says, "For the time being we need do nothing more than register our protest against this all too common caricature of the Scripture doctrine of inspiration. [12]

So Young joins with Gresham Machen, with Warfield, with Engelder, and with Harris against that dishonest "caricature" of the Bible doctrine of verbal inspiration. Mark you, it is as clear as it can be that Ferre, Buttrick, Fosdick, Brunner and Karl Barth are not answering any fundamentalists who really teach a mechanical theory of inspiration. They simply ridicule verbal inspiration and make it appear hateful by calling it "mechanical." As Machen said, "It is so much easier to content one's self with a few opprobrious adjectives such as 'mechanical,' or the like. Why engage in serious criticism when the people prefer ridicule? Why attack a real opponent when it is easier to knock down a man of straw?"

The Bible does not teach a mechanical inspiration without using people and oftentimes their thoughts and feelings or devotions or prayers, and revealing their thoughts. The words are God's words and the Scripture is the Word of God, but it comes through men. And I do not know of a single book on the subject, or a single reputable Bible teacher or preacher who holds that despised "mechanical view of inspiration."

Neither do the unbelieving critics know of such a reputable

---

11. *Inspiration and Canonicity of the Bible*, p. 21. (Machen's quotation is from *Christianity and Liberalism*, p. 73.)
12. *Thy Word Is Truth*, p. 26.

Bible teacher or book that claims that the writers were merely machines. They only pretend to be defending against "mechanical inspiration." They really are attacking the integrity of the Bible and the Bible doctrine of verbal or word-for-word inspiration.

III. HOW GAUSSEN GLORIES IN THE WAY GOD USED MEN TO WRITE HIS WORD!

Gaussen is at once the most thorough, the most scholarly and perhaps the most tender and devoted in his marvelous discussion of the inspiration of the Scriptures. We do not wonder that Spurgeon was entranced with it, that James M. Gray had his lifetime position settled by it, and that multiplied thousands have found here most beautifully and charmingly expressed the truth of God about inspiration.

Gaussen does not hesitate to use "dictation" on occasion, hated by infidels, but he does not mean that inspiration is mechanical or that the men whom God used to write the Bible were simply machines. So for the readers' pleasure and blessing we take an extended passage from his book. This is what we believe.

9. That the style of Moses, Ezekiel, David, St. Luke, and St. John, may be at the same time God's style, is what a child might tell us.

Let us suppose that some modern French author had thought good, at the commencement of the present century, to aim at popularity by borrowing for a time the style, we shall say, of Chateaubriand; might it not then be said with equal truth, but in two different senses, that the style was the author's and yet the style too of Chateaubriand? And if, to save the French from some terrible catastrophe by bringing them back to the Gospel, God should condescend to employ certain prophets among them, by the mouths of whom he should proclaim his message, would not these men have to preach in French? What, then, would be their style, and what would you require in it, in order to its being recognized as that of God?

If such were his pleasure, one of these prophets might speak like Fenelon, another like Bonaparte; in which case there is no doubt that it would be, in one sense, the curt, barking, jerking style of the great captain; also, and in the same sense, the sustained and varied flow of the priest of Cambray's rounded eloquence; while in another, and a higher and truer sense, it would, in both these mouths, be the style of God, the manner of God, the word of God. No doubt, on every occasion on which he has revealed himself, God might have caused an awful voice to resound from heaven, as of old from the top of Sinai, or on the banks of the Jordan. His messengers, at least, might have been only angels of light. But even then what languages would these angels have spoken? Evidently those of the earth! And if he behoved on this earth to substitute for the syntax of heaven and the vocabulary of the archangels, the words and the constructions of the Hebrews or the Greeks, why not equally have borrowed their manners, style, and personality?

10. This there is no doubt that he did, but not so as that any thing was left to chance. "Known unto him are all his works from the beginning of the world"; and just as, year after year, he causes the tree to put forth its leaves as well for the season when they respire the atmospheric elements, and, co-operating with the process at the roots, can safely draw nourishment from their juices, as for that in which the caterpillars that are to spin their silk on its branches are hatched and feed upon them; just as he prepared a gourd for the very place and the very night on which Jonah was to come and seat himself to the east of Nineveh, and when the next morning dawned, a gnawing worm when the gourd was to be withered; so, too, when he would proceed to the most important of his doings, and cause that Word to be written which is to outlast the heavens and the earth, the Lord God could prepare long beforehand each of those prophets, for the moment and for the testimony to which he had foreordained them from eternity. He chose them, in succession, for their several duties, from among all men born of women; and, with respect to them, fulfilled in its perfection that saying, "Send, O Lord, by the hand thou shouldst send."

As a skilful musician, when he would execute a long score by himself, takes up by turns the funereal flute, the shepherd's pipe, the merry fife, or the trumpet that summons to battle; so did Almighty God, when he would make us hear his eternal word, choose out from of old the instruments which it seemed fit to him to inspire with the breath of his spirit. "He chose them before the foundation of the world, and separated them from their mother's womb."

Has the reader ever paid a visit to the astonishing organist, who so charmingly elicts the tourist's tears in the Cathedral at Freiburg, as he touches one after another his wondrous keys, and greets your ear by turns with the march of warriors on the river-side, the voice of prayer sent up from the lake during the fury of the storm, or of thanksgiving when it is hushed to rest? All your senses are electrified, for you seem to have seen all, and to have heard all.

Well, then, it was thus that the Lord God, mighty in harmony, applied, as it were, the finger of his Spirit to the stops which he had chosen for the hour of his purpose, and for the unity of his

celestial hymn.   He had from eternity before him all the human
stops which he required; his Creator's eye embraces at a glance
this range of keys stretching over threescore centuries; and when
he would make known to our fallen world the everlasting counsel
of his redemption, and the coming of the Son of God, he put his
left hand on Enoch, the seventh man from Adam, and his right
on John, the humble and sublime prisoner of Patmos.   The
celestial anthem, seven hundred years before the flood, began
with these words, "Behold, the Lord cometh with ten thousand of
his saints, to execute judgment upon all"; but already, in the
mind of God, and in the eternal harmony of his work, the voice
of John had answered to that of Enoch, and closed the hymn,
three thousand years after him, with these words, "Behold, he
cometh with clouds, and every eye shall see him, and they also
which pierced him! Even so, Lord Jesus, come quickly.   Amen!"
And during this hymn of thirty centuries, the Spirit of God
never ceased to breathe in all his messengers; the angels, an
apostle tells us, desired to look into its wondrous depths. God's
elect were moved, and life eternal came down into the souls of
men.

Between Enoch and St. John, listen to Jeremiah, twenty-four
centuries after the one, and seven hundred years before the other,
"Before I formed thee in the belly," saith the Lord, "I knew thee;
and before thou camest forth out of the womb I sanctified thee,
and I ordained thee a prophet unto the nations." In vain did
this alarmed man exclaim, "Ah, Lord God! behold, I cannot
speak: for I am a child." The Lord answers him, "Say not, I
am a child: for thou shalt speak whatsoever I command thee";
and the Lord put forth his hand and touched his mouth, "Behold," said he, "I have put my words in thy mouth."

Between Enoch and Jeremiah, listen to Moses. He, too, struggles on Mount Horeb against the call of the Lord, "Alas, O my
Lord, I am not eloquent; send, I pray thee, by the hand of him
whom thou wilt send."   But the anger of the Lord is kindled
against Moses. "Who hath made man's mouth?" he says to
him.   "Now therefore go, and I will be with thy mouth, and
will teach thee what thou shalt say."

Between Jeremiah and John, listen to Paul of Tarsus, "When it
pleased God, who separated me from my mother's womb, to
reveal his Son in me, he called me by his grace, that I might
preach him among the heathen."

You see, then, that it was sometimes the artless and sublime simplicity of John; sometimes the impassioned, elliptical, rousing,
and logical energy of Paul; sometimes the fervour and solemnity
of Peter; it was Isaiah's magnificent, and David's lyrical poetry;
it was the simple and majestic narratives of Moses, or the sen-
tentious and royal wisdom of Solomon—yes, it was all this; it
was Peter, it was Isaiah, it was Matthew, it was Job, it was
Moses; yet it was God.

"Are not all these which speak Galileans?" the people exclaimed on the day of Pentecost; yes, they are so; but the message that is on their lips comes from another country — it is from heaven. Listen to it; for tongues of fire have descended on, their heads, and it is God that speaks to you by their mouths.

11. Finally, we would fain that people should understand that this human individuality to which our attention is directed in the Scriptures, far from leaving any stain there, or from being an infirmity there, stamps upon them, on the contrary, a divine beauty, and powerfully reveals to us their inspiration.

Yes, we have said that it is God who speaks to us there, but it is also man; — it is man, but it is also God. Admirable Word of God! it has been made man in its own way, as the eternal Word was! Yes, God has made it also come down to us full of grace and truth, like unto our words in all things, yet without error and sin! Admirable Word, divine Word, yet withal full of humanity, much-to-be-loved Word of my God!

Yes, in order to our understanding it, it had of necessity to be put upon mortal lips, that it might relate human things; and, in order to attract our regard, behoved to invest itself with our modes of thinking, and with all the emotions of our voice; for God well knew whereof we are made. But we have recognised it as the Word of the Lord, mighty, efficacious, sharper than a two-edged sword; and the simplest among us, on hearing it, may say like Cleopas and his friend, "Did not our hearts burn within us while it spoke to us?"

With what a mighty charm do the Scriptures, by this abundance of humanity and by all this personality with which their divinity is invested, remind us that the Lord of our souls, whose touching voice they are, does himself bear a human heart on the throne of God, although seated on the highest place, where the angels serve him and adore him for ever! It is thus, also, that they present to us not only that double character of variety and unity which already embellishes all the other works of God, as Creator of the heavens and the earth; but, further, that mingling of familiarity and authority, of sympathy and grandeur, of practical details and mysterious majesty, of humanity and divinity, which is recognisable in all the dispensations of the same God, as Redeemer and Shepherd of his Church.

It is thus, then, that the Father of mercies, while speaking in his prophets, behoved not only to employ their manner as well as their voice, and their style as well as their pen; but, further, often to put in operation their whole faculties of thought and feeling. Sometimes, in order to show us his divine sympathy there, he has deemed it fitting to associate their own recollections, their human convictions, their personal experiences, and their pious emotions, with the words he dictated to them; sometimes, in order to remind us of his sovereign intervention, he has preferred dispensing with this unessential concurrence of their recollections, affections, and understanding.

Such did the Word of God behove to be.

Like Immanuel, full of grace and truth; at once in the bosom of God and in the heart of man; mighty and sympathizing; heavenly and of the earth; sublime and lowly; awful and familiar; God and man!

Studied under this aspect, considered in this character, the Word of God stands forth without its like; it presents attractions quite unequalled; it offers to men of all times, all places, and all conditions, beauties ever fresh; a charm that never grows old, that always satisfies, never palls.　With it, what we find with respect to human books is reversed; for it pleases and fascinates, extends and rises in your regard the more assiduously you read it.　It seems as if the book, the more it is studied and studied over again, grows and enlarges itself, and that some kind unseen being comes daily to stitch in some fresh leaves.　And thus it is that the souls, alike of the learned and the simple, who have long nourished themselves on it, keep hanging upon it as the people hung of old on the lips of Jesus Christ.　They all think it incomparable; now powerful as the sound of mighty waters; now soft and gentle, like the voice of the spouse to her bridegroom; but always perfect, "always restoring the soul, and making wise the simple."[13]

Gaussen did not believe that inspiration was mechanical: he would not deny that God could use David's prayers and praises nor that God, in the following epistles, could not express the compassion and the burden of Paul's heart which He Himself had created in the apostle and so expressed His own heart through him.　So we suggest that honest readers look with scorn on the insincere charges of "mechanical dictation," and that fundamental teachers, preachers and writers do not fall into the trap of either defending or demolishing this "man of straw," as Machen says it is of "mechanical dictation."

IV. CONSERVATIVES HAVE BEEN FAR TOO SENSITIVE ABOUT THE TERM "MECHANICAL DICTATION"

Conservative, Bible-believing scholars, constantly reading the books of unbelievers and anxious not to appear unscholarly or traditional, have, unconsciously, in most cases, soaked up the coloring, some of the phraseology, even some of the secondary

---

13. *The Inspiration of Holy Scripture,* pp. 49-55.

ideas of liberals, the enemies of the Bible. Hear the warning of
Dr. Edward J. Young:

> There is today a tendency among evangelicals to yield to some
> of the demands of modern unbelief. This is seen both in a
> general depreciation of doctrine and a lack of clarity and posi-
> tiveness in stating it, and also in acceptance of some of the
> tenets of "higher" criticism. Sometimes it is also seen in an un-
> willingness to come out resolutely in opposition to the trends of
> the times and to bear the reproach of Christ. It is to those who
> may have yielded somewhat to the prevailing trend that this
> work is directed.
>
> Many scholars are concerned only with, what they call, the
> human side of the Bible. If this meant that they merely wished
> to study the languages, geographical and historical background,
> and questions of special introduction, always paying due heed to
> the supernatural character of the Bible, there could be no ob-
> jection. Such is, however, not the case. Rather, that which en-
> gages their attention is a study of the above-mentioned and
> kindred subjects in complete disregard of the Bible's attestation
> to its own divinity. One receives the impression from reading
> many modern books on the Bible that there is no real coming to
> grips with the doctrine of special revelation and all that it in-
> volves.[14]

The more or less unthinking absorption of the liberal viewpoint, or more or less being influenced by it, failing to resist it,
is deplored by R. Laird Harris:

> But how about the Church itself? Surely the leaders of our
> great Protestant denominations have resisted the "acids of mo-
> dernity." Unfortunately, it is not so. Painful it is to have to
> relate how our church leaders have for the most part felt that
> they could neutralize these acids simply by diluting them slightly.
> The effort has been not to meet the attack head on but to appease
> the gathering unbelief at every point and meanwhile try to
> salvage some shreds of faith from the general ruin. The result
> has been a preaching without conviction, a religion without
> authority, a Christ of human proportions. And in a world sick
> unto death the Church has turned to the panacea of ecumeni-
> calism to present to the world a united front — united in unbelief.[15]

Now look for the tendency to cater to the terminology of
liberals about so-called "mechanical dictation."

---

14. *Thy Word Is Truth*, p. 5.
15. *Inspiration and Canonicity of the Bible*, p. 37.

1. Orr Says "All Intelligent" Believers
"Repudiate Dictation"

Dr. James Orr of Scotland (Professor of Apologetics and Systematic Theology in the United Free Church College in Glasgow) was a great scholar and very influential in theology. And he regarded himself as a defender of the faith. His book, *Revelation and Inspiration*, has had great influence.

Unfortunately, Orr was too much influenced by higher criticism and the attacks of unbelievers on the Bible. He says he believes in verbal inspiration. But, he says, "'Verbal inspiration,' however, is often taken to mean much more than this. It is apt to suggest a *mechanical* theory of inspiration, akin to dictation, which all intelligent upholders of inspiration now agree in repudiating."[16]

But it is *not true* that "all intelligent" upholders of inspiration "agree in repudiating" that God gave the very words of the Bible, "dictated" them, if you wish the word. Calvin, Gaussen, Warfield (*Inspiration and Authority of the Bible*, p. 87), Pieper and Lenski, all used the word "dictate" or "dictation" to describe inspiration, and they were not unintelligent. Orr, a compromising conservative, was very wrong when he made the statement above.

But before you are too much impressed with Orr's statement, you must remember that what he means by verbal inspiration is not what the Bible claims for itself at all. He openly accepted the Darwinian theory of evolution.[17] He insisted on "progressive revelation" and differing degrees of inspiration in various parts of the Bible.[18] He believes that part of the Bible is based on "oral traditions and records."[19] He says the Bible cannot be proved errorless.[20] He denies the accuracy of the Bible in historical and scientific matters.[21] And even on the very page where he warns about "*mechanical* theory of inspiration, akin to dictation, which all intelligent upholders of inspiration now agree in repudiating," he really is repudiating what we believe and what Gaussen, Warfield, Engelder, Laird Harris, B. H.

---

16. *Revelation and Inspiration*, p. 210.
17. *Revelation and Inspiration*, pp. 101,108.
18. *Revelation and Inspiration*, pp. 102,103.
19. *Revelation and Inspiration*, p. 156.
20. *Revelation and Inspiration*, p. 199.
21. *Revelation and Inspiration*, p. 212.

Carroll, Edward Young, Machen, Robert Dick Wilson believed. On the same page he stresses that "the *reports of the Lord's own sayings* in the Gospels" are variously reported, so evidently the Synoptic writers did not give the very words of Christ, he thinks.

No, Dr. Orr, with your ideas of errors in the Bible, scientific and historical inaccuracies, old traditions incorporated, you are no defender of a "God-breathed Book," given "not in the words which man's wisdom teacheth, but which the Holy Ghost teacheth" (I Cor. 2:13).

2. Urquhart, English Editor and Scholar, Although Much More Faithful to the Scriptures Than Orr, Falls Into the Same Error of Language

In his great book John Urquhart says:

> What, then, is "the traditional view," which not very long ago ruled unquestioned in the churches of this land, and which today, for hundreds of thousands, is bound up with Christianity itself? The reply can be given fully only in the two words — Verbal Inspiration. But here again we have to guard against misconception. Opponents of this view ran away with the inference that verbal inspiration must imply that the words were **dictated** to the inspired writers. The belief is, therefore, labelled "a mechanical theory," and is frequently at once thrown aside with contempt. Those who act in this way have no idea that they are doing injustice to the ordinary view; but such is, nevertheless, the fact. The presence of the word "inspiration," ought to have prevented them confounding it with dictation. The merchant does not inspire his clerk when he dictates to him. Dictation excludes the possibility of inspiration as completely as anything can. [22]

Note that he says that opponents of verbal inspiration "run away with the inference that verbal inspiration must imply that the words were *dictated* to the inspired writers. The belief is, therefore, labelled 'a mechanical theory,' and is frequently at once thrown aside with contempt." Unfortunately, while he believes in verbal inspiration and the accuracy of the Bible, Urquhart did not go into what the Bible clearly teaches about inspiration, and he was too much impressed with the complaint

---

22. *The Inspiration and Accuracy of the Holy Scriptures*, p. 12.

of unbelievers.   Unbelievers are against verbal inspiration, and not because they think it is mechanical.

Again Urquhart says, "The presence of the word 'inspiration' ought to have prevented them confounding it with dictation. The merchant does not inspire his clerk when he dictates to him."   But he thinks of inspiration as a certain divine afflatus with which the writers were inspired, as men may be inspired by great music, by mountain scenery, by a tremendous orator, by a holy thought!   If he had grasped the idea that God is not promising that the men were inspired but only that the Scriptures themselves were inspired, he would not have fallen into this error.   Men writing the Bible wrote more than they understood.   The words were inspired and the content of the Scripture goes far beyond what men who wrote the Scriptures understood.   The prophecy of Isaiah is exalted, not because the man was a spiritual genius; perhaps he was, perhaps not; but that is not the explanation of the prophecy of Isaiah.   It came from God, and whatever God wanted to use of Isaiah, He used.   And well He might.   He had prepared him from before his birth.

But the Bible doctrine of inspiration has nothing to do with how the men felt when they wrote or how exalted was their state or how clear was their understanding.   That question is not involved in determining what men wrote, when they wrote the Scriptures, breathed out from God,   "in words which the Holy Ghost teacheth."   The Bible is not inspired because it inspires us.   The Bible is God-breathed.   And Urquhart was wrong in using the dictionary definition instead of the Bible definition for II Timothy 3:16.

We will speak about "dictation" a little later.   But Urquhart was too much impressed with the complaints of unbelievers and he did the Bible doctrine of inspiration a disservice by his inadequate defense.

Urquhart believed in verbal inspiration, believed that the very words were inspired and said so repeatedly.   But he was too sensitive to the criticisms of Driver and others.

3. Henry Thinks Divine Dictation Erroneous

Dr. Carl Henry says in the book edited by Walvoord:

In view of the stylistic differences and personality factors which distinguish the various writings, it would be clearly erroneous to conceive of inspiration in terms of divine dictation. Yet the fact remains that, in the giving of the Law, written on stone, we are confronted by the recording of revelation by absolute miracle entirely apart from human means. [23]

Yet Dr. Henry defends the inspiration of the Bible. He says on the same page, "Nowhere is any hint to be found of the compatibility of inspiration with error, or that some parts of Scripture are to be segregated from others as more, or less, trustworthy." Dr. Henry thinks it erroneous "to conceive of inspiration in terms of divine dictation." He says, "The message of the Bible is not the message of men merely; it is the veritable Word of God, since all Scripture is God-breathed." [24] He says, "No distinction of inspiration exists between parts of the Bible." [25]

But his trouble is that he has a contradictory position. If God gave the words, that is dictation. He does not realize that God had called men before they were born, prepared them all their lives, formed their character, their personality, their idiosyncrasies, their vocabulary, their style of speech, then used the men He had formed to say exactly what He wanted them to write down. If Dr. Henry had thought through the fact that the Scriptures were all settled in Heaven before they were revealed on earth (Ps. 119:89), and that God prepared certain things for those who loved Him before He revealed them by His Spirit (I Cor. 2:9,10), he could see how God could dictate to men and use their vocabularies and their personalities. We think that it is probably true that most very scholarly men who read predominantly the work of unbelieving scholars are influenced in their language and even in their thinking, away from the simplicity of what the Bible says on such matters.

4. Custer, Following Thomas, Says "Dictation Is Not Inspiration"

Dr. Stewart Custer of Bob Jones University has out a very fine, small book. In it he takes a good, strong, clear stand

---

23. *Inspiration and Interpretation*, p. 275.
24. *Inspiration and Interpretation*, p. 255.
25. *Inspiration and Interpretation*, p. 257.

that the Bible is inerrant.   In chapter 7 on "The Conservative View of Inspiration" he has the following paragraph under the heading, "Denial of Dictation":

> Again and again Conservatives repudiate the theory of mechanical dictation. Griffith Thomas wrote, "Verbal inspiration does not mean mechanical dictation, as if the writers were only passive; dictation is not inspiration."   Hodge is just as emphatic, "The Church has never held what has been stigmatized as the mechanical theory of inspiration.   The sacred writers were not machines. Their self-consciousness was not suspended; nor were their intellectual powers superseded. Holy men spake as they were moved by the Holy Ghost. It was men, not machines; not unconscious instruments, but living, thinking, willing minds, whom the Spirit used as his organs. Moreover, as inspiration did not involve the suspension or suppression of the human faculties, so neither did it interfere with the free exercise of the distinctive mental characteristics of the individual.' [26]

Again, Dr. Custer, like Griffith Thomas and others before him, has his thinking too much colored by the liberals with whom he differs.   He defends what does not need to be defended.   He answers the complaint of the liberals which is not an honest complaint.   And in doing so, he unfortunately does discredit to the Bible doctrine which he earnestly seeks to defend.   To connect "mechanical" with "dictation" is itself a mistake.

Most people who are against what they call mechanical dictation are really against verbal inspiration, that is, they deny that God gave the words, that men wrote "the words which the Holy Ghost teacheth."   We do not agree with them, and ought not encourage them in attacks on verbal inspiration.

5. Thomas Thinks God "Breathed Into" the Words of Men in Scripture Instead of Breathing Out the Words

W. H. Griffith Thomas makes the same mistake as Urquhart because he misunderstands what the word "inspired," in II Timothy 3:16, means. In his book he says:

> Let us notice 2 Timothy 3:16. Whether we follow the Authorized Version or the Revised Version, (he means the American Standard Version) the thought is: "Every writing is God-

---

26. *Does Inspiration Demand Inerrancy?* p. 85.

breathed." God, **somehow or other, breathed into these writings** (emphasis added), and therefore we are concerned with words.

And then he calls attention to the express statement of I Corinthians 2:13:

> "**Words** which the Holy Ghost teacheth." Could anything be more definite and clear than this? Not the words which man's wisdom teacheth, but the **words** which "the Holy Ghost teacheth." And so there is an intimate, a necessary connection, between thoughts and words. Whether it be for our own thinking, or for intercourse between man and man, thoughts must be expressed in words. [27]

But he has misunderstood what II Timothy 3:16 says. The Greek word there translated "inspired of God" is *Theopneustos*. And that does *not* mean that "God, somehow or other, *breathed into these writings*" as Thomas says, but it means that God Himself *breathed out* these writings. Thomas was misled, we suppose, by the word "inspired" from the Latin, and the usual dictionary definition, but that is a mistake. God did not breathe on men's words. He breathed out His own words through men.

But what Thomas is saying is that God breathed on words of men's choice, because in the preceding paragraph he said, "3. *The Media of the Bible.* — I do not know any other term than this that will better express my idea. I mean the words of the men (2 Pet. 1:21)." But the good man finds himself on both sides of the fence! He admits that the Bible says the Scripture is in "Words which the Holy Ghost teacheth," and yet he thinks that really means they are men's words and that God someway breathed into the words which the men selected. No, the words were from God, and only secondarily and incidentally were they men's words.

Now here is where Dr. Thomas' mistake leads him. On pages 89 and 90 he says further:

> But some one says: Does not this mean "verbal inspiration"? Well, we can call it verbal inspiration if we like, or we can call it plenary inspiration, if we prefer, so long as we do not call it dictation. When a man dictates a letter to his secretary, he does not inspire her. It is mechanical dictation, and he expects her to reproduce exactly what he tells her. But in Scripture we do not have mechanical dictation, but inspiration. [28]

---

27. *God Spake All These Words*, p. 89.
28. *God Spake All These Words*, pp. 89,90.

He continues that "inspiration extends to the form as well as to the substance, that *it reaches to the words as well as to the thoughts.*" But Dr. Thomas conceives of inspiration as God inspiring the men and then supervising and breathing into their words. That is not what the Bible teaches. God Himself breathed out the words.

So Dr. Thomas, a scholarly man too much impressed by the critics, equates mechanical inspiration with dictation. He dodges the term hated by the liberals because they hate verbal inspiration, and thus he, I am sure, without intention, takes away from the authority which God Himself clearly gives to the very words of the Bible in the original autographs.

And let us say it again, it is not the men who are inspired but the writings. God used men, used their feelings, their emotions, their personalities, no doubt, in little degree or much, exactly as He wished. He had prepared the men, prepared the circumstance, prepared their vocabulary, their viewpoints, their thoughts. He had planned the men before they were born and now He could use them perfectly for the purposes that He intended and for which He had prepared them. So God breathed out the very words of Scripture and had men write them down. And the men, in some fashion, little or much, participated.

Again, let us be plain and clear as the Bible itself is clear and plain, God Himself gave the words. Jesus said of the Scriptures, "Every word...proceedeth out of the mouth of God." The Bible is "God-breathed" (*Theopneustos*), and is written "not in the words which man's wisdom teacheth, but which the Holy Ghost teacheth." God did not breathe on the words of men, He breathed out the words Himself. They are men's words but their source was God. They are not mechanical, but if God giving the words means dictation, then they were dictated.

Men may properly deny that inspiration was "mechanical," but we should take care lest we throw out the baby with the bath water. God still says that He gave the very words of Scripture.

CHAPTER XV

DID GOD DICTATE THE BIBLE?

I. GOD GAVE THE VERY WORDS

1. All Bible Believers Agree Certain Parts of Scripture Are the Very Words of God

2. Of Course God Used Men and Their Language

3. When Man Takes Part in a Miracle, It Is God Who Does It

II. BUT IF THE WORDS ACTUALLY CAME FROM GOD, THAT IS "DICTATION"

1. God Did Not Give Just the Thought

2. Inspiration Is Not Simply Superintendence

3. Why Would It Bemean Bible Writers for God to Give the Words?

III. BLESSED MEN OF GOD HAVE SAID THE BIBLE IS "DICTATED"

1. Calvin Said Scriptures Were "Dictated by the Holy Spirit"

2. Warfield Says "It Is a Process of Nothing Other Than 'Dictation'"

3. Gaussen Speaks of "the Divine Wisdom Which Has Dictated the Scriptures"

DID GOD DICTATE THE BIBLE?

Did God dictate the very words in the original autographs as men wrote them down? Webster says *dictate* comes from the Latin *dictatus*—"to say." He defines the word

1. To tell or utter so that another may write down...
2. To say, utter, or communicate authoritatively...

Now, did God "say," did He "utter so that another may write down" the Scriptures? Did He "say, utter or communicate authoritatively" the words men wrote down in the Scriptures? We think it clear that He did. Was that, then, dictation?

I. GOD GAVE THE VERY WORDS

Here we must simply face what the Scriptures claim for themselves.

1. All Bible Believers Agree Certain Parts of Scripture Are the Very Words of God

He gave the very words of the Ten Commandments speaking from Mount Sinai, and later wrote them with the finger of God in tables of stone. Of course, God gave the very words on the plaster of Belshazzar's palace. God spoke the very words from Heaven at the baptism of Jesus. In the case of all the angels who spoke to men, certainly God gave the very words. In some three thousand cases, Griffith Thomas tells us, the Bible says, "And God said," or "The word of the Lord came saying," or similar statements.

And so if the statements given are exact quotations from

God, then certainly God dictated the words in those cases. But whether speaking through Balaam's ass or through wicked High Priest Caiaphas or through Old Testament prophets who did not understand what they had written, or through Moses and Paul, the two greatest men of the Old and New Testaments, perhaps, did God give to them the very words?

2. Of Course God Used Men and Their Language

I do not ask, Did God use men? Of course He did. And the question is not, Did the various writers, as God's penmen, use different styles and vocabularies? Everyone knows there are differences and variations, and Bible believers all say that God not only chose the men to write the Scripture before they were born but prepared them to write and used them in writing. The Bible believers all agree that God used men to write the Scriptures and that this was not mechanical. And we think it clear that God not only chose the men to write the Scripture before they were born but prepared them through the years, controlled the circumstances, built their character, their viewpoint, their vocabulary, then used them to write for Him what He had prepared ahead of time and now revealed "not in the words which man's wisdom teacheth, but which the Holy Ghost teacheth."

We note what God said to Jeremiah in Jeremiah 1:5, and then what Jeremiah said in verse 6:

"Ah, Lord God! behold, I cannot speak: for I am a child. But the Lord said unto me, Say not, I am a child: for thou shalt go to all that I shall send thee, and whatsoever I command thee thou shalt speak. Be not afraid of their faces: for I am with thee to deliver thee, saith the Lord. Then the Lord put forth his hand, and touched my mouth. And the Lord said unto me, Behold, I have put my words in thy mouth."

Does not that teach us that God not only knew Jeremiah before he was born but set him up, sanctified him, and ordained him to be a prophet? And does it not say that Jeremiah could not of himself have brought these messages in the prophecy, but God touched his mouth and said, "Behold, I have put my words in thy mouth"? Surely God is saying that He prepared Jeremiah and prepared the message and was the author of both. So the words of Jeremiah and his prophecy are exactly the words of God. The style is God's, the vocabulary is God's. God put some of the feelings and emotions and experiences in Jeremiah also, and though they are in some secondary sense Jeremiah's words, God Himself breathed out the words of the Scripture.

3. When Man Takes Part in a Miracle, It Is God Who Does It

God and Mary together brought into the world the Baby Jesus. Jesus was the Son of Mary, but were not any characteristics He had like His mother—by birth or social inheritance as He grew up—just as perfectly planned and brought about as the deity who resided in that body? Luke could say when he wrote his Gospel, "It seemed good to me also...to write unto thee in order...." Is it too much to believe, then, that it seemed good to God first, God who called Luke and ordained him and appointed him before he was born and then prepared him to write and gave him the words in which to write?

We are not asking, Did it seem good to Luke to write that Gospel? We are asking, Did it not seem good to God first and was not that attitude of mind in Luke planned and planted by the Lord?

Christ in His incarnation is the proof that when God and man (or in this case the woman Mary) work together in a miracle, it is man who cooperates or submits or trusts, passively, but God Himself plans and does the supernatural work. Mary could be glad to say yes to God's plan, but Mary did not create the One who came from God through her. So the Bible writers could lend their pens and whatever personal participation, feeling, testimony, praises, or admonition God had prepared them for and allowed to be in them. But God who prepared the men and the circumstances gave the words to include or express the things God Himself had prepared. God gave the words through men, but they are God's words.

On this matter Warfield says:

> It is vain to say that the message delivered through the instrumentality of this tongue is conditioned at least in its form by the tongue by which it is spoken, if not, indeed, limited,

curtailed, in some degree determined even in its matter, by it. Not only was it God the Lord who made the tongue, and who made this particular tongue with all its peculiarities, not without regard to the message He would deliver through it; but His control of it is perfect and complete, and it is as absurd to say that He cannot speak His message by it purely without that message suffering change from the peculiarities of its tone and modes of enunciation, as it would be to say that no new truth can be announced in any language because the elements of speech by the combination of which the truth in question is announced are already in existence with their fixed range of connotation. The marks of the several individualities imprinted on the messages of the prophets, in other words, are only a part of the general fact that these messages are couched in human language, and in no way beyond that general fact affect their purity as direct communications from God. [1]

We believe that men wrote the Bible because that is the clear claim of the Bible itself. Well, why cannot we believe that the very words are from God since the Bible expressly says so?

On a sudden impulse, God did not look about to find somebody through whom He could give part of the Scripture. In that case, either He would prevent those personalities from coloring the Scripture or He would necessarily limit the Scriptures by using their personalities, vocabulary style, etc. No, that is not the way Scripture came into being. God planned the message ahead of time. It was settled in Heaven. It was "prepared for those who love him" before it was "revealed... unto us by his Spirit" (I Cor. 2:9,10). The men themselves were called, ordained, appointed before they were born, as was Jeremiah (Jer. 1:5); as in the case of Isaiah, "called from the womb" and given a name (Isa. 49:1). His mouth was made like a sharp sword as the personality and character of Isaiah came into being, molded by the hand of God through the years and by God's circumstances who was made into a "polished shaft" and then hidden until it was time for God to use him. And then the Lord who, Isaiah said, "formed me from the womb to be his servant" would use him (Isa. 49:5). Whatever style Isaiah had was God's style; whatever personality Isaiah had was a personality God had created for His own use.

Come back to the one most solid, clear thought in the Scripture about inspiration: God Himself gave the words.

1. *The Inspiration and Authority of the Bible*, p. 94.

II. BUT IF THE WORDS ACTUALLY CAME FROM GOD, THAT IS "DICTATION"

Is the word *dictation* hateful? Then liberals and infidels made it hateful. Men, too anxious to please unbelievers and too anxious to disavow the straw man of "mechanical dictation," have avoided and feared the term. But that is not straight thinking, and it is not quite intellectually honest, it seems to me. Griffith Thomas' book is labeled, *God Spake All These Words.* And that quotation from Exodus 20:1, referring to the words of the Ten Commandments, is really a proper name for a book about the inspiration of the Bible. Well, if God gave all the words in the Bible, then is not that dictation?

Suppose I dictate a letter to a secretary. That means I tell her word-for-word what to write. Well, did not God tell the men who wrote the Bible word-for-word what to write?

1. God Did Not Give Just the Thought

As editor of *THE SWORD OF THE LORD*, I might counsel with some man and suggest that he write an article for *THE SWORD OF THE LORD* on some particular subject. We might talk it over and agree about the general thought. Then the man might write the article and express the thoughts we agreed upon in his own words. That would not be dictation, but it would not be verbal inspiration either.

Or I might be a little more specific in my requirements for an article for *THE SWORD OF THE LORD*. I might counsel with the author from time to time to make sure that he said as nearly as possible what I felt should be published, and then I might read the article over very carefully to approve it or to have it further corrected before printing. You understand that would not be dictation, but it would not be word-for-word inspiration either. It would be supervision. The words would be his words, not mine in any sense. That is not the way the Bible was written.

2. Inspiration Is Not Simply Superintendence

Let's carry the illustration a little further. Suppose he and I sat at the same desk and suppose I watched every sentence that he wrote, and allowed him to write what he understood ought to be the substance of the article on which we agreed. But suppose that I carefully supervised him just to see that no error crept in. That would not be dictation, but it would not be verbal inspiration either. It would be superintendence. Some people think that is the way the Bible came, but it is not. God gave the words; they were breathed out from God.

3. Why Would It Bemean Bible Writers for God to Give the Words?

Do you really think you honor God by insisting that God was not so strict and not so all-powerful and all-pervasive in the inspiration of the Bible? Why would one be more anxious for men to get the credit and God get less credit? In the Bible itself the question is never brought as if there were some strange paradox, some awful mystery about how the Bible could be the word of men and the Word of God, too! No, it is obviously clear that God used men. But it is equally clear that He gave them the very words. If God saw no contradiction, if God did not feel the need to hedge and trim on this question, why should we? Why should we try to put into this plan that men copied down oral tradition or from ancient records or from their memories or from eyewitnesses? Why do you want more of men and less of God?

"Dictation," says someone, "dishonors the men who wrote the Bible." Shame! Shame! So you want big prophets and a little God, do you? You do not want a man simply hearing what God says and writing it down, do you? Well, then, your attitude is simply the carnal attitude of the unbelieving world that always wants to give man credit instead of God, whether for salvation or inspiration. A secretary is not ashamed to take dictation from man. Why should a prophet be ashamed to take dictation from God?

Face it honestly, if God gave the very words and men wrote them down, that is dictation. It was not *mechanical* dictation.

It ought not to be hard for us to understand that God, who could give the very words by a miracle, could also express the feelings and character and personality of the men whom He had formed and through whom He gave the words.

III. BLESSED MEN OF GOD HAVE SAID THE BIBLE IS "DICTATED"

Are you ashamed to say boldly that God gave the very words of the Bible, that He dictated them? If so, then you do not feel about it as John Calvin and Warfield and Gaussen and many another saint and scholar felt.

1. Calvin Said Scriptures Were "Dictated by the Holy Spirit"

Commenting on the classic text II Timothy 3:16 saying that all Scripture is God-breathed, John Calvin says:

> This is a principle which distinguishes our religion from all others, that we know that God hath spoken to us, and are fully convinced that the prophets did not speak at their own suggestion, but that, being organs of the Holy Spirit, they only uttered what they had been commissioned from heaven to declare. Whoever, then, wishes to profit in the Scriptures, let him, first of all, lay this down as a settled point, that the Law and the Prophets are not a doctrine delivered according to the will and pleasure of men, but dictated by the Holy Spirit. ... This is the first clause (of the text) that we owe to the Scripture the same reverence which we owe to God; because it has proceeded from Him alone, and has nothing belonging to man mixed with it.[2]

Note carefully the first settled point one must decide in order to profit in the Scriptures. It is, says Calvin, "that the Law and the Prophets are not a doctrine delivered according to the will and pleasure of men, but *dictated by the Holy Spirit.*" *Dictated*, Calvin says, not mechanical dictation but dictation; not with no color of human personality, for the Scriptures had that, but nevertheless "dictated by the Holy Spirit." We now

---

2. Cited by Urquhart in *The Inspiration and Accuracy of the Holy Scriptures,* pp. 129,130.

ask you, who know the same truth as Calvin knew but avoid the term *dictation* because of the sneers of the Fosdicks and Buttricks and Brunners: Where among all of them was a mighty, exact scholar like Calvin? We should be as logical and mentally honest as Calvin. If God gave the words, what is wrong with saying, "Dictated by the Holy Spirit"?

2. Warfield Says "It Is a Process of Nothing Other Than 'Dictation'"

Warfield says:

> (Deut. xviii. 18), **"and I will put my words in his mouth,** and he shall speak unto them all that I shall command him." The process of revelation through the prophets was a process by which Jehovah put His words in the mouths of the prophets, and the prophets spoke precisely these words and no others. So the prophets themselves ever asserted. "Then Jehovah put forth his hand, and touched my mouth," explains Jeremiah in his account of how he received his prophecies, "and Jehovah said unto me, Behold, I have put my words in thy mouth" (Jer. i. 9; cf. v. 14; Isa. li. 16; lix. 21; Num. xxii. 35; xxiii. 5. 12. 16). Accordingly, the words "with which" they spoke were not their own but the Lord's: "And he said unto me," records Ezekiel, "Son of man, go, get thee unto the house of Israel, and speak with my words unto them" (Ezk. iii. 4). It is a process of nothing other than "dictation" which is thus described (2 S. xiv. 3. 19), though, of course, the question may remain open of the exact processes by which this dictation is accomplished.[3]

Note carefully that Warfield describes word-for-word inspiration and he said, "It is a process of nothing other than 'dictation' which is thus described," and leaves open the question of the "exact processes by which this dictation is accomplished." What a mighty scholar was Warfield! What do those people gain who, for fear of displeasing the liberals, will not use Warfield's language? The real enemy the liberals fight is verbal and plenary inspiration of the Bible. And those who are not willing to give that up need not shun the language of Calvin and Warfield that if God gives the very words, "and the prophets spoke precisely these words and no others," then "it is a process of nothing less than 'dictation.'"

---

3. *The Inspiration and Authority of the Bible,* pp. 86,87.

3. Gaussen Speaks of "the Divine Wisdom Which Has Dictated the Scriptures"

Speaking boldly for plenary, complete and verbal inspiration of the Scriptures, Gaussen rejoices "respecting the living and personal form under which the Scriptures of God have been given to us." That is, he believes thoroughly that God used these human personalities as well as their pen. So Gaussen says:

> We begin by declaring how far we are from contesting the fact alleged, while, however, we reject the false consequences that are deduced from it. So far are we from not acknowledging this human individuality stamped throughout on our sacred books, that, on the contrary, it is with profound gratitude—with an ever-growing admiration—that we contemplate this living, actual, dramatic, humanitary character diffused with so powerful and charming an effect through all parts of the book of God. Yes (we cordially unite with the objectors in saying it), here is the phraseology, the tone, the accent of a Moses; there, of a John: here, of an Isaiah; there, of an Amos: here, of a Daniel or of a Peter; there, of a Nehemiah, there again of a Paul. We recognise them, listen to them, see them. Here, one may say, there is no room for mistake. We admit the fact; we delight in studying it; we profoundly admire it; and we see in it, as we shall have occasion more than once to repeat, one additional proof of the divine wisdom which has dictated the Scriptures.[4]

Note carefully Gaussen is not speaking of mechanical dictation, but in this human element discernible in the Scriptures he finds "one additional proof of *the divine wisdom which has dictated the Scriptures.*" God dictated the Scriptures, says Gaussen.

Here are three of the mightiest Bible scholars and Bible defenders who agree that God dictated the Scriptures. Now do those who tremble at such a term know some Scripture truth that Calvin and Warfield and Gaussen did not find? Have some of the unbelievers proved false the conclusions to which Calvin and Gaussen and Warfield were driven by the Scriptures themselves?

We would have to say that word-for-word inspiration, verbal inspiration, is necessarily divine dictation. We do not deny that God used men; we simply say that God gave the men the words

---

4. *The Inspiration of the Holy Scriptures,* pp. 41,42.

they wrote down and we say it because the Bible says it so plainly and so often that honest Bible believers must accept it.

We do not insist that one must use the term *dictation* about the Scriptures. But if one scurries to cover from the insincere terminology used by unbelievers and thus tries to avoid the odium which unbelievers find in verbal inspiration, then the retreat seems to be not only unnecessary but seriously wrong.

CHAPTER XVI

PROPHECIES FULFILLED PROVE THE BIBLE IS THE SUPERNATURALLY INSPIRED BIBLE

I. CONSIDER THE AMAZING FULFILLMENT OF PROPHECIES ABOUT THE NATION ISRAEL

1. The Great Promises About Israel Begin With the Promise to Abraham

2. The Backslidings, Captivity, Regathering and Dispersal Again of Israel Clearly Prophesied and Fulfilled

3. A Later Dispersal of Jews to All the Nations of the World Was Foretold in Scripture

4. One of the Most Amazing Parts of God's Prophecy About Israel Is That the Nation Cannot Be Destroyed

II. THE BIBLE OUTLINE OF THE HISTORY OF THE WORLD HAS BEEN FULFILLED THUS FAR TO THE LETTER

III. WITH INFINITE DETAIL THE COMING OF CHRIST, HIS LIFE, DEATH AND RESURRECTION, ARE FORETOLD IN THE OLD TESTAMENT

IV. MANY LESSER PROPHECIES ADD UNIMPEACHABLE TESTIMONY THAT THE BIBLE IS SUPERNATURALLY INSPIRED

1. Jeremiah 49:17,18 Tells of the Desolation of Edom:

2. Destruction and Ruin of Moab and Ammon Just as Clearly Foretold

3. The Utter and Permanent Destruction of Babylon Is Emphatically Foretold in Isaiah 13:19-22:

PROPHECIES FULFILLED PROVE THE BIBLE IS THE SUPERNATURALLY INSPIRED BIBLE

There are many evidences that the Bible is the Word of God. But one evidence stands above all others as the obvious one, the proof that every person, sinner and saint, beginning student or scholar, can use. The Bible proves itself. What it predicts comes to pass. What it says proves true to all who try it out.

In Deuteronomy 18, verses 20 to 22, God Himself proposes this infallible test:

"But the prophet, which shall presume to speak a word in my name, which I have not commanded him to speak, or that shall speak in the name of other gods, even that prophet shall die. And if thou say in thine heart, How shall we know the word which the Lord hath not spoken? When a prophet speaketh in the name of the Lord, if the thing follow not, nor come to pass, that is the thing which the Lord hath not spoken, but the prophet hath spoken it presumptuously: thou shalt not be afraid of him."

How can we know whether a prophet speaks the truth? If the thing he prophesied follows as he promised in the name of God that it would, then the man's prophecy is true and he spoke for God. But if the man speaks presumptuously, pretending to speak for God when God does not speak through him, or when he speaks in the name of other gods, and the thing which he promised does not follow, in punishment "even that prophet shall die."

What a simple and fair test this is of the Bible.

The reason millions of common Christians everywhere, I mean people who love God and try to please Him, accept the

Bible as the very inspired Word of God is that it proves itself. That is why the apostles and early Christians accepted it absolutely. That is why down through the centuries the great creeds of Christendom declare that the Bible is the inspired, errorless Word of God.

The Bible itself is prophecy. There are other evidences that accumulate to make the Bible "the impregnable rock of Holy Scripture," as Prime Minister Gladstone called it. These evidences are like those for the resurrection of Christ, which the Scripture itself says was proved "by many infallible proofs" (Acts 1:3). But we give a whole chapter to this matter of fulfilled prophecy since the Bible itself is prophecy, and since the matter is so incontestably proved where every honest heart seeks to know the truth.

To prophesy in the Bible generally means to speak in the power and wisdom of the Spirit of God. So we read again and again that the Spirit of the Lord came on this one or on that one "and they prophesied." So it was with Zacharias and Elisabeth (Luke 1:41,67). So it is promised in Joel 2:28-32 for the New Testament age, called "the last days," and that began to be fulfilled at Pentecost as Peter plainly says in Acts 2:14-21.

But in a peculiar, infallible sense, the Bible is prophecy. It calls itself that repeatedly.

Second Peter 1:19-21 speaks of the Scripture:

"We have also a more sure word of prophecy; whereunto ye do well that ye take heed, as unto a light that shineth in a dark place, until the day dawn, and the day star arise in your hearts: Knowing this first, that no prophecy of the scripture is of any private interpretation. For the prophecy came not in old time by the will of man: but holy men of God spake as they were moved by the Holy Ghost."

"We have also a more sure word of prophecy," said Peter, more sure than the eyewitnesses of Peter and James and John who were with Jesus "in the holy mount" and saw Him transfigured. Dr. Scofield says, "That is, made more sure by fulfilment in part." No, more sure because personal testimony might be colored by human frailty in understanding or in memory or in expression, but the inspired Scripture is more sure because it is breathed out from God Himself, as II Timothy 3:16 tells us. This Scripture is "a more sure word of prophecy," and verse 20 tells us that "no prophecy of the scripture is of any private interpretation." The Scripture is prophecy. And verse 21 tells us, "For the prophecy came not in old time by the will of man: but holy men of God spake as they were moved by the Holy Ghost." The Scripture is "a more sure word of prophecy."

We see from this passage that all the Old Testament Scriptures are included in the term prophecy.

Five times the book of Revelation calls itself a prophecy. Revelation 1:3: "Blessed is he that readeth, and they that hear the words of this prophecy." Revelation 22:7: "Blessed is he that keepeth the sayings of the prophecy of this book." Verse 10 of the same chapter says, "Seal not the sayings of the prophecy of this book." Verse 18: "For I testify unto every man that heareth the words of the prophecy of this book, If any man shall add unto these things, God shall add unto him the plagues that are written in this book." And verse 19 again calls it the book of prophecy: "And if any man shall take away from the words of the book of this prophecy, God shall take away his part out of the book of life."

In fact, the Scripture tends here not only to call the book of Revelation a book of prophecy, but the whole book of Scriptures is "the book of this prophecy," and the blessing and the plagues connected with Revelation are true about all the Scriptures.

It is common talk in the New Testament to say that "Esaias prophesied of this people," or similar statements about the Scriptures in the book of Isaiah.

The resurrected Christ talked to the two on the road to Emmaus, "And beginning at Moses and all the prophets, he expounded unto them in all the scriptures the things concerning himself" (Luke 24:27). Note, "Moses and all the prophets." Similarly, the same day, to all the disciples assembled in Jerusalem, He said, "...that all things must be fulfilled, which were written in the law of Moses, and in the prophets, and in the psalms, concerning me." But in Deuteronomy 18:15 and 18 Moses is called a prophet, and in Acts 2:30 Peter says about David, "Therefore being a prophet, and knowing that God had sworn with an oath to him...." So the law of Moses is prophecy and the Psalms are prophecy, and, of course, the writings of what we call the Major and Minor Prophets are prophecy. The Bible, then, is in a special sense prophecy.

So now we have a simple and honest proposition that honest men must face: Are the prophecies and foretellings in the Word of God obviously from God? Does what God promise come to pass? Are Bible prophecies from time to time fulfilled, proving the Bible is the Word of God? Beyond any shadow of doubt every honest person can find for himself that the Bible proves itself the very infallible Word of God, proves it by prophecies already fulfilled.

Dr. W. A. Criswell, president of the Southern Baptist Convention, says:

> The outstanding, differentiating characteristics of Israel's religion is predictive prophecy. Only in the Bible will you find the phenomenon of prophecy. [1]

He continues:

> Where is there a god or gods; where is there a founder of religion such as Confucius, Buddha, Muhammad, or Zoroaster; or where is there any other who could with such certainty predict the future? Where is there a statesman who, in these times, can foretell what will be the condition of things in Europe or in America one hundred years from now or even ten years from now? Yea, I can tell any man how he can become a multimillionaire within a relatively short time. If he can predict what will happen even in the course of an hour, he can make himself fabulously rich by playing the market on the New York Stock Exchange. We do not know the future. It is the prerogative of God to know what tomorrow will bring. The fulfilled prophecies of the Bible bespeak the omniscience of its author.
>
> In Isaiah 41:21-23 we have what is probably the most remarkable challenge to be found in the Bible. "Produce your cause, saith the Lord; bring forth your strong reasons, saith the King of Jacob. Let them bring them forth, and shew us what shall happen: let them shew the former things, what they be, that we may consider them, and know the latter end of them; or declare us things for to come. Shew the things that are to come hereafter, that we may know that ye are gods: yea, do good, or do evil, that we may be dismayed, and behold it together." This Scripture reference has both a negative and a positive value. Negatively, it suggests an infallible criterion by which we may test the claims of religious impostors. Positively, the passage calls attention to an unanswerable argument for the truthfulness of God's Word. Jehovah bids the prophets of false faith successfully to predict events lying in the distant future; their success or failure will show whether or not they are true sages or merely

---

1. *Why I Preach That the Bible Is Literally True*, p. 30.

pretenders and deceivers. On the other hand, the demonstrated fact that God alone knows the future and in his Word declares the end from the beginning shows that he is God and that the Scriptures are his inspired revelations to mankind.[2]

How strong is the statement of God in Isaiah 46:9-11:

"Remember the former things of old: for I am God, and there is none else; I am God, and there is none like me, Declaring the end from the beginning, and from ancient times the things that are not yet done, saying, My counsel shall stand, and I will do all my pleasure: Calling a ravenous bird from the east, the man that executeth my counsel from a far country: yea, I have spoken it, I will also bring it to pass; I have purposed it, I will also do it."

I. CONSIDER THE AMAZING FULFILLMENT OF PROPHECIES ABOUT THE NATION ISRAEL

Since all the Old Testament, except the first 11 chapters, deal principally with Israel, we find an amazing number of prophecies given from time to time and later fulfilled.

1. The Great Promises About Israel Begin With the Promise to Abraham

"And in thee shall all families of the earth be blessed" (Gen. 12:3). That promise was restated to Abraham in Genesis 13:14-17. It included giving Abraham the whole land of Canaan, included a nation of unnumbered descendants, and the promise to continue forever. The promise was repeated in Genesis 15. Abraham was told that his descendants would go into Egypt but later "the fourth generation shall come hither again," and the covenant was promised in verse 18.

The covenant is repeated again in Genesis 17:6-8, and particularly in verses 15 to 19 and included the promise of Abraham's famous "seed," the Lord Jesus. And that nation should come through Sarah, yet barren when the promise was given.

---

2. *Why I Preach That the Bible Is Literally True,* pp. 30,31.

Some 430 years went by, and Abraham's grandson, Jacob, and his family, the patriarchs, all went down to Egypt and in the fourth generation were brought out with a mighty hand as God had promised.

In these enlightened days, let no man say that there was no man Abraham, no Ur of the Chaldees, no going into Egypt and no returning as a nation. Ur of the Chaldees has now been excavated; Abraham was a real man; the events in Egypt in the return of the nation Israel is history. The fact that kings should come from the loins of Abraham was fulfilled in David's dynasty and eventually in Christ.

2. The Backslidings, Captivity, Regathering and Dispersal Again of Israel Clearly Prophesied and Fulfilled

Criswell says of Deuteronomy 28: "Here is prewritten the sad history of Israel."

The land of Palestine was a land "flowing with milk and honey." It supported vast populations. It was a prize sought by the world kingdoms, by the great kingdoms — the Canaanites, the Hittites, the Egyptians, the Medes and Persians, the Babylonians, Greece and Rome. The great cedars in Lebanon were like no other forests in the world. Solomon's kingdom over Israel was the richest then in the world. Now and then the great sands in the Arabian desert blow away to reveal parts of great cities which were once inhabited but which now are starved for lack of water. There are remnants of canals for irrigation, where now there is no water to fill them. The land once principally covered by great forests, is now barren hills. Where once there was the abundant "early and the latter rain," now it is often drouth. Why is that? Because of the sins of Israel. God foretold in Deuteronomy 28:23,24, "Thy heaven that is over thy head shall be brass, and the earth that is under thee shall be iron. The Lord shall make the rain of thy land powder and dust: from heaven shall it come down upon thee, until thou be destroyed."

Because of their sins, the destruction and captivity of the

nation Israel by their enemies is plainly foretold in Deuteronomy 28:25,26:

"The Lord shall cause thee to be smitten before thine enemies: thou shalt go out one way against them, and flee seven ways before them: and shalt be removed into all the kingdoms of the earth. And thy carcase shall be meat unto all fowls of the air, and unto the beasts of the earth, and no man shall fray them away."

Verse 33 says, "The fruit of thy land, and all thy labours, shall a nation which thou knowest not eat up; and thou shalt be only oppressed and crushed alway." Now we know that Israel was carried into captivity to Babylon, and Judah for full seventy years. Then, as the books of Ezra and Nehemiah tell us, the decree went forth from the Emperor Cyrus and a remnant of Jews came back, built Jerusalem, built the Temple and populated the land again. That regathering itself had been prophesied by Jeremiah before the captivity and in Jeremiah 29:11-14 he said:

"For I know the thoughts that I think toward you, saith the Lord, thoughts of peace, and not of evil, to give you an expected end. Then shall ye call upon me, and ye shall go and pray unto me, and I will hearken unto you. And ye shall seek me, and find me, when ye shall search for me with all your heart. And I will be found of you, saith the Lord: and I will turn away your captivity, and I will gather you from all the nations, and from all the places whither I have driven you, saith the Lord; and I will bring you again into the place whence I caused you to be carried away captive."

3. A Later Dispersal of Jews to All the Nations of the World Was Foretold in Scripture

The captivity in Babylon is not the only dispersal of Israel foretold in the Scriptures. In Deuteronomy 30:1-6 we have that dispersal foretold and the regathering prophesied:

"And it shall come to pass, when all these things are come upon thee, the blessing and the curse, which I have set before thee, and thou shalt call them to mind among all the nations, whither the Lord thy God hath driven thee, And shalt return

unto the Lord thy God, and shalt obey his voice according to all that I command thee this day, thou and thy children, with all thine heart, and with all thy soul; That then the Lord thy God will turn thy captivity, and have compassion upon thee, and will return and gather thee from all the nations, whither the Lord thy God hath scattered thee. If any of thine be driven out unto the outmost parts of heaven, from thence will the Lord thy God gather thee, and from thence will he fetch thee: And the Lord thy God will bring thee into the land which thy fathers possessed, and thou shalt possess it; and he will do thee good, and multiply thee above thy fathers. And the Lord thy God will circumcise thine heart, and the heart of thy seed, to love the Lord thy God with all thine heart, and with all thy soul, that thou mayest live."

When was the second dispersal of the Jews to take place? We know it happened in A.D. 70 when Jews rebelled against the Roman Empire and the Roman general Titus (later emperor), took the city. It has been said that over a million Jews, crowded into the area, were slain and a hundred thousand or more sold as slaves. Then later in the year 135 A.D. some Jews came back and there was rebellion again and this time such utter destruction that a team of oxen plowed across the face of the once populace city, now destroyed.

Was that scattering of Israel foretold? Yes, the Lord Jesus, weeping over Jerusalem, foretold its destruction in Luke 19: 41-44:

"And when he was come near, he beheld the city, and wept over it, Saying, If thou hadst known, even thou, at least in this thy day, the things which belong unto thy peace! but now they are hid from thine eyes. For the days shall come upon thee, that thine enemies shall cast a trench about thee, and compass thee round, and keep thee in on every side, And shall lay thee even with the ground, and thy children within thee; and they shall not leave in thee one stone upon another; because thou knewest not the time of thy visitation."

And again in Luke 21:20-24 the destruction of the city and the wholesale scattering of Jews in all the world is foretold in the words of Jesus:

"And when ye shall see Jerusalem compassed with armies, then know that the desolation thereof is nigh. Then let them

which are in Judaea flee to the mountains; and let them which are in the midst of it depart out; and let not them that are in the countries enter thereinto. For these be the days of vengeance, that all things which are written may be fulfilled. But woe unto them that are with child, and to them that give suck, in those days! for there shall be great distress in the land, and wrath upon this people. And they shall fall by the edge of the sword, and shall be led away captive into all nations: and Jerusalem shall be trodden down of the Gentiles, until the times of the Gentiles be fulfilled."

Jesus gave these prophecies about A.D. 30, and Luke wrote them before the forty years were expired, up to the destruction of Jerusalem. Sir William Ramsay and other famous scholars have now so authenticated the historical accuracy of the book of Luke that only the ignorant or the intentional unbeliever would doubt that these actual prophecies were made, were written down, and then were fulfilled to the letter.

4. One of the Most Amazing Parts of God's Prophecy About Israel Is That the Nation Cannot Be Destroyed

In Matthew 24:34 and 35 Jesus said, "Verily I say unto you, This generation shall not pass, till all these things be fulfilled. Heaven and earth shall pass away, but my words shall not pass away." The word "generation" here is the Greek *genea*, "the primary definition of which is, 'race, kind, family, stock, breed.' (So all lexicons.)" says the Scofield Bible notes. The race of Jews will not be destroyed, neither will the words of Christ.

God promised to Abraham, "All the land which thou seest, to thee will I give it, and to thy seed FOR EVER." Then the seed of Abraham cannot disappear. And Genesis 17:13 calls circumcision "an everlasting covenant" with Israel. God promised David,"And thine house and thy kingdom shall be established for ever before thee: thy throne shall be established for ever" (II Sam. 7:16). That promise is yet future. It was future when it was given, but it involves the kingdom of David over Israel. In the prophets, God promised again and again that Israel would be regathered and be converted to God. And Jeremiah 31:35,36 tells us how permanent and unchangeable are these promises to Israel the nation:

"Thus saith the Lord, which giveth the sun for a light by day, and the ordinances of the moon and of the stars for a light by night, which divideth the sea when the waves thereof roar; The Lord of hosts is his name: If those ordinances depart from before me, saith the Lord, then the seed of Israel also shall cease from being a nation before me for ever."

The fact that there are Jews as a nation, Jews in blood, Jews in national consciousness, Jews in tradition, Jews in separation from the Gentiles everywhere in the world, prove that the mighty hand of God is on the nation Israel. I do not think the little nation Israel in Palestine today is a fulfillment of the great prophecy of the future. But at least it proves the Jews are a separate people, with a separate language, a separate consciousness, with a definite national inheritance coming down through the centuries undestroyed.

Again Dr. Criswell says:

> There were many ancient people cited in the Old Testament. There were the Hittites, the Hivites, the Jebusites, the Ammonites, the Moabites, but nobody today has ever seen anybody who ever saw anyone who ever heard of anyone who ever saw a Hittite or a Jebusite or a Hivite or a Moabite. But Jesus said the Jews will be here until he comes again. Are they? Do you know a Jew? [3]

Other great cities and areas have been devastated with war and the people murdered or displaced. But where are the people of Nineveh? of Babylon? of Edom? of Tyre? Where are the people of the great nation Carthage, in North Africa? Other peoples may scatter and dissolve into the surrounding population and appear no more in their racial and national integrity. Not so the Jews. They are still Jews and there will be Jews until Christ returns and gathers the remnant, purges out the remnant, and sets up the kingdom of David again over Israel.

---

3. *Why I Preach That the Bible Is Literally True*, p. 32.

II. THE BIBLE OUTLINE OF THE HISTORY OF THE WORLD HAS BEEN FULFILLED THUS FAR TO THE LETTER

The Lord controls the destinies of the nations of the earth. "The king's heart is in the hand of the Lord, as the rivers of water: he turneth it whithersoever he will" (Prov. 21:1).

King Nebuchadnezzar, the first world emperor, learned "that the most High ruleth in the kingdom of men, and giveth it to whomsoever he will, and setteth up over it the basest of men" (Dan. 4:17). It is remarkable, even miraculous, the way God foretold His plans for the nation Israel and has carried them out. It is even more amazing, perhaps, that He gives in advance an outline of all the world empires and the course of human history, in the Bible.

In Daniel 2 we read that the first world emperor Nebuchadnezzar, greatly moved by the fact that he was the first man ever to rule the then known world, had a vision from God of a great statue of a man with a head of gold, breast and arms of silver, belly and thighs of brass, legs of iron, feet part of iron and part of clay (Dan. 2:31-33). In the king's vision, he saw a stone cut out without hands which smote the image upon his feet and ground it to powder and the wind blew it away. And the interpretation in God's meaning in the dream is clearly told us in Daniel 2:37-44:

"Thou, O king, art a king of kings: for the God of heaven hath given thee a kingdom, power, and strength, and glory. And wheresoever the children of men dwell, the beasts of the field and the fowls of the heaven hath he given into thine hand, and hath made thee ruler over them all. Thou art this head of gold. And after thee shall arise another kingdom inferior to thee, and another third kingdom of brass, which shall bear rule over all the earth. And the fourth kingdom shall be strong as iron: forasmuch as iron breaketh in pieces and subdueth all things: and as iron that breaketh all these, shall it break in pieces and bruise. And whereas thou sawest the feet and toes, part of potters' clay and part of iron, the kingdom shall be divided; but there shall be in it of the strength of the iron, forasmuch as thou sawest the iron mixed with miry clay. And as the toes of the feet were part of iron, and part of clay, so the kingdom shall be partly strong, and partly broken. And

whereas thou sawest iron mixed with miry clay, they shall mingle themselves with the seed of men: but they shall not cleave one to another, even as iron is not mixed with clay. And in the days of these kings shall the God of heaven set up a kingdom, which shall never be destroyed: and the kingdom shall not be left to other people, but it shall break in pieces and consume all these kingdoms, and it shall stand for ever."

Here four world kingdoms are described. They were in this order: Babylon, represented by the head of gold; the breast and arms representing Media-Persia, to follow; then the belly and thighs of brass, picturing the Grecian Empire under Alexander the Great; then the legs of iron and the feet, part of iron and part of clay, representing the Roman Empire—the two legs picturing the divided Roman Empire, east and west, with two capitals, at Constantinople and at Rome; and the ten toes representing the disintegration of the Roman Empire into ten principal nations. And the prophecy clearly leaves no room for any other. The statue represents the kings of this earth down to the coming of Christ, who will destroy these kingdoms and set up a kingdom that "shall break in pieces and consume all these kingdoms, and it shall stand for ever."

There is no room for the infidel critics to say that all these things were foretold after they had become fact, that is, that Daniel was writing history instead of prophecy. No, the more scholars know about the years before Christ, the more certain it becomes that Daniel was a historical character in Babylon, that the book of Daniel was written then, and that God foretold the four great world empires when only one of them had come into existence. The world empires had been foretold about 600 years B.C. Daniel lived to see the Babylonian Empire become that of the Medes and Persians. The Septuagint included the book of Daniel, already accepted in the Old Testament canon, and the *Encyclopaedia Britannica* says:

> It was natural to begin with the law, and the Greek version of the Pentateuch dates from the beginning of the 3rd century B.C. In the 2nd century B.C., when it had become customary to read not only the law but the prophets in public worship, the bulk of this second section of the Hebrew scriptures was similarly translated (p. 336, Vol. 20).

Only those who do not believe the Bible, are not Christian in attitude and convictions, deny that the book of Daniel was written by the man and at the time which it claims. And the world empires proceeded in exactly the form and the nature foretold in Daniel 2. At last appeared the Roman Empire, then it was divided into the eastern and western empires, represented by the two legs of the statue. Then no other world empire followed, as the Scripture makes clear they will not follow. The papacy, Charlemagne, Kaiser Wilhelm of Prussia, Hitler, Stalin, Mao of China, all have aspired the world empire as the communists do today, but they have all failed and all must fail. The remnants of the Roman Empire are still divided into the ten toes, and will be at Christ's second coming and His return to reign.

The four world empires are pictured again in prophecy in Daniel 7. The four beasts: a lion with eagle's wings, the bear with three ribs in its mouth, the leopard with four wings and four heads, and the fourth beast, dreadful and terrible, with ten horns. There we see in Daniel 7:8 the prophecy of a king who will partially restore the Roman Empire, and he is none else than the Man of Sin, the Antichrist. Then "the prince that shall come" is mentioned again in Daniel 9:26 and 27, and even the seven years of his power is foretold. And the Roman beast appears again in Revelation 13, combining the characters of the previous world empires with ten horns representing ten kings. This ruler, dictator, antichrist, "the beast" and the confederation of the kings uniting with him, will be destroyed at Christ's coming, the Scripture says.

But it is important to note that no other world empire, like Babylon, Media-Persia and Rome, is to come except this short revival of the Roman Empire itself. And that cannot come until "he that now letteth," or restrains the influence of the Holy Spirit on Christians, is removed at the rapture. "The mystery of iniquity doth already work" toward such a world empire, but it cannot succeed.

Who but God could possibly have foretold the entire major events and course of human history?

III. WITH INFINITE DETAIL THE COMING OF CHRIST, HIS LIFE, DEATH AND RESURRECTION, ARE FORETOLD IN THE OLD TESTAMENT

Again Dr. Criswell says:

> The marvelous portrait of Jesus to be found in the Old Testament is a miracle of the omniscient God. Who could draw a picture of a man not yet born? Surely God and God alone. Nobody knew a thousand years ago that Milton was going to be born or five hundred years ago that Washington was to be born or two hundred years ago that Churchill was to be born. Yet here in the Bible we have the most striking and unmistakable likeness of a man portrayed, not by one, but by twenty or twenty-five artists, none of whom had ever seen the man they were painting. The man was Jesus, the Christ.[4]

Then on the same page Dr. Criswell says:

> The messianic prophecies and their fulfilments in Christ are simply amazing in their number and in their detail. Let us consider just a few of them:
> (1) Genesis 3:15 says he is to be born the seed of the woman.
> (2) Isaiah 7:14; 49:1; Micah 5:3 tell us he is to be born of a virgin.
> (3) Genesis 9:18,27 says he is to be a descendant of Shem.
> (4) Genesis 12:3; 18:18; 22:18 tell us he is to be a descendant of Abraham.
> (5) Genesis 17:19; 21:12; 26:4 tell us he is to be a descendant of Isaac.
> (6) Genesis 28:4-14; Numbers 24:17; Isaiah 49:3 tell us he is to be a descendant of Israel, that is, of Jacob.
> (7) Genesis 49:9-10; I Chronicles 5:2; Micah 5:2 tell us he is to be born of the tribe of Judah.
> (8) 2 Samuel 7:12-15; 23:1-5, and other passages too numerous to mention, tell us that he is to be born of the house of David.
> (9) Micah 5:2 tells us that he is to be born in Bethlehem, the City of David.
> (10) The passages in the Bible that describe the characteristics of his life and work are too numerous even to mention.
> (11) Isaiah 62:11 and Zechariah 9:9 describe his triumphal entry into Jerusalem.
> (12) Psalm 41:9 and Zechariah 11:12-13 describe his betrayal by a friend and disciple even at the cost of thirty pieces of silver.
> (13) Genesis 3:15; Psalm 22:1-21; Isaiah 50:6; 53:1-12; and

---

4. *Why I Preach That the Bible Is Literally True*, p. 34.

Zechariah 13:7 describe his sufferings on the cross and his death for our sins.

(14) Psalm 22:16 and Zechariah 13:6-7 describe the piercing of his hands and his feet.

(15) Psalm 22:16 and Isaiah 53:8-12 describe his death on the cross.

(16) Psalm 22:18 describes the lots cast for his vesture.

(17) Psalm 16:10 and Isaiah 53:9 describe his being embalmed and his being entombed.

(18) Psalm 16:10; 17:15; and Jonah 1:17 portray his resurrection on the third day.

(19) Psalm 8:5-6 and 110:1 describe his ascension into heaven.[5]

Dr. Criswell here did not mention the fact that it was clearly foretold exactly when Christ would come—sixty-nine weeks of years, 483 years, from the going forth of the commandment of Cyrus to rebuild Jerusalem after the captivity (Dan. 9:25). And by the type of the passover lamb, slain on the fourteenth day of Nisan, in midafternoon, every year for some 1500 years, show that "Christ our passover" (I Cor. 5:7) would die at a certain hour on a certain day, after He came.

Wise men from the east having the prophecies of Daniel knew when to expect the coming of the Saviour. When they got to Jerusalem and found the prophecy of Micah 5:2, they knew that He should be born in Bethlehem. And types all through the ceremonial law, the sacrifices, the priesthood, the tabernacle furniture, all pictured the Saviour revealing His life and person and work so much in detail that one would be dull and stubborn in his unbelief indeed who does not find the Bible the very infallible Word of God!

The sacrifices pictured that Jesus would die. The shewbread in the Tabernacle pictured Him as the Bread from Heaven, just as the manna had done. The golden lampstand burning pure olive oil pictured Christ filled with the Spirit during all His ministry, as "the Light of the world." The anointed high priest pictured Christ our High Priest in His intermediatorial work.

It is fair to say that the only people who do not believe that the Bible is the infallible, divinely inspired Word of God are

---

5. *Why I Preach That the Bible Is Literally True*, pp. 33,34.

those who will not even check the overwhelming evidences which are available to all.

IV. MANY LESSER PROPHECIES ADD UNIMPEACH-ABLE TESTIMONY THAT THE BIBLE IS SUPERNATURALLY INSPIRED

1. Jeremiah 49:17,18 Tells of the Desolation of Edom:

"Also Edom shall be a desolation: every one that goeth by it shall be astonished, and shall hiss at all the plagues thereof. As in the overthrow of Sodom and Gomorrah and the neighbour cities thereof, saith the Lord, no man shall abide there, neither shall a son of man dwell in it." So the rose-red city of Petra, cut out of the solid rock with infinite labor, a marvel of the world, still lies desolate as was prophesied.

The utter destruction of Nineveh is foretold carefully. The minor prophet Nahum was occupied wholly with "the burden of Nineveh." In 1:8 Nahum says, "But with an overrunning flood he will make an utter end of the place thereof, and darkness shall pursue his enemies." In 2:13 he says, "Behold, I am against thee, saith the Lord of hosts, and I will burn her chariots in the smoke, and the sword shall devour thy young lions: and I will cut off thy prey from the earth, and the voice of thy messengers shall no more be heard." Yes, God has made "an utter end" of Nineveh and "the voice of thy messengers shall no more be heard."

Zephaniah 2:13 says also, "And he will stretch out his hand against the north, and destroy Assyria; and will make Nineveh a desolation, and dry like a wilderness." Nineveh was one of the largest cities in the world but it was utterly destroyed. Other cities of like age — Damascus, Jerusalem, Athens, Rome — have lived on, have been rebuilt, have continued despite wars and desolations. But not Nineveh. The prophecy is fulfilled.

2. Destruction and Ruin of Moab and Ammon Just As Clearly Foretold

Zephaniah 2:9 says, "Therefore as I live, saith the Lord of

hosts, the God of Israel, Surely Moab shall be as Sodom, and the children of Ammon as Gomorrah, even the breeding of nettles, and saltpits, and a perpetual desolation: the residue of my people shall spoil them, and the remnant of my people shall possess them." Where now are any Moabites or Ammonites? Rather, Arabs, descended from Ishmael, now inhabit what was once the countries of the Moabites and Ammonites.

3. The Utter and Permanent Destruction of Babylon Is Emphatically Foretold in Isaiah 13:19-22:

"And Babylon, the glory of kingdoms, the beauty of the Chaldees' excellency, shall be as when God overthrew Sodom and Gomorrah. It shall never be inhabited, neither shall it be dwelt in from generation to generation: neither shall the Arabian pitch tent there; neither shall the shepherds make their fold there. But wild beasts of the desert shall lie there; and their houses shall be full of doleful creatures; and owls shall dwell there, and satyrs shall dance there. And the wild beasts of the islands shall cry in their desolate houses, and dragons in their pleasant palaces: and her time is near to come, and her days shall not be prolonged."

First Peter 5:13 sends greeting from "the church that is at Babylon," where Peter preached, but we think rather the Babylon country and area, not the ancient city. The Scriptures have been marvelously fulfilled.

The destruction of Tyre, one of the great kingdom cities of the ancient world, is foretold in Ezekiel 26:3-5:

"Therefore thus saith the Lord God; Behold, I am against thee, O Tyrus, and will cause many nations to come up against thee, as the sea causeth his waves to come up. And they shall destroy the walls of Tyrus, and break down her towers: I will also scrape her dust from her, and make her like the top of a rock. It shall be a place for the spreading of nets in the midst of the sea: for I have spoken it, saith the Lord God: and it shall become a spoil to the nations."

Tyre was so strong that neither Shalmaneser nor the world ruler Nebuchadnezzar could take it. The Phoenician people from Tyre and Sidon ruled the commerce of the seas. But Tyre was to be destroyed. Tyre is broken down, and this amazing prophecy has been fulfilled: "I will also scrape her dust from her, and make her like the top of a rock." How did that come to pass? In the days of Nebuchadnezzar, the city moved out to an island nearby and could not be taken. But in 332 Alexander the Great took the city after a seige of seven months, "by his constructing a mole connecting it with the mainland" (Young's Analytical Concordance). To make that causeway from the coast out to the island, he destroyed all the houses in the mainland, scraped even the dirt down to the rock to make a highway to the island. Thus Tyre was taken, dwindled and disappeared and the site of the ancient city is scraped bare of dust where fishermen spread their nets. How amazingly God uses men to fulfill His prophecies!

Three cities in Galilee received a special curse in the time of Christ because they did not repent under His mighty, miracle-working ministry. In Matthew 11:20-23 He said:

"Then began he to upbraid the cities wherein most of his mighty works were done, because they repented not: Woe unto thee, Chorazin! woe unto thee, Bethsaida! for if the mighty works, which were done in you, had been done in Tyre and Sidon, they would have repented long ago in sackcloth and ashes. But I say unto you, It shall be more tolerable for Tyre and Sidon at the day of judgment, than for you. And thou, Capernaum, which art exalted unto heaven, shalt be brought down to hell: for if the mighty works, which have been done in thee, had been done in Sodom, it would have remained until this day."

Note the three cities named: Chorazin, Bethsaida and Capernaum. As Sodom and Gomorrah were destroyed under God's curse, so were these cities to be.

Seven times I have gone through the land of Palestine. Tiberius on the Sea of Galilee still remains. So does Nazareth. But we have only a vague idea where the two cities of Chorazin and Bethsaida are. In recent years the ruins of the second century synagogue at Capernaum have been discovered and it is fairly sure we know the site of the city which has utterly disappeared.

Does it not become increasingly clear that God knows all the future and that in the Bible He has foretold much of it?

I do not wonder that Peter said:

"We have also a more sure word of prophecy; whereunto ye do well that ye take heed, as unto a light that shineth in a dark place, until the day dawn, and the day star arise in your hearts: Knowing this first, that no prophecy of the scripture is of any private interpretation. For the prophecy came not in old time by the will of man: but holy men of God spake as they were moved by the Holy Ghost." — II Pet. 1:19-21.

CHAPTER XVII

AMAZING SCIENTIFIC ACCURACY OF THE BIBLE

I. WE SEEK GOD'S TRUTH IN NATURE AND IN THE BIBLE

1. Christians Have No Quarrel With Known Facts, True Science

2. The Quibbles of Dishonest Unbelievers Are Not Important

3. They Are Wrong Who Deny That the Bible Never Speaks on Matters of Science

II. SCIENTIFIC FACTS REVEALED IN THE BIBLE NOT THEN KNOWN TO SCIENCE

1. "For the Life of the Flesh Is in the Blood" — Lev. 17:11

2. Out in Space the World Hangs on Nothing, Is Round, Revolves

3. There Are an Uncounted Multitude of Stars

4. Plants and Animals Reproduce Themselves Only "After Their Kind"

5. Many Other Scientific Facts Are Inferred in the Scriptures, Written Before Men Could Have Known They Were True

III. HOW AMAZING THAT THE BIBLE MAKES NO ERRORS IN FACTUAL STATEMENTS

1. Consider the Blunders of Other Ancient Writings Not Found in Scripture

2. Scientists' Fickle, Changeable Theories: Not the Bible

AMAZING SCIENTIFIC ACCURACY
OF THE BIBLE

Men sometimes like to say that the Bible is not a textbook of science, but that it was given to show the way of salvation, not to tell the facts of science. Some like to say that therefore the Bible is to show us the Rock of Ages, not to show us the age of the rocks.

Thus they try to make a foundation for saying that the Bible story of creation in six days, the creation of Eve and the fall of man are all allegorical, poetic, figurative but not literally factual. Thus they would make room in their thinking for the theory of origin and development of plants and animals and man by evolutionary processes, or by "progressive creation," as a process extending for ages. Thus they would make the flood of Genesis a local matter or a refinement of Babylonian legend.

Such men would also eventually be compelled either to deny the inerrancy of the Bible or to say that the Bible is simply written in the terms of the culture of the times, that it is absolutely correct only in matters of religion and then only as the New Testament progresses in accuracy and corrects the Old. They would eventually then be led to deny the perfection and sinlessness of Jesus Christ or that He was either a product of His times, without perfect knowledge, or that He spoke in the culture of His age with veiled truth, knowing better.

No! If "every word of God is pure," as Proverbs 30:5 says; if "every word...proceedeth out of the mouth of God," as Jesus Himself quoted in Matthew 4:4, then God talks as correctly about scientific matters as about spiritual matters. He speaks as truly when He mentions a fact incidentally as when He discusses a matter at more length.

The Bible is literally the Word of God. It does not deal

primarily with what we call scientific matters, but when it does mention them, it mentions them correctly with the perfect knowledge of God and with the accuracy of a divinely inspired Scripture.

I. WE SEEK GOD'S TRUTH IN NATURE AND IN THE BIBLE

Dr. Cornelius Van Til, in his syllabus, *The Doctrine of Scripture*, says, "Dealing first with science, we accept the distinction made by Dr. Enno Wolthuis between science 'as no more than a technique' and science as 'an interpretation of nature.' 'For example,' says Wolthuis, 'anyone who studies the behavior of electrons must conclude, simply on the basis of experimental data, that they possess wave properties similar to those of light' (*Science, God and You*, Grand Rapids, 1965, p. 67)."[1]

1. Christians Have No Quarrel With Known Facts, True Science

And I suggest that here we have no quarrel with science "as no more than a technique." Known facts discovered by investigation and experiment show that scientific achievement, in the sense of modern medicine, invention, manufacturing techniques, does not contradict or question the Bible.

But science as "an interpretation of nature" is strictly a philosophy of guesswork, not a scientific knowledge of facts, and so it is godless and usually not only untrue but the enemy of God's revealed truth.

The Christian has no battle with truth. All truth is from God, whether truth in nature or in the Bible. The Ten Commandments are from God but just as certainly the earth about us, the musical scale, the multiplication table, the chemical composition of water, the specific gravity of iron or lead, and such settled, permanent, factual principles, are from God. And we need have no fear that anyone will ever discover a scientific fact that is contradictory to the plain statements of the Scripture

---

1. *The Doctrine of Scripture*, p. 46.

properly interpreted. Scientists may presumptuously step out of
the field of their specialty and deal in theological speculation
about the origin of the universe and the origin of man and the
history of this planet. Thus their suppositions may be utterly
contrary to the Bible because they are only false suppositions.
Or, a Christian may wrongly interpret some Scripture. John
Jasper, a famous Negro preacher of Richmond, Virginia, had
a famous sermon, "The Sun Do Move," to prove that the
earth is flat and stationary and the sun moves around the earth.
Thus the theologian's interpretation may be contrary to known
facts. But there can be no conflict between scientific facts and
the Scriptures themselves. God made the universe and then
God tells about it in the Bible. God is Himself the Master
Scientist and His revelation in the Scripture will never contradict
His own science.

2. The Quibbles of Dishonest Unbelievers
Are Not Important

Let us not quibble here. Intelligent and honest people who
want to know the truth will not be impressed with the foolish
slander of Harry Emerson Fosdick.

> In the Scriptures the flat earth is founded on an underlying
> sea; it is stationary; the heavens are like an upturned bowl or
> canopy above it; the circumference of this vault rests on pillars;
> the sun, moon, and stars move within this firmament of special
> purpose to illumine man; there is a sea above the sky, "the
> waters which were above the heavens," and through the "win-
> dows of heaven" the rain comes down.... [2]

Who is there who reads the Bible and believes it and thinks
that that is an honest report of what the Bible teaches about
the world?

And other infidels have mocked that the Bible teaches that
the earth is flat and that it has four corners, because it says
that in the kingdom age God "shall assemble the outcasts of
Israel, and gather together the dispersed of Judah from the
four corners of the earth" (Isa. 11:12). Literate people know

---

2. *The Modern Use of the Bible*, pp. 46,47.

that that colorful language simply means the four directions: north, east, south and west, even as the Lord Jesus in Matthew 24:31 speaks of gathering Israel "from the four winds." And surely no serious and intelligent person would claim that the Bible is unscientific when it speaks of the rising and the setting of the sun any more than the weather bureau is unscientific when it announces the minute of the rising and the exact time of the setting of the sun daily. As far as our earthly horizon is concerned, the sun does rise and set, of course, and sensible people speak of it in that way. I say, let us have no insincere quibbles that offend good sense and reveal infidel intentions.

3. They Are Wrong Who Deny That the Bible Never Speaks on Matters of Science

Bernard Ramm says, "...in that inspiration came through the mold of the Hebrew culture, the hyperorthodox is wrong." He also says,

> If God spoke through the Hebrew and Greek languages, He also spoke in terms of the cultures in which these languages were embedded. The eternal truths of the Hebrew-Christian religion are clothed and garbed not only in the Hebrew and Greek languages but also in the cultural molds of the times of the composition of the Bible. [3]

That is, God speaks on scientific matters, says Ramm, only as to the appearance and accommodates the statement to the culture of the times! And then Ramm goes into great detail to answer Rimmer and others and explicitly denies that there are any scientific statements in the Bible. He further says,

> Our summary is but a restatement of our premise that the Holy Spirit conveyed infallibly true theological doctrines in the cultural mold and terms of the days of the Bible writers, and did not give to the writers the secrets of modern science. It is a misunderstanding of the nature of inspiration to seek such secrets in various verses of the Bible. [4]

But as we believe Ramm is radically wrong in supposing that God could not give inspiration except to the culture of the

---

3. *The Christian View of Science and Scripture*, p. 71.
4. *The Christian View of Science and Scripture*, p. 136.

times, in giving early inspiration to be corrected later, even so he is radically wrong, we believe, in supposing that there are no scientific statements in the Bible. Our position is simple and easily stated. Since the Bible says that all Scripture is God-breathed and that every word proceeded from the mouth of God, then everything that the Bible mentions is true when stated as the truth, whether it is about science, history or theology. If one insists that the Bible is not a textbook in science, we agree. It is not even a *textbook* on systematic theology. But that does not mean that it is untrue either in matters of science or of theology.

Thus, since Jesus said that the Genesis flood occurred in the days of Noah, and approved it, it happened: "...and the flood came, and destroyed them all" (Luke 17:27). And since the Lord Jesus said that "the same day that Lot went out of Sodom it rained fire and brimstone from heaven, and destroyed them all," then that happened exactly that way. That is an exact factual statement (Luke 17:29). Since Jesus said that "Jonas was three days and three nights in the whale's belly," (Matt. 12:40) so it happened that way. These are actual scientific statements. And just so, all the statements about creation, the statements about history, the statements about this universe are scientifically accurate.

That man is no special friend of the Bible who gives away half the truth to defend the rest of it. If the Bible is simply an accommodation to the cultures of ancient times, and has errors in the Old Testament that must be corrected in the New, and has errors in science but not in theology, who is to prove that the theology is correct if the science is not? Who is to prove that Jesus was right about some things if He was ignorant or wrong in others? So, whatever the Bible says is so. That is what the Scriptures expressly claim and what we believe.

II. SCIENTIFIC FACTS REVEALED IN THE BIBLE NOT THEN KNOWN TO SCIENCE

1. "For the Life of the Flesh Is in the Blood"—Lev. 17:11

The Bible gives the most accurate, definite, brief statement of the use of the blood in the body, a statement which is absolutely scientific.   Scientists have never been able to form a better statement.   But the Bible made its scientific statement about 3,500 years ago, and science has only discovered the use of the blood in the last one hundred years!

Leviticus 17:11 says, "For the life of the flesh is in the blood."

Leviticus 17:14 says, "For it is the life of all flesh; the blood of it is for the life thereof: therefore I said unto the children of Israel, Ye shall eat the blood of no manner of flesh: for the life of all flesh is in the blood thereof...."

And before that, Genesis 9:4 says, "But flesh with the life thereof, which is the blood thereof, shall ye not eat."

The life is in the blood!

It is the blood that carries on all the life processes of the body.

It is the blood that absorbs the oxygen from the air in the lungs and carries this oxygen throughout the body.

It is the blood that collects the carbon dioxide and other wastes that are then discharged by the blood into the lungs, and breathed out of the body.

It is the blood that collects digested food, takes it from the little cilia in the intestines and distributes it to the various parts of the body.

It is the blood that causes growth, builds new cells, grows bone and flesh, stores fat, makes hair and nails.

It is the blood that feeds and supports all the organs of the body.   If the blood supply be cut off from an arm, that arm will immediately begin to die and rot.   If the blood be not sufficiently supplied to the scalp, the head becomes bald.

It is blood that repairs the body.   The blood can make new bone and knit the break together.   The blood can close wounds and grow new flesh, new skin, and even new nerves.

It is the blood which fights disease.   We now know that infectious germs are destroyed by white corpuscles in the blood and the pus from a sore is simply white corpuscles that have been killed in this battle against the enemies of the body.   "*The life of the flesh is in the blood*"!   All nourishment, all growth, all repair of tissues, all the fight against disease within the body is carried on by the blood.

If the body is to be immunized against certain diseases, it is the blood which must make it immune.

If disease is about to overcome the body, often the only remedy is a transfusion of blood.

Certainly the Bible is exactly scientifically accurate when it says that "the life of the flesh is in the blood."

But remember that though the Bible has said so for about 3,500 years, the scientists are just now finding it out!

For example, in 1799, George Washington died, 155 years ago. This greatest man in America, one of the greatest in world's history, had a doctor called. The doctor bled Washington three times, and the last time took more than a quart of blood! From his sickness Washington might have recovered if he had had his blood. But the doctor, the scientist of his day, had not yet discovered what the Bible had been saying for many centuries. He did not know he was draining away the life of the father of his country into a bucket, when he took the blood from Washington's veins. He foolishly thought that most illnesses were caused by too much blood. And practically all the scientists of his day were agreed with that poor doctor.

William Harvey had discovered that the arteries contained blood instead of air about 1628 and thought that the blood circulated but had not proven it. Practically nothing was known of the life-sustaining work of the blood until modern times.

Lister, who first proved the presence of germs and introduced the antiseptic system of modern surgery, died as recently as 1912. The scientists of George Washington's day did not know that the blood, which is the life of the flesh, must destroy germs.

If blood be shut off from the brain four or five minutes, the brain is destroyed and the victim, if he lives, is an imbecile. "The life of the flesh is in the blood" is a scientific statement in the Bible.

2. Out in Space the World Hangs on Nothing, Is Round, Revolves

Long before men learned by scientific investigation the facts about the earth and the universe, the Bible reveals some of these facts.

(a) The earth hangs out in space on nothing. Job 26:7

says, "He stretcheth out the north over the empty place, and hangeth the earth upon nothing." Even Ramm, who believes in progressive revelation, thinks the Old Testament was written only in accommodation to the culture of the day, admits about this passage: "Such men as Fausset, Cook, and Leathes, are very strong in their statements that this verse through divine inspiration gives us a hint of the world being suspended in nothing as modern astronomy teaches."[5] What else could it teach?

Ellicott's Commentary says: "If these words mean what they seem to do — and it is hard to see how they can mean anything else — then they furnish a very remarkable instance of anticipation of the discoveries of science. Here we find Job, more than three thousand years ago, describing in language of scientific accuracy the condition of our globe, and holding it forth as a proof of Divine power."[6]

The Bible, divinely inspired, is scientifically accurate when it speaks on scientific matters.

(b) The Bible speaks of the earth as a sphere or globe. Isaiah 40:22 says, "It is he that sitteth upon the circle of the earth, and the inhabitants thereof are as grasshoppers; that stretcheth out the heavens as a curtain, and spreadeth them out as a tent to dwell in." On this passage Dr. Scofield says, "A remarkable reference to the sphericity of the earth." The word translated "circle" here rather means arch or roundness and not a circle in one plane. So a round earth hangs out in space on nothing, and this was written thousands of years before Galileo, Columbus and Magellan learned that the earth is round.

(c) This round earth revolves on its axis.

Speaking of His Second Coming in Luke 17:34-36, the Lord Jesus said: "I tell you, in that night there shall be two men in one bed; the one shall be taken, and the other shall be left. Two women shall be grinding together; the one shall be taken, and the other left. Two men shall be in the field; the one shall be taken, and the other left."

Note that when Jesus comes it will be night on some parts of the earth; the people will be in bed. In some parts of the earth it will be morning; women will be grinding the meal for

---

5. *The Christian View of Science and Scripture*, p. 133.
6. *Ellicott's Commentary*, p. 46.

the day at the mill. It will be midday some places; men will be working in the fields.

But the coming of Christ will be "in a moment, in the twinkling of an eye, at the last trump" (I Cor. 15:52). It will be "as the lightning, that lighteneth out of the one part under heaven, shineth unto the other part under heaven; so shall also the Son of man be in his day" (Luke 17:24). So in one moment of time it would be night at one place on the earth, daybreak at another place and midday at another place. The Lord Jesus knew, and the evangelist was inspired to write, this scientific fact about the revolution of the earth which makes night and day on opposite sides of the earth at the same time.

3. There Are an Uncounted Multitude of Stars

Ancient people thought there were a few hundred stars. Scientists tell us now that with the naked eye, counting both from the northern and the southern hemispheres, about 5,000 stars may be seen by good eyesight.

But the Lord promised Abraham that his seed should be as the stars uncountable (Gen. 15:5). In Genesis 22:17, He told Abraham that "in multiplying I will multiply thy seed as the stars of the heaven, and as the sand which is upon the sea shore." That is, that the stars are as innumerable, uncountable, as the sand. In Deuteronomy 1:10, Moses was inspired to say to Israel, "The Lord your God hath multiplied you, and, behold, ye are this day as the stars of heaven for multitude." And the next verse says, "The Lord God of your fathers make you a thousand times so many more as ye are...." And twice more in Deuteronomy, when the nation Israel had at least three and a half million people, they were likened unto the stars in multitude (Deut. 10:22; 28:62).

But are the stars really as innumerable, uncountable as the sand by the seashore? Are there literally millions of stars?

Yes, there are. The stars are uncountable. Although to the naked eye there are only some 5,000 stars visible from all over the earth, now that there are giant telescopes to look into the heavens many millions of miles further, we find there are uncounted millions of stars. They are as uncountable as the sands of the sea, as the Scripture said.

You see, this scientific statement was made in the Bible before anyone, by human means, could know that it was true.

4. Plants and Animals Reproduce Themselves Only "After Their Kind"

Ten times in Genesis, chapter 1, we are told that in God's creation, the grass and herbs, fruit trees, fish and animals in the water, and birds of the air, cattle, creeping things should all reproduce "after his kind" and "after their kind." Sometimes men say that *kind* here means a *species*. But since men's definitions about a species do not agree, we simply use the word the Bible uses. Animals and plants reproduce only "after their kind." There may be development within a kind and so we may have red roses, yellow roses, pink roses, white roses, and the beautiful orange-red Tropicana which grows in my yard, but they are all roses, and roses produce only roses.

We may have many kinds and sizes of dogs — short-haired, long-haired, the racing greyhound, the giant Saint Bernard, the shepherd, the bulldog, the tiny Chihuahua, with colors of black or white or spotted or all in-between, but they are still dogs. Dogs never bring forth cats nor pigs. And even some very closely related animals that may be of the same "kind" according to Bible terminology, when they breed, the results are usually sterile. And so it is with the mule — a cross between the horse and the ass. So it is with the cataloes which Colonel Goodnight tried so hard to develop from crossing cattle and buffaloes or the American bison.

Not until the days of Pasteur and Lister did science know that insects and germs did not arise by spontaneous generation! Pasteur finally proved that life never begins except where there is already life. With dismay, early evolutionists found that acquired characteristics are never inherited. For thousands of years sheep have had their fat tails cut off, but lambs still grow such tails. Ever since Abraham, Hebrew boy babies have been circumcised, but the circumcision is never inherited. Giraffes do not grow long necks by stretching them! And scientists have searched in vain ever since Darwin for "missing links" between the different kinds of animals and plants. There are none at all! All reputable scientists now agree it is proven that animals and plants reproduce only "after their kind." When Moses wrote this, nearly all the people in the world thought differently, but God stated the scientific fact before scientists ever proved it.

5. Many Other Scientific Facts Are Inferred in the Scriptures, Written Before Men Could Have Known They Were True

(a) Hebrews 1:2 says that "by his Son" God "made the worlds." *Worlds* is plural. Yet, when the book of Hebrews was written, there was not a single telescope by which anybody could tell that there are other planets in our solar system, and others besides our solar system. No one could tell by the unaided human eye that the planets we see are more than points of light, more or less bright. But God, who made all the planets, referred to them here.

(b) Job 28:25 tells us that God makes "weight for the winds; and he weigheth the waters by measure." Long before men had ever had instruments and methods of learning it, God says that the air has weight. We now know that at sea level a column of air weighs about fourteen pounds to the square inch. But God said it before.

The Bible speaks of "the paths of the seas" (Ps. 8:8). Isaiah 43:16 says, "Thus saith the Lord, which maketh a way in the sea, and a path in the mighty waters." Does not this speak of ocean currents regularly established by the hand of God? And it was written when men had only sailed around the Mediterranean Sea and the east coast of Africa, as far as we know, and so no one knew about the Japan current, the Gulf Stream and other well-defined great currents or paths in the sea.

What the Bible mentions incidentally is just as true as the part that God gives great detail to, and what God mentions about scientific fact is just as accurate and true as what He mentions about theology and the plan of salvation.

III. HOW AMAZING THAT THE BIBLE MAKES NO ERRORS IN FACTUAL STATEMENTS

The Bible was written in an age when there were no telescopes, practically no scientific instruments, and little scientific knowledge. In the areas of biology, geology, astronomy and chemistry, for example, there was very little knowledge beyond what ordinary people could observe with the naked eye and judge by appearances. Yet the Bible makes no mistakes.

1. Consider the Blunders of Other Ancient Writings Not Found in Scripture

A beautiful, extended passage by Gaussen exclaims over the amazing freedom from error in the Word of God. He says:

First Fact: There Is No Physical Error in the Word of God

If there were any, we have admitted it, the book would not be from God. "God is not man that he should lie," nor the son of man that He should be mistaken. He behoves, no doubt, in order to His being understood, to stoop to our weakness, but without in the least partaking in it; and His language will always be found to witness to His condescension, never to His ignorance.

This remark is still more serious than one would suppose before having reflected on it. It becomes very striking on a close examination.

Examine all the false theologies of the ancients and moderns; read in Homer or in Hesiod, the religious codes of the Greeks; study those of the Buddhists, those of the Brahmins, those of the Mohammedans; you will not only find in these repulsive systems on the subject of the Godhead but will meet with the grossest errors on the material world. You will be revolted with their theology no doubt; but their natural philosophy and their astronomy also, ever allied to their religion, will be found to rest on the most absurd notions.

Read in the Chou-king and the Y-king of the Chinese, their fantastic systems on the five elements (wood, fire, earth, metal, and water), and on their omnipotent influences on all divine and human affairs. Read in the **Shaster**, in the **Pouran**, in the four books of the **Vedham**, or law of the Hindus, their revolting cosmogony. The moon is 50,000 leagues higher than the sun; it shines with its own light; it animates our body. Night is caused by the sun's setting behind the mountain Someyra, situated in the middle of the earth, and several thousand miles high. Our earth is flat and triangular, composed of seven stages, each with its own degree of beauty, its own inhabitants, and its own sea, the first of honey, another of sugar, another of butter, another of wine; in fine, the whole mass is borne on the heads of countless elephants which, in shaking themselves, cause earthquakes in this nether world! In one word, they have placed the whole history of their gods in relations at once the most fantastic and the most necessary with the physical world and all the phenomena of the universe. Thus, the missionaries of India have often repeated that a telescope, silently planted in the midst of the holy city of Benares, or in the ancient Ava, would prove a battery, powerful as lightning, for overturning the whole system of Brahma, and the whole of that of Boudhou.

Read farther the philosophers of Greek and Roman antiquity, Aristotle, Seneca, Pliny, Plutarch, Cicero. How many expressions of opinion will you not find there, any single one of which would be enough to compromise all our doctrines of inspiration, if it could be met with in any book of Holy Scripture! Read Mahomet's Koran, making mountains to be created "to prevent the earth from moving, and to hold it fast as if with anchors and cables." What do I say? Read even the cosmogony of Buffon, or some of Voltaire's sneers on the doctrine of a deluge, or on the fossil animals of a primitive world.

Second Fact: Not Even Christian Leaders Could Write Without Scientific Errors

We will go much farther. Read again, we do not say the absurd reasonings of the pagans, of Lucretius, of Pliny, or of Plutarch, against the theory of the antipodes, but even the fathers of the Christian Church. Hear the theological indignation of the admirable Augustine, who says that it is opposed to the Scriptures; and the scientific eloquence of Lactantius, who considers it so opposed to common sense: "**Num aliquid loquuntur!**" he exclaims; "is there any man so silly as to believe that men exist having their feet above their heads, trees with their fruit hanging downwards, rain, snow, and hail falling topsy turvy!" "They would answer you," he adds, "by maintaining that the earth is a globe! **Quid dicam de iis nescio, qui cum semel aberraverint, constanter in stultitia perseverant, et vanis vana defendunt!**" "One knows not what to say of such men, who, when they have once run into error, persist in their folly, and defend one absurdity by another!"

Listen, farther, to the legate Boniface, who brought Virgilius, for his opinion in this matter, as a heretic before the Pope; listen to Pope Zachary treating that unhappy bishop as **homo malignus.** "If it be proved," says he, "that Virgilius maintains the existence of other men under this earth, call a council, condemn him, put him out of the Church, depose him from the priesthood!"

Listen, at a later period, to the whole clergy of Spain, and especially to the imposing Council of Salamanca, indignant at the geographical system by which Christopher Columbus was led to look for a whole new continent. Listen, at the epoch of Newton's birth, to the great Galileo, who "ascended," says Kepler, "the highest ramparts of the universe," and who justified at once by his genius and by his telescope the disowned and condemned system of Copernicus; behold him groaning, at the age of eighty, in the prisons of Rome, for having discovered the movement of the earth, after having had to pronounce these words, ten years before (28th June 1633), before their Eminences, at the palace of the Holy Office: "I, Galileo, in the seventieth year of my age, on my knees before your Eminences, having before my eyes, and touching with my own hands, the Holy Scriptures, abjure, curse, and detest, the error of the earth's movement."

What might we not have been entitled to say of the Scriptures, had they expressed themselves on the phenomena of nature, as these have been spoken of by all the ancient sages?—had they referred all to four elements, as people did for so long a period? —had they said the stars were of crystal, as did Philolaus of Crotona; and had they, like Empedocles, lighted up the two hemispheres of our world with two suns?—had they taught, like Leucippus, that the fixed stars, set ablaze by the swiftness of their diurnal movement round the earth, feed the sun with their fires? —had they, like Diodorus of Sicily, and all the Egyptian sages, formed the heavens and the earth by the motion of the air and the natural ascent of fire?—or had they thought, like Philolaus, that the sun has only a borrowed light, and is only a mirror, which receives and sends down to us the light of the celestial spheres?—had they, like Anaxagoras, conceived it to be a mass of iron larger than the Peloponnesus, and the earth to be a mountain, whose roots stretched infinitely downwards?—had they imagined the heaven to be a solid sphere, to which the fixed stars are attached, as was done by Aristotle, **and almost all the ancients**?—had they called the celestial vault a **firmamentum**, or a στερέωμα, as their interpreters have done, both in Latin and in Greek?—had they spoken, as has been done so recently, and even among people professing Christianity, of the influence exerted by the movements of the heavens on the elements of this lower world, on the characters of men, and on the course of human affairs?

Such is the natural proneness of all nations to this superstition, that, notwithstanding their religion, the ancient Jews, and the Christians themselves, equally fell into it. "The modern Greeks," says D'Alembert, "have carried it to excess; hardly do we find one of their authors who does not, on all occasions, speak of predictions by the stars, of horoscopes, and talismans, so that there was hardly an edifice in Constantinople, and in all Greece, that had not been erected according to the rules of the **apotelesmatic astrology**." French historians observe, that astrology was so much in fashion under Catherine de Medicis, that people dared not undertake any thing of importance without having consulted the stars; and even under Henry III. and Henry IV., the predictions of astrologers formed the engrossing subject of ordinary conversation at court. "We have seen, towards the close of the last century," says Ph. Giulani, "an Italian send Pope Innocent XI. a prediction, in the manner of a horoscope, on Vienna, at that time besieged by the Turks, and which was very well received." And in our own days the Count de Boulainvilliers has written very seriously on the subject.

Third Fact: Some Fifty Human Authors in 1500 Years, Not a Contradiction, Not an Error of Fact in the Bible

Open now the Bible; study its fifty sacred authors, from that wonderful Moses who held the pen in the wilderness, four hundred years before the war of Troy, down to the fisherman, son of Zebedee, who wrote fifteen hundred years afterwards, in Ephesus and in Patmos, under the reign of Domitian; open the Bible, and try if you can to find any thing of this sort there. No. None of those blunders which the science of every successive age discovers in the books of those that preceded it; none of those absurdities, above all, which modern astronomy points out, in such numbers, in the writings of the ancients, in their sacred codes, in their systems of philosophy, and in the finest pages even of the fathers of the Church; no such errors can be found in any of our sacred books; nothing there will ever contradict what, after so many ages, the investigations of the learned world have been able to reveal to us of what is certain in regard to the state of our globe or of that of the heavens.

Carefully peruse our Scriptures from one end to the other, in search of such blemishes there; and while engaged in this research, remember that it is a book which speaks of every thing, which describes nature, which proclaims its grandeur, which tells the story of its creation, which informs us of the structure of the heavens, of the creation of light, of the waters, of the atmosphere, of the mountains, of animals, and of plants; — it is a book that tells us of the first revolutions of the world, and foretells to us also the last; a book that relates them in circumstantial narratives, exalts them in a sublime poesy, and chants them in strains of fervent psalmody; — it is a book replete with the glow of oriental rapture, elevation, variety, and boldness; — it is a book which speaks of the earth and of things visible, at the same time that it speaks of the celestial world and of things invisible; — it is a book to which nearly fifty writers of every degree of mental cultivation, of every rank, of every condition, and separated by fifteen hundred years from each other, have successively put their hand; — it is a book composed first in the centre of Asia, among the sands of Arabia, or in the deserts of Judea, or in the fore-court of the temple of the Jews, or in the rustic schools

of the prophets of Bethel and of Jericho, or in the sumptuous
palaces of Babylon, or on the idolatrous banks of Chebar; and
afterwards, at the centre of western civilisation, amid the Jews
with their manifold ignorance, amid polytheism and its ideas,
as well as in the bosom of pantheism and its silly philosophy;
— it is a book the first writer of which had been for the space
of forty years a pupil of the magicians of Egypt, who looked
upon the sun, and the stars and the elements as endowed with
intelligence, as re acting upon the elements, and as governing
the world by continual effluxes; — it is a book the first chapters
of which preceded by more than NINE HUNDRED YEARS
the most ancient philosophers of ancient Greece and of Asia,
the Thaleses, the Pythagorases, the Zaleucuses, the Xenophaneses,
the Confuciuses; — it is a book which carries its narratives even
into the field of the invisible world, even into the hierarchies of
the angels, even into the remotest realms of futurity, and the
glorious scenes of the last day; — well then, search through
these 50 authors, search through these 66 books, search through
these 1189 chapters, and these 31,173 verses....search for one
single error of those thousands with which ancient and modern
books abound, when they speak either of the heaven or of the
earth, or of their revolutions, or of their elements; search, but
you will search in vain.

Fourth Fact: Exalted, Poetic Language But
No Slips, No Errors

There is nothing constrained or reserved in its language; it
speaks of all things and in all tones; it is the prototype, it is the
unapproachable model; it has been the inspirer of all the most
exalted productions of poetry. Ask this of Milton, of the two
Racines, of Young, of Klopstock. They will tell you that this
divine poesy is of all the most lyrical, the boldest in its flights,
and the most sublime: it rises on a cherub and soars on the
wings of the wind. And yet never does this book do violence to
the facts or to the principles of a sound philosophy of nature.
Never will you find it in opposition, in the case of a single
sentence, with the correct notions which science has enabled us to
reach with regard to the form of our globe, its size, or its
geology; on the vacuum and on space; on the inert and obedient
materiality of all the stars; on the planets, on their masses, on
their courses, on their dimensions, or on their influences; on the
suns that people the depths of space, on their number, on their
nature, or their immensity. Just as in speaking of the invisible
world, and of a subject so new, so unknown, and so delicate, as
that of the angels, this book has not one of its authors that, in
the course of the 1560 years which it took to write it, has varied
in the character of charity, humility, fervour, and purity which
belongs to those mysterious beings; just as in speaking of the
relations of the celestial world with God, never has one of these

fifty writers, either in the Old or in the New Testament, uttered a single word that favours that constant leaning to pantheism which characterises the whole philosophy of the Gentiles; so likewise you will not find one of the authors of the Bible who, in speaking of the visible world, has suffered a single one of those expressions of opinion to escape him, which, in other books, contradict the reality of facts — not one which makes the heaven to be a firmament, as has been done by the Septuagint, St. Jerome, and all the Fathers of the Church — not one that makes the world, as Plato did, an intelligent animal — not one that reduces all things here below to the four elements of the physical system of the ancients — not one that holds with the Jews, with the Latins, with the Greeks, with the finest minds of antiquity, with the great Tacitus among the ancients, with the great De Thou among the moderns, with the sceptic Michael Montaigne, that "the stars have domination and power, not only over our lives and the conditions of our fortune, but even over our inclinations, our discourses, our wills; that they govern, impel, and agitate them at the mercy of their influences; and that (according as our reason teaches us and finds it to be) the whole world feels the impulsion of the slightest celestial movements. **Facta etenim et vitas hominum suspendit ab astris;**" — not one that speaks of the mountains as Mahomet has done, of the cosmogony like Buffon, of the antipodes like Lucretius, like Plutarch, like Pliny, like Lactantius, like St. Augustine, like Pope Zachary. — Assuredly, were there to be found in the Bible a single one of those errors that abound among philosophers, as well ancient as modern, our faith in the plenary inspiration of the Scriptures would be more than compromised by it; we should have to acknowledge that there are errors in the Word of God, and that these delusive expressions are those of a fallible writer, not those of the Holy Ghost; for God is not man that He should lie; in Him there is no variableness, neither shadow of falsity; and He to whom lying lips are an abomination, could not have been capable of contradicting Himself and dictating that which is false.

There is no physical error, then, in the Scriptures; and this great fact, which becomes all the more striking the more narrowly we look into it, is the manifest proof of an inspiration carried into their choice of the smallest expressions they employ. [7]

When all the other literature in the world was filled with fantastic and often monstrous errors of fact concerning the world, its animals, its people, and its science, is it not amazing that the Bible was scientifically accurate?

All over America — in great auditoriums and citywide campaigns in Chicago, Buffalo, Cleveland, Seattle, Miami and

---

7. *The Inspiration of the Holy Scriptures,* pp. 253-260.

elsewhere, and on radio broadcasts and in print — we have challenged any man with a Ph.D. degree from a recognized university to meet us in public debate if he would affirm there were scientific and historical errors in the Bible. Although we have offered to pay expenses and provide the audience and remuneration, there have been no responses.

Dr. Harry Rimmer and the Research Science Bureau offered $1,000 reward for anyone "finding and proving a scientific error in the Scriptures." One man claimed the reward and took the matter to court in 1929 claiming that the number of quail God sent to answer the plea of the Israelites in the wilderness was scientifically impossible. However, he lost his case in court and no one else tried it.

It is an amazing thing that the Scriptures, on everything that they touch, are meticulously, perfectly accurate. It is the Book of God and the words are God's words.

2. Scientists' Fickle, Changeable Theories: Not the Bible

It is said that Dr. Henry Drummond, in the university he served in Scotland, was brought to question: A new shipment of scientific books for the library were received but there was no room for them on the shelves. What should they do?

Drummond answered, it is said, that the library should go through the scientific books and every book more than ten years old should be taken off the shelves and put in the basement to make room for new books. Any book of science is becoming obsolete and out of date after ten years!

Oh, the changing vagaries of science! First, the scientist believed in the Ptolemaic system which "supposed the earth to be the fixed center of the universe about which the sun and stars revolved." Then the Copernican system replaced the former idea holding that "the earth rotated daily on its axis and the planets revolved in orbits around the sun." And now that system of thought has been modified in several ways and it is thought that the sun itself and our planetary system is only a part of another giant system revolving about a far-off fixed star!

We were taught as an axiom of physics, when I was in school, that matter is indestructible, that although it might be burned it would still be existent in the forms of gases and ashes. That matter might be changed from solid to liquid or to gas, but it was still in existence. Now we know that matter may be converted into energy by the fission of the atom.

Mechanical refrigeration is a modern idea. The fact that by compression men could take heat from matter and place it in the air outside, thus cooling a refrigerator or a room, is a modern idea.

Where is now the theory widely accepted that a certain "ether" fills space?

Some scientists speak of evolution by slow, gradual micro-evolution taking millions of years. Others think that evolution came in great jumps — macroevolution. Darwin thought that evolution had taken fifty million years. His son thought later it had taken 500 million years. Now many think it has taken four or five billion years. The simple truth is, there are no observable steps in evolution now taking place so that they must push God millions of miles further into the past in order to make room for the supposed but unproven infinitely slow changes of supposed evolution.

CHAPTER XVIII

MORE EVIDENCES THAT THE BIBLE IS THE
INERRANT, INSPIRED WORD OF GOD

I. SOME BASIC PRINCIPLES ABOUT BIBLE EVI-
DENCES

1. We Take the Bible by Faith

2. We Do Not Need to Know All the Answers to Know
That the Bible Is True

3. Men Will Not Submit to the Bible Who Do Not Sur-
render to Christ

II. THERE IS AN OVERWHELMING PRESUMPTION
THAT THE BIBLE IS THE WORD OF GOD

1. Such a Surpassing Revelation by Its Very Nature Obviously Fits and Claims the Designation As the Word
of God

2. The Character of the Writers Indicates That What
They Say Is True

3. The Centuries-Old Conviction of the Church and of the
Mass of Christians That the Bible Is the Word of
God Cannot Be Ignored

III. THE HISTORICAL ACCURACY OF THE BIBLE

1. The Mosaic Authorship of the Pentateuch

2. Dr. Robert Dick Wilson's Investigation of the Old Testament

3. Sir William Ramsay Testifies to the Accuracy of the
New Testament

IV. TEN REASONS WHY DR. R. A. TORREY BELIEVED
THE BIBLE TO BE THE WORD OF GOD

MORE EVIDENCES THAT THE BIBLE IS THE INERRANT, INSPIRED WORD OF GOD

The primary concern of this book as it must be for every Christian, is to find and understand what the Bible claims and teaches about itself. For we as students of the Bible are to reverence it, study it, obey it and not to judge it. What God Himself says in His Word is more important than anything anybody else says about the Bible, and its inspiration, its character and its authority.

Although this book is not primarily about evidences that the Bible is the Word of God but more particularly what the Bible claims for itself, yet we seek to give a few overwhelming evidences that the Bible is the infallible Word of God and so comfort the heart of Christians and to give them assurance and boldness.

The simple fact is that anyone denying the divine inspiration of the Bible thus blinds himself to great areas of truth and brings up a thousand unsolvable problems. Unbelief is more credulous than belief, and unbelief in the Bible is more unreasonable than simple acceptance of it as the Word of God. It is simply impossible to explain or even to conceive of such a book as the Bible without a divine element as the very Word of God.

So let us be not much troubled about some apparent contradiction or some alleged mistake in the Bible.

I. SOME BASIC PRINCIPLES ABOUT BIBLE EVIDENCES

We need to start from the right premise and step out with

the right foot.   There are some settled principles on which a Christian may confidently act.

1. We Take the Bible by Faith

The Scripture says, "Through faith we understand that the worlds were framed by the word of God" (Heb. 11:3).

Note, we do not go without understanding.   But our understanding goes with our faith!

We who are Christians already know God our Father and Jesus Christ our Saviour.   Already we have known and experienced blessings from the Bible and from the Christ of the Bible, internal evidence that Christ is the Son of God, our Saviour.   To us He says that the Bible is true.   Already we have the evidence of experience that the Bible is the Word of God, so we believe what the Bible claims and what Christ claims about the infallible, inerrant Scriptures.

We CHOOSE to believe.   Wicked scoffers do not choose to believe.   The Apostle Peter was inspired to remind us of all the things spoken on this matter by the holy prophets and of the command of the apostles of Christ.

"Knowing this first, that there shall come in the last days scoffers, walking after their own lusts, And saying, Where is the promise of his coming? for since the fathers fell asleep, all things continue as they were from the beginning of the creation.   For this they willingly are ignorant of, that by the word of God the heavens were of old, and the earth standing out of the water and in the water." — II Pet. 3:3-5.

So scoffers, who walk after their sinful lusts, choose not to believe.   They are "willingly...ignorant."   That is, they ignore the evidences as a matter of choice and so they do not choose to believe.

But Christians choose to believe the Word of God.   Our understanding and our faith work together.

So if there are a thousand statements in the Scripture I do not understand, yet am I assured by faith it is all it claims to be, all it is proved to be in the past, proved to my heart and to the hearts of millions of others.   I already have so much evidence, what does it matter if my limited understanding, my lack of experience, my inadequate scholarship leaves some things I cannot explain? My heart is so sure from a thousand proofs that I can trust God that He knows what I do not know. Through the years innumerable problems and questions about the Bible have been wonderfully settled in my mind. And so I am sure that there are proper logical answers to all the other problems and that one day I shall know them.

So Christians are wise to take the counsel of a saint of God, to "believe your beliefs and doubt your doubts." What we do know makes us certain. What we do not know we take by faith.

2. We Do Not Need to Know All the Answers to Know That the Bible Is True

We know where Cain got his wife. That is easy: There were many sisters and nieces from which he could choose and did. But if I cannot prove that Moses wrote the Pentateuch and that Isaiah wrote both the first and the last parts of Isaiah, Jesus knew and He said it was true. If I cannot explain some apparent discrepancy, that does not make it a real contradiction to the facts or with other Scriptures. If I find there is a gloss of a word or a line inserted by some copyist, or that there is some bad translation of a word or two in my language, I know there are over two thousand manuscripts that can be checked to find the original statement of Scripture. I know that God has not left His Scripture unprotected, and that it shall never pass away.

Of course there are problems about the Bible. This is not a little book about one subject. It has the most profound discussions of all the great themes the human mind could ever approach. It has much about God, eternity, the unseen world, about mysteries no man knows all about. Who can explain regeneration—that miracle which changes the penitent, believing sinner into a born-again child of God? Who can explain the incarnation—how Christ Jesus, the Creator, came from eternity into time, from Heaven to earth, from God to man, that is, became God in the garments of man? Who can understand fully the Creator?

There are a thousand things in nature about which we know

little. Can you explain life itself? Heredity? Can you explain electricity? The mystery of the atom? Of the electrons and neutrons? What are the boundaries of space? Do you understand the theory of relativity? Of curved space? Can you understand how a caterpillar becomes a butterfly? How a tadpole becomes a frog? How the chromosomes in a tiny ovum or sperm cell carry all the hereditary characteristics of parents? There are a thousand marvels in nature that we cannot explain; we simply accept them as true because they obviously are. We need not be surprised if there are riches in the Bible yet unexplored, questions about the Bible which we cannot immediately and easily answer. The finite man with limited knowledge cannot explain fully the infinite.

So we will find questions about the Bible which we cannot explain, questions we cannot answer. Of course that is to be expected. The simplest person can understand the plan of salvation, but many mysteries of the Bible require study.

We are told that prophets of old "inquired and searched diligently, who prophesied of the grace that should come unto you: Searching what, or what manner of time the Spirit of Christ which was in them did signify, when it testified beforehand the sufferings of Christ, and the glory that should follow" (I Pet. 1:10,11). If prophets searched diligently in their own inspired writings to find more fully the meaning and could not, should we be surprised if there are riches in the Scriptures yet uncovered and questions answerable but to which we do not know the answer?

And Peter speaks of the writings of "our beloved brother Paul," and says, "As also in all his epistles, speaking in them of these things; in which are some things hard to be understood, which they that are unlearned and unstable wrest, as they do also the other scriptures, unto their own destruction" (II Pet. 3:15,16). So Paul's writings and other Scriptures are "hard to be understood." And *they that are unlearned and unstable* wrest and misuse these Scriptures and do not understand them. So it is only sensible to know that anything as marvelous and supernatural and eternal as the Word of God has mysteries that are not revealed to the careless and unbelieving or to those who are not willing to learn and study and pray and be led by the Spirit.

Oh, these Scriptures are "the word of God, which liveth and abideth for ever," as I Peter 1:23 and Isaiah 40:8 tell us. And some of the riches of Scripture will only be understood in eternity. So, in Ephesians 2:7, the Lord tells us that because of God's rich mercy and great love, He saves us by grace: "That in the ages to come he might shew the exceeding riches of his grace in his kindness toward us through Christ Jesus." And, oh, some of the marvels of Scripture will be wonderfully clear in eternity, though they be beyond mortal comprehension now. So do not be surprised if there are some mysteries about the Bible. That is part of its eternal and divine quality.

The more men study the Word of God prayerfully and with the leading of the Holy Spirit, the more they understand it and the fewer problems arise. The more ancient cities and records are uncovered with the archaeologist's spade, the more the historical accuracy of the Bible is proven. The more the unbelieving scientists find themselves defeated in trying to prove a creation without God, the more the perfection of the Scriptures appears.

Surely, at least nine out of ten of all the charges and questions of infidels about the so-called untrustworthiness of the Bible have long been answered with compelling truth by Bible scholars. Unbelievers often still quote these objections because they read after infidels and do not seek and do not know the answers which believing scholars have found.

But there are evidences so compelling that anyone who wants to know must be convinced beyond a doubt that the Bible is the inspired, trustworthy, inerrant Word of God.

The testimony of Jesus Christ alone is overwhelming proof. The prophecies fulfilled show that the Bible is written with supernatural knowledge of the future which no mere man could have without divine inspiration. The amazing lack of errors of fact in the Bible surely must show why millions take it as the inerrant Word of God.

We will not give all the evidence but to encourage the question, we here give more evidence that the Bible is what it claims to be — the inerrant, infallible Word of God, thoroughly trustworthy and true in every statement it makes.

3. Men Will Not Submit to the Bible Who Do Not Surrender to Christ

We do not expect every scholar to accept the Bible's claim

to be infallibly inerrant, the God-breathed Word of God. One who has not been converted, born of the Spirit, cannot understand the Word of God. Such an one is not spiritually perceptive of spiritual truth. First Corinthians 2:14 says, "But the natural man receiveth not the things of the Spirit of God: for they are foolishness unto him: neither can he know them, because they are spiritually discerned."

So Dr. Fosdick will still read the Bible with his bias and willful blindness and write, "In the Scriptures the flat earth is founded on an underlying sea; it is stationary; the heavens are like an upturned bowl or canopy above it; the circumference of this vault rests on pillars...."[1] He will believe that silly lie — "As the early writings of the Old Testament clearly reveal, Jehovah, at first one among many gods, dwelt with his own special people and exercised no jurisdiction beyond their boundaries."[2]

So an unconverted Buttrick will read or hear expounded Galatians 3:13: "Christ hath redeemed us from the curse of the law, being made a curse for us," and say, "Such a God, we suggested, has earned the verdict of the French sceptic: 'Your God is my Devil.'"[3]

So an Albert Schweitzer will read the Bible and write his book, *The Quest of the Historical Jesus*, and an unbelieving Ferre will write his book on *The Sun and the Umbrella*, teaching that Jesus and the Bible shut out God from man! The unconverted heart does not easily accept the claims of the Bible, just as it has not surrendered to the demand of Christ for repentance and faith. We should remember that in God's sight it is "the fool" who hath "said in his heart, There is no God" (Ps. 53:1). And the resurrected Saviour Himself said to His disciples, "O fools, and slow of heart to believe all that the prophets have spoken..." (Luke 24:25).

Why this rebellion of the unconverted heart against the Bible? Why this enmity toward the truth? Because the Bible demands repentance of sin and absolute submission to Christ as Saviour and to the instruction and commands of the Scripture.

---

1. *Modern Use of the Bible*, p. 46.
2. *Modern Use of the Bible*, p. 13.
3. *The Christian Fact and Modern Doubt*, p. 174.

J. I. Packer sees this problem and says:

> We shall argue that subjection to the authority of Christ in-
> volves subjection to the authority of Scripture. Anything short
> of unconditional submission to Scripture, therefore, is a kind of
> impenitence; any view that subjects the written Word of God to
> the opinions and pronouncements of men involves unbelief
> and disloyalty towards Christ.[4]

Does some scholar come to the Bible, honestly seeking to
study it fairly? Well, if he has an impenitent heart, an unconverted heart, he already has a bias, a bent against Christ and
against the Scriptures, and the impenitence of his heart is reflected in the unbelief in his mind.

That the natural man has a natural hostility to the Bible
was recognized by Bannerman, who says:

> Once more, the singular, and to many minds the offensive,
> assumption which the Bible makes to rule the belief and practice
> of men with an authority from which there is no appeal, ex-
> poses it to hostility of yet another but not less formidable kind.[5]

The unconverted, sinful heart even of a Bible scholar reacts
to the claims and demands of the Bible just as the prodigal son
did to the authority of his father. The unconverted man, the
unbeliever in the deity of Christ and the supernatural authority
of the Scriptures as the very Word of God, cannot be expected
to approach the Bible with an unbiased and objective approach,
seeking the truth. When the Bible demands submission of the
will and the life as the authority of God, unconverted men who
will not admit that demand will not approach the Bible with
the favor and love and humble-hearted reverence which it
deserves and demands.

So we frankly cannot expect ever to get all unconverted men
over on the side of the Bible. If one comes to Christ as a
penitent sinner, comes for mercy and forgiveness and a new
heart, and relies on Christ as the divine, atoning substitute, to
redeem him and save him, then only can he be expected to have
the heart attitude that is open to understand and believe the
Scriptures fully.

Then we ought to say also that those scholars who have been
converted but who feel a great desire to appease the unconverted

---

4. *"Fundamentalism" and the Word of God*, p. 21.
5. *Inspiration of the Scriptures*, p. 47.

and longs to have standing among the "scholars," thus limits his own capacity to take the Scriptures at face value.

Oh, when one comes to the Scripture, he should come ready to submit to Christ as Saviour and to every command of God and plan of God made clear in the Scriptures. We cannot expect full acceptance of the Bible by the sinful world.

II. THERE IS AN OVERWHELMING PRESUMPTION THAT THE BIBLE IS THE WORD OF GOD

The mass of evidence even to the general public and those with only a casual acquaintance with the Scriptures, is still overwhelming evidence. We insist that there is a tremendous presumption that the Bible is all it claims to be.

1. Such a Surpassing Revelation by Its Very Nature Obviously Fits and Claims the Designation As the Word of God

Aside from its claim to inspiration, the Bible speaks as if it were the Word of God, speaks about things about which only the Word of God could tell, speaks with authority that only the Word of God could claim. It speaks with a certainty and dogmatic authority that do not fit the uninspired writings of men.

Dr. Lewis Sperry Chafer says:

> The Scriptures are in themselves a phenomenon of such a character — presenting truth on so vast a scale and so marvelous that the added claim to divine accuracy appears, **a fortiori,** as a necessary corollary to the whole. Such surpassing revelation could hardly be presented in its perfection of form apart from divine inspiration. [6]

As the master of the house walks in his own door without hesitation and with complete knowledge of the place and with the certainty that he is expected and has a right there, even so the Bible claims to speak for God as if it were the very words of God and deals with subjects only God could know, and

---

6. *Systematic Theology,* Vol. 1, p. 67.

demands such obedience as only God has a right to demand.

This presumption that the Bible is the Word of God is so strong that Bettex says:

> If we accept a God at all, who is Spirit and reveals Himself to His creatures, the inspiration of the Bible is rather a conclusion so irresistible, and a concept so clear, that we should be obliged to construct it **a priori** if the Bible were silent concerning it. [7]

The one who even approaches the matter of whether the Bible is the Word of God and does not come with the presumption that God has revealed Himself in the Scriptures, reveals some animus against God, some evidence that he is "slow of heart to believe all that the prophets have spoken" as Jesus said in Luke 24:25. The facts of a God who made man and of man who has instinctive hope of a hereafter, an instinctive sense of such a God, indicates an overpowering presumption that the Bible is inspired of God and has the authority of God's own Word.

2. The Character of the Writers Indicates That What They Say Is True

The men who were used of God to write the Bible claim that they were inspired of God, claim that God put His words in their mouths, claim that the Holy Spirit spoke by them. Now are the writers of the Bible lying, deceitful men? Was Moses a charlatan? Was there no sincerity in David? Were the apostles who wrote the New Testament and were willing to die to back their claim that Christ was the unique Son of God and that Scriptures were the very Word of God — were they deceivers, mountebanks? Only one answer is thinkable.

Moses again and again claimed to write down the words of the Lord. Since he was so signally blessed in leadership, since his forty years' ministry was all good and not bad, since he made a triumphant nation out of a rabble of slaves, and since what he built lasted through the centuries, we are inclined to listen very carefully when Moses claims to be inspired of God. When Isaiah says that God called him from the womb, and made him a polished shaft that he might speak God's words,

---

7. *The Bible, the Word of God,* p. 173.

and when Jeremiah insisted God put His words in his mouth, and when Ezekiel says the same thing, we begin to feel the increasing weight of evidences.   When David says that the Holy Spirit spoke by his tongue and when Paul and Peter and the other New Testament apostles claim that they spoke the very words of God, then the united voice of between forty and fifty writers of the Bible has to be considered.   These were good men. They were willing to die for their convictions.   They spoke for God and built no selfish empires.   The presumption is, then, that there is a great probability that they spoke the truth when they claimed inspiration.   Until you can discredit the writers of the Bible, you must consider at face value their unanimous claim to write as inspired of God.

Dr. Chafer, mentioned above, sees this evidence also.   He says:

> The men who served as human authors of the books of the Bible were in themselves trustworthy witnesses. As such, they are to be credited whether they speak under inspiration or not. These men were not deceived nor were they deceivers. Apart from the claims of inspiration, the basis of faith remains, established, as it is, by credible witnesses. Their claim to inspiration cannot be discredited until the witnesses are discredited. Similarly, it is no small evidence in the case that the human authors — and there were upwards of forty of them extending over a period of 1600 years —, whether inspired or not, are in perfect agreement as to the things which they teach; nor has one of them at any time recorded one intimation that the Bible is **not** the inspired Word of God written. [8]

Thus, there is an overwhelming presumption to begin with that the Bible is the Word of God.

3. The Centuries-Old Conviction of the Church and of the Mass of Christians That the Bible Is the Word of God Cannot Be Ignored

How united are the great church fathers on the inspiration of the Scriptures!   Dr. Edward J. Young quotes many of them in

---

8. *Systematic Theology*, Vol. 1, p. 67.

the introduction to his chapters in the book, *Thy Word Is Truth*:

Justin Martyr said, "...we must not suppose that the language proceeds from men who are inspired, but from the Divine Word which moves them."

Gregory of Nyssa said, "Whatsoever the Divine Scripture says is the voice of the Holy Spirit."

Augustine said, "Therefore we yield to and agree to the authority of the Holy Scripture which can neither be deceived nor deceive."

Origen said, "We cannot say of the writings of the Holy Spirit that anything in them is useless or superfluous, even if they seem to some obscure."

Clement of Alexandria said, "There is no discord between the Law and the Gospel, but harmony, for they both proceed from the same Author."

Irenaeus says, "All Scripture, as it has been given to us by God, will be found to be harmonious."[9]

Engelder quotes Martin Luther: "But it is cursed unbelief (*der verfluchte Unglaube*) and the odious flesh which will not permit us to see and know that God speaks to us in Scripture and that it is God's Word, but tells us that it is the word merely of Isaiah, Paul, or some other mere man, who has not created heaven and earth (IX:1800)."[10]

And we could quote Jerome, Calvin and other leaders of the reformation alike.   The Bible has always been regarded by the mass of Christians as the Word of God.

Dr. Benjamin Warfield calls attention to "the church doctrine of inspiration," and says:

> Thus they themselves introduce us to the fact that over against the numberless discordant theories of inspiration which vex our time, there stands a well-defined church-doctrine of inspiration. This church-doctrine of inspiration differs from the theories that would fain supplant it, in that it is not the invention nor the property of an individual, but the settled faith of the universal church of God; in that it is not the growth of yesterday, but the assured persuasion of the people of God from the first planting of the church until to-day; in that it is not a protean shape, varying its affirmations to fit every new change in the ever-shifting thought of men, but from the beginning has been

---

9. *Thy Word Is Truth*, pp. 12,39.
10. *Scripture Cannot Be Broken*, p. 51.

the church's constant and abiding conviction as to the divinity of the Scriptures committed to her keeping. It is certainly a most impressive fact, — this well-defined, aboriginal, stable doctrine of the church as to the nature and trustworthiness of the Scriptures of God, which confronts with its gentle but steady persistence of affirmation all the theories of inspiration which the restless energy of unbelieving and half-believing speculation has been able to invent in this agitated nineteenth century of ours. Surely the seeker after the truth in the matter of the inspiration of the Bible may well take this church-doctrine as his starting-point.

What this church-doctrine is, it is scarcely necessary minutely to describe. It will suffice to remind ourselves that it looks upon the Bible as an oracular book, — as the Word of God in such a sense that whatever it says God says, — not a book, then, in which one may, by searching, find some word of God, but a book which may be frankly appealed to at any point with the assurance that whatever it may be found to say, that is the Word of God.[11]

He further says:

Nor do we need to do more than remind ourselves that this attitude of entire trust in every word of the Scriptures has been characteristic of the people of God from the very foundation of the church. Christendom has always reposed upon the belief that the utterances of this book are properly oracles of God. The whole body of Christian literature bears witness to this fact. We may trace its stream to its source, and everywhere it is vocal with a living faith in the divine trustworthiness of the Scriptures of God in every one of their affirmations. This is the murmur of the little rills of Christian speech which find their tenuous way through the parched heathen land of the early second century. And this is the mighty voice of the great river of Christian thought which sweeps through the ages, freighted with blessings for men. Dr. Sanday, in his recent Bampton lectures on "Inspiration" — in which, unfortunately, he does not teach the church-doctrine — is driven to admit that not only may "testimonies to the general doctrine of inspiration" from the earliest Fathers, "be multiplied to almost any extent; but (that) there are some which go further and point to an inspiration which might be described as 'verbal' "; "nor does this idea," he adds, "come in tentatively and by degrees, but almost from the very first." He might have spared the adverb "almost." The earliest writers know no other doctrine. If Origen asserts that the Holy Spirit was co-worker with the Evangelists in the composition of the Gospel and that, therefore, lapse of memory, error or falsehood was impossible to them, and if Irenaeus, the pupil of Polycarp, claims for Christians a clear knowledge that

---

11. *The Inspiration and Authority of the Bible*, p. 106.

"the Scriptures are perfect, seeing that they are spoken by God's Word and His Spirit"; no less does Polycarp, the pupil of John, consider the Scriptures the very voice of the Most High, and pronounce him the first-born of Satan, "whosoever perverts these oracles of the Lord."

Nor do the later Fathers know a different doctrine. Augustine, for example, affirms that he defers to the canonical Scriptures alone among books with such reverence and honor that he most "firmly believes that no one of their authors has erred in anything, in writing." To precisely the same effect did the Reformers believe and teach. Luther adopts these words of Augustine's as his own, and declares that the whole of the Scriptures are to be ascribed to the Holy Ghost, and therefore cannot err. Calvin demands that whatever is propounded in Scripture, "without exception," shall be humbly received by us, — that the Scriptures as a whole shall be received by us with the same reverence which we give to God, "because they have emanated from him alone, and are mixed with nothing human." The saintly Rutherford, who speaks of the Scriptures as a more sure word than a direct oracle from heaven, and Baxter, who affirms that "all that the holy writers have recorded is true (and no falsehood in the Scriptures but what is from the errors of scribes and translators)," hand down this supreme trust in the Scripture word to our own day—to our own Charles Hodge and Henry B. Smith, the one of whom asserts that the Bible "gives us truth without error," and the other, that "all the books of the Scripture are equally inspired;...all alike are infallible in what they teach;...their assertions must be free from error." Such testimonies are simply the formulation by the theologians of each age of the constant faith of Christians throughout all ages. [12]

We feel we must add to the above a reminder that the great minds, the educated modern mind of godly men who are not theologians have joined in this belief in the Bible. So it was with Shakespeare, Tennyson, Browning, Milton, Wordsworth, writers of England. So it was with Cromwell, Gladstone, Lloyd George, Winston Churchill, Queen Victoria, Abraham Lincoln, George Washington, President Adams, Daniel Webster, Thomas Carlyle, John Ruskin, Robert E. Lee, Theodore Roosevelt, and President Wilson. All these have been ardent believers in the Bible as the very Word of God. The witness of the church and the testimony of the best men and women of all ages give a great presumption that the Bible is what it claims to be—the very Word of God.

---

12. *The Inspiration and Authority of the Bible,* pp. 107-109.

III. THE HISTORICAL ACCURACY OF THE BIBLE

Whole books have been written on this subject and we can deal with it only briefly.

1. The Mosaic Authorship of the Pentateuch

That Moses wrote the first five books in the Bible is claimed throughout those books. For example, after long chapters giving detailed laws and rules, Exodus 24:4 tells us, "And Moses wrote all the words of the Lord, and rose up early in the morning, and builded an altar under the hill, and twelve pillars, according to the twelve tribes of Israel."

Throughout the rest of the Bible, Moses is acknowledged as the human writer of the Pentateuch. Joshua, in Joshua 1:7, is commanded, "Only be thou strong and very courageous, that thou mayest observe to do according to all the law, which Moses my servant commanded thee."

Dr. Oswald T. Allis calls attention to the fact that in the last book in the Old Testament, Malachi 4:4, Israel was commanded, "Remember ye the law of Moses my servant, which I commanded unto him in Horeb for all Israel, with the statutes and judgments." As we have seen elsewhere, the Lord Jesus Himself quoted again and again from Moses and said, "Moses ...wrote of me" (John 5:46). And John 1:17 declares, "For the law was given by Moses, but grace and truth came by Jesus Christ." All the Jews in the time of Christ believed that the Pentateuch was written by Moses.

However, higher critics did not know much about the ancient civilizations and so they said that there was no writing in the time of Moses, and that the history of Israel must have been written from long repeated, oral editions. Hence, they said Moses could not have written the Pentateuch. Then Astruc, Eichhorn, Graff, Wellhausen and others formed the documentary theories that the Pentateuch was a hodge-podge of pieces from different manuscripts patched together by some nice lying crook, either in the days of King Josiah or later, in the days of Ezra after the captivity. Dr. Oswald T. Allis says, "In like manner history may not tell us all we would like to know about Moses, but of another than Moses as author of the Pentateuch history knows absolutely nothing."[13]

However, archaeology continues to make amazing contributions to our knowledge of ancient times. For example, Hammurabi, king of Babylon, about 2,000 B.C., was a contemporary of Abraham and some Assyriologists identify him with Amraphel of Genesis 14, one of the kings Abraham pursued to rescue Lot. In 1902, Hammurabi's code of laws was found engraved on a big stone in the ruins of Susa. So, several hundred years before Moses there was a high civilization, a well-defined code of laws, all carefully written down and recorded.

In 1888, in the ruins of Tel-el-Amarna in Egypt, about 400 clay tablets were found. They were part of the royal archives of Amenhotep, III, and Amenhotep, IV, who reigned about 1400 B.C. They contained official correspondence from various kings of Palestine and Syria written in Babylonian cuneiform script about the time of Moses, showing that many people could write in the days of Moses. So Dr. W. F. Albright says, "Only a very ignorant person can now suggest that writing (in many forms) was not known in Palestine and the immediately surrounding regions during the entire second millennium B.C."[14] *Halley's Bible Handbook* has a record of many such evidences of early writing.

There never was any factual basis for denying that Moses wrote the first five books in the Bible exactly as the Scriptures claim and as Jesus Christ Himself said. Only infidel speculation would argue against it.

The Graff-Wellhausen theory has been answered wonderfully in *The Five Books of Moses* by Dr. Oswald T. Allis of Princeton and later Westminster Seminary and we recommend that book to anyone who has been disturbed by the foolish claims of unbelievers against the Mosaic authorship of the Pentateuch.

2. Dr. Robert Dick Wilson's Investigation of the Old Testament

Dr. Robert Dick Wilson was professor of Semitic Philology

---

13. *The Five Books of Moses*, pp. 4,5.
14. Bulletin #60, American Schools of Oriental Research, Dec., 1935.

in Princeton Theological Seminary. Dr. Edward J. Young, who
revised and introduced the latest printing of Dr. Wilson's book,
A Scientific Investigation of the Old Testament, says that this
scholar "was at home in some forty-five languages and dialects, even including the Armenian." And point by point this
great and devoted Christian scholar shows that the higher
critics are wrong and unscholarly in their conclusions and their
speculations. He shows that the Old Testament proves itself
to be the very Word of God. He called his book *A Scientific
Investigation of the Old Testament* and he said:

> I presume that the prima-facie evidence of the documents of
> the Old Testament is to be received as true until it shall have
> been proved false. I hold, further, that the evidence of manu-
> scripts and versions and of the Egyptian, Babylonian, and
> other documents outside the Bible confirms the prima-facie evi-
> dence of the Biblical documents in general both as to text and
> meaning; and that this text and meaning cannot be corrected
> or changed simply in order to be brought into harmony with
> the opinions of men of our generation. To demand that we
> should verify every statement of any ancient document (or
> modern for that matter) before we can reasonably believe it, is
> demanding the impossible. The most that we can reasonably
> require is that the author of the document and the document
> itself shall stand the test of veracity wherever their statements
> can be examined in the light of other testimony of the same
> age and provenance and of equal veracity. Examined in this
> way, I contend that our text of the Old Testament is presump-
> tively correct, that its meaning is on the whole clear and trust-
> worthy, and that we can as theists and Christians conscientiously
> and reasonably believe that the Old Testament as we have it
> is what it purports to be and what Christ and the apostles
> thought it to be — the Word of God and the infallible rule of
> faith and practice.

He said, "In my discussion of the text, therefore, it is my
endeavor to show from the evidence of manuscripts, versions,
and the inscriptions, that we are scientifically certain that we
have substantially the same text that was in the possession of
Christ and the apostles and, so far as anybody knows, the same
as that written by the original composers of the Old Testament
documents."

Since Dr. Wilson died, among the Dead Sea Scrolls found in
Qumran caves, there was a manuscript of Isaiah, by far the
oldest known to exist (some 200 years B.C.), and this fits

almost to the minutest detail with the Masoretic text which we already had.

In concluding the author's preface, Dr. Wilson said, "In conclusion, let me reiterate my conviction that no one knows enough to show that the true text of the Old Testament in its true interpretation is not true."[15]

All good Christians have a great reverence for the truth. We are not against scholarship. We simply know that Christ and the Bible can be trusted, and the speculation of ungodly scholars, which deny the authenticity of the Bible, are false.

3. Sir William Ramsay Testifies to the Accuracy of the New Testament

Sir William Ramsay was for the greater part of his life professor of humanity at the University of Aberdeen. For thirty-four years he spent his vacations in a study exploring in Asiatic Turkey and thus he became the acknowledged authority on the life of Paul and the history of the early church. He wrote *St. Paul the Traveller and the Roman Citizen, The Cities of St. Paul,* and many other books, including *The Bearing of Recent Discovery on the Trustworthiness of the New Testament.* His discoveries and scholarly work earned him a knighthood from the British Government. Sir William Ramsay tells us:

> Among other old books that described journeys in Asia Minor the Acts of the Apostles had to be read anew. I began to do so without expecting any information of value regarding the condition of Asia Minor at the time when Paul was living. I had read a good deal of modern criticism about the book, and dutifully accepted the current opinion that it was written during the second half of the second century by an author who wished to influence the minds of people in his own time by a highly wrought and imaginative description of the early Church. His object was not to present a trustworthy picture of facts in the period about A.D. 50, but to produce a certain effect on his own time by setting forth a carefully coloured account of events and persons of that older period. He wrote for his contemporaries, not for truth. He cared nought for geographical or historical surroundings of the period A.D. 30 to 60. He thought only of the period A.D. 160-180, and how he might paint the heroes of old time in situations that should touch the conscience of his

---

15. *A Scientific Investigation of the Old Testament,* pp. 8,9,10,13.

contemporaries. Antiquarian or geographical truth was less than valueless in a design like this: one who thought of such things was distracting his attention from the things that really mattered, the things that would move the minds of men in the second century.

Such was the commonly accepted view in the critical school about 1870 to 1880, when I had been studying modern opinions. It is now utterly antiquated. There is not one point in it that is accepted. Everything is changed or discarded. But about 1880 to 1890 the book of the Acts was regarded as the weakest part of the New Testament. [16]

But thirty-four years of following the steps of the Apostle Paul in his missionary journeys, checking all the historical archaeological sources possible, now, convinced after long years of checking fact after fact, sentence after sentence in the book of Luke and the book of Acts, Ramsay wrote in this book:

I describe no striking discoveries. My aim is to state certain principles that result from modern discovery, and to illustrate their bearing on the New Testament. The method is to show through the examination, word by word and phrase by phrase, of a few passages, which have been much exposed to hostile criticism, that the New Testament is unique in the compactness, the lucidity, the pregnancy and the vivid truthfulness of its expression. That is not the character of one or two only of the books that compose the Testament: it belongs in different ways to all alike, though space fails in the present work to try them all. [17]

We could give great details showing how the critics have retreated further and further from their attacks on the Bible. Now, those who say that the book of Daniel is not authentic but was written later, retreat. The Graff-Wellhausen theory is discredited. It has been shown that Belshazzar really did rule in Babylon as co-king along with his father Nabonidus. But sufficient for our purpose here is to show that great scholars have now answered the critics and intelligent scholarship accepts the Bible as historically accurate and true.

---

16. *The Bearing of Recent Discovery on the Trustworthiness of the New Testament,* pp. 37,38.
17. *The Bearing of Recent Discovery on the Trustworthiness of the New Testament,* p. v.

IV. TEN REASONS WHY DR. R. A. TORREY BELIEVED THE BIBLE TO BE THE WORD OF GOD

Dr. R. A. Torrey, one of the greatest Bible scholars America has produced, an eminent evangelist, trained in Yale and two German universities, co-worker and successor of D. L. Moody, has given "ten reasons why I believe the Bible to be the Word of God." They are published in a book by that name by Moody Press and in this author's collection, *A Coffer of Jewels About...the Bible.* Without much discussion, we list these important evidences here.

1. On the ground of the testimony of Jesus Christ.
2. On the ground of its fulfilled prophecies.
3. On the ground of the unity of the Book.

When sixty-six books, written by some forty authors, through fifteen hundred years or more, and in different countries, provide a book without a single contradiction and united on the great doctrines and principles taught, that has to be supernatural.

4. On the ground of the immeasurable superiority of the teachings of the Bible to those of any other and all other books.
5. On the ground of the history of the Book, its victory over attack.
6. On the ground of the character of those who accept and those who reject the Book.
7. On the ground of the influence of the Book.
8. On the ground of the inexhaustible depth of the Book.
9. On the ground of the fact that as we grow in knowledge and holiness we grow toward the Bible.
10. On the ground of the direct testimony of the Holy Spirit.

There is such a well of overwhelming evidence that the Bible is the Word of God, that there is no excuse for any honest heart not coming to know this truth.

CHAPTER XIX

GOD PRESERVES HIS ETERNAL WORD

I. THERE ARE PROBLEMS OF COPIES, TRANSLATION AND CANON OF SCRIPTURE

1. How Do We Know That the Copies Are Exact and True? The Translations? The Canon?

2. Jesus Had Faced All Those Problems About the Old Testament

3. How Wonderfully God Has Preserved His Word

II. THE SCRIPTURES CLEARLY CLAIM TO BE ETERNAL AND INDESTRUCTIBLE

1. Psalm 119 Declares That All the Scriptures Are Settled Forever in Heaven and Endure Forever

2. Isaiah and Peter Were Inspired to Say That the Word of God Is Incorruptible, Abides Forever

3. The Lord Jesus Plainly Promises That the Scriptures "Shall Not Pass Away"

III. WE HAVE ALL THE INSPIRED SCRIPTURE IN OUR BIBLE CANON

1. The Old Testament Canon Already Settled in the Time of Christ

2. The New Testament Canon

3. God Has Guided So We Have a Correct Canon of Scripture

IV. THOUSANDS OF COPIES AVAILABLE, TOGETHER AND COMPARED, GUARANTEE THE FAITHFULNESS OF OUR BIBLES TO THE ORIGINAL AUTOGRAPHS

GOD PRESERVES HIS ETERNAL WORD

A disreputable publisher advertises that he has found and published "the lost books of the Bible" and that you should buy them. But have we lost some books out of the Bible, some books inspired of God but not preserved for us? No, we have not. There are no "lost books of the Bible." There are certain apocryphal books, long known, which never have been a part of the Bible and do not claim to be, although the Catholic Bible prints them between the Old and New Testaments. God has promised that His Word abides forever, and so the world has all the portions that God inspired for the Bible.

I. THERE ARE PROBLEMS OF COPIES, TRANS-
LATION AND CANON OF SCRIPTURE

But when we speak of inspiration, we speak of the original autographs, the original manuscripts. We have none of the original manuscripts. All we have are copies of copies.

1. How Do We Know That the Copies Are Exact
and True? The Translations? The Canon?

Well, we know of the meticulous care with which the scribes copied the Scriptures, even counting the letters. And we have thousands of manuscripts; so if one copyist made a mistake, accidentally altering or leaving out a letter or adding a word, and if perhaps two or three others copied his mistake, yet we have hundreds of other manuscripts that did not make the same mistake so that we can compare them and almost certainly come to the very original words. God has promised to preserve His Word forever and we are sure He has.

But the inspiration dealt with provided the Old Testament written down in Hebrew (and a few chapters of Daniel in Chaldaic).   And the New Testament was written in the Koine, the Greek language of the common people in the market place. How do I know that the translation of the Scriptures which I have in English are well done?

Well, there are many, many translations.   The differences in the translations are so minor, so insignificant, that we can be sure not a single doctrine, not a single statement of fact, not a single command or exhortation, has been missed in our translations.   And where the Word of God is not perfectly translated in one instance, it is corrected in another translation. And if the Word of God is not perfectly portrayed in one translation, it is portrayed, surely, in the winnowed sum of them all. And besides, one can go back to the original Greek and Hebrew texts to check for himself the translations. Or those who do not know Hebrew and Greek may use Young's Analytical Concordance.   There you will find in every single case the original Greek or Hebrew word, find how it is used, and thus can check the translations.

Yes, we are interested in the questions about the Bible.   Do we have the correct canon of Scripture, with all the inspired writings enclosed?   There is abundant evidence that we do. Have copyists passed on to us any major errors so that in any particular matter we miss the Word of God?   There is abundant evidence that they have not.   Do the various translations differ materially on any doctrine, any fact of history, any Christian duty, on the plan of salvation, or the Person of Christ, or any comfort or instruction?   No, they do not!   God has preserved His Scriptures.

2. Jesus Had Faced All Those Problems
About the Old Testament

But very fortunately for us, the questions of the canon, of the copyists and the translators is greatly simplified by the fact that Jesus faced all these problems.   The Old Testament Scriptures which Jesus read and loved and quoted, He had only in copies.   Scriptures from the writing of Moses nearly fifteen hundred years before, and the writings of Malachi, the last of the minor prophets, over four hundred years before, had all been copied many times in Jesus' day.

Not only so, but about fourteen apocryphal books had been written in the time between the Testaments, and yet they were not included in the Jewish canon of Old Testament Scriptures and Jesus did not count them the Word of God nor refer to them as such.   He faced the same problem people have now about the canon of Scriptures.

And Jesus had the problem of translation also.   The Old Testament Scriptures were written in Hebrew, but now the Jews spoke the Aramaic language.   And if Jesus talked to the people in the Aramaic language, He must have the translation of the Scriptures in that language.   Or, if He spoke in the Koine Greek, which doubtless He knew, He would have the Scriptures in the Septuagint, the translation of the seventy elders who put the Old Testament from the Hebrew into Greek. You see, Jesus faced all the problems of the canon, of the copies, of the translations, yet He gave not a hint that these problems detracted from the eternal verity of the Word of God. He still said, "The scripture cannot be broken" (John 10:35). He still said of the Scriptures that "man shall not live by bread alone, but by every word that proceedeth out of the mouth of God" (Matt. 4:4).   He still said, "Think not that I am come to destroy the law, or the prophets: I am not come to destroy, but to fulfil.   For verily I say unto you, Till heaven and earth pass, one jot or one tittle shall in no wise pass from the law, till all be fulfilled" (Matt. 5:17,18).

So in New Testament times God had preserved His Word so it was utterly trustworthy, and you may be sure He has continued to preserve it.   Our problems have already been faced, and God has guaranteed that the Scriptures are indestructible, eternal.

3. How Wonderfully God Has Preserved His Word!

Dr. A. Z. Conrad, long minister of the Park Street Church in Boston, has these encouraging words:

> It would be a strange contradiction of evidence to ignore or
> deny the fact that the hand of God has been definitely engaged

in protecting and preserving his Word. Charles T. Bateman in his interesting volume, "The Romance of the Bible," follows with great care the history of the writing and preservation of the Word of God. Its existence seemed again and again imperiled by neglect, by apostasy, by violent and determined efforts to annihilate it. In the ten great Roman persecutions the Book of the Christians, the Bible, was the especial object of attack; in each of the persecutions the effort at its annihilation was coextensive with the imperial power of the day. Nero, Domitian, Trajan, Hadrian, Septimus Severus, Marcus Aurelius, Valerian, and Diocletian successively undertook the obliteration of the Bible from civilization. Each effort proved not only abortive, but finally resulted in the multiplication of the copies of the Word of Life.

Not only has the Bible proved its indestructibility at the hands of its enemies, but it has withstood even the greater danger, that of overthrow and defeat at the hands of its supposed friends. There are few chapters in human history more weighted with significance than those which relate to the attitude of the Catholic Church toward the Bible at the time of Henry IV. The dungeon, the rack, and the flame were all employed to prevent the common people from having the benefit of a free reading of the Bible. The fires of Smithfield were again and again proving the tremendous hold of the Bible upon the martyr spirits that suffered death because of their loyalty to the ever-living Word. The years following 1533 repeatedly witnessed the most agonizing martyrdom in the interests of an open Bible. Fryth, Anne Askew, Alexander Campbell were the first of many to lay down their lives for the Book of books.[1]

We can rejoice then that God thus preserves His Word.

II. THE SCRIPTURES CLEARLY CLAIM TO BE ETERNAL AND INDESTRUCTIBLE

There is abundant material evidence that the Scriptures, as we have them today, correctly represent the original autographs. But our principal concern is what the Bible claims for itself. If God has plainly promised that His Word abides forever, we may safely rest on that and we will find that all the evidence fits in with what God has promised. Historical evidence can never disprove but only substantiate what God Himself has plainly said about the Scriptures.

---

1. *The Seven Finalities of the Faith*, pp. 85,86.

1. Psalm 119 Declares That All the Scriptures Are Settled Forever in Heaven and Endure Forever

What a claim is here! "For ever, O Lord, thy word is settled in heaven" (Ps. 119:89). Whether or not the Word of God is incorruptible as it is written down in the language of men, here certainly we are told the Word of God is settled forever in Heaven. We think that infers that the Scriptures will be preserved among men but it certainly teaches the eternal character of the Scriptures, settled and preserved in Heaven.

But in the same Psalm 119, verse 160 says, "Thy word is true from the beginning: and every one of thy righteous judgments endureth for ever." I think there can be no doubt that this promise refers to the Word of God on earth and among men and it is not only true from the very beginning, but "every one of thy righteous judgments endureth for ever."

2. Isaiah and Peter Were Inspired to Say That the Word of God Is Incorruptible, Abides Forever

In Isaiah 40:8 is this blessed promise, "The grass withereth, the flower fadeth: but the word of our God shall stand for ever."

This Scripture is quoted and enlarged upon in the New Testament. In I Peter 1:23-25, it is written:

"Being born again, not of corruptible seed, but of incorruptible, by the word of God, which liveth and abideth for ever. For all flesh is as grass, and all the glory of man as the flower of grass. The grass withereth, and the flower thereof falleth away: But the word of the Lord endureth for ever. And this is the word which by the gospel is preached unto you."

We are born again by hearing the Gospel from the Scriptures. Psalm 19:7 says, "The law of the Lord is perfect, converting the soul." So here we read that one is born again by the incorruptible Seed, by the Word of God. So God speaks here of the Word of God on earth among men, which Word has the Gospel through which people are born again. And this written Word of God lives and abides forever.

The eternal Word of God here is contrasted with mankind:

"for all flesh is as grass." It is contrasted with the human glory of our civilization: "...and all the glory of man as the flower of grass. The grass withereth, and the flower thereof falleth away: But the word of the Lord endureth for ever." So indestructible and eternal is the Word of God. Not like mankind himself, not like the glories of our civilization and of this world. "But the word of the Lord endureth for ever." And it is this Word, this written Scripture, by which men preach the Gospel!

What a strong, clear statement that the Word of God is indestructible, incorruptible, that it abides forever!

3. The Lord Jesus Plainly Promises That the Scriptures "Shall Not Pass Away"

Jesus refers to His second coming, a doctrine that many men despise. But there is a vast amount of Scripture concerning the second coming, the regathering of Israel, judgments of Christ on the people, the destruction of the nations of this world, the millennial kingdom, the last judgment, etc. So, speaking of these prophetic matters, Jesus says, "Heaven and earth shall pass away, but my words shall not pass away" (Matt. 24:35; Mark 13:31; Luke 21:33). Here thrice repeated is the promise of Christ, "My words shall not pass away." Here the Scriptures in their eternal nature are contrasted with the earth and the heavens about it, which are under a curse and which must be purged by fire and, in their present state, pass away. Not so the Word of God! In Psalm 19 there is this same contrast, "The heavens declare the glory of God." But the heavens are not perfect. Nature is under a curse for man's sake. Nature shows that there is a God but it doesn't tell about the plan of salvation through faith in the atoning Saviour, but verse 7 says, "The law of the Lord is perfect, converting the soul." The Scriptures are more perfect and eternal than the natural world around us, says the Scripture.

When Jesus says, "My words shall not pass away," He refers certainly to all the Scriptures. Colossians 3:16 exhorts us, "Let the word of Christ dwell in you richly," referring to the Bible. All the words of the Bible are the words of Christ, and they shall never pass away!

So Jesus says of the Scripture, "The scripture cannot be broken" (John 10:35).

And the Scriptures that are eternal will judge the lost at the last judgment, for Jesus said in John 12:48, "He that rejecteth me, and receiveth not my words, hath one that judgeth him: the word that I have spoken, the same shall judge him in the last day."

Did Jesus come to destroy the law? He gives a wonderful pronouncement on that in Matthew 5:17,18:

"Think not that I am come to destroy the law, or the prophets: I am not come to destroy, but to fulfil. For verily I say unto you, Till heaven and earth pass, one jot or one tittle shall in no wise pass from the law, till all be fulfilled."

By the law and the prophets Jesus refers to all the Old Testament and He says that "till heaven and earth pass, one jot or one tittle shall in no wise pass from the law, till all be fulfilled."

Circumcision, commanded in the law for Jews, is not now required, but the circumcision of the heart which it pictured is required, so the Scripture does not pass away. Jesus makes it clear in what intricate detail the Scriptures will be preserved. Not a jot nor a tittle will pass away! The Lord here guarantees even the verbal accuracy of the translations and copies — not of one particular copy nor of one particular translation but of the inspired Word in all of them together.

Here, then, is a clear Bible doctrine that the Word of God abides forever, it endures forever, it shall never pass away! So, if we know the detailed methods by which God preserves His Word, well and good. If we do not know how providence has overruled the wrath of men, the errors of copyists, the bias of translators, we can still know that He does overrule them. And not altogether, perhaps, in one copy or in one translation, but in them all collectively God has His perfect Word, never to be destroyed, never to pass away. The Word of God abides forever.

III. WE HAVE ALL THE INSPIRED SCRIPTURE IN OUR BIBLE CANON

We have not here the space, even if we had the scholarship,

to give in great detail all the evidences that we have properly the complete and perfect canon of Scripture.

Dr. Laird Harris's book on the *Inspiration and Canonicity of the Bible* and the discussion in the *International Bible Encyclopaedia*, written by George L. Robinson, and other sound books, including introductions to the Old and New Testaments, deal properly with this matter. But our main concern here is to find what the Bible teaches and claims for itself. And the Bible does clearly claim an indestructible, eternal perfection, as we have seen.

So here we need only sum up some of the principal evidences for our canon of the Scriptures, as contained in all Protestant Bibles.

1. The Old Testament Canon Already Settled in the Time of Christ

It is generally acknowledged that the Old Testament canon of Scriptures, containing exactly the same books as we now have in the Protestant Bibles, was accepted by the Jews in Christ's time. The Jewish historian Josephus lists the Old Testament Scriptures as we have them.

The fourteen books of the apocrypha were written in the time between the Testaments, but they were not accepted as canonical. They do not claim to be the inspired Scripture. They were included in the copies we now have of the Septuagint (not necessarily in original Jewish copies) and are published in the Latin Vulgate and adopted officially by the Catholic church. But the apocryphal books do not have the marks of Scripture, they were not accepted as Scripture in their own day by Jewish people, and they are never quoted as Scripture by the Lord Jesus. No, the canon of the Old Testament Scripture was already decided without the apocrypha, and is referred to repeatedly in the New Testament as if it were a settled group of writings clearly recognized as the Word of God.

The foolish and untrue claim of some Catholics, that the church decided the canon of Scriptures and that Protestants owe to Catholics their Bible, is utterly foolish and untrue. And when men take on themselves the authority of God, they simply confuse matters, as our Catholic friends did in trying to make the apocrypha the Word of God.   They are not that.   They never have been.   They do not even claim to be the Word of God.

On this matter, the sensible and sure attitude of a Christian ought to be that he accepts just what Jesus Christ accepted — the Old Testament Scriptures as the Word of God.

2. The New Testament Canon

The books that are accepted in our New Testament have simply earned their way there.   They have proved to the mass of Christians that they are the Word of God.   They claim to be inspired.   They deal with matters that inspired Scripture would deal with.   They speak with authority.

Luke tells us that in his day there were many people who had undertaken to give an orderly outline of the life of Christ as they had gotten it from eyewitnesses (Luke 1:1 and 2).   But it was necessary for Luke "having had perfect understanding of all things *anothen* [from above]," to make known the certainty of the things already written which were not certain.   Thus Luke claims a perfection that involves inspiration and he claims he got it "from above."

Likewise, Paul's epistles clearly claim to be inspired, as you see in I Corinthians 2:10-14; I Thessalonians 2:13; Galatians 1:8-12 and elsewhere.   And so with all the books in the New Testament we can see they have earned their place in claiming to be the Word of God.   They prove themselves to be that as they are read and studied and followed by millions.   According to Revelation 22:18, that book seems to close the canon of Scripture as a warning, "If any man shall add unto these things, God shall add unto him the plagues that are written in this book."

3. God Has Guided So We Have a
Correct Canon of Scripture

Let us make sure we understand this: No decision of councils, nor decree of pope, no confession of faith of a denomination, could make any part of Scripture the Word of God.   It is already the Word of God.   Then it got its place in the canon because it was already the inspired Word of God.

Some godly theologians make much of the fact that New Testament books are in the canon because they are apostolic. It is true that Jesus promised the Holy Spirit would come to the disciples and guide them into all truth.   In John 16:13 Jesus said, "Howbeit when he, the Spirit of truth, is come, he will guide you into all truth: for he shall not speak of himself; but whatsoever he shall hear, that shall he speak: and he will shew you things to come."   He even promised of this Holy Spirit, "He shall teach you all things, and bring all things to your remembrance, whatsoever I have said unto you" (John 14:26).   And that is true, no doubt, about the inspiration of the Gospels, and the Holy Spirit did, to a perfect degree, guide those who wrote the New Testament books.   However, this promise of the Spirit seems to be for all Christians in some measure and to others besides the Bible writers it would mean illumination and not necessarily revelation and inspiration. And the Apostle Paul was not then converted so he would not necessarily be in the immediate group to whom that promise was originally given.

People would like to say that Luke wrote on the authority of Paul or sponsored by Paul and that Mark wrote his Gospel under the sponsorship of Peter.   However, the Scripture says nothing like that and we have a far more certain evidence that the Scriptures, as we have them, are inspired than any sponsorship by Paul or by Peter would give them.   We have the assurance of Jesus Christ that His words will never pass away. We have the certainty from the Scriptures that the Word of God endures forever, that it will never pass away.   So by faith a Christian accepts what God promises.   He keeps His Word incorruptible.

IV. THOUSANDS OF COPIES AVAILABLE, TOGETHER AND COMPARED, GUARANTEE THE FAITHFULNESS OF OUR BIBLES TO THE ORIGINAL AUTOGRAPHS

The providence of God in preserving manuscripts and copies of the Scriptures makes a fascinating story.

Although we do not have any of the original autographs of
the Bible, we have so many copies of the Old Testament in
Hebrew and in the Greek Septuagint, so many copies of the
New Testament in Koine Greek, so many copies in Latin,
that comparing one copy with other copies, one can find with
almost perfect certainty any gloss, any mistakes by the scribe
in copying, any addition of a word or change in a letter, from
the original copy.

1. The Romance of God's Preservation of Scripture

The way God has preserved many of these old manuscripts
makes an amazing and happy story.

Dr. Lobegott Tischendorf, sponsored by the Russian and
German governments, in 1844 and fifteen years later, visited
the monastery of St. Catherine at the foot of Mt. Sinai and
found there an ancient manuscript of the Old Testament Greek
Septuagint, a copy that had been made in about the year 350.

Buried in the sands of Egypt, archaeologists uncovered many
letters and records and accounts by common people written in
the Greek and it was discovered for the first time that the language of the New Testament was not some strange and holy
kind of Greek, not the classic language of Homer, but the
everyday language of the Greek people.

A few years ago in the Qumran caves near the north end of
the Dead Sea were found the ruins of an Essene colony. Preserved in earthenware jars in these dry caves were manuscripts,
including many portions of Scripture, a complete Isaiah, etc. It
is thought that the copy of Isaiah goes back to 200 years
B.C. and is many centuries older than any other Old Testament
manuscript.

In their letters and sermons, the early church fathers quoted
many verses from the New Testament. One scholar said that
he had been able to copy all the New Testament from the
writings of these fathers excepting only eleven verses! And
thus we have many ways to check one manuscript against
others to find the slightest deviation from the original manuscripts. Some copyists made a mistake but, of course, they
did not all make the same mistake, and on any particular
passage more of the manuscripts would be right than could

be wrong since they came from such widely scattered places in Egypt and the Eastern Roman Empire and the West. The New Testament Scriptures were quoted by the fathers, some were translated in Latin manuscripts, some Old Testament Scriptures in the Septuagint Greek and some in the original Hebrew.

Sir Dalrymple was the man who discovered that every verse in the New Testament except eleven could be reproduced from the published works of the early church fathers. [2]

2. From Thousands of Sources We Know the True Text

Dr. W. A. Criswell, president of Southern Baptist Convention and pastor of the First Baptist Church of Dallas, Texas, has the following clear, good statement:

Our Assurance of the True Word of the Text

It is thus that from every part of the ancient world, from the tombs, from the rubbish heaps, from the libraries, from the writings of the Fathers, from the versions, there comes evidence piled on top of evidence for the authenticity of the text of the Word of God. The multiplication of these ancient manuscripts is unbelievable. They come from every part of the ancient world, and they cover every portion of the New Testament and of the whole Bible.

For example, one scholar estimates that there are 4,105 ancient Greek manuscripts of the New Testament. It has also been variously estimated that there are as many as 15,000 to 30,000 Latin versions of the Holy Scriptures. Besides these, there are at least 1,000 other early versions of the Sacred Word. When all those thousands of documents are checked, compared, combined, grouped, studied, we have a certain and final answer regarding the text.

When we remember that there is but a single manuscript that preserves the annals of Tacitus; when we remember that there is but a single manuscript that preserves the Greek Anthology; when we remember that the manuscripts of Sophocles, of Thucydides, of Euripides, of Virgil, of Cicero, are most rare and the very few in existence are, for the most part, very late; then we can see with what profusion of evidence God supported the truth of the transcription of His Sacred Word.

With complete and perfect assurance I can pick up my Bible and know that I read the revealed Word of God. The God who

2. W. A. Criswell in *These Issues We Must Face*, p. 58.

inspired it also took faithful care that it be exactly preserved through the fire and the blood of the centuries.[3]

Radical scholars have been disappointed and Bible believers greatly encouraged by the fact that the finding of the manuscript of Isaiah in the Dead Sea Scrolls is centuries older than any other manuscript of Isaiah we have, and follows in meticulous detail almost perfectly the Masoretic text we already had from many copies. So we know that there have been no important changes made in the copying by scribes through long centuries.

3. Only a Scattered Few Insignificant Details of Difference in Manuscripts Are Unsure

Gaussen was well acquainted with all the radical scholars of his day and their efforts to find errors in the Scriptures, in the Received Text of the New Testament particularly. By comparing with all the manuscripts available, he found that the most radical of the liberals could only point to tiny differences, insignificant and only rare, about which there was any uncertainty whatever. He compared and listed all the criticisms and all the studies on the book of Romans, as an example. He says:

> We will present the differences between **our received text** and ALL THE MANUSCRIPTS that one has been able to collect down to Griesbach. That learned and indefatigable person, for the Epistle to the Romans, scrutinized first of all seven manuscripts written WITH UNCIAL LETTERS (or Greek capitals), and it is thought, from thirteen to fourteen centuries old, (the **Alexandrine**, in the British Museum; that of the **Vatican**, and that of Cardinal **Passionei** at Rome; that of Ephrem at Paris; that of St. Germain, that of Dresden, and that of Cardinal **Coislin**); and after that, a hundred and ten manuscripts **in small letters**, and thirty others, brought for the most part from Mount Athos, and consulted by the learned Matthei, who travelled long for that purpose in Russia and the East.
>
> For the four Gospels, the same Griesbach had opportunities of consulting as many as three hundred and thirty-five manuscripts.[4]

Then after giving detail, point by point, all the preferred

---

3. *These Issues We Must Face*, pp. 59,60.
4. *The Inspiration of the Holy Scriptures*, p. 177.

readings by the liberal Griesbach and those that he mentioned as not preferable but perhaps doubtful, Gaussen says again:

> We see, then, the amount of the whole: such is the admirable integrity of the Epistle to the Romans. According to Griesbach **five insignificant corrections**, in the whole epistle — according to more modern critics ONLY TWO, and these the most insignificant of the five; — and according to Scholz THREE! [5]

Then Gaussen says:

> It is reckoned, that of the seven thousand nine hundred and fifty-nine verses of the New Testament, there hardly exist ten or twelve in which the corrections that have been introduced by the new readings of Griesbach and Scholz, as the result of their immense researches, have any weight at all. Further, in most instances they consist but in the difference of a single word, and sometimes even of a single letter. [6]

And it has been shown again and again that with every possible variation found in any of the manuscripts, there is not a single doctrine of the Bible changed, not a single historical event affected, not a single duty commanded that is thus clouded. God has wonderfully preserved His Scripture.

And we are sure that while in any particular single manuscript, there may be some gloss or mistake in copying, as between an "a" or "the" or between one letter in a word and another letter, we know that in all the manuscripts together there abides the incorrupt Word of God, and that every honest Bible reader thus can find the will of God for himself and divine truth on everything he needs to learn from the Scriptures.

4. We Rejoice With Gaussen Over the Obvious Providence of God in Thus Preserving His Word

In that classic book by Gaussen, *The Inspiration of the Holy Scriptures*, he finds, as we do, the providence of God amazing and we rejoice with him. He says:

> When one thinks that the Bible has been copied during thirty centuries, as no book of man has ever been or ever will be; that it was subjected to all the catastrophes and all the captivities of

---

5. *The Inspiration of the Holy Scriptures*, p. 188.
6. *The Inspiration of the Holy Scriptures*, p. 189,190.

Israel; that it was transported seventy years to Babylon; that
it has seen itself so often persecuted, or forgotten, or interdicted,
or burnt, from the days of the Philistines to those of the Seleu-
cidae; — when one thinks that, since the time of Jesus Christ, it
has had to traverse the first three centuries of the imperial
persecutions, when persons found in possession of the holy
books were thrown to the wild beasts; next the 7th, 8th, and
9th centuries, when false books, false legends, and false decretals
were everywhere multiplied; the 10th century, when so few could
read, even among princes; the 12th, 13th, and 14th centuries,
when the use of the Scriptures in the vulgar tongue was punished
with death, and when the books of the ancient fathers were
mutilated, when so many ancient traditions were garbled and
falsified, even to the very acts of the emperors, and to those of
the councils; — then we can perceive how necessary it was that
the providence of God should have always put forth its mighty
power, in order that, on the one hand, the church of the Jews
should give us, in its integrity, that Word which records its
revolts, which predicts its ruin, which describes Jesus Christ; and,
on the other, that the Christian churches (the most powerful of
which, and the Roman sect in particular, interdicted the people
from reading the sacred books, and substituted in so many ways
the traditions of the middle ages for the Word of God) should
nevertheless transmit to us, in all their purity, those Scriptures,
which condemn all their traditions, their images, their dead
languages, their absolutions, their celibacy; which say, that
Rome would be the seat of a terrible apostasy, where "the
Man of Sin would be seen sitting as God in the temple of God,
waging war on the saints, forbidding to marry, and to use
meats which God had created;" which say of images, "Thou
shalt not bow down to them" — of unknown tongues, "Thou
shalt not use them" — of the cup, "Drink ye all of it" — of the
virgin, "Woman, what have I to do with thee?" — and of marriage, "It is honourable in all."

Now, although all the libraries in which ancient copies of the
sacred books may be found have been called upon to give their
testimony; although the elucidations given by the fathers of all
ages have been studied; although the Arabic, Syriac, Latin,
Armenian, and Ethiopian versions have been collated; although
all the manuscripts of all countries and ages, from the third to
the sixteenth century, have been collected and examined a thousand times over, by countless critics, who have eagerly sought
out some new text, as the recompense and the glory of their
wearisome watchings; although learned men, not content with
the libraries of the West, have visited those of Russia and carried
their researches into the monasteries of Mont Athos, Turkish
Asia, and Egypt, there to look for new instruments of the sacred
text; — "Nothing has been discovered," says a learned person,
already quoted, "not even a single reading, that could throw
doubt on any one of the passages before considered as certain.

All the **variantes**, almost without exception, leave untouched the essential ideas of each phrase, and bear only on points of secondary importance;'' such as the insertion or the omission of an article or a conjunction, the position of an adjective before or after its substantive, the greater or less exactness of a grammatical construction. [7]

V. THE INCORRUPTIBLE WORD OF GOD IN TRANSLATIONS

Since no translation is perfect, can we have the Word of God preserved today when nearly everybody in the world must have the Bible in some translation from the original Scriptures? Yes, we say again that in the translations we have still the perfect Word of God.

1. All the Translations Together Are the Word of God

God has promised that His Word "liveth and abideth for ever." That did not mean that all of the Word of God was in one manuscript, as the autographs were originally given. That does not mean that all the Bible as a unit was perfectly preserved in one copy through the centuries.

For example, among the Dead Sea Scrolls found in the Qumran caves near the Dead Sea, the book of Isaiah was perfectly complete but other books of the Bible were not. In the *Codex Sinaiticus* manuscript discovered by Tischendorf at the Monastery of St. Catherine near Mt. Sinai, was not all of the Scriptures. The *Codex Ephraem* manuscript has only a part. So let us say then that it is not necessary that all the Word of God be in any one manuscript or bound volume in order for it to be true that the Bible is kept perfectly and incorruptible in this world and that it shall never pass away. All of the translations together and all of the copies together guarantee that God's Word is perfectly preserved.

A preacher preaches the Gospel but not all of the truth in one sermon — no, nor in a lifetime of Bible preaching! As a young man I made a holy vow to set out to preach everything

---

7. *The Inspiration of the Holy Scriptures,* pp. 169,170.

in the Bible. I soon found out that I could never catch up.
There is more to the Bible than I have ever been able to understand fully or to expound to the people. Yet the Word of God
is preached and added together, all of it is preached somewhere,
sometime.

If we had every gloss removed, every translation perfect in
a copy of the Word of God, no one man, nor any hundred
men, could understand it all, learn it all fully, expound it all.

You see, it is not necessarily God's promise that in one particular bound copy all the Word of God would be retained, nor
in the mouth of one preacher all of it would be preached.

Besides, "it pleased God by the foolishness of preaching to
save them that believe" (I Cor. 1:21). So by the foolishness
of fallible men He has had Scriptures copied, translated, printed
and preached. It is not bad but good that God, in loving
mercy, chooses us frail, human agents to spread the Gospel —
to copy, to translate, to preach His eternal Word. Behind the
obvious personality of Paul or David or Moses present in the
Scriptures, God miraculously gives His own perfect Word. So
God, overruling and providentially protecting, preserves His
Word, keeps it "living and abiding for ever" in this world,
though one may see or think he sees incidental human flaws in
some translation or in some copy.

This is the way God works among men. Men looked on
Jesus and saw a Jewish peasant, a carpenter, a provincial
from Galilee. Many did not see that He is God, Creator of
all things, hidden in the garments of humanity, in "the form
of a servant" who "was made in the likeness of men" (Phil.
2:7).

Just so God's eternal Word is, in small part, hidden under a
word miscopied here, a biased translation there. Actually no
translation can perfectly, wholly reveal the Word of God. The
nuances of language, the color of tradition, the accretion of
corollary meaning besides the lexicon definition, cannot all
pass from one language to another.

Let me illustrate. In Bombay, India, I was preaching through
an interpreter to a great revival crowd in Byculla High School
Auditorium. There I saw this truth afresh. Preaching, I cried
out, "You cannot get by with sin!" The interpreter stopped,
nonplussed. He turned to me inquiringly, "Get by?" He
stood helplessly. The American idiom has a definite meaning,

but it is not in the dictionary meaning of the word "get" and the word "by." So I lamely changed my statement to "sin will certainly be punished," but I lost some of the punch because the full force of the idiomatic proverb could not be put into Telugu language in simple, direct translation. So no translation can be perfect.

Jesus intentionally spoke in parables. He had the deliberate intent that among the wicked who had no heart to hear His truth, it should be hidden. He said:

"By hearing ye shall hear, and shall not understand; and seeing ye shall see, and shall not perceive: For this people's heart is waxed gross, and their ears are dull of hearing, and their eyes they have closed; lest at any time they should see with their eyes and hear with their ears, and should understand with their heart, and should be converted, and I should heal them." — Matt. 13:14,15.

God chooses weak men to work His work, the foolishness of preaching to save them that believe.

So the Lord Jesus Himself appeared "as a root out of a dry ground...and when we shall see him, there is no beauty that we should desire him" (Isa. 53:2). God leaves the Bible with problems that appear as contradictions to a Voltaire, a Tom Paine, a Robert Ingersoll, or other wicked-hearted, determined unbelievers. He leaves imprecatory psalms and tells of the commanded destruction of the Amalekites so that a self-righteous Fosdick or Buttrick, presuming to judge God and the Word, can say they are immoral. God does not force the meaning nor the impact of Scripture on the unbelieving, critical, rebellious heart. As in parables the Lord Jesus deliberately made it so one must have a believing, seeking heart to understand, so He made it with the Bible, in its copies and translations and problems, that the wicked heart need not believe it unless he has a heart to believe it.

Even so, leaving room for His people to have faith and study, and leaving room for higher critics to scoff, God leaves the problems of copying, translating, preaching and interpreting to frail, fallible men, led and empowered by the Holy Spirit, but always, on the whole, preserving His Word forever. The Word may, in some tiny, insignificant detail, seem hidden under the frailties of human scribes and translators, but God has guaranteed it is preserved forever and will never pass away!

2. The Holy Spirit Continually Works Preserving and Using the Word of God

The Apostle Paul praises God, "Who also hath made us able ministers of the new testament; not of the letter, but of the spirit: for the letter killeth, but the spirit giveth life" (II Cor. 3:6). The Holy Spirit must help one to understand the Scriptures. And He some way guarantees that the seeking heart finds the truth, though that person may not be wise enough to get the literal wording. One way that the Holy Spirit keeps the incorruptible Word is that the Spirit-led man preaches more than the letter of the Word that he may use.

There is a great deal in the Old Testament Scriptures which are not apparent to one who first reads them. But when we have seen them interpreted in the New Testament, how much richer in meaning they are than the letter would tell! So we now know that the circumcision in the Old Testament really pictured regeneration, circumcision of heart. Though the command in Exodus 20:14 was, "Thou shalt not commit adultery" Jesus tells us that the meaning is far more than that: "Whosoever looketh on a woman to lust after her hath committed adultery with her already in his heart" (Matt. 5:28). And the Old Testament said that one ought to honestly pay back any restitution that fitted, he should pay back what he had taken — an eye for an eye and a tooth for a tooth (Exod. 21:24). But Jesus added more to that. He said that one should not resist it if this rule were badly enforced and one should go, if need be, the second mile for the one mile he owed, and he should turn the other cheek for a second blow if he deserved only one (Matt. 5:38-41).

So no man can understand all the Bible well enough to preach it all. But wonderfully the Holy Spirit gets the meaning of all of it, as needed, out through consecrated and Spirit-filled lips just the same.

In St. Paul, Minnesota, a preacher preached on the sin of Achan that brought the curse on Israel, from Joshua 7. One man heard it and he understood little of the letter of it. He understood the word "Achan" as meaning "acorn." So, in some agitation he told the preacher, "I have an acorn in the camp!" He was penitent and turned from sin to trust the

Saviour. He did not get the letter but he got the spiritual impact just the same!

A pioneer preacher preached on that text in Acts 2:40, "Save yourselves from this untoward generation." The word means crooked, perverse, but he understood the word to mean "untowered," that is, a people without a tower of refuge, without a safe place to hide! And he wonderfully preached so that sinners repented and fled to Christ, the Tower of Refuge! He did not understand the letter but the Holy Spirit of God, who understood the word, guided the preacher's preaching just the same! I do not advise that one preach on Scriptures without earnestly studying the meaning, but it is still true that only the Holy Spirit of God will preach all the Scriptures that are hidden within human words.

And God is so determined that His Word will remain and be preached that He had wicked, murderous Caiaphas preaching the word on the substitutionary death of Christ when he said, "Ye know nothing at all, Nor consider that it is expedient for us, that one man should die for the people, and that the whole nation perish not" (John 11:49,50). Then we are told, "This spake he not of himself: but being high priest that year, he prophesied that Jesus should die for that nation; And not for that nation only, but that also he should gather together in one the children of God that were scattered abroad" (vss. 51,52).

You see, then, that God is determined His Word shall be known and He has wonderfully preserved it, though sometimes it be not all in one translation, nor in one copy, nor in the preaching of one preacher.

And let us not grieve but rather let us rejoice that God has mercifully allowed men to unite with Him in His saving plan. He chose Mary to be the mother of Jesus. He chose frail men to write the Scriptures. He chose the weakest of this world to preach the Gospel and to win souls. And in it all He had the perfection of Christ and the perfection of the Bible and the perfection of the miracle of regeneration, wrought of God but using human tools.

This writer has been sometimes wonderfully blessed to find how the blessed Spirit led to the meaning of a Scripture. Once I was troubled as I read Hebrews 4:9-11:

"There remaineth therefore a rest to the people of God. For

he that is entered into his rest, he also hath ceased from his own works, as God did from his. Let us labour therefore to enter into that rest, lest any man fall after the same example of unbelief."

Here in verse 10 we are told that one enters into the heavenly rest by ceasing from his own works. But verse 11 says in the King James Version, "Let us *labour* therefore to enter into that rest." I thought then, as I do now, that labor is not the way to get salvation and to have the heavenly rest. I felt certain the meaning was different, the translation faulty. So I looked in Young's Analytical Concordance and found every way that the word there translated *labor* was used, and it means rather to "give diligence." One should give diligence, that is, he should urgently set out to "enter into that rest." Not "labor," but earnestly attending to the matter at once, is taught here.

You see, the blessed Holy Spirit within made the meaning clear despite what seems to be a faulty translation. God never lets His Word perish.

CHAPTER XX

BIBLE TRANSLATIONS, PRINCIPLES AND COMMENTS

I. SOME BASIC PRINCIPLES ABOUT TRANSLATIONS OF THE BIBLE

1. Each Translation Is Primarily the Word of God

2. Translations by Reverent, Responsible Groups of Scholars Are More Reliable Than One-Man Translations

3. Unbelief in Christ and the Bible Disqualifies One to Translate Scriptures

II. NOTES ON SOME TRANSLATIONS

1. The King James or Authorized Version Is the Most Popular and Useful English Translation

2. The King James Version Is Now Available With Archaic Expressions Corrected

3. The American Standard Version

4. The Revised Standard Version

5. Several Modern Speech Translations Pattern After the RSV

6. Amplified and Expanded Versions

7. Phillips Translation, the New Testament in Modern English

8. Several One-Man Translations

BIBLE TRANSLATIONS, PRINCIPLES AND COMMENTS

The Scripture "cannot be broken" (John 10:35), and every one of God's righteous judgments "endureth for ever" (Ps. 119:160). They are "incorruptible" according to I Peter 1:23. Therefore the various translations contain, together, the eternal, unchangeable Word of God. But there are virtues and faults in each particular translation which we should note. And there are certain principles and problems about translations of the Bible which we should bear in mind.

I. SOME BASIC PRINCIPLES ABOUT TRANSLATIONS OF THE BIBLE

A perfect translation of the Bible is humanly impossible. The words in one language do not have exactly the same color and meaning as opposite words in another language, and human frailty and imperfection enter in. So, let us say, there are no perfect translations. God does not inspire particular translations, although He may illuminate and give spiritual wisdom to the translator.

1. Each Translation Is Primarily the Word of God

When we speak of a flaw in this translation or that, we should remember that the flaws are so few in any criticised translation as to be a minor and almost insignificant part of the whole. Suppose there are one hundred places in the Revised Standard Version which I think are bad translations — and there probably are. That would be one verse, perhaps, in each thirteen pages of the approximate 1300 pages in the edition! If liberals, biased against the deity of Christ, change "virgin" in Isaiah 7:14 to "young woman," as I think is wrong, or leave out "begotten" in John 3:16, which seems to be weak scholarship and take indefensible liberty, yet all the great truths of God are taught in this version, all the comfort, all the commands.

Whatever their faults, all translations have the very Word of God. If in the King James Version the word "conversation" in I Peter 3:1 and 2 does not now mean "manner of life," as it did in 1611 when translators used that word, and if "prevent" in I Thessalonians 4:15 does not now mean "precede" in modern speech, as it did when translated, these words are still no serious obstacle to understanding the Word of God and obeying it.

So the translations are the Word of God, and our serious effort to have good translations and a proper opposition to liberal bias to translations and irresponsible paraphrases should not keep us from rejoicing that in any translation we know we can find Christ and salvation, can know the will of God and be comforted by His promises.

2. Translations by Reverent, Responsible Groups of Scholars Are More Reliable Than One-Man Translations

In government, a Congress or Parliament can better represent the people than one man. The President is wise to have a cabinet of responsible men, each concerned with some particular phase of government work. The Bible says, "In the multitude of counsellors there is safety" (Prov. 11:14). And a proverb says, "Two heads are better than one." A school superintendent needs a school board.

So a one-man translation will carry the bias of one man. Inevitably a translator tends to translate not only what the Scripture literally says but what he thinks it means. So Anglican J. B. Phillips will translate "elder" as "priest." So the Catholic Douay Version will translate "repent" as "do penance." So Gesenius, a foremost German radical unbeliever, in his Hebrew lexicon said the Hebrew word *alma* means "young woman" instead of "virgin" (contrary to usage in the Bible), and Brown, Driver and Briggs, all notorious liberals in America, then gave it the same meaning, "young woman," in their American edition. The natural human tendency to understand the Scriptures according to preconceived opinions and to put interpretation in the translation means that a translation by a responsible, scholarly, reverent, believing group is a more accurate, more exact translation of the original languages than if done by one man of equal scholarship and devotion.

That means that a one-man translation may be helpful and sometimes consulted, but it should never be the norm for Bible reading and interpretation and preaching.

3. Unbelief in Christ and the Bible Disqualifies One to Translate Scriptures

In I Corinthians 2:14, the inspired apostle, after speaking in detail about divine revelation and inspiration of Scripture, says, "But the natural man receiveth not the things of the Spirit of God: for they are foolishness unto him: neither can he know them, because they are spiritually discerned." So, scholarship and education do not fit any man to understand the Scriptures, nor to teach them, nor to translate them. So teaches the plain Word of God.

One who does not accept Christ as the very Son of God, God in human form atoning for our sins, who does not accept the Bible account about Christ as infallibly correct, is not a Christian and the Holy Spirit does not live within him. He does not have the help of the Holy Spirit in understanding the Bible. The man who has not submitted his will to Christ, who does not bow to the authority of the Bible, has no heart to understand it. He ought not even to teach a Sunday school class, he certainly is not capable of preaching the Scriptures in the pulpit, of teaching them in a classroom, or translating them into another tongue. A man who does not understand what the Bible says in one language cannot properly translate it into another language.

So, an unconverted Moffatt, a Weigle or the Jew Orlinsky, however scholarly, is incompetent to translate Scriptures, just as an infidel Ferre is incompetent to teach in a theological seminary and a scoffer Buttrick incompetent to edit a Bible commentary. No version of the Bible, translated in whole or in part by liberal unbelievers, can be regarded as reliable in certain key matters.

To translate God's Word adequately while rebelling against Christ and trying to take the crown of deity from His head, is unthinkable. If the bias of one man creeps into his solitary translation, the bias of a group of unbelievers is accumulated, reinforced bias, expressed in a translation dominated by liberals as in the Revised Standard Version and the New English Testament. The fact that "everybody does it" does not make it right, it only makes it more respectable. So the fact that there are many scholars in a translation may make the translation more respectable, but it does not make the liberal translation accurate. No unconverted, unbelieving liberal has enough spiritual perception to be a trustworthy translator.

II. NOTES ON SOME TRANSLATIONS

It is not necessary nor wise to take the space to comment on all the translations of the Bible in English. I have seventeen or eighteen translations of the Bible in English on my shelves; one French version; I have the Nestle's Greek Version and the Westcott and Hort Greek Version; but it seems wise to discuss some of the versions most widely spread and used.

1. The King James or Authorized Version Is the Most Popular and Useful English Translation

Since 1611 the King James Version of the Bible has been more widely spread and more greatly used than all the other English translations of the Bible combined. The beauty, the stately dignity and reverence of the language is far beyond that of any other translation. It has done more to influence Western civilization, Western language, viewpoints and morals than anything else in England or America in these three and a half centuries. Of course the translation itself is not inspired, is not infallibly correct, but as the Holy Spirit some way led the Christian millions to a consensus of opinion on the Scriptures that should be accepted in our canon as our Bible, so surely the Holy Spirit and God's providence have led millions to love and favor the King James Version.

In all pulpit reading of the Bible and nearly all quotations of the Bible from the pulpit I have used the King James Version. It is known to the people and there is a certain authority in the familiar language. Just as Jesus often, when He had occasion, quoted the Septuagint translation of the Old Testament because that was the one the people knew, so it is wise now for Bible-believing preachers to use the King James Version in the public service. The minister's memory work and the memory verses, and passages taught children, ought generally to be in the King James Version.

A preacher should refer, when necessary, to other versions, as I do many times. When I quote John 5:24 in a message, then I may quote the same verse from the American Standard Version because "and cometh not into judgment, but hath passed out of death into life" seems to add emphasis to the King James statement, "and shall not come into condemnation; but is passed from death unto life." But a preacher needs to be careful about displaying his scholarly knowledge of other versions in the pulpit, and he should feel very reverently toward the translation that is familiar to the multitudes and loved by them. There are many reasons why the principal translation used in the pulpit and the Sunday school and the home should be the King James Version.

There are some complaints against the King James Version, particularly by the liberals. They say there are "so many archaic words." Actually, you will not find one archaic word of clouded meaning to every three pages. The context nearly always makes the sense of any such word clear. Where Proverbs 13:24 says, "He that spareth his rod hateth his son: but he that loveth him chasteneth him *betimes*"—"betimes" really means "early" but the meaning is clear anyway. If "prevent" means to "go before" or "precede" in I Thessalonians 4:15, one can hardly miss the meaning, even with the archaic usage of a word now changed in meaning.

But someone exclaims, "Today young people cannot understand the King James Version." The complaint is silly. I taught college sophomores Shakespeare and there are ten times as many obsolete or archaic terms in Shakespeare as in our

King James translation of the same period, and the translation in the King James Version is more classic, more influential and more eternal than all the writings of Shakespeare. Chaucer is studied in English classes with hardly a sentence in the language as we now know it, and students learn that. One archaic word in three or four chapters does not faze any interested reader. Again and again we have read the whole Bible through at the breakfast table and each child from seven or eight years on read her part daily.

Some enthusiastic teachers may get young people interested in a modern version and so think that they learn it more easily. But the same enthusiasm would get them to enjoy the King James Version as much.

"I can't understand it," says some querulous youthful voice; or, "I don't enjoy the King James Version." You can't understand "the Lord is my shepherd; I shall not want" and other sweet cadences of the 23rd Psalm? You cannot understand "in my Father's house are many mansions: if it were not so, I would have told you. I go to prepare a place for you," in that most comforting chapter of John 14? You cannot understand the Beatitudes such as, "Blessed are the pure in heart: for they shall see God"?

There are really no uninteresting parts of the Bible; there are just some uninterested people. And the antagonism or indifference which one may have toward the Bible is not really intellectual; it is spiritual. Some people do not love the Bible and do not read it, not because of archaic words but because of the natural, human antipathy to spiritual things, the indifference of the sinful, human heart to divine things. Their real antipathy is not toward the King James Version but toward the Bible itself.

There is no evidence that any translation of the Bible now in existence will ever supersede the King James Version in the love and usage by common Christians.

2. The King James Version Is Now Available With Archaic Expressions Corrected

The Scofield Reference Bible, using the King James Version and scholarly, fundamentally sound notes, has been in wide use for many years. In the new Scofield Bible there has been some enlargement of notes, some corrections, and we find words as used today substituted for the archaic expressions. We think that is a good thing.

Also the "Modern King James Version," copyright by Jay P. Green, likewise corrects archaic words, and changes "thou" and "thee" to you, etc., except when referring to deity. And so do the companion Children's Version and Teen-Age Version. These are not new translations but the King James Version with the occasional obsolete word replaced by a word in common usage.

3. The American Standard Version

We do not deal here in detail with the Revised Version of England, with the New Testament published in 1881, the Old Testament in 1885. The American Standard Version was published fourteen years later by the section of American scholars who helped on the English Revised Version. Charles Leach says:

> The main differences between the English and American revisions are as follows:
> The latter retains the name "JEHOVAH" in the text, instead of translating it as "LORD" or "GOD." It is more strictly uniform in the translation and use of other words. It has modernized some expressions passed over by the English revision, and in many cases returns to the Authorized version's readings. It may perhaps therefore be said that the American revision is the best and latest result of Christian scholarship in giving a translation from the original languages into present-day English. [1]

So here we say a word about the American Standard Version, which is much more widely used in America than the English Revision.

The translators of the American Standard Version had the advantage of having access to the three oldest manuscripts with which we are familiar — the Vatican, the Alexandrian, and the Sinaitic manuscripts.

It corrects some mistakes in the King James Version. One very serious error in the translation of the King James Version

---

1. *Our Bible — How We Got It*, p. 113.

makes Revelation 22:14 say, "Blessed are they that do his commandments, that they may have right to the tree of life, and may enter in through the gates into the city." That would seem to make the plan of salvation by works and that people go to Heaven by keeping God's commandments. But it is not a good translation. The American Standard Version correctly says: "Blessed are they that wash their robes, that they may have the right to come to the tree of life, and may enter in by the gates into the city."

One greatly criticised error in the American Standard Version changes the II Timothy 3:16 statement, "All scripture is given by inspiration of God, and is profitable..." into "every scripture inspired of God is also profitable...."

Now there is available the new American Standard Bible New Testament, published by Moody Press. The American Standard Version of 1901, widely acclaimed for its word-for-word fidelity to the Greek, has been painstakingly revised by the Lockman Foundation in the light of the latest textual advances. Dr. Wilbur M. Smith says, "Certainly the most accurate and most revealing translation of the New Testament that we now have."

The scholar and the preacher would do well to have the American Standard Version at hand and to consult it when necessary, but generally would do well, we think, to use the King James Version in the pulpit, in memory work, and in class teaching, since it is actually the translation of the mass of people. And the beauty of its language is not equalled in other translations, we think.

4. The Revised Standard Version

This translation of 1952 claims to be "translated from the original tongues being the version set forth in A.D. 1611, revised A.D. 1881-1885 and A.D. 1901 compared with the most ancient authorities and revised A.D. 1952." But as the justly revered Princeton scholar, Dr. Oswald T. Allis, says in his book, *Revision or New Translation?* there are far too many changes and the translation entirely too free to be called a translation of the King James Version or even of the American Standard Version.

It is a new translation in modern speech by liberal trans-

lators. It is often merely a paraphrase. The words added to
the original which are not in the original manuscript are not
honestly put in italics as in the King James and the American
Standard Versions. The translators often presume that the
texts were wrong and that they could guess the words that
ought to be in the manuscripts instead of the words that are
there.

Dr. Allis says:

> That the question would be raised whether the **Revised Stand-
> ard Version** is a "liberal" or "higher critical" version, was
> inevitable. There are two reasons for this, neither of which is
> far to seek. The first is the theological viewpoint of at least
> the majority of the committee of revisers. The other is the
> translation itself. Unless the distinction between "conservative"
> and "higher critic" or "liberal" is to pass utterly into the dis-
> card, few if any will endeavor to maintain that this revision
> was prepared by a group of conservative scholars. Evidence
> to the contrary is too clear and too abundant. [2]

Dr. Allis also says:

> If by a "liberal" version is meant a version which represents
> a lax and "liberal" attitude to the question of the plenary,
> verbal inspiration and the divine authority of Scripture, then
> RSV is clearly such a version. Sufficient evidence has been
> given in the preceding pages to show that it is governed by a
> very different conception of what is meant by an "accurate"
> version from that to be found in AV and RV. This was to
> be expected. Thirty-five years ago Doctor Moffatt in the Preface
> to his **New Testament: A New Translation** (1913), in dis-
> cussing the difficulties which the translator faces in trying to
> make an accurate and idiomatic translation, made this signifi-
> cant statement: "But once the translator of the New Testament
> is freed from the influence of the theory of verbal inspiration,
> these difficulties cease to be so formidable." Moffatt's own
> translations give a clear indication of the amount of freedom
> which he felt a translator was entitled to exercise in this regard.
> And while RSV does not go as far as he did, it shows the
> same determination not to be fettered by the **ipsissimaverba** of
> Scripture. RSV, as we have seen, inserts words, it omits words;
> its "idiomatic" renderings often give the gist of the passage and
> constitute a paraphrase rather than a translation. While insist-
> ing that the translator must confine himself to translation, its
> authors have also insisted that it is the duty of the translator
> to assume the role of interpreter, and to regard it as his function

---

2. *Revision or New Translation?* p. 143.

not only to tell us what the writers said, but what they meant by what they said.

In justification of this broad conception of the role of the translator Doctor Cadbury tells us: "As they (the first Christian authors) wrote with neither grammatical precision nor absolute verbal consistency, he (the modern translator) is willing to deal somewhat less meticulously with the data of a simple style that was naturally not too particular about modes of expression or conscious of some of the subtleties which some later interpreters read into it" (p. 52).

This, it will be noted, is merely another way of saying what Moffatt had said years ago, that the theory of verbal inspiration, by which is meant a divine trustworthiness and authority which extends to the very words of Scripture, is not to be held any longer. For, if the New Testament writers wrote "without grammatical precision," the implication is that the translator need not attempt to translate precisely. If they did not show "absolute verbal consistency," he need not seek to secure it. If they were "naturally not too particular about modes of expression," he need not be particular either. In short, if they did not write accurately, he need not translate accurately. So runs the argument. And the corollary is this, as we have pointed out more than once: since they did not express themselves accurately, there may be considerable difference at times between what they said and what they meant to say or were trying to say. So the translator must try to make clear what he believes they meant to say. Or, as Doctor Cadbury puts it: "To this (the mere translation) he adds whatever he may modestly claim to have achieved of real insight into the meaning of the original." [3]

So in the sense of a translation being often a paraphrase and not a literal translation, and in the sense that the revisers did not regard the Scriptures as verbally inspired and did not feel obligated to represent the words of the Scripture but their own interpretation of the words, the Revised Standard Version is a liberal translation, and thus unreliable.

First Corinthians 2:14 plainly tells us, "The natural man receiveth not the things of the Spirit of God: for they are foolishness unto him: neither can he know them, because they are spiritually discerned."

Jay Green, in the introduction to the Modern King James Version, says about the Revised Standard Version:

What then will be written down in the "loss" column for the new versions?

---

3. *Revision or New Translation?* pp. 143-145.

The first loss, easily demonstrated were space available, is the loss of thousands of words, hundreds of verses, dozens of phrases which have either been completely removed or else have had doubt thrown upon them. Most people mourn their loss.

Secondly, thousands of verses engraved in the hearts of God's people are now unnecessarily changed as a matter of policy, with the effect that one quoting the King James Version to young people is cast in the role of an "old fogie" who lives in the past.

Other losses tumble over one another as a search is made of various versions: The virgin birth is clouded by translating "young woman" in Isaiah 7:14; by translating that Joseph was the father of Jesus; by removing "first-born" from Matthew 1:25. The Godhood of the Lord Jesus becomes dubious when the new versions accord a "Thou" to God, but only a "you" to Jesus. In similar vein, the Son of God is rendered "God's son" or "a son of God." The handling of Romans 9:5 and I Timothy 3:16 remove two solid proof-verses to the divinity of Christ. The use of "only son" instead of "only begotten Son" is in the same category.

Propitiation becomes merely a "remedy for the defilement of sins."

Justification by faith is marred by presenting faith as a meritorious work which procures righteousness: "He who through faith is righteous shall live" replaces the wonderful statement, "the just shall live by faith" (Rom. 1:17).

The God-breathed inspiration of the Scriptures is diluted until only "every inspired scripture has its use" (II Tim. 3:16).

Peter and John and the beast are worshiped, even idols are worshiped, but the Lord Jesus is not worshiped: all only "pay him homage," or "do obeisance."

Redemption becomes a mere "release"; faith is only an "awakening"; believing degenerates into a simple "yielding of allegiance"; righteousness in the modern version is but "goodness"; the miraculous darkness on Resurrection Day is translated "eclipse"; and the demon-possession so prevalent in Jesus' day becomes nothing more than "epilepsy." Not one of these can be claimed to be precise translation of the Greek words God's apostles wrote.

Another massive loss occurs because myriads of words are **added** to the Holy Scriptures. The reader, however, is not given the slightest inkling as to which are God's words and which are words added by the translators. Very few are aware of what is being done to the original by these added words. Professor Beegle, in the book cited above, readily admits: "In the case of the modern versions which have neither italics nor footnotes there are, obviously, no means of discerning difficult passages where the translation has elements of uncertainty, and so the reader must rely solely on the judgment and interpretation of the translator." Readers of the new versions "must

rely solely upon the judgment and interpretation of the translator" in **thousands upon thousands** of verses of the Bible! No
wonder the reader feels ripped from his moorings![4]

The most active opposition to the Revised Standard Version
has been about changing the translation of Isaiah 7:14 from,
"Behold, a virgin shall conceive," to, "Behold, a young woman
shall conceive and bear a son." Dr. Luther Weigle, chairman
of the translators, said that in the Hebrew English lexicon the
word "alma" means simply "young woman," not necessarily
"virgin," and he said that the word for "virgin" in the Hebrew
was *bethulah.* He did not tell you, however, that the lexicon
he uses was prepared by unbelieving critics. Gesenius, the
"German orientalist and biblical critic," is described in the
Encyclopaedia Britannica in these words:

> To Gesenius, who was an exceptionally popular teacher, be-
> longs in a large measure the credit of having freed Semitic
> philology from theological and religious prepossession, and of
> inaugurating the strictly scientific (and comparative) method.
> His chief work, **Hebraisches u. Chaldaisches Handworterbuch**
> (1810-12), has passed through several editions (Eng. ed.:
> Francis Brown, S. R. Driver and Charles A. Briggs, **A Hebrew
> and English Lexicon of the Old Testament,** 1907).[5]

Gesenius, a notorious liberal, specialized in changing the
theological terminology of the Bible into that of liberals.
Brown, Driver and Briggs, translators of the lexicon in English
were, all three of them, radical liberals and two of them were
tried in the Presbyterian church for outrageous infidelity.

The simple truth is that every time the word *alma,* the controversial Hebrew word in Isaiah 7:14, appears in the Old
Testament, it would fit virgin and would properly be translated
that way. It was translated so by the seventy elders of Israel
in the Septuagint version, translating the Hebrew into the Greek
two centuries before Christ. It was so translated by the King
James translators, by the English revisers, by the American
Standard revisers. Most important of all, it was so translated
by the Lord Himself in Matthew 1:23, quoting Isaiah 7:14!
There the word in the Greek is *parthenos,* which even the biased
Revised Standard Version must translate as virgin. The Holy
Spirit surely knew what the word meant!

---

4. *Modern King James Version,* pp. 9,10.
5. *Encyclopaedia Britannica,* p. 316.

On the other hand, despite the liberal lexicons and the liberal translators, the word *bethulah* could not always mean virgin, as one can easily see by checking in the original Old Testament Hebrew.   For example, Joel 1:8 says, "Lament like a virgin girded with sackcloth for the husband of her youth." The word for virgin is the Hebrew *bethulah,* yet it refers to a widow lamenting for the husband of her youth.   So *bethulah* may mean young woman; it does not necessarily mean virgin. Another example is Isaiah 23:12, "And he said, Thou shalt no more rejoice, O thou oppressed virgin, daughter of Zidon ...." The word virgin refers here to the wicked city Zidon. A heathen city whose destruction is being prophesied is here called "virgin, daughter of Zidon." The word *bethulah* used here is often used for a city, even the most wicked cities, and does not necessarily mean virgin.

In Isaiah 47:1, the city of Babylon is called a virgin, although the passage is promising the destruction of the city for their sins. The word for virgin is *bethulah,* and does not mean virgin.   Jeremiah 18:13 says, "...the virgin of Israel hath done a very horrible thing." And the context expresses amazement at the wickedness of Israel.   Verses 14 to 17 following say:

"Will a man leave the snow of Lebanon which cometh from the rock of the field? or shall the cold flowing waters that come from another place be forsaken? Because my people have forgotten me, they have burned incense to vanity, and they have caused them to stumble in their ways from the ancient paths, to walk in paths, in a way not cast up; To make their land desolate, and a perpetual hissing; every one that passeth thereby shall be astonished, and wag his head. I will scatter them as with an east wind before the enemy; I will shew them the back, and not the face, in the day of their calamity."

And the word for "virgin" here in Jeremiah 18:13 is *bethulah.* It certainly does not mean virgin here.   And so with other places in the Scripture, as one can find using Young's Analytical Concordance, for example.

If there is any word for virgin in the Hebrew, it is *alma,* and the Jewish leaders who translated the Septuagint, and the translators of the King James Version, the English Revised Version, the American Standard Version, yes, and God Himself who translated it in Matthew 1:23, as virgin, are right.   And the Revised Standard Version translators were wrong.   They put virgin in the margin, knowing it could mean virgin. A liberal bias caused the mistranslation here.

Other places in the translation show a distinct liberal bias against the deity of Christ and against the verbal inspiration of the Scriptures themselves.

5. Several Modern Speech Translations Pattern After the RSV

Liberals made so much of the Revised Standard Version, and liberals were so free in their criticism of the King James and the American Standard Versions that other translations by liberals have appeared. Among these is the New English Bible, the New Testament, which has appeared and it has the flaws generally of the Revised Standard Version.

Among these also is the American Bible Society's *Good News for Modern Man*, the New Testament in today's English version. It is very free in its translation, and much of it is paraphrased instead of literal translation. For example, instead of "Joseph was a just man," we have "Joseph, to whom she was engaged, was a man who always did what was right." Instead of "In the beginning was the Word, and the Word was with God, and the Word was God," this version has it, "Before the world was created, the Word already existed; he was with God, and he was the same as God. From the very beginning, the Word was with God." That is no translation but a paraphrase. It is not careful of doctrine and not scholarly in translation, for the translation of Acts 2:38 is, "Peter said to them: 'Turn away from your sins, each one of you, and be baptized in the name of Jesus Christ, so that your sins will be forgiven; and you will receive God's gift, the Holy Spirit." But "so that your sins will be forgiven" following baptism, is not an accurate translation. The King James Version has it, "Repent, and be baptized every one of you in the name of Jesus Christ for the remission of sins." But the word translated "for" is the Greek preposition *eis*, an indefinite preposition of reference occurring some 1800 times in the New Testament, and its meaning *referring to, at, in, from,* etc. One should repent and be baptized referring to, pointing to, or reminding one of the remission of sins. But the translation here, "so that your sins will be forgiven," is wholly unjustified, for the

Greek preposition *eis* should never be translated "so that" or "in order to." The preposition for that would be *hina*, and God would have said that if He had meant that. This is a sample of the careless, unscholarly way of the modern speech translations, paraphrasing instead of translating and putting one's interpretation into the translation instead of literally saying exactly what the original Scriptures said.

6. Amplified and Expanded Versions

There are two such versions: one, a New Testament Expanded Translation by Kenneth S. Wuest, published by Eerdmans, and the other, the Amplified New Testament by the Lockman Foundation, published by Zondervan, which in each case put in a number of extra words to try to amplify or expand the meaning of the Scriptures. Actually they amount to commentaries. They are not literal and exact translations. The Scriptures do not have all those words in them. Although one may enjoy reading them, they should never be quoted as Scripture, and they should not be studied as Scripture for they thus water down the Word of God and necessarily they interpret it instead of literally translating it.

7. Phillips Translation, the New Testament in Modern English

This translation is very popular. It is easy reading. However, it is not reliable. In the translator's Preface to the epistles, that is, *Letters to Young Churches*, he says, "Without holding fundamentalist views on 'inspiration'...," and again, "When necessary the translator should feel free to expand or explain ...." Again he said, "The translation (or in some cases the paraphrase) should 'flow' and be easy to read." And he frankly admits, "For close, meticulous study, existing modern versions should be consulted." In other words, his translation does not claim to be accurate, does not claim to be always more than a paraphrase, does not hold to the verbal inspiration and thus the infallible accuracy of the Scriptures. An interestingly written paraphrase, not meticulously accurate, should not be counted a translation of the Bible.

8. Several One-Man Translations

Moffatt's translation, the first in modern speech, has been very popular but has the faults of the Revised Standard Version and more.

Weymouth's translation is some better than Moffatt's, but the notes are often wrong and unreliable.

Charles G. Williams' translation of the New Testament was by a reverent, godly, Bible believer, and a good scholar. However, his greatest concern was to emphasize the tense of the Greek verbs, which is sometimes perhaps overdone. Otherwise, it has the virtues of orthodoxy and the limitations of a one-man translation.

Living Gospels and Living Letters, translations or rather paraphrases of the four Gospels, the book of Acts, and of the epistles, by Kenneth Taylor, clearly announce themselves as paraphrases, not translations. Therefore they are interpretations, interesting reading but not reliable. They are generally sound, without being reliable translations. Taylor, as a ridiculous example, makes Peter and his wife writing from Rome instead of Babylon, following the Roman tradition instead of historical facts that Peter probably never saw Rome, that he was not there when Paul was there, not there when Paul wrote to Rome, and his wife was not mentioned in the Scripture. He was the apostle to the Jews, not to the Gentiles.

Way's translation has a number of faults. We have also the Berkeley Version by Verkuyl, a modern one-man translation.

In conclusion, let us suggest again that every Christian, every minister, every scholar make the King James Version the principal basis of his Bible study. Students and ministers probably ought to have the American Standard Version to consult and a Young's or Strong's Analytical Concordance by which he may look up the usage in the Bible of any particular Greek or Hebrew word and thus check the translation by its inspired use in more than one place. Generally speaking, we would discourage the use of paraphrases, amplified and expanded versions, and modern-speech versions, since they tend to take away from the impact of the inspiration of the very words in the original manuscript and the soberness and serious sense of responsibility with which we should approach the very Word of God. If a verse of Scripture could mean any one of several things, as one might get the impression from using many modern versions or paraphrases, then the word itself in its original, literal meaning would probably not be held so sacredly.

We suggest *The English Bible*, A History of Translations from the earliest English Versions to the New English Bible, by F. F. Bruce, Oxford Press, for further study, although it is more liberal than we would be.

ANNOTATED BIBLIOGRAPHY

Here we give a brief analysis of some of the principal books on inspiration, with the author's estimate of the importance and relative reliability of those mentioned. This is not a complete bibliography but, we believe, lists and evaluates most of the important books in the English language on the subject, the most important books with which we are acquainted.

1. *The Inspiration of the Holy Scriptures*, by L. Gaussen (or *Theopneustia, the Plenary Inspiration of the Scriptures*), published in America by Moody Press, Chicago, probably the most useful book ever written on inspiration of the Scripture. Gaussen was a Swiss theologian, born 1790, died 1863.

J. Theodore Mueller of Concordia Seminary, in *Concordia Theological Monthly*, says: "Dr. Gaussen put into this book about every essential that can be said on biblical inspiration, both positively, in stating the doctrine, and negatively, in defending it against the attacks of unbelieving critics. The basic theme which he proves is that the orthodox Christian Church has always believed in, and confessed, verbal and plenary inspiration."

Charles Spurgeon said: "If we have in the Word of God no infallible standard of truth, we are at sea without a compass, and no danger from rough weather without can be equal to this loss within. 'If the foundation be removed, what can the righteous do?' and this is a foundation loss of the worst kind. In this work the author proves himself a master of holy argument. Gaussen charms as he proclaims the divine veracity of Scripture. His testimony is clear as a bell."

Dr. James M. Gray, president of Moody Bible Institute, said: "The milestones on my spiritual pathway have been marked by certain books I have read, and one that stands out in my memory more than any other is Gaussen's great work, *The Plenary Inspiration of the Scriptures*. The day it came into my hands as a young minister just beginning his work marks an epoch, and I speak from experience when I say that a Christian who reads and studies it need never again be troubled by attacks on the Word of God."

The book was translated from the French by David D. Scott of Glasgow.   Even in his translation the book has wonderful literary charm and a warmth of devotion that makes it a joy, while it is a must for the scholarly study of the Bible doctrine of inspiration.

2. *The Inspiration and Authority of the Bible*, by Benjamin Breckinridge Warfield of Princeton Seminary.   Introduction by Cornelius Van Til.   A collection of Dr. Warfield's articles on inspiration of the Bible.   On the essentials concerning inspiration, Warfield is at the very top, and perhaps had more influence on theologians of the present day than Gaussen.   This book, with Gaussen's, stands above others in scholarly defense of the verbal, plenary inspiration of all the Scriptures and their infallible accuracy and authority.

3. The article on *Inspiration* in *The International Standard Bible Encyclopaedia*, Volume 3, written by Benjamin B. Warfield.   Although Orr himself had written on inspiration, acknowledged the belief in evolution, in progressive inspiration of the Scriptures, and had other weaknesses, he came to believe, we suppose, that Warfield was a better authority and so Orr, editor-in-chief of *The International Standard Bible Encyclopaedia*, five-volume set, asked Warfield to write the passage on *Inspiration*.   There are twenty-two extended columns in this remarkable write-up on inspiration of the Scriptures.   It is scholarly, inclusive, powerful, thoroughly authoritative.

4. *Thy Word Is Truth*, by Dr. Edward J. Young.   Dr. Young, recently deceased, was professor of Old Testament in Westminster Seminary, Philadelphia.   The book has 287 pages and the author says, "The present work is not a technical theological treatise.   It is simply a popular book, designed to acquaint the intelligent layman with the biblical doctrine of inspiration and to convince him of its importance.   It would specifically appeal to the modern evangelical not to cast aside the time-honored biblical view of inspiration."   A strong, good book holding to the verbal plenary inspiration of the Scripture, its inerrancy, proper approach to the Scriptures, some modern views answered, the Bible and salvation, etc.   There is an Appendix on the Westminster Confession of Faith and an

index of names and subjects and one of Scripture. A very, very fine book by a genuine scholar and reverent Christian. Eerdmans Publishers.

5. *Scripture Cannot Be Broken*, Six Objections to Verbal Inspiration Examined in the Light of Scripture, by Theodore Engelder, Concordia Publishing House, St. Louis, 1944. Publication in book form of a series of articles that appeared in the *Concordia Theological Monthly*. The contents include: I. Does the Bible Contain Errors? (some 200 pages). II. Has the Bible Moral Blemishes? III. Does the Bible Deal in Trivialities? IV. The Disastrous Results of Criticizing and Correcting Scripture (A Resume); V. Is Verbal Inspiration Mechanical Inspiration? VI. Does Verbal Inspiration Imply an Atomistic Conception and Use of Scripture? VII. Does Verbal Inspiration Establish a "Legalistic Authority of the Letter"? VIII. The Battle for Verbal Inspiration (Final Resume). There is an extended index, which is needed, because an enormous number of scholars are quoted. More unbelieving scholars are quoted and answered than in any other book we know.

There is some limitation to the usefulness of the book. One minor limitation is that the book was written primarily for Lutherans, it quotes primarily Lutheran scholars, it sometimes quotes from the German without translating. The book is not as easy reading as Gaussen and Warfield, but is very, very valuable. 498 pages. It is thoroughly for verbal, word-for-word inspiration, absolute authority of the Scriptures.

6. *Inspiration and Canonicity of the Bible*, by R. Laird Harris of the Covenant Seminary, St. Louis. This was the First Prizewinner in Zondervan's $2500.00 Christian Textbook Contest. The first 128 pages are given to the inspiration of the Bible, and are very valuable. The balance of the 304 pages are given to the canonicity of the Old and New Testaments with extended notes and index. The book is very helpful and beyond any serious criticism for the out-and-out believer.

7. *Inspiration of the Bible*, by B. H. Carroll, Fleming H. Revell Company. From 1926 to 1930 there was a serious controversy among Texas Baptists and Southern Baptists on the question of inspiration of the Scriptures. Dr. J. M. Dawson, in a message before the pastors and laymen's conference preceding the Texas state convention, gave a message, widely published in pamphlet form, on the inspiration of the Bible, denying the verbal inspiration but asserting what he called

"dynamic" inspiration, that is, inspiration of thought, not the words. We did extended correspondence with greatly respected Bible teachers, including Dr. I. M. Haldeman of New York City, Dr. James M. Gray of Moody Bible Institute, Dr. Mark Matthews of Seattle, and others, and published articles on verbal inspiration in the magazine, *The Fundamentalist.* At length Dr. W. W. White, state Baptist secretary, (later president of Baylor University, now retired) wrote in *The Baptist Standard*, a good article for the verbal inspiration of the Scriptures. Meantime, Dr. J. B. Cranfill, former editor of *The Baptist Standard*, very influential among Texas Baptists, and the editor of commentaries and sermons by the late Dr. B. H. Carroll, got together some lectures by Dr. Carroll and had them published in the book, *Inspiration of the Bible*, by B. H. Carroll. Dr. Carroll was founder and first president of Southwestern Baptist Theological Seminary, the most eminent theologian among Southern Baptists.   His book had a profound effect. In introductions to the book, both Dr. George W. Truett and Dr. Lee Scarborough state their belief in the verbal inspiration of the Bible.

The book has only 122 pages, and the lectures are of the popular form, but are very valuable, easily understood, and, I think, cannot be successfully answered by any unbeliever.

8. *All About the Bible:* Its Origin, Its Language, Its Translation, Its Canon, Its Symbols, Its Inspiration, Its Alleged Errors and Contradictions, Its Plan, Its Science, Its Rivals, by Sidney Collett. An English book, now published by Revell, in the 26th printing.   Translations have appeared in eight languages and the book is very valuable.   It is more the popular in its approach, has restored the faith of many to the Scriptures.   The chapter on science and the Bible is not as valuable as the rest of it but it is a beautiful and very useful book.

9. *Many Infallible Proofs*, The Evidences of Christianity, by Arthur T. Pierson, Fleming H. Revell Publishers.   An old but very valuable book for the general reader. Arthur T. Pierson was a Presbyterian minister in the late 19th century, a widely known editor; supplied the pulpit for Charles Spurgeon.   Not as full of scholarly detail as Gaussen and Warfield's books.

10. *Does Inspiration Demand Inerrancy?*   A paper-bound volume by Professor Stewart Custer of Bob Jones University, Craig Press, New Jersey.   A study of biblical doctrine of in-

spiration in the light of inerrancy. 120 pages, limited primarily to the matter of inerrancy. Good and reliable.

11. *A Scientific Investigation of the Old Testament*, by Robert Dick Wilson, eminent Semitic scholar of Princeton University and Seminary. Published by Moody Press. A very important witness by perhaps the greatest Semitic scholar in the world in his day. He sums up his treatment of the matter as follows: "In conclusion, let me reiterate my conviction that no one knows enough to show that the true text of the Old Testament in its true interpretation is not true."

He was an earnest and devoted Bible believer, familiar with some forty-five languages and dialects.

12. *The Five Books of Moses*, by Oswald T. Allis, fundamental, reliable answer to the Graff-Wellhausen theory, and other critical attacks on the Pentateuch. Scholarly, very helpful, 319 pages. Presbyterian and Reformed Publishing Company.

13. *The Bible the Word of God*, by F. Bettex, a classic book on inspiration by a German author. My copy was published by the German Literary Board, Burlington, Iowa. Not dated, so probably now out of print. It is warm and sweet. Studies carefully the great connecting matters of knowledge and faith, the Bible and what it is and what it claims to be, objections to the Bible and biblical criticism. There are 314 pages and the book is valuable but not as documented nor up-to-date in answering objections as some others.

14. *Inspiration: The Infallible Truth and Divine Authority of the Holy Scriptures*, by James Bannerman. An old classic on this subject, published in 1865 in London. Bannerman was a Scot. There are fourteen chapters, 595 pages, including the index, and the book deals very carefully with the whole theory and philosophy of inspiration from the viewpoint of a Bible believer. He answers philosophical objections to the inspiration of the Scripture. Not as direct and practical and all-inclusive as Gaussen nor with as much practical and definite exegesis of Scripture as Warfield and Young, but generally helpful, philosophical, devoted and good.

15. *God Spake All These Words*, by W. H. Griffith Thomas, a Moody Colportage book, paper-bound, giving details of how we got our Bible and why we believe it is God's Word. Generally good, popular. It teaches verbal inspiration but does not go into the corollary truths.

16. *The Inspiration of the Scriptures*, by Loraine Boettner.

Published by Eerdmans Publishing Company. This popular, scholarly Reformed theologian teaches the verbal inspiration of the Bible. His position is: "We do not separate the divine and human elements, but insist that the two are united in perfect harmony so that every word of Scripture is at one and the same time the word of God and also the word of man. The writers themselves make it plain that in this process the divine influence is primary and the human secondary, so that they are not so much the originators but rather the receivers and announcers of these messages" (p. 39). Only 88 pages but very definite and clear on the doctrine of inspiration by an accepted Reformed scholar.

17. *The Divine Inspiration of the Bible*, by Arthur W. Pink, published in 1917 by Bible Truth Depot. Not a big book but offers evidence that there is a presumption in favor of the Bible, the Bible's perennial freshness, the honesty of the writers, the character of its teaching, fulfilled prophecies, typical significance, the unity of the Bible, influence of the Bible, miraculous power of the Bible, its completeness, its indestructibility and inward confirmation; and five pages on verbal inspiration, then the application of the argument. Generally good, popular but not profound.

18. *A Coffer of Jewels About Our Infallible, Eternal Word of God, the Bible*, compiled by John R. Rice, has 16 chapters, including Spurgeon, Talmage, Torrey, William Jennings Bryan, James M. Gray, L. W. Munhall, R. G. Lee, W. A. Criswell, B. H. Carroll, J. R. Graves, Dyson Hague, Sidney Collett and this author. We think the richest compilation of testimony and preaching and defense of the Scripture in print, gathered from writers in England, Canada, and America. The matchless sermon by Spurgeon, the wisdom of R. A. Torrey's "Ten Reasons," the effervescent and jolting and learned attack of Bryan against evolution, the sweet beauty of Dyson Hague and Sidney Collett, the scriptural defense of the Scripture by James M. Gray, L. W. Munhall and B. H. Carroll, and the fine preaching of Lee, Criswell, Talmage, make this extraordinary. Published by Sword of the Lord Publishers. 318 pages.

19. *Our Bible—How We Got It*, by Charles Leach, and *Ten Reasons Why I Believe the Bible Is the Word of God*, by R. A. Torrey, Moody Colportage, paperback. A history of manuscripts and translations of the Bible, very useful with Torrey's "Ten Reasons" listed elsewhere in this book.

20. *Why I Preach That the Bible Is Literally True*, a fine volume, "From the bottom of my heart and the top of my head," by W. A. Criswell, pastor of the great First Baptist Church, Dallas, Texas, a warmhearted, fervent preacher with a Ph. D. degree. Very readable, helpful and impressive. Broadman Press.

21. *The Fundamentals for Today*, Volume 1, the new edition edited by Dr. Charles Feinberg. The articles, especially number 14, "Inspiration of the Bible," by Dr. James M. Gray; "Inspiration," by Dr. L. W. Munhall, and the other articles by Bishop, Pierson, and Gaebelein are particularly helpful on inspiration. Kregel Publications, Grand Rapids, Michigan, revised in two volumes in 1958.

22. *Revelation and Inspiration*, by James Orr. Because Orr was professor of apologetics and systematic theology in the United Free Church in Glasgow, this book, published in 1910, has been so influential that we list it here. We need to remember that nineteen years later, in 1929, *The International Standard Bible Encyclopaedia*, edited by Orr, had Dr. Warfield's wonderful article on inspiration. Since Orr chose Warfield for that task, it seems likely that his own ideas about inspiration greatly matured and some of the errors of his book were corrected in his own thinking. Certainly Warfield did not go along with the general teachings of Orr, that evolution was a fact, that there had been a progressive revelation so that mistakes in the earlier books of the Bible were corrected by the later and particularly by the New Testament. Orr defended the Scriptures, and we are sorry for the many concessions made to liberal, destructive scholarship and trust that when he asked Warfield many years later to prepare his wonderfully orthodox and scholarly article on inspiration that Orr had come to a similar position. We do not recommend Orr's book, *Revelation and Inspiration*, though the man was a devout Christian and after making many concessions, still insisted the Bible is the Word of God.

23. *Inspiration and Interpretation*, edited by John Walvoord, has the good and the bad. Discusses principally the positions of Augustine, Calvin, Irenaeus, Rowley, John Wesley, Emil Brunner, William Sanday, Martin Luther, Reinhold Niebuhr. Only Carl F. H. Henry, in the chapter on "Divine Revelation and the Bible," comes to grip directly with the problem of inspiration as taught in the Scriptures. Henry, although "New

Evangelical" in his emphasis and viewpoint, seeking to mediate between the unbelieving scholars and conservative Bible believers, nevertheless takes a clear-cut stand for verbal inspiration and equal inspiration of all parts of the Bible. Eerdmans Publishing Company.

24. *The Inspiration and Accuracy of the Holy Scriptures*, by John Urquhart, published in 1895 in England. This book is a classic. The first six chapters in Book I are on the Scripture Doctrine of Inspiration. The next thirteen chapters in Book II are on the Genesis of Rationalism. The last sixteen chapters in Book III are on Critical Results Tested by Modern Discovery. Then there is an Appendix; Archdeacon Farrar on Daniel. The book is a classic, very fine. 582 pages. We think out of print.

25. *The Christian View of Science and Scripture*, by Bernard Ramm, Eerdmans Publishing Company, 1954. Ramm takes the position of James Orr and John Pye Smith. He believes in evolution, or progressive creation, believes in progressive inspiration, that the Bible is limited by the culture and knowledge of the age in which the writers lived. Because it comes to grips with the question, it is counted an important book. We have reviewed the book, not favorably, in great detail in our book, *Earnestly Contending for the Faith*, Sword of the Lord Publishers. We cannot recommend Ramm's book, and mention it only because it was widely used among the new evangelicals trying to mediate between unbelieving scholars and Bible believers.

26. *Christ and the Scriptures*, by Adolph Saphir. An old book, only 142 pages. Out of print, but very valuable. Adolph Saphir was a German Jew, won to Christ by a Scottish missionary. He went to Scotland, then did mission work among the Jews and others. Despite his German origin, the English is beautiful, limpid, clear. A wonderful spirit of Christian devotion in the book. Saphir was converted in 1843, preached and wrote in the last century. Dr. A. C. Gaebelein, who introduced the American edition, said, "It is the strongest book on the divinity and infallibility of the Bible we know." The biographer of Saphir said, "He seemed to combine the gentleness and simplicity of a child with the firm grasp of a strong man, when he dealt with holy Scripture. No halting or hesitating utterance could be detected in his voice or manner, as he dwelt upon the deep things of God, and lucidly spread out before a

hushed audience the magnificent truths concerning Jesus Christ and God's way of salvation."

The chapters are:

    I. The Book and the Person
    II. Jesus and the Scriptures
    III. The Testimony of the Apostles
    IV. Five Characteristics of the Bible — Evidences of Its Divine Origin
    V. Israel's Messiah — the Living and the Written Word
    VI. Scripture and the Holy Spirit
    VII. Practical Observations, With Special Reference to the Present Age

Heartwarming, greatly strengthens the faith, reliable. Should be reprinted.

27. *"Fundamentalism" and the Word of God,* by J. I. Packer, copyrighted by The Inter-Varsity Fellowship, printed in England and published in America by Eerdmans, pocket edition, paperback. Packer believes in fundamentalism, but doesn't like fundamentalists and tries to avoid the reproach that goes with belief in the Bible. He takes generally Warfield's stand on verbal and plenary inspiration, and defends it. However, he slanders American fundamentalists.

He says on page 33, "We must not judge the original fundamentalists too harshly. Their resources of scholarship were certainly limited, but their desire to defend the evangelical faith against a militant and aggressive Liberalism was equally certainly right. It was better to fight clumsily than not to fight at all. However, there is no doubt that their Evangelicalism was narrowed and impoverished by their controversial entanglements. Their Fundamentalism was Evangelicalism of a kind, but of a somewhat starved and stunted kind — shrivelled, coarsened and in part deformed under the strain of battle."

Such a description of the men whose works were collected and printed in the series of volumes on *The Fundamentals,* for example, is carelessly inadequate, unjustly critical and lacking in genuine study of sources. To account Warfield, Hodge, Robert Dick Wilson, Oswald T. Allis, James M. Gray, R. A. Torrey, W. B. Riley, William Jennings Bryan, Machen, Scofield, Munhall, and Ironside, without resources of scholarship, clumsy, narrow, impoverished, and so on, is foolish, one-sided, inadequate judgment. The only Americans Packer seems to have studied were N. B. Stonehouse and Dr. Carl Henry. So he adopts theirs and The Inter-Varsity Fellowship New Evangelical viewpoint.   He is against coming out from apostate denominations, against an all-out fight against liberalism.   He is against premillennial truth and against revivals and evangelism.   He is against the "Anabaptist" position of independent local churches not following denominational tradition.   So he is a sheep among the goats.   He is a Bible believer more friendly to infidels than aggressive Christians.   He would like to avoid the term "fundamentalist" because it is in disrepute by infidels and unbelieving scholars.   He would like to drop the term "inerrancy" concerning the Bible, also, although he believes the Bible is inerrant.

It is notable that his kind of fundamentalism has turned England principally over to the liberals, and there is no strong evangelical and evangelistic leadership, there are no great fundamental, soul-winning churches in Great Britain to compare with the fundamentalists and the great soul-winning churches in America.   Many good things in the book are marred by a narrow and unbrotherly viewpoint. 191 pages.

There are other good books by Kuyper, William Gladstone, some good things by Dr. Wilbur Smith in *Therefore Stand,* some earnest discussion in the *Systematic Theology* textbooks by Hodge, Strong, Lewis Sperry Chafer (better).

INDEX

BIOGRAPHICAL

SCRIPTURE

TOPICAL